Guide to the National Environmental Policy Act

Guide to the National Environmental Policy Act

Interpretations, Applications, and Compliance

Valerie M. Fogleman

QUORUM BOOKS
Westport, Connecticut • London

Library of Congress Cataloging-in-Publication Data

Fogleman, Valerie M.
    Guide to the National Environmental Policy Act : interpretations,
    applications, and compliance / Valerie M. Fogleman.
       p.   cm.
    Includes bibliographical references (p.).
    ISBN 0-89930-486-9 (lib. bdg. : alk. paper)
    1. Environmental law—United States. I. United States. National
Environmental Policy Act of 1969. II. Title.
KF3775.A315F64   1990
344.73'046—dc20
[347.30446]   90-8413

British Library Cataloguing in Publication Data is available.

Library of Congress Catalog Card Number: 90-8413
ISBN: 0-89930-486-9

First published in 1990

Quorum Books, 88 Post Road West, Westport, CT 06881
An imprint of Greenwood Publishing Group, Inc.

Printed in the United States of America

The paper used in this book complies with the
Permanent Paper Standard issued by the National
Information Standards Organization (Z39.48-1984).

10 9 8 7 6 5 4

To my mother, Tanya, David, Nicole, and Joe

Contents

Preface

The National Environmental Policy Act (NEPA) is a short, broadly written statute that has been interpreted by between one thousand and two thousand published judicial decisions. The act applies to thousands of federal agency actions each year. These agency actions are as diverse as consideration of applications by scientists to field test genetically engineered plants, proposals by land managers to spray herbicides, and proposals by architects and engineers to construct post offices and roads in urban communities.

Because NEPA is so broadly written and because it has such a broad application, it is impossible to understand how to comply with NEPA or how to participate meaningfully in the NEPA process merely by reading the statute. In addition to the statute, NEPA's implementing regulations written by the Council on Environmental Quality must be consulted as well as relevant judicial decisions and occasionally regulations of individuals agencies. This book draws together these various sources of NEPA law and presents the law in a readable format designed to be a practical guide to compliance with the NEPA process as well as a comprehensive legal analysis of every aspect of NEPA law.

The book is intended for several major groups of people. The first group consists of people who must comply with NEPA: federal agency personnel; contractors and consultants hired by the agencies to aid in the NEPA process; and applicants for federal permits, funding, and approval. The second group consists of public interest groups and members of the general public who wish to participate in the NEPA process. The third group includes people and entities involved in NEPA litigation: agency personnel, applicants, environmental organizations, members of the general public, and lawyers retained by any of the above. The final group consists of people with an academic interest in NEPA and its evolution. In addition to the above groups, the book provides a source of NEPA law for people and entities in states that have adopted statutes based on NEPA, and for people who and entities that are required to comply with other state statutes similar to the NEPA process.

Because the book is intended for use by lawyers as well as non-lawyers, the notes section at the end of each chapter contains lengthy citations to case law. A statement in the text may thus be supported by cases in several jurisdictions to aid lawyers in researching case law in a particular jurisdiction.

Acknowledgments

I would like to thank the many people who aided me in writing this book, especially personnel from federal and state agencies who provided me with information about agency practices and procedures. I would also like to thank personnel of the Nueces County law library who aided me in my accumulation of NEPA case law, especially Richard Mungia.

I would like to thank particularly Harry L. Marks of the law firm of Gary, Thomasson, Hall & Marks Professional Corporation, whose constant encouragement and support enabled me to write this book, and the other people of the law firm who encouraged me, especially Rosemary Hutchinson for her secretarial skills and Pat Garcia for her help in researching.

My thanks also go to Michael C. Blumm and James L. Huffman of Northwestern School of Law of Lewis and Clark College for their aid in preparing an early version of chapters 3 and 4, and to the Oregon Department of Land Conservation and Development for providing funding for that study with funds obtained from the National Oceanic and Atmospheric Administration, appropriated under the Coastal Zone Management Act of 1972. The early version of chapters 3 and 4 was published as "Threshold Determinations Under the National Environmental Policy Act," in 15 Boston College Environmental Affairs Law Review 59 (1987), with the able assistance of law review staff members.

Last, but certainly not least, I would like to thank Frank F. Skillern of Texas Tech University School of Law, who first interested me in environmental law and who has unfailingly encouraged my endeavors in it.

Acronyms

AEC	Atomic Energy Commission
CEQ	Council on Environmental Quality
CEQA	California Environmental Quality Act
DEA	Drug Enforcement Administration
EA	Environmental Assessment
EAF	Environmental Assessment Form
EIR	Environmental Impact Report
EIS	Environmental Impact Statement
EPA	Environmental Protection Agency
ERC	Economic Regulatory Administration
FAA	Federal Aviation Administration
FCC	Federal Communications Commission
FDA	Food and Drug Administration
FERC	Federal Energy Regulatory Commission
FONSI	Finding of No Significant Impact
FPC	Federal Power Commission
HUD	Department of Housing and Urban Development
ICC	Interstate Commerce Commission
MEPA	Michigan Environmental Protection Act
NEPA	National Environmental Policy Act
NOAA	National Oceanic and Atmospheric Administration
NPDES	National Pollutant Discharge Elimination System
NRC	Nuclear Regulatory Commission
SEC	Securities and Exchange Commission
SEQRA	New York State Environmental Quality Review Act
TVA	Tennessee Valley Authority

The National Environmental Policy Act

1.1 INTRODUCTION

The National Environmental Policy Act (NEPA) was signed into law on January 1, 1970. The act was described by one of its authors as "the most important and far-reaching environmental and conservation measure ever enacted by the Congress."[1] NEPA is broad. It applies to all federal agencies and to every major action taken by the agencies that significantly affects the quality of the human environment. NEPA supplements all statutes not in conflict with it. Thus not only does NEPA give federal agencies the power to consider the environmental effects of their proposed actions, it requires them to consider the effects before proceeding with the actions.

NEPA's brevity contrasts sharply with the lengthy and complex environmental laws enacted after it. NEPA's brevity, however, is matched by its ambiguity. As Justice Thurgood Marshall stated: "[T]his vaguely worded statute seems designed to serve as no more than a catalyst for development of a 'common law' of NEPA."[2] This book analyzes NEPA, the court decisions interpreting NEPA, the Council on Environmental Quality (CEQ) regulations implementing NEPA, and court decisions interpreting those regulations.

Chapter 1 examines NEPA's legislative history and its provisions. The extent of NEPA's application to federal agencies is examined, as is its application to ongoing agency actions at the time of its enactment. The continuing debate on whether NEPA extends to agency actions conducted in the United States when the only environmental effects of the actions occur outside the United States is also discussed.

The interaction of NEPA and other statutory procedures required to be followed by an agency is analyzed. Finally, the continuing issue of whether NEPA is substantive or purely procedural is briefly discussed.

1.2 LEGISLATIVE HISTORY

NEPA's legislative history is sparse. Before NEPA was signed into law in 1970, bills had been proposed for several years on the need for the federal government to consider environmental matters in its decision making and in formulating its policies.[3] Congressional committees and subcommittees had held hearings and published reports on assessing the environmental effects of technological advances and on establishing a national policy for the environment.[4]

In 1969, the bills that became NEPA were introduced in the House and the Senate.[5] After a series of hearings before House subcommittees, the House bill was amended and unanimously reported out of committee.[6] The House bill focused on establishing a five-member Council on Environmental Quality in the Executive Office of the President.[7]

The Senate bill also was amended and reported out of committee.[8] The Senate bill, which was more comprehensive than the House bill, had three titles. Title I was a declaration of national environmental policy. "Title II authorized research and data gathering on environmental matters. Title III authorized the creation of a three-member Board of Environmental Quality Advisers in the Executive Office of the President."[9]

The Senate bill passed the Senate by voice vote on July 10, 1969.[10] The House amended the Senate bill to contain the House's version of NEPA. The amended bill passed the House on September 23, 1969, by a vote of 372 to 15 with 43 representatives not voting.[11] The Senate subsequently disagreed with the House amendments and agreed to the House's request for a conference committee.[12]

The conference committee considered the bills passed by the Senate and the House together with companion legislation containing the Environmental Quality Improvement Act, which authorized the creation of the Office of Environmental Quality to support the CEQ.[13] The conference committee subsequently reported out a version of NEPA containing additions as well as compromises. These changes are discussed in section 1.3 together with a section-by-section discussion of NEPA.

After minimal debate, the Senate agreed to the conference report on December 20, 1969, by voice vote.[14] The House subsequently agreed to the conference report by voice vote after minimal debate on December 22, 1969.[15] On January 1, 1970, President Richard Nixon signed NEPA into law.[16]

1.3 SECTION-BY-SECTION DISCUSSION

1.3.1 Purpose

NEPA's purpose is:

To declare a national policy which will encourage productive and enjoyable harmony between man and his environment; to promote efforts which will prevent or eliminate damage to the environment and biosphere and stimulate the health and welfare of man; to enrich the understanding of the ecological systems and natural resources important to the Nation; and to establish a Council on Environmental Quality.[17]

NEPA has two titles. Title I contains a declaration and a mandate to the federal government. Title II establishes the CEQ in the Executive Office of the President.

Title I of NEPA has two major sections. Section 101 contains a broad declaration of policy. Agencies have discretion to determine the specific ways in which they comply with this congressional policy.[18] Section 102 contains NEPA's action-forcing, or procedural, requirements. These procedures, which are designed to ensure that environmental protection is considered by agencies, require a strict standard of compliance.[19]

The Supreme Court has described NEPA as having two major purposes or aims. The first purpose is to place "upon an agency the obligation to consider every significant aspect of the environmental impact of a proposed action." The second aim is to ensure "that the agency will inform the public that it has considered environmental concerns in its decision making process."[20]

1.3.2 Congressional Declaration of Policy

The "strong precatory language" of section 101 declares "a broad national commitment to protecting and promoting environmental quality."[21] Congress recognized the environmental effect of human activities and "the critical importance of restoring and maintaining environmental quality to the overall welfare and development of man."[22] In order "to create and maintain conditions under which man and nature can exist in productive harmony, and fulfill the social, economic, and other requirements of present and future generations of Americans," Congress declared that the federal government would cooperate with "State and local governments, and other concerned public and private organizations, to use all practicable means and measures, including financial and technical assistance."[23]

In addition, Congress declared that the federal government had: the continuing responsibility . . . to use all practicable means, consistent with other essential considerations of national policy, to improve and coordinate Federal plans, functions, programs, and resources to the end that the Nation may—

(1) fulfill the responsibilities of each generation as trustee of the environment for succeeding generations;
(2) assure for all Americans safe, healthful, productive, and esthetically and culturally pleasing surroundings;
(3) attain the widest range of beneficial uses of the environment without degradation, risk to health or safety, or other undesirable and unintended consequences;
(4) preserve important historic, cultural, and natural aspects of our national heritage, and maintain, wherever possible, an environment which supports diversity and variety of individual choice;
(5) achieve a balance between population and resource use which will permit high standards of living and a wide sharing of life's amenities; and
(6) enhance the quality of renewable resources and approach the maximum attainable recycling of depletable resources.[24]

Finally, Congress recognized "that each person should enjoy a healthful environment and that each person has a responsibility to contribute to the preservation and enhancement of the environment."[25] This provision has been held not to vest anyone with any rights.[26]

In the Senate bill, this section had formerly declared that "each person has a fundamental and inalienable right to a healthful environment and that each person has a responsibility to contribute to the preservation and enhancement of the environment."[27] The Senate's language was dropped by the conference committee despite strong arguments for its retention by Senator Henry Jackson, one of NEPA's authors, who declared that he believed that the language reaffirmed existing law.[28]

1.3.3 "To the Fullest Extent Possible"/Statutory Conflicts

Section 102, which was added to the House amendment to NEPA by the conference committee is based on the Senate bill.[29] The section contains a broad directive that "to the fullest extent possible" federal policies, public laws, and regulations should be "interpreted and administered in accordance with the policies set forth in [NEPA]."[30] NEPA's house managers amplified this latter phrase in the conference report by adding explanatory remarks, not reviewed and agreed to by the Senate conference members, that NEPA was to be complied with unless there was "a clear conflict between [an agency's] statutory authority and [NEPA]."[31]

The term "to the fullest extent possible" applies to every requirement of section 102.[32] The District of Columbia Circuit declared early in NEPA's history that the term was not "an escape hatch for footdragging agencies."[33] Instead, the court held that the term made compliance with NEPA's procedural requirements nondiscretionary.[34] The Supreme Court subsequently interpreted the term to be "a deliberate command that the duty NEPA imposes upon the agencies to consider environmental factors not be shunted aside in the bureaucratic shuffle."[35] Thus, unless there is a "clear and unavoidable conflict in statutory authority," an agency must comply with NEPA.[36] Administrative difficulty, delay, or economic cost does not excuse an agency's noncompliance.[37]

The term has been interpreted as a directive to the courts as well as the agencies. Thus, if there is a legitimate difference of opinion regarding whether a statutory conflict exists, arguably the difference should be resolved in favor of applying NEPA's policies.[38]

Because NEPA is a supplementary statute applying to all major federal actions significantly affecting the quality of the human environment, it is not surprising that courts have found some conflicts between it and other statutes. The major conflict is timing. Compliance with NEPA is time consuming, particularly if an environmental impact statement (EIS) is required.[39] Thus, if an agency must act within a short time period, for example thirty days, and the agency's action requires preparation of an EIS, there is an irreconcilable statutory conflict because the agency could not draft, circulate, receive comments on, and subsequently review and revise an EIS within that limited period. In such a case, the agency is not required to comply with NEPA to the extent of the conflict.[40] However, if an agency is able to comply with NEPA together with the agency's other statutory duty, it must do so.[41]

Similarly, if Congress directs an agency to conduct an emergency action and that action requires preparation of an EIS, there is a statutory conflict. In such cases, courts have excepted an agency from NEPA's requirement that an EIS be prepared[42] or have permitted the agencies to proceed with the action before the EIS was completed.[43]

Another type of statutory conflict arises if Congress imposes a mandatory duty on an agency[44] or does not permit an agency to consider environmental factors in making a decision to act.[45] Compliance with NEPA in these cases would not serve any purpose because the decision maker would not be permitted to consider the results of the NEPA process in making his decision. Except for the examples discussed above, courts rarely find a statutory conflict between NEPA and another statute.[46] The circuits are split on whether an agency must file an explicit statement of reasons why it is unable to comply with NEPA because of a statutory conflict.[47]

Just as NEPA does not require an agency to comply with its requirements when there is a clear statutory conflict, Congress has created equivalent "conflicts" in enacting legislation since the enactment of NEPA. Congress has declared that a specific action is exempt from NEPA,[48] or that a specific type of action is exempt.[49] The courts differ on whether congressional intent must be specific or whether compliance with NEPA may be precluded by implication.[50]

A corollary of the congressionally created conflict with NEPA occurs when Congress declares that a specific type of judicial challenge to a specific action is barred.[51] In effect, such an action by Congress is equivalent to Congress anticipating or mooting a cause of action.[52] The reverse occurs when Congress directs an agency to prepare an EIS for a specific action.[53]

1.3.4 EIS Requirement

Section 102 contains NEPA's "action-forcing procedures."[54] The section contains a mandate for "all agencies to the Federal Government" to perform certain procedures.

The procedure that has become the focal point of NEPA is preparation of a detailed statement to accompany "every recommendation or report on proposals for legislation and other major Federal actions significantly affecting the quality of the human environment."[55] The term "detailed statement" in NEPA replaced an earlier requirement for a "finding."[56]

The term "major Federal action significantly affecting the quality of the human environment" has been litigated extensively to define almost every word in the term. Chapter 3 analyzes activities that are considered to be major federal actions affecting the human environment. Chapter 4 examines the process by which it is determined whether such actions have a significant environmental effect.

The detailed statement, which is known as an environmental impact statement (EIS) must contain:

(i)   the environmental impact of the proposed action,

(ii) any adverse environmental effects which cannot be avoided should the proposal be implemented,

(iii) alternatives to the proposed action,

(iv) the relationship between local short-term uses of man's environment and the maintenance and enhancement of long-term productivity, and

(v)   any irreversible and irretrievable commitments of resources which would be involved in the proposed action should it be implemented.[57]

Chapter 5 describes and analyzes all aspects of the preparation of EISs and determinations regarding their adequacy. Chapter 6 analyzes issues that arise in NEPA litigation. Chapter 7 discusses state or mini-NEPAs and compares them to NEPA.

1.3.5 Consultation and Commenting Procedures

The agency official preparing the EIS must consult with federal agencies that have legal jurisdiction or special expertise on the proposed action's environmental effects; obtain comments from the above agencies and make the comments available to the president of the United States, the CEQ, and the public; also make available, "comments and views of the appropriate Federal, State, and local agencies, which are authorized to develop and enforce environmental standards"; and attach the above comments and views to the proposal as it passes through existing agency review processes.[58]

Sections 5.8.5 and 5.8.6 discuss NEPA's consulting and commenting procedures. The public availability of information generated by the NEPA process is limited to information that is available under the Freedom of Information Act.

1.3.6 Freedom of Information Act Limitations

NEPA declares that data made available to the public is limited to data that is available under the Freedom of Information Act.[59] This does not mean, however, that an agency does not need to comply with NEPA for actions involving classified information. The Supreme Court has held that an agency must consider the environmental effects of its actions regardless of whether the proposed actions are classified or whether the required environmental documentation, including any environmental assessments (EAs) and EISs, would contain classified information.[60] Thus, there is no national defense exemption under NEPA.[61]

However, because the agency's duty under NEPA to consider the environmental effects of its actions is not necessarily coextensive with the requirement that it publicly disclose the environmental considerations, the agency is not required to publicly release any information that is not available to the public under the Freedom of Information Act. The agency may thus prepare internal environmental documentation in certain cases.[62]

In effect, because no public participation is involved in these cases, the resulting documentation is unchallengeable whatever the state of the documentation. Cases involving a classified action are rare, however. If the agency action involves national defense policy but NEPA may be complied with without disclosing classified information, the agency is required to comply with NEPA[63] including the public participation requirements.

1.3.7 Interdisciplinary Analysis

Section 102 mandates that agencies shall utilize "a systematic interdisciplinary approach which will insure the integrated use of the natural and social sciences and the environmental design arts in planning and in decisionmaking which may have an impact on man's environment."[64] This provision, which applies whether or not an agency prepares an EIS, means that agencies have a duty to conduct an interdisciplinary analysis of a proposed action's environmental effects. The provision does not require an agency to involve specific disciplines in the analysis or to consider all documents that could possibly be relevant.[65] The provision also does not require an agency necessarily to include a formal and mathematically precise cost-benefit analysis in an EIS.[66]

1.3.8 Quantification of Environmental Values

Section 102 requires agencies to "identify and develop methods and procedures, in consultation with the [CEQ], which will insure that presently unquantified environmental amenities and values may be given appropriate consideration in decision making along with economic and technical considerations."[67] This provision means that agencies must "search out, develop and follow procedures reasonably calculated to bring environmental factors to peer status with dollars and technology in their decision making."[68] Agencies are not required to promulgate specific regulations quantifying environmental values.[69] Nor are agencies necessarily required to give environmental values dollar values as long as environmental values are considered, for example, by recognizing, discussing, and weighing the beneficial and adverse environmental effects of an agency action.[70]

The agency's choice of methodology in quantifying environmental and other values must be justifiable in light of current scientific practices,[71] but it need not be the best scientific methodology available.[72] Courts cannot require an agency to use one methodology instead of another. A court must simply ensure that the procedure followed by the agency resulted in a reasoned analysis of the evidence.[73] If the agency uses methodologies in an EIS, it must discuss the methodology[74] but it is not required to disclose all the assumptions underlying a methodology.[75]

1.3.9 Consideration of Alternatives

Under section 102, an agency must "study, develop, and describe appropriate alternatives to recommended courses of action in any proposal which involves unresolved conflicts concerning alternative uses of available resources."[76] This requirement is independent of the section 102 requirement that alternatives must be considered in an EIS.[77] Whereas alternatives to be considered in an EIS are alternatives to the proposed action,[78] this independent requirement applies to alternative uses of available resources, which requires consideration of different alternatives from the EIS requirement. The independent requirement, therefore, applies to all agency actions covered by NEPA. In effect, the requirement applies to actions for which an EA is prepared in addition to actions for which an EIS is prepared.[79]

To comply with the provision, agencies must "actively seek out and develop alternatives" to their actions rather than merely speculating about which options exist.[80] The extent of the search for alternatives decreases as the environmental effects of an action decrease.[81] An agency need only consider reasonable alternatives.[82] The alternative use of funds to be expended by the agency is not an alternative use of available resources, and, thus, need not be considered.[83]

1.3.10 International Cooperation in Environmental Protection

Section 102 recognizes "the worldwide and long-range character of environmental problems" and supports efforts to anticipate and prevent a decline in the world environment.[84] Senator Jackson added this provision to the Senate bill that became NEPA. The provision's purpose is to give agencies statutory authority to participate in developing a program of international cooperation in environmental protection.[85]

Legislation pending in Congress in 1990 would add the policy that the United States will provide world leadership in ensuring a healthy and stable global environment. The legislation would require the CEQ to issue regulations extending NEPA to federal actions significantly affecting the extraterritorial and global environments.[86]

1.3.11 Provision of Environmental Information

The other procedures contained in section 102 are making information on how to maintain and enhance the quality of the environment available to states, counties, municipalities, institutions, and individuals, and giving advice on those matters;[87] initiating and utilizing "ecological information in the planning and development of resource-oriented projects";[88] and assisting the CEQ.[89]

1.3.12 Delegation

NEPA provides that "the responsible federal official" shall prepare an EIS.[90] A 1975 amendment to section 102 provides that in specified instances, EISs prepared by certain state agencies or officials were not legally inadequate for that reason.[91] Judicial interpretation of this provision of NEPA is discussed in section 5.6. Delegation of EA preparation is discussed in section 4.4.

1.3.13 Review of Agency Procedures

Section 103 ordered the federal agencies to conduct a one-time review of their statutory authority, administrative regulations, and current policies and procedures to determine whether deficiencies or inconsistencies existed that prohibited full compliance with NEPA's purposes and provisions. Measures to overcome deficiencies or inconsistencies were to be proposed to the president by July 1, 1971.[92]

1.3.14 Supplementary Nature of NEPA

Section 104 states that NEPA does not affect a federal agency's statutory obligations to comply with environmental laws, coordinate or consult with federal and state agencies, or act, or refrain from acting, contingent upon another federal or state agency's recommendations or certification.[93] In essence, the provision states that compliance with NEPA is not a defense to the listed obligations.

The District of Columbia Circuit rejected an interpretation of this section that would have undermined an agency's obligation to comply with NEPA. The court held that the provision does not permit an agency to abdicate consideration of the environmental effects of its proposed action.[94]

Section 105 states that "[t]he policies and goals set forth in [NEPA] are supplementary to those set forth in existing authorizations of Federal agencies."[95] That is, NEPA does not modify or repeal existing law. Agencies must comply with NEPA unless compliance would cause them to violate their existing statutory authorizations.[96] Agencies are not required to promote environmental values in specific ways.[97]

It is well settled that NEPA grants federal agencies authority to consider the environmental effects of their proposed actions[98] and imposes a duty on agencies to do so.[99] Equally well settled is the proposition that NEPA does not grant agencies authority to act outside their statutory mandate.[100] Actions taken by the agency must be authorized by its organic statute.[101] NEPA does not expand an agency's range of final decisions.

Thus, NEPA accords an agency authority to postpone a proposed action until it complies with the NEPA process,[102] impose environmental conditions on a permit, or deny a permit if such actions are within its statutory mandate.[103] An agency may not, however, order a private action to be postponed in order to enable subsequent NEPA compliance when the private action is not subject to NEPA.[104] Similarly, an agency may base a substantive decision on environmental consequences identified by the NEPA process,[105] but not if the agency decision maker is precluded by Congress from considering environmental consequences in reaching his decision.[106]

1.3.15 The Council on Environmental Quality

Title II of NEPA established the Council on Environmental Quality (CEQ) and outlined its responsibilities. This title and CEQ responsibilities under NEPA and other statutes are discussed in chapter 2.

1.4 APPLICATION TO FEDERAL AGENCIES

NEPA applies to "all agencies of the Federal Government."[107] Congress,[108] the judiciary,[109] the states,[110] the governments of trust territories,[111] and "the performance of staff functions for the President in his Executive Office"[112] are excluded.

In order to be a federal agency for purposes of NEPA, an entity must have substantial authority to act on behalf of the federal government.[113] An entity that administers a program for the federal government is generally considered to be a federal agency under NEPA[114] unless Congress specified otherwise.[115] Entities administered mainly by the states are not federal agencies even though they may have been created by Congress.[116]

Several federal agencies vigorously opposed the application of NEPA to their programs. For example, the post office initially argued that it was exempt from NEPA because Congress exempted it from certain types of federal statutes.[117] By the mid-1970s, however, the courts rejected this argument.[118]

The Environmental Protection Agency (EPA) argued initially that it was exempt from NEPA.[119] When NEPA was enacted the EPA did not exist. There are statements in NEPA's legislative history, however, that may be interpreted to mean that Congress did not intend NEPA to be applicable to environmentally protective regulatory agencies.[120] The CEQ initially considered the EPA to be exempt from compliance with NEPA[121] but abandoned the exemption in 1973.[122]

The EPA thus failed to gain a blanket exemption from NEPA but was successful in gaining exemptions from specific environmental regulatory procedures, both from Congress[123] and the courts. When a procedure conducted pursuant to another environmental law is the "functional equivalent" of NEPA, courts have held that the EPA's compliance with that procedure fulfills the procedure mandated by NEPA.[124] The functional equivalence doctrine thus ensures that when the EPA is protecting the environment, it is not required to engage in duplicative procedures forestalling that protection.

1.5 APPLICATION TO ONGOING ACTIONS

Agencies were required to comply with NEPA beginning January 1, 1970.[125] Neither NEPA nor its legislative history indicated whether NEPA was to be applied retroactively to actions begun before that date. Courts resolved the issue, not by deciding whether the statute could be applied retroactively, but by determining whether there was agency action that occurred after January 1, 1970.

Thus, if an agency project was not completed by January 1, 1970, but the agency had taken all major federal actions involved in the project before that date, NEPA did not apply.[126] On the other hand, if major federal actions remained to be taken by the agency on an ongoing project, NEPA applied to the project.[127]

1.6 EXTRATERRITORIAL APPLICATION

The issue of whether NEPA has extraterritorial application is not settled. The issue has several facets. The first facet is determining whether NEPA applies only to the fifty states or whether it also applies to trust territories and other territory outside the fifty states. The broad language of NEPA referring to the "nation" rather than the "United States" has been interpreted to include trust territories.[128]

The other facet of NEPA's extraterritorial application has two components: whether NEPA applies to actions that affect the global commons such as the oceans and Antarctica, and whether NEPA applies to actions that only affect the territory of foreign nations. These issues caused considerable debate during the 1970s,[129] with the CEQ taking the position that NEPA applied to both types of actions.[130] In 1977, the CEQ proposed procedures for each type of action, with an abbreviated procedure for actions that only affected foreign nations.[131]

The CEQ subsequently excluded its proposed regulations on extraterritoriality from the final CEQ regulations. Instead, the issue of extraterritorial application was addressed in Executive Order 12,114, issued in 1979.[132] The executive order, which was drafted in consultation with the CEQ and the Department of State,[133] requires EISs for major federal actions significantly affecting the global commons. The executive order has many exemptions. An abbreviated environmental review, or participation in bilateral or multilateral environmental studies, is required under specified circumstances for major federal actions affecting foreign countries.

Courts have not directly reached the issue of whether NEPA has extraterritorial application for all major federal actions significantly affecting the quality of the human environment.[134] The District of Columbia Circuit provided some guidance by holding that NEPA did not apply to nuclear export licensing decisions by the Nuclear Regulatory Commission. The commission's actions only affected the environment of a foreign nation not the United States. However, the court limited its decision to the type of major federal action at issue in the case.[135] Thus, the extraterritoriality issue remains unsettled.

In 1989, Congress required multilateral development banks to develop procedures for, and to assess, the environmental effects of

their proposed actions.[136] Proposed amendments to NEPA, pending in
Congress in 1990, would require the CEQ to issue regulations extending NEPA to proposed federal actions significantly affecting the extraterritorial environment and requiring agencies to consider the
effects of their proposed actions on the global environment including
effects on global climate change, depletion of the ozone layer, loss of
biological diversity, and transboundary pollution.[137]

1.7 INTERACTING STATUTES

Because NEPA supplements other statutes, many agencies must
comply with procedures mandated by statutes other than NEPA
before they may conduct an action. When an agency must comply with
environmental procedures of other statutes, the CEQ regulations state
that compliance should be integrated with the NEPA process.[138] Thus,
NEPA concerns may be required to be considered in procedures
conducted under other statutes.[139] Similarly, if an agency is required
to perform certain procedures under NEPA, it may be required to
consider issues mandated by another statute.[140] The interaction of the
NEPA procedures and those of another statute has been held not to
result in application of one statute's procedural provision to the other
statute.[141]

Thus, although the procedures may be integrated, the statutory
requirements remain independent. Compliance with one statute does
not necessarily equate with compliance under NEPA and vice versa.
If the requirements of one statute generally duplicate NEPA's requirements, compliance with NEPA may equate with compliance with
another environmental statute,[142] but only as far as NEPA duplicates
the provisions of the other statute.[143] Similarly, if another statute
declares that one of its procedures may be conducted as part of the
agency's compliance with NEPA, the procedure must comply with all
requirements of both statutes.[144] NEPA may require additional procedures to be conducted when considerations required by NEPA and the
other statute overlap.[145]

1.8 SUBSTANTIVE OR PROCEDURAL EFFECT

A debate has continued for many years regarding whether NEPA is
purely procedural or whether it has substantive content.[146] Early
decisions of the circuits split on the issue.[147] In 1978, the Supreme
Court stated that "NEPA does set forth significant substantive goals
for the Nation, but its mandate to the agencies is essentially proce-

dural."[148] The Court added that administrative decisions should be set aside "only for substantial procedural or substantive reasons as mandated by statute."[149]

Two years later, the Supreme Court elaborated on its earlier statement, stating that "once an agency has made a decision subject to NEPA's procedural requirements, the only role for a court is to insure that the agency has considered the environmental consequences."[150] The Court held that NEPA did not require an agency to elevate environmental concerns over other appropriate considerations.[151] The Court further developed its previous NEPA statements in 1989 by declaring that once an agency complied with NEPA's procedural prerequisites it would not violate NEPA if it proceeded with an unwise action that was environmentally destructive.[152]

Whether an agency action that violates NEPA's policies is only ever unwise and can not be arbitrary or capricious if the agency complies with NEPA's procedures has not been squarely decided by the Supreme Court.[153] Although an unwise decision is not necessarily arbitrary and capricious,[154] the District of Columbia Circuit has declared that an agency must exercise some scrutiny over the agency's substantive decision to determine the decision's rationality.[155]

Nevertheless, by stating that an agency action may proceed after the agency complies with NEPA's procedures even though the action is environmentally destructive,[156] the Supreme Court seems to have ruled out any possibility of interpreting NEPA to have any substantive content. Thus, it appears that an agency's actions are not arbitrary or capricious even if the actions are directly contrary to NEPA's purposes as long as the agency complied with NEPA's procedures. If this is the position taken by the Supreme Court, it is difficult to reconcile with the purpose of NEPA's action-forcing provisions which is "to insure that the policies enunciated in section 101 are implemented."[157] Of course, if the documentation required by NEPA revealed a potential violation of other environmental laws, plaintiffs could base a challenge on those violations.

A Senate bill pending in Congress in 1990 would give NEPA substantive content by requiring agencies to consider in EISs, "measures that will be taken to mitigate adverse environmental effects if the proposed action is implemented" as well as "a description of how the proposed action or chosen alternative and selected mitigation measures conform to the policies of [NEPA]."[158] In contrast, a bill passed by the House would require agencies to implement mitigation measures, monitoring, and other conditions if the conditions are in the EIS and are selected by an agency as part of its final decision.[159]

NOTES

1. 115 Cong. Rec. 40,416 (1969) (remarks of Sen. Jackson).

2. Kleppe v. Sierra Club, 427 U.S. 390, 421 (1976) (Marshall, J., concurring in part and dissenting in part).

3. *See generally* S. Rep. No. 296, 91st Cong., 1st Sess. 11–12 (1969); H. Rep. No. 378, 91st Cong., 1st Sess., *reprinted in* 1969 U.S. Code Cong. & Admin. News 2751, 2752.

4. *See* Senate Comm. on Interior and Insular Affairs and House Comm. on Science and Astronautics, Congressional White Paper on a National Policy for the Environment, 90th Cong., 2d Sess. (1968); *Environmental Quality; Hearings on H.R. 7796, H.R. 13211, H.R. 14605 and H.R. 14627 Before the Subcomm. on Science, Research and Development of the House Comm. on Science and Astronautics,* 90th Cong., 2d Sess. (1968); Subcommittee on Science, Research and Development of the House Comm. on Science and Astronautics, Technology Assessment, 90th Cong., 1st Sess. (1967); *Technology Assessment Seminar; Proceedings Before the Subcomm. on Science, Research and Development of the House Comm. on Science and Astronautics,* 90th Cong., 1st Sess. (1967); Subcomm. on Science, Research and Development of the House Comm. on Science and Astronautics, Environmental Pollution: A Challenge to Science and Technology, 89th Cong., 2d Sess. (1966).

5. *See* S. 1075, 91st Cong., 1st Sess. (1969); H.R. 6750, 91st Cong., 1st Sess. (1969). *See generally* H. Rep. No. 378, 91st Cong., 1st Sess., *reprinted in* 1969 U.S. Code Cong. & Admin. News 2751, 2752.

6. *See* 1969 U.S. Code Cong. & Admin. News at 2752–53.

7. *See id.* at 2759.

8. *See* S. Rep. No. 296, 91st Cong., 1st Sess. 1–4 (1969); *see also* 115 Cong. Rec. 19,008 (1969).

9. *See* 115 Cong. Rec. 40,415 (1969) (remarks of Sen. Jackson).

10. *Id.* at 19,013.

11. *Id.* at 26,590.

12. *See id.* at 40,415; *see also id.* at 26,591 (conferees appointed by House).

13. *See* Council on Environmental Quality, *Environmental Quality 1972: Third Annual Report* 223; *see also* 115 Cong. Rec. 29,050–89 (1969) (Senate consideration of Environmental Quality Improvement Act).

14. 115 Cong. Rec. 40,415–27 (1969).

15. *Id.* at 40,923–28.

16. Pub. L. No. 91–190, 83 Stat. 852 (1970).

17. 42 U.S.C. § 4321 (1988).

18. Calvert Cliffs' Coordinating Comm., Inc. v. AEC, 449 F.2d 1109, 1112, 1128 (D.C. Cir. 1971); *see also* National Citizens Comm. for Broadcasting v. FCC, 567 F.2d 1095, 1106 n.47 (D.C. Cir. 1977) (agency could determine how to accommodate mandate of NEPA with its own mandate), *cert. denied,* 436 U.S. 926 (1978); Public Interest Research Group v. FCC, 522 F.2d 1060, 1068 (1st Cir. 1975) (same), *cert. denied,* 424 U.S. 965 (1976).

19. Calvert Cliffs' Coordinating Comm. v. AEC, 449 F.2d 1109, 1112 (D.C. Cir. 1971); *see* Environmental Defense Fund, Inc. v. Andrus, 619 F.2d 1368, 1374 (10th Cir. 1980).

20. Baltimore Gas & Elec. Co. v. Natural Resources Defense Council, Inc., 462 U.S. 87, 97 (1983).

21. Robertson v. Methow Valley Citizens Council, 109 S. Ct. 1835, 1844–45 (1989).

22. 42 U.S.C. § 4331(a) (1988).

23. *Id.*

24. *Id.* § 4331(b).

25. *Id.* § 4331(c).

26. *See* Environmental Defense Fund, Inc. v. Corps of Eng'rs, 325 F. Supp. 749, 755 (E.D. Ark. 1971); *see also* Noe v. Metropolitan Atlanta Rapid Transit Auth., 644 F.2d 434, 438–39 (5th Cir.) (elimination of provision is one reason why NEPA does not grant a private right of action), *cert. denied*, 454 U.S. 1126 (1981).

27. S. 1075 § 101(b), 91st Cong., 1st Sess. (1969), *reprinted in* S. Rep. No. 296, 91st Cong., 1st Sess. (1969).

28. Conf. Rep. No. 765, 91st Cong., 1st Sess., *reprinted in* 1969 U.S. Code Cong. & Admin. News 2767, 2768; *see* 115 Cong. Rec. 40,416 (1969) (remarks of Sen. Henry Jackson).

29. Conf. Rep. No. 765, 91st Cong., 1st Sess., *reprinted in* 1969 U.S. Code Cong. & Admin. News 2767, 2769.

30. 42 U.S.C. § 4332 (1988).

31. Conf. Rep. No. 765, 91st Cong., 1st Sess., *reprinted in* 1969 U.S. Code Cong. & Admin. News 2767, 2771; *see* 115 Cong. Rec. 40,422 (1969) (remarks of Sen. Jackson) (explanatory statements were not reviewed and agreed to by Senate conferees); *id.* at 40,423 (remarks of Sen. Muskie) (concern that revision of language not change legislative mandates of agencies with authority in environmental improvement field).

32. Flint Ridge Dev. Co. v. Scenic Rivers Ass'n, 426 U.S. 776, 787 (1976); *see also* Major Changes in S. 1075 as Passed by the Senate, *reprinted in* 115 Cong. Rec. 40,417, 40,418 (1969) (term applies to clauses 1 and 2 of section 102).

33. Calvert Cliffs' Coordinating Comm., Inc. v. AEC, 449 F.2d 1109, 1114 (D.C. Cir. 1971).

34. *See id. See, e.g.,* Steubing v. Brinegar, 511 F.2d 489, 495 (2d Cir. 1975) ("'to the fullest extent possible' means that plaintiffs' delay in bringing a suit should not prevent a court from enjoining construction pending compliance if it appears that such a stay would best serve the public interest"). *See also* Silva v. Romney, 473 F.2d 287, 292 (1st Cir. 1973) ("We cannot think of any stronger language which could have been used to underscore the importance of protecting the environment").

35. Flint Ridge Dev. Co. v. Scenic Rivers Ass'n, 426 U.S. 776, 787 (1976).

36. *Id.* at 788; Calvert Cliffs' Coordinating Comm., Inc. v. AEC, 449 F.2d 1109, 1115 (D.C. Cir. 1971); *see* Louisiana v. FPC, 503 F.2d 844, 877 (5th Cir. 1974) (rejecting agency's argument that environmental impact of action was uncertain; court stated agency should "make a good faith effort to describe the reasonably foreseeable environmental impact of each [action]").

37. Calvert Cliffs' Coordinating Comm., Inc. v. AEC, 449 F.2d 1109, 1115 (D.C. Cir. 1971).

38. Romer v. Carlucci, 847 F.2d 445, 468 (8th Cir. 1988) (Arnold, C. J., concurring in part and dissenting in part).

39. *See* Flint Ridge Dev. Co. v. Scenic Rivers Ass'n, 426 U.S. 776, 789 n.10 (1976); *see also* section 5.8 (EIS process).

40. Flint Ridge Dev. Co. v. Scenic Rivers Ass'n, 426 U.S. 776, 791 (1976); *see also* Colorado Public Interest Research Group, Inc. v. Hills, 420 F. Supp. 582, 588 (D. Colo. 1976) (agency need not comply with NEPA in areas in which statute conflicted).

41. *See, e.g.,* Texas Comm. on Natural Resources v. Bergland, 573 F.2d 201, 207 (5th Cir.), *cert. denied,* 439 U.S. 966 (1978). *Cf.* Natural Resources Defense Council, Inc. v. NRC, 647 F.2d 1345, 1386 (D.C. Cir. 1981) (Robinson, J., concurring) (period for NRC to act on export license may not be sufficient for NRC to comply with EIS requirement).

42. *See, e.g.,* Gulf Oil Corp. v. Simon, 502 F.2d 1154, 1157 (Temp. Emer. Ct. App. 1974) (emergency legislation mandating allocation of crude oil); Dry Colors Mfrs. Ass'n, Inc. v. Department of Labor, 486 F.2d 98, 107–08 (3d Cir. 1973) (promulgation of emergency temporary standard on carcinogens in the workplace; draft EIS was adequate); Atlanta Gas Light Co. v. FPC, 476 F.2d 142, 150 (5th Cir. 1973) (interim gas curtailment order); Alaska v. Carter, 462 F. Supp. 1155, 1161 (D. Alaska 1978) (emergency withdrawal of public lands under Federal Land Policy and Management Act). *See also* Cohen v. Price Comm'n, 337 F. Supp. 1236, 1241–42 (S.D.N.Y. 1972) (temporary agency that was required to act promptly was not required to comply with NEPA). *Cf.* Louisiana Power & Light Co. v. FPC, 557 F.2d 1122, 1125–26 (5th Cir. 1977) (all interim curtailment plans do not necessarily create statutory conflict with NEPA's EIS requirement); Louisiana v. FPC, 503 F.2d 844, 875–76 (5th Cir. 1974) (FPC required to prepare EIS for permanent gas curtailment plan); Consolidated Edison Co. of New York, Inc. v. FPC, 512 F.2d 1332, 1346 (D.C. Cir. 1975) (declining to agree that it is well settled that agency is not required to prepare EISs for interim gas curtailment plans).

43. *See, e.g.,* Cities of Lakeland & Tallahassee v. FERC, 702 F.2d 1302, 1314 (11th Cir. 1983) (interim gas curtailment plan).

44. *See* Pacific Legal Found'n v. Andrus, 657 F.2d 829, 841 (6th Cir. 1981) (listing species as endangered or threatened under Endangered Species Act).

45. *See* Milo Community Hosp. v. Weinberger, 525 F.2d 144, 148 (1st Cir. 1975) (decertification of hospital as provider under Medicare Act for continued noncompliance with fire protection provisions); *see also* Burkey v. Ellis, 483 F. Supp. 897, 909 (N.D. Ala. 1979) (Congress specified values to use in cost-benefit analysis; NEPA balancing was, therefore, obviously upset).

46. *See* Jones v. Gordon, 792 F.2d 821, 825 (9th Cir. 1986); Forelaws on Board v. Johnson, 743 F.2d 677, 685 (9th Cir. 1985), *cert. denied,* 478 U.S. 1004 (1986); Public Serv. Co. v. NRC, 582 F.2d 77, 85 (1st Cir.), *cert. denied,* 439 U.S. 1046 (1978); Ely v. Velde, 451 F.2d 1130, 1134–38 (4th Cir. 1971); Ocoee River Council v. TVA, 540 F. Supp. 788, 798 (E.D. Tenn. 1982).

47. *Compare* Pacific Legal Found'n v. Andrus, 657 F.2d 829, 841 (6th Cir. 1981) (statement of reasons is not required as a matter of law where an EIS is not required) *with* Cities of Lakeland & Tallahassee v. FERC, 702 F.2d 1302, 1315 n.17 (11th Cir. 1983) (explicit findings required to demonstrate statutory conflict

prohibiting compliance with NEPA); American Smelting & Ref. Co. v. FPC, 494 F.2d 925, 948 (D.C. Cir.) (same), *cert. denied*, 419 U.S. 882 (1974). *Cf.* Consolidated Edison Co. of New York, Inc. v. FPC, 512 F.2d 1332, 1346–47 (D.C. Cir. 1975) (express findings demonstrating statutory conflict are required but remand would probably not benefit plaintiffs).

48. *See* Romer v. Carlucci, 847 F.2d 445, 467 (8th Cir. 1988) (Arnold, C. J., concurring in part and dissenting in part) (noting that Congress did not require report from Scowcroft Commission on basing MX missiles); Environmental Defense Fund, Inc. v. Higginson, 655 F.2d 1244, 1246 n.3 (D.C. Cir. 1981) (noting that rider to appropriations bill declared that action should proceed as if EIS had been filed); Colon v. Carter, 633 F.2d 964, 965 (1st Cir. 1980) (noting that EIS was not required on assistance to Cuban and Haitian refugees under Refugee Education Assistance Act).

49. *See* Clean Water Act, 33 U.S.C. § 1371(c) (1988) (no action by EPA administrator under Act "shall be deemed a major Federal action significantly affecting the quality of the human environment within the meaning of the National Environmental Policy Act" except for provision of federal financial assistance for constructing publicly owned treatment works and issuance of National Pollutant Discharge Elimination System permits for new sources); *see* Simons v. Gorsuch, 715 F.2d 1248, 1251 (7th Cir. 1983) (purpose of section 1371(c) is to exclude certain actions under Clean Water Act from requirement to prepare EIS, not to require EPA to prepare EIS for those types of actions); *see also* Idaho v. Hanna Mining Co., 882 F.2d 392, 396 (9th Cir. 1989) (interpreting provision in Comprehensive Environmental Response, Compensation and Liability Act excepting liability from act if damages "were specifically identified as an irreversible and irretrievable commitment of natural resources" in an EIS).

After the EPA approves state National Pollutant Discharge Elimination System (NPDES) permit programs, states issue NPDES permits directly and the EPA has the right to object. *See* 33 U.S.C. § 1342(d) (1988). The decision of the EPA not to object to a permit's issuance has been held not to trigger NEPA. *See* District of Columbia v. Schramm, 631 F.2d 854, 862 (D.C. Cir. 1980); Chesapeake Bay Found'n, Inc. v. Virginia State Water Control Bd., 453 F. Supp. 122, 125–26 (E.D. Va. 1978). Thus, NEPA applies to the issuance of NPDES permits in states with unapproved state NPDES permit programs but not in states with approved programs.

50. *See* Limerick Ecology Action, Inc. v. NRC, 869 F.2d 719, 729–30 (3d Cir. 1989) (requiring specific intent); Environmental Defense Fund, Inc. v. Froehlke, 473 F.2d 346, 355 (8th Cir. 1972) (appropriations bill enacted after NEPA did not change NEPA's requirements); Davis v. Morton, 469 F.2d 593, 598 (10th Cir. 1972) (general statement in subsequent statute did not imply actions were not subject to NEPA). *But see* Izaak Walter League of Am. v. Marsh, 655 F.2d 346, 367 (D.C. Cir.) (describing cases finding implied repeal of NEPA as to specific action), *cert. denied*, 454 U.S. 1092 (1981); Kansas *ex rel.* Stephan v. Adams, 608 F.2d 861, 866 (10th Cir. 1979) (Congress' review of the report was stronger expression of intent than appropriations measure), *cert. denied*, 445 U.S. 963 (1980); Environmental Defense Fund, Inc. v. Hoffman, 566 F.2d 1060, 1071 (8th Cir. 1977) (appropriation of funds for proposed action after "exhaustive review process and despite the

recommendations of the President, clearly represents a determination by Congress as to the adequacy of the mitigation plan" in the EIS); Burkey v. Ellis, 483 F. Supp. 897, 909 (N.D. Ala. 1979) (mandatory cost-benefit ratio in statute repealed NEPA by implication). *Cf.* Environmental Defense Fund, Inc. v. Corps of Eng'rs, 325 F. Supp. 749, 762 (E.D. Ark. 1971) (Congress, in making annual appropriations for agency action probably assumed that agency was complying with applicable laws).

51. *See* Portland Audubon Soc'y v. Lujan, 884 F.2d 1233, 1236–40 (9th Cir. 1989) (interpreting H.R. Res. 395 § 314, Pub. L. No. 100–446, 102 Stat. 1825 (1988)).

52. *See* section 6.5.

53. *See* Romer v. Carlucci, 847 F.2d 445, 448 (8th Cir. 1988) (citing section 110 of Department of Defense Authorization Act of 1984; proposed deployment and peacetime operations of MX missiles in Minuteman silos); Southeast Alaska Conservation Council v. Watson, 697 F.2d 1305, 1310 (9th Cir. 1983) (citing Pub. L. No. 96–487 § 503(h), 94 Stat. 2371, 2400–01 (1980)).

54. *See* Robertson v. Methow Valley Citizens Council, 109 S. Ct. 1835, 1844 (1989) (quoting 115 Cong. Rec. 40,416 (1969) (remarks of Sen. Jackson)).

55. 42 U.S.C. § 4332(2)(C) (1988).

56. *See* City of New York v. United States, 344 F. Supp. 929, 940 n.16 (E.D.N.Y. 1972) (citing 115 Cong. Rec. 29,055, 20,058 (1969)).

57. 42 U.S.C. § 4332(2)(C) (1988).

58. *Id.*

59. *Id.* (citing 5 U.S.C. § 552 (1988)).

60. Weinberger v. Catholic Action of Hawaii/Peace Educ. Project, 454 U.S. 139, 146 (1981); *see* 40 C.F.R. § 1507.3(c) (1989).

61. No Gwen Alliance of Lane County, Inc. v. Aldridge, 855 F.2d 1380, 1384 (9th Cir. 1988); Concerned About Trident v. Rumsfeld, 555 F.2d 817, 822–23 (D.C. Cir. 1977).

62. Weinberger v. Catholic Action of Hawaii, 454 U.S. 139, 143–46 (1981); *see also* Hudson River Sloop Clearwater, Inc. v. Department of Navy, 891 F.2d 414, 423 (2d Cir. 1989); Laine v. Weinberger, 541 F. Supp. 599, 601–03 (C.D. Cal. 1982).

63. *See* section 6.2 (jurisdiction).

64. 42 U.S.C. § 4332(2)(A) (1988).

65. Nucleus of Chicago Homeowners Ass'n v. Lynn, 524 F.2d 225, 232 (7th Cir. 1975), *cert. denied*, 424 U.S. 967 (1976); *see also* Pennsylvania Protect Our Water & Envtl. Resources, Inc. v. Appalachian Regional Comm'n, 574 F. Supp. 1203, 1221 (M.D. Pa. 1982) ("omission of environmental planners did not preclude the team of preparers from adequately complying with NEPA requirements"). *Cf.* Save Our Invaluable Land, Inc. v. Needham, 542 F.2d 539, 542 (10th Cir. 1976) (describing provision as declaration of policy effectuated by EIS requirement), *cert. denied*, 430 U.S. 945 (1977).

66. Robinson v. Knebel, 550 F.2d 422, 426 (8th Cir. 1977); *see* section 5.10.4 (cost-benefit analyses).

67. 42 U.S.C. § 4332(2)(B) (1988).

68. Environmental Defense Fund, Inc. v. Corps of Eng'rs, 492 F.2d 1123, 1133 (5th Cir. 1974). *Cf.* Save Our Invaluable Land, Inc. v. Needham, 542 F.2d 539, 542

(10th Cir. 1976) (describing provision as declaration of policy effectuated by EIS requirement), *cert. denied*, 430 U.S. 945 (1977).

69. *See* Natural Resources Defense Council, Inc. v. SEC, 606 F.2d 1031, 1053 (D.C. Cir. 1979); *see also* Cape Henry Bird Club v. Laird, 359 F. Supp. 404, 414 (W.D. Va.) (EIS was not deficient because agency was unable to quantify environmental values at issue), *cert. denied*, 484 F.2d 453 (4th Cir. 1973).

70. Robinson v. Knebel, 550 F.2d 422, 426 (8th Cir. 1977).

71. City of New York v. United States Dep't of Transp., 715 F.2d 732, 751 (2d Cir. 1983), *cert. denied*, 465 U.S. 1055 (1984); *see also* C.A.R.E. NOW, Inc. v. FAA, 844 F.2d 1569, 1573 (11th Cir. 1988) (agency's methodology was legally adequate).

72. Tribal Village of Akutan v. Hodel, 869 F.2d 1185, 1192 (9th Cir. 1988).

73.*See* Friends of Endangered Species, Inc. v. Jantzen, 760 F.2d 976, 986 (9th Cir. 1985); Environmental Defense Fund, Inc. v. Corps of Eng'rs, 492 F.2d 1123, 1133 (5th Cir. 1974).

74. 40 C.F.R. § 1502.24 (1989).

75. Tribal Village of Akutan v. Hodel, 869 F.2d 1185, 1192 (9th Cir. 1988).

76. 42 U.S.C. § 4332(2)(E) (1988).

77. *See* Nucleus of Chicago Homeowners Ass'n v. Lynn, 524 F.2d 225, 232 (7th Cir. 1975), *cert. denied*, 424 U.S. 967 (1976); Wicker Park Historic Dist. Preservation Fund v. Pierce, 565 F. Supp. 1066, 1079–81 (N.D. Ill. 1982).

78. *See* 42 U.S.C. § 4332(2)(C)(iii) (1988).

79. *See* section 4.5 (scope of an EA).

80. Olmsted Citizens for a Better Community v. United States, 793 F.2d 201, 208 (8th Cir. 1986); *see also* Trinity Episcopal School Corp. v. Romney, 523 F.2d 88, 93 (2d Cir. 1975) (alternatives must be studied, developed, and described); Environmental Defense Fund, Inc. v. Corps of Eng'rs, 492 F.2d 1123, 1135 (5th Cir. 1974) (agency must thoroughly consider appropriate methods of accomplishing action's aim).

81. River Road Alliance, Inc. v. Corps of Eng'rs, 764 F.2d 445, 452 (7th Cir. 1985), *cert. denied*, 475 U.S. 1055 (1986); *see* City of New York v. United States Dep't of Transp., 715 F.2d 732, 744 (2d Cir. 1983), *cert. denied*, 465 U.S. 1055 (1984).

82. *See* Environmental Defense Fund, Inc. v. Corps of Eng'rs, 470 F.2d 289, 297 (8th Cir. 1972), *cert. denied*, 412 U.S. 931 (1973).

83. Aertsen v. Landrieu, 637 F.2d 12, 20 (1st Cir. 1980). *But see* Save the Niobrara River Ass'n, Inc. v. Andrus, 483 F. Supp. 844, 861–62 (D. Neb. 1979) (alternative use of federal funding to meet agency's objectives by alternative method deserved consideration in EIS).

84. 42 U.S.C. § 4332(2)(F) (1988).

85. 115 Cong. Rec. 40,416–17 (1969); *see also* Pub. L. No. 101–240, 103 Stat. 2511 (1989) (to be codified at 22 U.S.C. § 262m-7 (requiring assessment of significant environmental effects of proposed multilateral development bank actions)).

86. H.R. 1113, 101st Cong., 1st Sess. (1989); H.R. 3847, 101st Cong., 2d Sess. (1990); S. 1089, 101st Cong., 1st Sess. (1989).

87. 42 U.S.C. § 4332(2)(G) (1988); *see* National Citizens Comm. for Broadcasting v. FCC, 567 F.2d 1095, 1106 n.47 (D.C. Cir. 1977) (FCC may determine best way to accommodate NEPA in its mandate), *cert. denied*, 436 U.S. 926 (1978).

88. 42 U.S.C. § 4332(2)(H1988).
89. *Id.* § 4332(2)(I).
90. *Id.* § 4332(2)(C).
91. *Id.* § 4332(2)(D).
92. *Id.* § 4333.
93. *Id.* § 4334.
94. *See* Calvert Cliffs' Coordinating Comm., Inc. v. AEC, 449 U.S. 1109, 1124 (D.C. Cir. 1971).
95. 42 U.S.C. § 4335 (1988).
96. Major Changes in S. 1075 as Passed by the Senate, *reprinted in* 115 Cong. Rec. 40,417, 40,418 (1969).
97. *See* Natural Resources Defense Council, Inc. v. SEC, 606 F.2d 1031, 1044–45 (D.C. Cir. 1979).
98. *See* Calvert Cliffs' Coordinating Comm., Inc. v. AEC, 449 F.2d 1109, 1112 (D.C. Cir. 1971); *see also* Consolidated Rail Corp. v. ICC, 646 F.2d 642, 655 (D.C. Cir.) (agency was entitled to rely on its EIS in making decision), *cert. denied*, 454 U.S. 1047 (1981); Detroit Edison Co. v. NRC, 630 F.2d 450, 452 (6th Cir. 1980) (agency could implement NEPA's environmental mandate through issuance of conditional licenses regulating off-site transmission lines).
99. *See* Grindstone Butte Project v. Kleppe, 638 F.2d 100, 103 (9th Cir.), *cert. denied*, 454 U.S. 965 (1981); Natural Resources Defense Council, Inc. v. SEC, 606 F.2d 1031, 1044 (D.C. Cir. 1979).
100. *See* United States v. Students Challenging Regulatory Agency Procedures, 412 U.S. 669, 696 (1973); Gage v. AEC, 479 F.2d 1214, 1220 n.19 (D.C. Cir. 1973). *See generally* Natural Resources Defense Council, Inc. v. EPA, 822 F.2d 104, 129 (D.C. Cir. 1987) (listing cases holding that NEPA "does not work a broadening of the agency's substantive powers").
101. *See* Natural Resources Defense Council, Inc. v. EPA, 859 F.2d 156, 169 (D.C. Cir. 1988); *see also* Colorado Public Interest Research Group, Inc. v. Hills, 420 F. Supp. 582, 587 (D. Colo. 1976) (nothing in statute gave Secretary of Housing and Urban Development authority to conduct continued monitoring).
102. *See* Shiffler v. Schlesinger, 548 F.2d 96, 102 (3d Cir. 1977). *Cf.* National Audubon Soc'y v. Watt, 678 F.2d 299, 310 (D.C. Cir. 1982) (Secretary of Interior could defer action until NEPA was complied with and "may also have had discretionary authority to delay construction until Congress had a reasonable opportunity to reconsider its earlier mandate in light of newly available environmental information. But he was not legally empowered to promise unconditionally to defer construction until 60 days after Congress took action . . . regardless of how long congressional action may be deferred").
103. *See* Natural Resources Defense Council, Inc. v. EPA, 859 F.2d 156, 170 (D.C. Cir. 1988).
104. *See* Natural Resources Defense Council, Inc. v. EPA, 822 F.2d 104, 128 (D.C. Cir. 1987).
105. *See* Marshall Minerals, Inc. v. FDA, 661 F.2d 409, 424 n.21 (5th Cir. 1982); *see also* Union Oil Co. v. Morton, 512 F.2d 743, 749 (9th Cir. 1975) (Secretary of Interior could consider environmental consequences in regulating drilling); Zabel v. Tabb, 430 F.2d 199, 213 (5th Cir. 1970) (Secretary of Army could reject

dredge and fill permit on nonnavigational (i.e., environmental) grounds), *cert. denied*, 401 U.S. 910 (1971); Environmental Defense Fund, Inc. v. Mathews, 410 F. Supp. 336, 338 (D.D.C. 1976) (NEPA provides agency with authority to consider environmental factors and to act on them). *Cf.* Gulf Oil Corp. v. Morton, 493 F.2d 141, 146 (9th Cir. 1974) (under NEPA and Outer Continental Shelf Lands Act, Secretary of Interior "has a continuing duty to guard all the resources of the outer Continental Shelf").

106. *See* Natural Resources Defense Council, Inc. v. Berklund, 609 F.2d 553, 558 (D.C. Cir. 1980) (Secretary of Interior had no discretion to deny coal lease to qualified applicant).

107. 42 U.S.C. § 4332(2) (1988).

108. League of Women Voters of Tulsa, Inc. v. Corps of Eng'rs, 730 F.2d 579, 583 (10th Cir. 1984); Minnesota v. Block, 660 F.2d 1240, 1259 (8th Cir. 1981), *cert. denied*, 455 U.S. 1007 (1982); 40 C.F.R. § 1508.12 (1989).

109. Citizens for a Better St. Clair County v. James, 648 F.2d 246, 250 (5th Cir. 1981); 40 C.F.R. § 1508.12 (1989).

110. Town of North Hempstead v. Village of North Hills, 482 F. Supp. 900, 903 (E.D.N.Y. 1979); *but see* 40 C.F.R. § 1508.12 (1989) (states are subject to NEPA when they assume NEPA responsibilities under section 104(h) of the Housing and Community Development Act of 1974).

111. People of Saipan v. United States Dep't of Interior, 502 F.2d 90, 95 (9th Cir. 1974), *cert. denied*, 420 U.S. 1003 (1975).

112. 40 C.F.R. § 1508.12 (1989). *Cf.* Alaska v. Carter, 462 F. Supp. 1155, 1160 (D. Alaska 1978) (recommendations by secretary of the interior on exercise of president's powers under Antiquities Act are not covered by NEPA when president requested recommendations).

113. Conservation Law Found'n of New England, Inc. v. Harper, 587 F. Supp. 357, 364 (D. Mass. 1984).

114. *See id.* at 363–64 (Property Review Board is a federal agency); Committee to Save the Fox Bldg. v. Birmingham Branch of the Federal Reserve Bank, 497 F. Supp. 504, 509 (N.D. Ala. 1980) (Federal Reserve Bank of Atlanta is a federal agency).

115. *See* Miltenberger v. Chesapeake & Ohio Ry., 450 F.2d 971, 974 (4th Cir. 1971) (AMTRAK).

116. *See* California Tahoe Regional Planning Agency v. Sahara Tahoe Corp., 504 F. Supp. 753, 762 (D. Nev. 1981) (interstate compact agency is not a federal agency); People by California Dep't of Transp. v. City of South Lake Tahoe, 466 F. Supp. 527, 534–36 (E.D. Cal. 1978) (same).

117. *See* City of Thousand Oaks v. United States, 396 F. Supp. 1306, 1307–08 (C.D. Cal. 1974) (upholding post office's argument that NEPA does not apply to it).

118. Chelsea Neighborhood Ass'ns v. United States Postal Serv., 516 F.2d 378, 382–86 (2d Cir. 1975); Morgan v. United States Postal Serv., 405 F. Supp. 413, 419 (W.D. Mo. 1975). *Cf.* Higgins v. United States Postal Serv., 449 F. Supp. 1001, 1002 (D. Mass. 1978) (post office voluntarily complied with NEPA).

119. *See generally* Lynch, *The 1973 CEQ Guidelines: Cautious Updating of the Environmental Impact Statement Process*, 11 Cal. Western L. Rev. 297, 309 (1975);

EPA's Responsibilities Under the National Environmental Policy Act: Further Developments, 3 Envtl. L. Rep. (Envtl. L. Inst.) 10,157 (1973).

120. *See* Portland Cement Ass'n v. Ruckelshaus, 486 F.2d 375, 380–84 (D.C. Cir. 1973) (discussing NEPA's legislative history), *cert. denied*, 417 U.S. 921 (1974); *see also* Dry Color Mfrs. Ass'n, Inc. v. Department of Labor, 486 F.2d 98, 107 (3d Cir. 1973) (OSHA is not generally exempt from NEPA).

121. 36 Fed. Reg. 7725 (1971).

122. 38 Fed. Reg. 10,865 (1973).

123. *See* Ethyl Corp. v. EPA, 541 F.2d 1, 54 (D.C. Cir.) (citing Congress' express exemption of the EPA from NEPA for actions taken under Clean Air Act, 15 U.S.C. § 793(c)(1) (1988)), *cert. denied*, 426 U.S. 941 (1976); 33 U.S.C. § 1371(c) (1988) (under Clean Water Act, NEPA applies only to EPA's funding assistance for constructing publicly owned treatment works and new source National Pollutant Discharge Elimination System permits). *See generally* Weyerhaeuser Co. v. Costle, 590 F.2d 1011, 1050–53 (D.C. Cir. 1978) (discussing EPA and NEPA).

124. *See* Wyoming v. Hathaway, 525 F.2d 66, 71–73 (10th Cir. 1975) (Federal Insecticide, Fungicide, and Rodenticide Act), *cert. denied*, 426 U.S. 906 (1976); Environmental Defense Fund, Inc. v. EPA, 489 F.2d 1247, 1257 (D.C. Cir. 1973) (same); Warren County v. North Carolina, 528 F. Supp. 276, 286–87 (E.D.N.C. 1981) (Toxic Substances Control Act); Maryland v. Train, 415 F. Supp. 116, 121–22 (D. Md. 1976) (Ocean Dumping Act); *see also* Indiana & Mich. Elec. Co. v. EPA, 509 F.2d 839, 842–43 (7th Cir. 1975) (exemption for EPA from activities conducted under Clean Air Act; prior to congressional exemption of act from NEPA); Amoco Oil Co. v. EPA, 501 F.2d 722, 749 (D.C. Cir. 1974) (same); Anaconda Co. v. Ruckelshaus, 482 F.2d 1301, 1306 (10th Cir. 1973) (same); Buckeye Power, Inc. v. EPA, 481 F.2d 162, 174 (6th Cir. 1973) (same), *cert. denied*, 425 U.S. 934 (1976); Appalachian Power Co. v. EPA, 477 F.2d 495, 508 (4th Cir. 1973). *Cf.* Merrell v. Thomas, 807 F.2d 776, 781 (9th Cir. 1986) (hesitating to adopt functional equivalence rationale but expressing confidence that Congress did not intend NEPA to apply to registrations under Federal Insecticide, Fungicide, and Rodenticide Act), *cert. denied*, 108 S. Ct. 145 (1987); Foundation on Economic Trends v. Heckler, 756 F.2d 143, 152–55 (D.C. Cir. 1985) (National Institutes of Health procedures for approving experiments under guidelines for activities involving genetically engineered organisms were not equivalent to EA).

125. *See* Calvert Cliffs' Coordinating Comm., Inc. v. AEC, 449 F.2d 1109, 1120 (D.C. Cir. 1971).

126. *See* Olivares v. Martin, 555 F.2d 1192, 1197 (5th Cir. 1977); San Francisco Tomorrow v. Romney, 472 F.2d 1021, 1025 (9th Cir. 1973); Pennsylvania Environmental Council, Inc. v. Bartlett, 454 F.2d 613, 624 (3d Cir. 1971).

127. *See* Morris County Trust for Historic Preservation v. Pierce, 714 F.2d 271, 277–78 (3d Cir. 1983); Arlington Coalition on Transp. v. Volpe, 458 F.2d 1323, 1330–31 (4th Cir.), *cert. denied*, 409 U.S. 1000 (1972).

128. *See* People of Enewetak v. Laird, 353 F. Supp. 811, 816–19 (D. Hawaii 1973).

129. *See generally* Council on Environmental Quality, *Environmental Quality 1979: Tenth Annual Report* 582.

130. Council on Environmental Quality, Memorandum on the Application of the EIS Requirement to Environmental Impacts Abroad of Major Federal Ac-

tions, 42 Fed. Reg. 61,068 (1977); *see* Natural Resources Defense Council, Inc. v. NRC, 647 F.2d 1345, 1386 n.156 (D.C. Cir. 1981) (Robinson, J., concurring).

131. *See generally* Comment, *Reinvigorating the NEPA Process: CEQ's Draft Compliance Regulations Stir Controversy*, 8 Envtl. L. Rep. (Envtl. L. Inst.) 10,045, 10,047 (1978).

132. Exec. Order No. 12,114, *reprinted in* 42 U.S.C. § 4321 note (1988); *see* section 2.2.2.

133. *See* Council on Environmental Quality, *Environmental Quality 1979: Tenth Annual Report* 582.

134. *See* Natural Resources Defense Council, Inc. v. NRC, 647 F.2d 1345, 1366 (D.C. Cir. 1981); Sierra Club v. Adams, 578 F.2d 389, 391 n.14 (9th Cir. 1978).

135. Natural Resources Defense Council, Inc. v. NRC, 647 F.2d 1345, 1366 (D.C. Cir. 1981).

136. Pub. L. No. 101–240, 103 Stat. 2511 (1989).

137. S. 1089 § 3(3), 101st Cong., 1st Sess. (1989); H.R. 1113 § 5, 101st Cong., 1st Sess. (1989); H.R. 3847 § 505, 101st Cong., 2d Sess. (1990).

138. 40 C.F.R. § 1502.25 (1989).

139. *See* City of Davis v. Coleman, 521 F.2d 661, 678 (9th Cir. 1975) (public hearings required by 28 U.S.C. § 128 (1988) should also consider factors enumerated in NEPA); Lathan v. Brinegar, 506 F.2d 677, 689 (9th Cir. 1974) (same).

140. *See* Sierra Club v. Penfold, 857 F.2d 1307, 1313 n.11 (9th Cir. 1988) (under Alaska National Interest Lands Act, 16 U.S.C. § 3120(b) (1988), an EA or EIS required to be prepared for NEPA must include a subsistence evaluation).

141. *See* Park County Resource Council, Inc. v. United States Dep't of Agriculture, 817 F.2d 609, 616–17 (10th Cir. 1987) (statute of limitations in Mineral Lands Leasing Act did not apply to NEPA challenge to oil and gas lease on federal forest land).

142. *See* Sagebrush Rebellion, Inc. v. Hodel, 790 F.2d 760, 767 (9th Cir. 1986) (NEPA hearing may fulfill Federal Land Policy and Management Act's hearing requirement); Environmental Defense Fund, Inc. v. Froehlke, 473 F.2d 346, 356 (8th Cir. 1972) (NEPA's agency consultation requirement fulfills Fish and Wildlife Coordination Act's consultation requirement); Missouri *ex rel.* Ashcroft v. Corps of Eng'rs, 526 F. Supp. 660, 677 (W.D. Mo. 1980) (same), *aff'd*, 672 F.2d 1297 (8th Cir. 1982); *see also* Texas Comm. on Natural Resources v. Marsh, 736 F.2d 262, 268 (5th Cir. 1984) (listing cases holding that compliance with NEPA satisfies provisions of Fish and Wildlife Conservation Act); section 1.4 (discussing functional equivalency doctrine). *Cf.* Half Moon Bay Fishermans' Marketing Ass'n v. Carlucci, 857 F.2d 505, 511 (9th Cir. 1988) (incorporation of EPA's comments on its compliance with Ocean Dumping Act in Corps of Engineers' EIS "saved the day" for the corps regarding its compliance with NEPA).

143. *See* Sagebrush Rebellion, Inc. v. Hodel, 790 F.2d 760, 764 (9th Cir. 1986) (notice of draft EIS and hearings did not comply in every respect with requirements of Federal Land Policy and Management Act but error was harmless); Stop 3–H Ass'n v. Coleman, 533 F.2d 434, 445 (9th Cir.) (compliance with NEPA did not demonstrate or establish compliance with 16 U.S.C. § 1653(f) (1988)), *cert. denied*, 429 U.S. 999 (1976); National Wildlife Fed'n v. Andrus, 440 F. Supp. 1245,

1255 (D.D.C. 1977) (requirement in Fish and Wildlife Coordination Act was not complied with by agency in complying with NEPA). *But see* Missouri Coalition for Env't v. Corps of Eng'rs, 678 F. Supp. 790, 803 (E.D. Mo. 1988) ("an agency's compliance with NEPA automatically satisfies the requirements of the [Fish and Wildlife Coordination Act]"); Cape Henry Bird Club v. Laird, 359 F. Supp. 404, 418 (W.D. Va.) ("compliance with NEPA is also a de facto compliance with the Fish and Wildlife Coordination Act"), *aff'd*, 484 F.2d 453 (4th Cir. 1973).

144. *See* Save the Yaak Comm. v. Block, 840 F.2d 714, 718 (9th Cir. 1988) (Congress' declaration that a biological assessment under Endangered Species Act may be prepared as part of NEPA process "does not indicate that a [biological assessment] may substitute entirely for an EA").

145. *See* Limerick Ecology Action, Inc. v. NRC, 869 F.2d 719, 730 (3d Cir. 1989) (actions under Atomic Energy Act do not necessarily preclude NEPA considerations).

146. *See, e.g.*, Environmental Defense Fund, Inc. v. Corps of Eng'rs, 492 F.2d 1123, 1139 (5th Cir. 1974) (describing split in circuits as to whether NEPA establishes substantive law to apply or has only procedural requirements); Andreen, *In Pursuit of NEPA's Promise: The Role of Executive Oversight in the Implementation of Environmental Policy*, 64 Ind. L.J. 205, 243–45 (1989); Liebesman, *The Council on Environmental Quality's Regulations to Implement the National Environmental Policy Act—Will They Further NEPA's Substantive Mandate*, 10 Envtl. L. Rep. (Envtl. L. Inst.) 50,039, 50,040 n.14 (1980) (listing articles discussing whether NEPA is substantive).

147. *Compare* Matsumoto v. Brinegar, 568 F.2d 1289, 1290 (9th Cir. 1978) ("[r]eview of the decision on the merits of the proposal is not required by NEPA") *with* Conservancy Council of N.C. v. Froehlke, 473 F.2d 664, 665 (4th Cir. 1973) (agreeing with Eighth Circuit that court had jurisdiction to substantively review substantive findings of agency). *See generally* National Wildlife Fed'n v. Morton, 393 F. Supp. 1286, 1296 n.12 (D.D.C. 1975) (listing cases on both sides of issue).

148. Vermont Yankee Nuclear Power Corp. v. Natural Resources Defense Council, Inc., 435 U.S. 519, 558 (1978).

149. *Id.*

150. Strycker's Bay Neighborhood Council, Inc. v. Karlen, 444 U.S. 223, 227 (1980) (per curiam).

151. *Id.*

152. Robertson v. Methow Valley Citizens Council, 109 S. Ct. 1835, 1846 (1989); *see also id.* at 1850 (NEPA does not require "a fully developed plan detailing what steps *will* be taken to mitigate adverse environmental impacts" (emphasis original)).

153. *See* Romer v. Carlucci, 847 F.2d 445, 465 n.2 (8th Cir. 1988) (Arnold, C. J., concurring in part and dissenting in part) (Supreme Court's decisions cast doubt on whether prior circuit law that substantive decisions under NEPA were reviewable, under arbitrary and capricious standard, for compliance with NEPA policies, is still valid).

154. *See* Jackson County v. Jones, 571 F.2d 1004, 1015 (8th Cir. 1978).

155. *See* Natural Resources Defense Council, Inc. v. SEC, 606 F.2d 1031, 1044 (D.C. Cir. 1979).

156. Robertson v. Methow Valley Citizens Council, 109 S. Ct. 1835, 1846 (1989).

157. *See* Environmental Defense Fund, Inc. v. Corps of Eng'rs, 470 F.2d 289, 297 (8th Cir. 1972) (quoting S. Rep. No. 296, 91st Cong., 1st Sess. 19 (1969)), *cert. denied*, 412 U.S. 931 (1973); *see also* Sierra Club v. Morton, 510 F.2d 813, 829 (5th Cir. 1975) (court may reject agency's "substantive decision only if it was reached procedurally without a full, good faith, individualized consideration or balancing of environmental factors, or if, according to the standards set forth in Sections 101(b) and 102(1) of NEPA, it is '[shown that] the actual balance of costs and benefits that was struck was arbitrary or clearly gave insufficient weight to environmental values'") (quoting Sierra Club v. Froehlke, 486 F.2d 946, 952 (7th Cir. 1973)).

158. S. 1089 § 1(b)(2), 101st Cong., 1st Sess. (1989).

159. H.R. 1113 § 1(d), 101st Cong., 1st Sess. (1989); H.R. 3847 § 501(d), 101st Cong., 2d Sess. (1990).

Administrative Structure for Implementing NEPA

2.1 INTRODUCTION

Chapter 2 examines the administrative structure for implementing NEPA. Each federal agency implements NEPA as NEPA pertains to its actions, using as its basis for NEPA procedures, regulations promulgated by the CEQ. This chapter traces the history of the CEQ and the development and substance of its guidelines and regulations for implementing NEPA. In addition, the chapter contains an overview of the supplementary regulations adopted by the federal agencies, noting similarities and differences between individual agencies' procedures.

The Environmental Protection Agency's responsibilities under NEPA and under section 309 of the Clean Air Act are discussed. The responsibilities are twofold. The EPA provides a public log of EISs by filing all draft and final EISs and by ensuring their public availability. Secondly, the EPA reviews agency actions and EISs and comments on their compliance with NEPA. The EPA has the power to refer environmentally unsatisfactory actions to the CEQ for a decision on the matter. Finally, chapter 2 examines the CEQ referral system.

2.2 THE COUNCIL ON ENVIRONMENTAL QUALITY

The CEQ was established by NEPA in the Executive Office of the President in 1970.[1] The CEQ was created to complement the Environmental Quality Council established by executive order in May 1969.

The Environmental Quality Council had had seven members: the president, the vice president, and five cabinet members.[2] In essence, Congress provided a statutory foundation for the CEQ, thus ensuring its continuation in the executive branch.

2.2.1 Structure

The CEQ, which is a federal agency,[3] has three members who are appointed by the president with the advice and consent of the Senate. One member of the CEQ is designated as chairman by the President.[4]

The Office of Environmental Quality, created by the Environmental Quality Improvement Act,[5] provides a small professional and administrative staff to support the CEQ.[6] The CEQ operates on the policy level; the Office of Environmental Quality operates on the staff level.[7] The chairman of the CEQ is director of the office.[8] The CEQ and the Office of Environmental Quality were planned together by Congress, with the CEQ being established a few months earlier than the Office of Environmental Quality.[9] In practice, the CEQ and the Office of Environmental Quality operate as one entity under one budget. The term CEQ refers both to the council and to the Office of Environmental Quality.[10]

The number of staff members supporting the CEQ has fluctuated. In the early 1970s, there were over seventy permanent and temporary staff members.[11] The number of CEQ staff members declined as the CEQ's budget rose during the 1970s as the CEQ relied on interagency agreements for projects and contracted many research projects and reports to consultants.[12]

In 1981, the CEQ suffered a drastic reduction in size when the employment with the CEQ of fifty-one staff members was terminated.[13] The CEQ's budget was also reduced and remained at a much reduced level during the following eight years.[14] The reduction in staff size and budget resulted in a general loss of prestige for the CEQ during the 1980s.[15] By 1986 there were fewer than ten staff members,[16] a level that continued into 1989.

The number of staff members is expected to increase in the 1990s as a result of a stated commitment to the CEQ by the Bush administration.[17] According to a 1989 statement by the then-nominee chairman of the CEQ, the Bush administration envisioned that the CEQ staff would increase to at least forty full-time employees by 1992 and that the CEQ's role in formulating environmental policy and its role as a mediator among the federal agencies would also increase.[18]

2.2.2 Responsibilities

The CEQ has advisory responsibilities under NEPA. The CEQ assists and advises the president in preparing and transmitting to Congress an environmental quality report; gathers information on and evaluates environmental conditions and trends; reviews and appraises federal programs and activities and makes recommendations to the president; develops and recommends to the president national policies fostering and promoting improvement of environmental quality; surveys, researches, and analyzes ecological systems and environmental quality; documents and defines changes in the national environment; reports at least annually on the state and condition of the environment; and prepares studies, reports, and recommendations on policy and legislation as requested by the president.[19]

The CEQ has responsibilities regarding the international as well as the national environment. A 1975 amendment to NEPA authorized the CEQ to make expenditures to support its international activities.[20] In 1979, the president published Executive Order 12,114 concerning the environmental effects abroad of major federal actions. The order provided for consultation with the CEQ by federal agencies during preparation of implementation procedures, and in certain instances, gave the CEQ the duty to make recommendations.[21]

In summary, the CEQ has three basic responsibilities: the analysis and development of national and international environmental policy; the interagency coordination of environmental quality programs; and the acquisition and assessment of environmental data.[22]

In 1989, the CEQ circulated draft procedures to federal agencies concerning the incorporation into EISs of information on global warming. The CEQ is expected to publish the procedures in 1990.[23] A proposed amendment to NEPA pending in Congress in 1990 would provide the CEQ with regulatory authority and would order the CEQ to issue guidelines under which federal agencies would review statistically significant samples of EISs to determine the effectiveness of mitigation measures, the accuracy of predictions, and the extent to which such mitigation measures were implemented.[24] The proposed legislation would also require the CEQ to prepare an annual policy report,[25] thus increasing the CEQ's role as a national policymaker in environmental matters.

The CEQ has various responsibilities other than those mentioned above. Primary among these is the CEQ's duty to act on referrals from the EPA concerning the unsatisfactory environmental impacts of proposed agency actions. This requirement is contained in section 309 of the Clean Air Act.[26] The CEQ also acts on referrals from agencies other than the EPA, under authority from NEPA.[27] These two latter requirements are discussed in section 2.10.

Other responsibilities of the CEQ include receiving annual compliance reports from agencies granted an exemption from the Endangered Species Act Amendments and making the reports publicly available,[28] and publishing and revising the national contingency plan for removing oil and hazardous substances from navigable waters.[29]

2.3 THE CEQ GUIDELINES

NEPA does not specifically direct the CEQ to issue regulations, or even guidelines, to implement NEPA.[30] Some authority to issue guidelines may be drawn from NEPA's mandate to the CEQ "to review and appraise the various programs and activities of the Federal Government in the light of the policy set forth in [NEPA],"[31] and the authority to develop and recommend to the president national environmental policies.[32] However, this language is far from being a clear grant of authority to issue guidelines or regulations.

The issue of whether the CEQ had authority to issue guidelines became largely academic on March 5, 1970, when the president expressly granted the CEQ authority to issue NEPA guidelines in Executive Order 11,514.[33] The CEQ acted swiftly to fulfill its "mandate for reform in the way Federal agencies make environmental decisions— from initial planning to implementation."[34]

On April 30, 1970, the CEQ published interim guidelines in the *Federal Register*.[35] The guidelines, which were developed with the assistance of the staffs of NEPA's principal congressional authors,[36] focused on preparation of the "detailed statements" required by NEPA.[37] Whereas NEPA only referred to a "detailed statement," the guidelines introduced a draft as well as a final EIS. The guidelines also interpreted the phrase "to the fullest extent possible" to mean that an agency must comply with NEPA unless a statutory conflict existed.[38] This strict interpretation had been adopted by NEPA's House managers and inserted in the explanatory remarks in the conference report on NEPA.[39] Generally, however, the CEQ left implementation of NEPA largely to the discretion of federal agencies,[40] which were to use the CEQ guidelines in preparing their own procedures.[41]

The cautious approach adopted by the CEQ was probably the only approach available to it whereby it could influence other federal agencies' compliance with NEPA. The agencies, nearly all of which were larger than the CEQ, were unaccustomed to having another agency direct them, especially regarding matters that were not included in their primary mandates. The CEQ publicly supported the agencies' efforts to comply with NEPA while it took small but sure steps to require the agencies to adopt the NEPA procedures contained in its guidelines.[42]

The agencies were reticent to formulate NEPA procedures, with some agencies contending that NEPA did not apply to them.[43] Agencies that did formulate procedures did not always publish or invite public comments on them. Although publication was not explicitly required, the CEQ, in an unchallenged action taken after repeatedly urging agencies to publish their procedures, published agency NEPA procedures in the *Federal Register*.[44]

In 1971, the CEQ published final guidelines for implementing NEPA in the *Federal Register*.[45] The final guidelines were more detailed than the interim guidelines with several major additions to encourage public participation in NEPA procedures. First, the CEQ stated that agencies were to consider the environmental effects of their proposed actions at the earliest possible time and always before making a decision on whether to proceed with the action. Secondly, agencies were to address more issues than previously in their NEPA procedures, including providing public information about NEPA procedures.[46]

The major addition in the final guidelines was a requirement that administrative actions not be taken sooner than ninety days after a draft EIS had been made public, circulated for comment, and furnished to the CEQ, or sooner than thirty days after a final EIS, together with comments to it, had been made available to the public and the CEQ.[47] This addition had been insisted upon by a congressional subcommittee overseeing the implementation of NEPA. The subcommittee had been highly critical of the agencies' suppression of environmental information until after an action had occurred and of the CEQ's position that only the final, not the draft EIS, was required to be published.[48]

Finally, the CEQ included in the final guidelines, interim procedures for referrals under section 309 of the Clean Air Act.[49] Due to the addition of the various new procedures in the final guidelines, the CEQ required agencies to revise their individual NEPA procedures in consultation with the CEQ.[50]

During the revision period, the District of Columbia Circuit published a landmark decision that was instrumental in persuading the agencies to incorporate CEQ's guidelines into their individual procedures. In *Calvert Cliffs' Coordinating Committee, Inc. v. AEC*, the District of Columbia Circuit rejected the AEC's "crabbed interpretation of NEPA" in its regulations for implementing NEPA.[51] In contrast to the AEC regulations' technical compliance with NEPA, the court favorably quoted the CEQ guidelines and their aim in assisting agencies to implement "not only the letter, but the spirit, of the Act."[52]

The CEQ's central role in implementing NEPA was assured after *Calvert Cliffs'*. Agencies continued to be slow in publishing NEPA procedures,[53] but the general form of their procedures was being set by the CEQ. Although some courts noted that the CEQ guidelines were only advisory,[54] courts, as well as agencies, often deferred to the CEQ's interpretation of NEPA.[55]

From 1971 to 1973, the CEQ supplemented its final guidelines with memoranda. Several of the memoranda discussed NEPA court decisions, especially noting decisions in which the courts had approved of the CEQ's interpretation of NEPA.[56] In 1972, the CEQ, for the first time, recommended that the agencies adopt its interpretation of what the content of their procedures should be. The CEQ memorandum was supported by discussions of judicial interpretations of NEPA.[57]

In 1973 the CEQ revised its final guidelines.[58] The 1973 guidelines were more detailed than the previous guidelines in specifying NEPA procedures to be adopted by agencies. Public participation procedures for EISs were strengthened. The revised guidelines were also more assertive in promoting the CEQ's interpretation of NEPA.

The scope of the guidelines increased beyond requiring draft and final EISs to include requiring consideration of environmental effects in all agency activities. The guidelines also required that EISs contain an evaluation of competing interests, including environmental and other interests.[59] The 1973 guidelines were not merely written more authoritatively in regulatory language; the CEQ published the guidelines in the *Code of Federal Regulations*, thus reinforcing the guidelines' regulatory appearance.

Once again, the agencies were slow to integrate the procedures in the revised guidelines into their individual procedures. Some agencies opposed the guidelines, arguing that compliance would require increases in staff and appropriations as well as interfering with the agencies' primary functions.[60] Every agency missed CEQ's deadline for publication of proposed changes to their procedures.[61] As late as 1976, some agencies still had not issued final procedures that complied with NEPA.[62]

2.4 THE CEQ REGULATIONS

In 1977, the CEQ's authority to implement NEPA was further strengthened. President Carter issued Executive Order 11,991, which empowered the CEQ to issue regulations that were binding on all federal agencies.[63] During the months following the executive order, the CEQ engaged in a lengthy rule-making process that included public hearings and numerous meetings with representatives of agencies, industry, and environmental groups. The rule-making process resulted in the CEQ's changing seventy-four out of ninety-two sections of the regulations.[64] Some agencies opposed the regulations, stating that the regulations exceeded the CEQ's authority under NEPA, case law, and Executive Order 11,991.[65]

In 1978 the CEQ promulgated final regulations,[66] whose major purpose was to provide uniform procedures for federal agencies that previously had each had varying NEPA procedures.[67] Other purposes included the reduction of paperwork and delay, and the accomplishment of NEPA's objective.[68] As had occurred with earlier NEPA procedures issued by the CEQ, many agencies were slow to supplement their individual procedures.[69]

The CEQ regulations are unusual. Issued eight years after enactment of the law they implement, the regulations are written by a small federal agency for use by other agencies, most of which greatly exceed the CEQ in size. Thus the regulations contain not merely the CEQ's interpretation of NEPA but, to a large extent, the CEQ's interpretation of NEPA as supported by case law, administrative experience from other federal agencies, and the lengthy rule-making process by which the regulations were finalized.[70] By codifying case law in the regulations, the CEQ made it more likely that courts would defer to its interpretation of NEPA. The codification of case law also caused the codified decisions to be applied nationwide.[71]

In addition to promulgating regulations guiding the NEPA process, the CEQ regulations set out procedures under section 309 of the Clean Air Act for referring environmentally unsatisfactory actions proposed by federal agencies to the CEQ,[72] and requirements for agency compliance with NEPA, including review by the CEQ of agency procedures implementing NEPA.[73] Section 309 of the Clean Air Act is discussed in section 2.10. Supplementary agency procedures are discussed in section 2.8.

The regulations' major change was the authority supporting them and their consequent ability to bind federal agencies. By applying the regulations to all federal actions covered by NEPA, the CEQ ensured that its interpretation of NEPA would become part of each agency's NEPA process. Other major changes in the regulations included the addition of more detailed procedures for determining the timing and scope of the NEPA process[74]; preparing draft and final EISs including commenting by other agencies and the public[75]; resolving disputes between agencies as to which agency is the lead agency, that is, which agency is primarily responsible for preparing an EIS and coordinating compliance in the NEPA process between other agencies.[76]

The regulations also introduced the "record of decision." The record of decision is prepared by an agency not less than thirty days after the agency issues a final EIS. In the record of decision, an agency must state its decision; identify and discuss the alternatives considered by its decision maker and state why one alternative was preferred over the others; state all factors entering into the agency's decision; and state whether "all practicable means to avoid or minimize environmental harm from the alternative selected have been adopted, and if not, why they were not."[77]

The record of decision was introduced to connect the means to the ends and "to see that the decisionmaker considers and pays attention to what the NEPA process has shown to be an environmentally sensitive way of doing things."[78] In the CEQ's opinion, the record of decision was "essential for the effective implementation of NEPA."[79]

The record of decision has not lived up to the CEQ's expectations. Most agencies do not routinely publish records of decision, thus the records are not subject to public review except for people who specifically request a copy. The CEQ referral process does not provide for review of agency actions based on records of decision.[80] Thus, by the time a record is made available, it is too late for the agency's action to be referred to the CEQ. Most importantly, the United States Supreme Court's interpretation of NEPA as an essentially procedural statute tends to, and may indeed, preclude judicial review of an agency's substantive decision once the agency has complied with NEPA's procedural requirements.[81] The CEQ regulations, as they apply to the preparation of EISs and records of decision are discussed in detail in chapter 5. The procedural/substantive interpretation of NEPA is briefly discussed in section 1.8.

Since promulgation of the CEQ regulations in 1978, only one regulation has been amended. The worst case analysis regulation required agencies to analyze the worst environmental consequences of a proposed action if the agency decided to proceed with the proposed action after discovering scientific uncertainty or gaps in scientific information when it evaluated the action's significant adverse environmental effects.[82]

In 1984, after controversial interpretations of the regulation by the Ninth Circuit,[83] the CEQ provided guidance on the regulation, and subsequently proposed withdrawing it and substituting a new regulation.[84] Two years later, the CEQ withdrew the worst case analysis regulation.[85] The withdrawal was upheld by the Supreme Court in 1989. The Supreme Court held that the CEQ had authority to withdraw the regulation because the regulation was not a codification of prior case law.[86] The withdrawn regulation and the new regulation, which does not require a worst case analysis, are discussed in section 5.10.2.

In October 1989, the chairman of the CEQ indicated that the CEQ may rewrite the regulations to clarify the types of actions requiring an EIS and those requiring an EA.[87] Also in 1989, the CEQ circulated draft procedures to federal agencies on including information on global warming in EISs. The CEQ is expected to publish the procedures in 1990. It is not certain whether the procedures will be in the form of guidelines or regulations.[88]

2.5 EFFECT OF THE CEQ REGULATIONS ON FEDERAL AGENCIES

The Supreme Court has recognized that Executive Order 11,991 made the CEQ regulations binding on federal agencies.[89] The CEQ regulations require federal agencies to comply with them regarding actions subject to NEPA in all circumstances except one. If emergency circumstances exist, an agency may conduct an action with significant environmental effects without complying with the regulations if it consults with the CEQ regarding alternative arrangements.[90] This narrow exception does not appear to have been widely used.

The independent regulatory agencies have long declared that they are not required to follow substantive directives originating from the executive branch and not the Congress.[91] During the rule-making process leading up to the CEQ regulations, the independent regulatory agencies bitterly criticized the CEQ for extending the regulations to them. The CEQ responded that NEPA applies to all federal agencies, and the regulations apply coextensively with NEPA because they simply interpret NEPA's procedural mandate.[92] As of mid-1990 the issue was still not settled. At least one independent regulatory agency continued to assert that its compliance with CEQ regulations was voluntary and conditional.[93]

The circuits are split on whether the CEQ regulations bind the independent regulatory agencies. The Ninth Circuit considers independent regulatory agencies to be bound by the CEQ regulations.[94] On the other hand, the Third Circuit considered the Nuclear Regulatory Commission (NRC) an independent regulatory agency, not to be bound by the CEQ regulations because the regulations were "not binding on an agency to the extent that the agency has not expressly adopted them."[95] The NRC had stated that it was not bound by any substantive regulations promulgated by the CEQ that the NRC had not adopted.[96] At issue was the worst case analysis regulation, which had been subsequently withdrawn by the CEQ.[97]

The rationale for the Third Circuit's holding is unclear. The CEQ regulations are binding on federal agencies, possibly excluding independent regulatory agencies, regardless of whether the CEQ regulations are expressly adopted by the federal agency. This proposition has been recognized by the United States Supreme Court when it stated that Executive Order 11,991 made the CEQ regulations mandatory and required the heads of federal agencies to comply with them.[98]

The Third Circuit seems to be stating that independent regulatory agencies are not bound by the CEQ regulations unless they expressly adopt them. Assuming that the court held that the independent regulatory agencies were not bound, this would create a split in the circuits. The issue in the Third Circuit would become whether NEPA and case law required an independent regulatory agency to follow the equivalent of the regulation. In such a situation, the CEQ's interpretation of NEPA as contained in the regulation would be entitled to substantial deference,[99] thus making it difficult but not impossible for an independent regulatory agency to prevail in an interpretation of NEPA contrary to that of the CEQ. Of course, if an independent regulatory agency adopts the CEQ regulations in its procedures, it is bound by them.[100]

Legislation pending in Congress in 1990 would give the CEQ regulatory authority thus ending the argument that the CEQ regulations do not apply to independent regulatory agencies.[101]

2.6 EFFECT OF THE CEQ REGULATIONS ON THE COURTS

The Supreme Court has stated that the "CEQ's interpretation of NEPA is entitled to substantial deference."[102] Thus, even when the CEQ's interpretation of NEPA conflicts with the interpretation adopted by a federal agency, a court may defer to the CEQ's interpretation.[103]

2.7 INFORMAL CEQ GUIDANCE

The CEQ publishes periodic guidance to the public and to agencies regarding NEPA procedures. Guidance published by the CEQ includes memoranda to federal agency heads on the CEQ's interpretation of NEPA,[104] a memorandum on the forty most often asked questions on the CEQ regulations,[105] guidance on agency implementation of the CEQ regulations,[106] and appendices to the CEQ regulations containing information on federal and state agencies with expertise on environmental quality issues.[107] The CEQ's informal advice is not binding on the agencies.[108]

Whereas the CEQ regulations are generally accorded substantial deference by the courts, courts may but do not necessarily accord the same deference to the CEQ's informal advice.[109] To be entitled to deference, the advice should be by the CEQ acting as a whole.[110]

2.8 SUPPLEMENTARY NEPA PROCEDURES OF INDIVIDUAL AGENCIES

The CEQ regulations require each federal agency to adopt NEPA procedures to supplement the CEQ regulations. The procedures are to be made available for public review as well as review by the CEQ for conformity with NEPA and the CEQ regulations.[111] This review by the CEQ is in addition to the review and possible referral of NEPA regulations to the CEQ by the EPA under section 309 of the Clean Air Act. The EPA may also influence the agencies' regulations by its ability to review and refer them.[112]

The CEQ regulations require agencies to include the following procedures in their individual procedures for implementing NEPA. First, the agency procedures must contain the procedures specified in NEPA for the preparation of EISs.[113] Second, the agencies must designate "major decision points for the agency's principal programs" that are likely to significantly affect the human environment. The individual agencies' NEPA process must correspond to these decision points.[114] Inclusion in agency procedures of an agency's principal decision points varies greatly depending on the nature of the agency. Decision points vary from the Department of State's negotiation of international agreements[115] to the National Aeronautics and Space Administration's conceptual study of an action followed by the detailed planning, subsequent implementation, and operation of the action.[116] Other agencies' decision points include notices of proposed rule making and the promulgation of the final rule in a rule-making proceeding.[117]

In identifying decision points, agencies may review environmental procedures for different categories of actions. For example, the EPA has separate environmental review procedures for its new source National Pollutant Discharge Elimination System program, its research and development programs, its solid waste demonstration project activities, and its facilities support activities.[118]

The third procedure that the CEQ requires in agencies' individual procedures is that the agency make "relevant environmental documents, comments, and responses . . . part of the record in formal rule-making or adjudicatory proceedings."[119] This requirement has greatly aided the public, especially plaintiffs, by opening up the agencies' decision-making procedures and by making the procedures subject to discovery. Agencies generally include this requirement in their procedures by restating the requirement.[120] Law enforcement proceedings may be exempt from this requirement.[121]

The fourth CEQ requirement is for "relevant environmental documents, comments, and responses [to] accompany the proposal through existing agency review processes so that agency officials use the [EIS] in making decisions."[122] Finally, the alternatives considered by the decision maker must be within the range of alternatives discussed in the relevant environmental documents. The decision maker must consider the alternatives in the EIS. Other documents containing information relevant to the alternatives in the EIS, which accompany the environmental documents, are encouraged to be made available in relevant parts to the public.[123] Some agencies simply reiterate either or both of the two latter requirements in their procedures.[124] The requirements are well settled in the case law.[125]

The NEPA procedures adopted by the individual agencies are varied. For example, the Department of Justice publishes general NEPA procedures supplemented by internal procedures in an appendix for such subdepartments as the Bureau of Prisons and the Drug Enforcement Administration.[126] The Department of Labor has taken an alternate approach. Because only three of the department's agencies routinely conduct actions to which NEPA applies, the department's NEPA procedures are tailored to these agencies' needs, with other agencies of the Department being required to use the procedures to the extent applicable.[127]

Several agencies publish voluminous manuals of procedures detailing the NEPA process.[128] The Department of the Interior includes its NEPA procedures as part of its departmental manual.[129] Appendices are published for each bureau such as the Fish and Wildlife Service, the Bureau of Land Management, the National Park Service, the Minerals Management Service, and so on. Each appendix contains information on the bureau's organizational responsibilities for complying with NEPA, and lists of actions normally requiring EISs, EAs, or categorical exclusions.[130]

Some agencies publish their procedures as regulations in the *Code of Federal Regulations* after initial publication in the *Federal Register*. Others merely publish the procedures and revisions to them in the *Federal Register*.[131] The Department of the Interior follows the latter practice. The Department publishes revisions to its NEPA procedures in the *Federal Register* and inserts those revisions into its internal loose-leaf manual. Changes to the appendices follow a similar format.[132]

Agencies generally list in their procedures different categories of actions typically conducted by them. The three major categories define the types of actions that require EISs, EAs, or that are categorical exclusions.[133] A categorical exclusion is generally not a major federal action significantly affecting the quality of the human environment, and it is thus generally not covered by NEPA.[134] The CEQ requires agencies to include a provision in their NEPA procedures whereby a proposed action will not be treated as a categorical exclusion if extraordinary circumstances exist.[135] The agencies' lists of types of actions may take the form of charts[136] or long lists of specific actions.[137] These lists are updated periodically.[138]

As noted, there are many similarities and differences between the procedures of the various federal agencies. Many differences are procedural. For example, an agency that prepares many EAs and EISs may have a detailed NEPA compliance manual,[139] whereas an agency whose actions are normally not covered by NEPA may publish a brief summary of procedures.[140]

Other differences are substantive. The Corps of Engineers revised its regulations to substitute a definition of federal action interpreted by the Fifth and Eighth Circuits. The definition narrowed the scope of the corps' regulations. In effect, like the CEQ, the corps adopted case law it agreed with and gave it nationwide application by incorporating it into its regulations. Whereas the CEQ's interpretation of NEPA in its regulations is routinely granted substantial deference by the courts, another agency's interpretation of NEPA may not necessarily be granted deference if a court finds that the agency does not have expertise in complying with NEPA. In this case, however, the CEQ added its authority to the corps' interpretation of NEPA by having approved the corps' regulations subject to modification following a referral by the EPA.[141]

Another example of an agency's regulations defining the scope of considerations in an EIS is the NRC's regulations, which contain a generic determination that the temporary storage of spent nuclear fuel after the cessation of operation of a nuclear reactor does not have significant environmental impacts.[142] In a challenge to the regulations, the United States Supreme Court deferred to the NRC's expertise in making scientific determinations within its special area of expertise.[143] There is thus a fine line between an agency's expertise in making scientific determinations and its nonexpertise in interpreting NEPA.

Location of this line in individual cases may well determine the outcome of the case.

The procedures of several agencies whose actions may affect the environment outside the United States have adopted NEPA procedures pursuant to Executive Order 12,114.[144] Executive Order 12,114 applies to actions having environmental effects either on the global commons, such as the oceans and Antarctica, or on foreign nations.[145]

Agencies that issue federal permits or that fund or approve projects often include instructions to potential applicants on the applicants' responsibilities in gathering and preparing data for the agency's use.[146] The issue of when applicants are permitted under NEPA to prepare environmental documentation is discussed in section 5.6.1.

2.9 EPA FILING SYSTEM FOR EISs

The EPA has two distinct responsibilities regarding draft and final EISs: an administrative process and a review process.

The CEQ regulations outline the EPA's administrative responsibilities for receiving and filing EISs, publishing a notice of filed EISs, and timing public comment deadlines to the filed EISs.[147] The EPA receives draft and final EISs from agencies and checks the documents for completeness. Each Friday the EPA publishes in the *Federal Register* a notice of availability for draft and final EISs that have been filed the previous week. The date of this notice is the date for calculating comment periods to the EISs. If the agency submitting the EIS withdraws, delays, or reopens a review period, it notifies the EPA and publishes a notice of its action.[148] The EPA thus provides an official log of EISs and ensures that filed EISs are publicly announced.[149]

2.10 SECTION 309 OF THE CLEAN AIR ACT

Section 309 of the Clean Air Act was enacted in 1970 to augment the administrative oversight of the agencies' compliance with NEPA in the face of widespread agency resistance to NEPA.[150] Section 309 provides that the administrator of the EPA shall review and comment publicly in writing on the environmental impact of proposed legislation and regulations and of newly authorized federal construction projects and major federal agency actions significantly affecting the quality of the human environment.[151] If the administrator determines that the legislation, regulation, or action "is unsatisfactory from the standpoint of public health or welfare or environmental quality, he shall publish his determination and the matter shall be referred to the [CEQ]."[152]

Section 309 thus provides broader powers than NEPA. Whereas plaintiffs in NEPA lawsuits may be precluded from challenging an agency's substantive decision to proceed with an action,[153] section 309 expressly grants the EPA administrator the power to comment on the substantive decision, to publish the decision, and to refer the matter to the CEQ. Once a matter is referred to the CEQ, agencies tend to accept the CEQ's suggestions or reach an agreement with the EPA.[154] Thus, the EPA has considerable power to ensure that environmentally destructive actions do not proceed. The power is increased substantially if the CEQ agrees with the EPA's comments. This power is largely undeveloped.

Section 309 has two components. First, it requires the administrator to review and comment on all actions requiring preparation of an EIS as well as additional actions, such as proposed legislation and regulations, and any federal construction projects. Second, section 309 authorizes the EPA to make and publish determinations of actions that it considers to be environmentally unsatisfactory and to refer such matters to the CEQ.

2.10.1 EPA Review

The environmental review process system is a distinct system from the EPA filing system for EISs described above.[155] Under authority of section 309, the EPA reviews and comments on draft and final EISs[156.] Summaries of the EPA's comments are published each week in the *Federal Register*. EISs on regulations are also reviewed by the EPA under section 309,[157] including any amendments to the CEQ regulations.[158] In addition to review of EISs under section 309, the EPA may comment on an EIS in its role as a cooperating agency.[159]

The EPA rates draft EISs and their underlying actions according to two sets of standards: a rating on the environmental effect of the underlying action and a rating on the adequacy of the draft EIS. Final EISs are not rated but are usually reviewed and commented on.[160] The four categories by which the EPA rates the action underlying a draft EIS are lack of objections (LO), environmental concerns (EC), environmental objections (EO), and environmentally unsatisfactory (EU).

The comment "lack of objections" means that the EPA did not identify any potential environmental effects requiring substantive changes to the proposed action. The EPA's review may have identified mitigation measures that could be achieved through minor changes in the proposed action.

A rating of "environmental concerns" indicates that the EPA identified environmental effects that it considers should be avoided if the environment is to be fully protected. In such a case, the EPA recommends that it work with the lead agency to apply mitigation measures or to change the preferred alternative.

The comment "environmental objections" indicates an intent by the EPA to work with the lead agency to avoid significant environmental effects. The EPA considers that corrective measures may require consideration of a different preferred alternative or substantial changes to the preferred alternative.

"Environmentally unsatisfactory" indicates that the EPA has identified adverse environmental effects "of sufficient magnitude that they are unsatisfactory from the standpoint of public health or welfare or environmental quality." In such a case, the EPA states that it intends to work with the lead agency to reduce the effects. If the EPA's efforts are unsuccessful and the potentially unsatisfactory effects are not corrected in the final EIS, the EPA guidance states that the proposed action will be recommended for referral to the CEQ.[161]

The three categories by which the EPA rates the adequacy of draft EISs are: Category 1—adequate; Category 2—insufficient information; Category 3—inadequate. A draft EIS receiving a category 1 rating does not require further analysis, although the EPA may suggest that additional or clarifying language be added. A draft EIS receiving a category 2 rating requires either additional information, data, analyses, or discussion to be included in the final EIS; a reasonably available alternative within the spectrum of alternatives considered in the EIS to be included in the final EIS; or the inclusion of necessary information to aid in assessing environmental effects.

A draft EIS rated category 3 requires formal revision or supplementation because it failed to adequately assess potentially significant environmental effects of the proposed action or it failed to include reasonably available alternatives outside the spectrum of alternatives analyzed in the draft EIS. The revised or supplemental draft EIS must be made available for public comment. Depending on the potential significant environmental effects of the proposed action, a draft EIS rated category 3 could be a candidate for referral to the CEQ.[162]

In addition to reviewing EISs and underlying actions, the EPA selectively reviews records of decision to determine if an agency has incorporated agreed upon mitigation measures into the proposed action.[163] In light of a 1989 Supreme Court decision, it is not clear whether the EPA has authority under NEPA to require incorporation of proposed mitigation measures into agency actions.[164]

If an agency refuses to include a mitigation plan in an EIS, the EPA could refer the matter to the CEQ under section 309 of the Clean Air

Act.[165] However, if the agency incorporates the plan in the EIS and then states in the record of decision that it is abandoning the plan, or simply abandons the plan without stating the fact, the remedy for the EPA or a person aggrieved by the agency action is unclear. As discussed below, by the time a record of decision is issued, it is too late for the EPA to refer an action to the CEQ. However, a person aggrieved by the agency action may have a cause of action based on the agency's bad faith.[166] One commentator has noted that the EPA's procedures do not fully implement section 309 because of the discretionary review of post-EIS procedures and the EPA's focus on the narrow issue of an agency's adoption of an agreed upon mitigation plan.[167]

The EPA's and CEQ's implementation of section 309 has other problems. The time limit for referring proposed actions to the CEQ does not allow the EPA to refer actions in which agreed upon plans were not included in the record of decision. Records of decision may not be issued until at least thirty days after the EIS is submitted to the EPA, whereas a referral must reach the agency within twenty-five days of the submission to the EPA of the final EIS. Therefore, the failure of an agency to base its record of decision on an EIS cannot be referred to the CEQ.[168]

As described above, the EPA reviews and comments on draft and final EISs. Typical comments by the EPA after reviewing draft EISs range from no objections[169] to the intent to consider referring the action to the CEQ if the EPA's concerns are not addressed in the final EIS.[170] Between these two extremes are requests by the EPA for additional information[171] or formulation of a monitoring plan,[172] concern that a proposed action violates other environmental laws,[173] a recommendation that a federal permit be denied,[174] or a declaration that the issuance of a permit under another environmental law is unlikely.[175]

Comments on final EISs range from the extreme of no formal comments because review of the final EIS was not deemed necessary[176] to the intent to consider referring the action to the CEQ if the EPA's concerns are not addressed.[177] Comments between these extremes include requests for commitments to be included in records of decision,[178] requests for the agency to prepare a supplemental EIS,[179] recommended denial of a federal permit,[180] or expression of a belief that implementation of the action will violate an environmental standard or law.[181]

The EPA is under no duty to refer an EIS a rating less severe than environmentally unsatisfactory to the CEQ.[182] Referral is not necessarily the only recourse open to the EPA, however, for actions it deems to be environmentally unsatisfactory. As well as being able to refer an action to the CEQ, the EPA also may state that it considers it unlikely that it will issue a permit required under the action[183] or that it may take administrative action under other environmental laws over which it has jurisdiction.[184] The EPA may also enter into a memorandum of agreement regarding concerns it wishes to be addressed in a final EIS.[185]

The nature of the EPA review of an agency action may affect a subsequent judicial challenge to the action. A favorable comment to a draft EIS by the EPA under its section 309 authority aids an agency in establishing the adequacy of the subsequent final EIS.[186] A referral to the CEQ by the EPA is also considered by a reviewing court and the agency may be entitled to deference if its proposed action is subsequently revised according to the CEQ's suggestions.[187] The failure of the EPA to review an EIS does not penalize the agency that submitted the EIS to the EPA for review.[188]

2.10.2 CEQ Referrals

A referral to the CEQ must concern a matter of national importance.[189] The CEQ regulations state that an agency that is considering referring a matter to the CEQ should consider the following factors in making that decision: possible violations of national environmental standards or policies; severity of the action; the action's geographical scope, duration, and precedential importance; and the availability of environmentally preferable alternatives.[190] The CEQ regulations, drawing on authority from NEPA, authorize referrals from agencies other than the EPA if the agency reviewing the EIS determines that the underlying action has environmentally unacceptable consequences.[191]

The CEQ regulations set out procedures for implementing section 309. The regulations include establishing a timetable for submitting referrals; detailing the procedures to be taken by an agency referring an action and the lead agency whose EIS is the subject of the complaint; and outlining the actions available to the CEQ.[192]

The referring agency must deliver its referral to the CEQ no later than twenty-five days after the final EIS has been made available to the EPA, commenting agencies, and the public, unless the lead agency grants an extension.[193] The lead agency must then deliver its response to the CEQ within twenty-five days following the date of the referral.[194] Within twenty-five days of the response, or of the notification of no response, the CEQ takes action,[195] and it concludes its actions no later than sixty days from the date it begins to act.[196]

The CEQ stresses that the referring agency must advise the lead agency at the earliest possible time of its intent to refer a matter to the CEQ. The referring agency must support its conclusion that the action is unsatisfactory with factual evidence and a reasoned explanation of why the action is unsatisfactory, and it must specify the remedial activities it considers necessary.[197] In its reply, the lead agency must fully address issues raised in the referral,[198] support them with evidence, and respond to the referring agency's recommendations. Interested parties may submit their views to the CEQ.[199]

The CEQ has several options when it receives a referral. It may conclude that the referral process has resolved the problem; mediate between the referring and lead agencies; obtain additional views and information by holding public meetings or hearings; refer the matter back to the referring and lead agencies because it is not an issue of national importance, or because it does not consider the difference to be irreconcilable; publish its findings and recommendations; or submit the referral, response, and its recommendation to the president for action.[200]

Although a decision on a referral by the CEQ does not bind the agencies involved, in general the agencies have accepted the CEQ's recommendations.[201] Agencies have agreed to modify the action,[202] they have compromised,[203] and they have adopted proposed changes by the CEQ.[204] Congress has helped persuade agencies to accept the CEQ's recommendations by use of its appropriations power.[205] Although an agency does not violate NEPA by rejecting the CEQ's and the EPA's advice subsequent to a review and referral it should articulate its reasons for doing so.[206] A referral by the EPA and a subsequent determination by the CEQ may influence a subsequent judicial challenge. The Ninth Circuit accorded deference to an agency's modifications to its regulations implementing NEPA when the regulations had been revised according to CEQ suggestions following a section 309 referral.[207]

The referral process has been used sparingly. From 1974–1984 there were twenty-two referrals: thirteen by the EPA, six by the Department of the Interior, one by the EPA and the Department of the Interior, one by the Department of Defense, and one from the Advisory Council on Historic Preservation.[208] The lead agencies in the above referrals were the Corps of Engineers in nine referrals, the Federal Highway Administration in four referrals, the Bureau of Land Management in four referrals, and the Department of Transportation in two referrals. The Atomic Energy Commission, the Department of Housing and Urban Development, and the Federal Aviation Administration were each referred once.[209]

NOTES

1. 42 U.S.C. § 4342 (1988).
2. *See* 115 Cong. Rec. 40,422 (1969) (remarks of Sen. Allott).

3. Pacific Legal Found'n v. CEQ, 636 F.2d 1259, 1263 (D.C. Cir. 1980).

4. 42 U.S.C. § 4342 (1988). *See generally* 20 Env't Rep. (BNA) 1059, 1059-60 (1989) (CEQ chairman stated that two member positions, both of which were vacant in October 1989, may be eliminated by statute).

5. 42 U.S.C. §§ 4371–4374 (1988).

6. *Id.* § 4371(c)(2).

7. *See* 115 Cong. Rec. 40,925 (1969) (Answers by Rep. John Dingell to Letter from Rep. George Fallon)); *see also id.* at 40,424 (remarks of Sen. Edmund Muskie) (remarking on relationship between CEQ and Office of Environmental Quality); *id.* at 40,425 (same).

8. 42 U.S.C. § 4372 (1988).

9. *See* Council on Environmental Quality, *Environmental Quality 1972: Third Annual Report* 223; *see also* 115 Cong. Rec. 29,050–89 (1969) (Senate consideration of Environmental Quality Improvement Act).

10. *See* General Accounting Office, *The Council on Environmental Quality: A Tool in Shaping National Policy* 1 (CED-81–66 1981); Davies & Lettow, *The Impact of Federal Institutional Arrangements* in *Federal Environmental Law* 126, 131 (Envtl. L. Inst. 1974).

11. *See CEQ's Role Declines Under Carter, Reagan After Serving as Major Policy-Making Body,* 16 Env't Rep. (BNA) 10 (1985).

12. General Accounting Office, *The Council on Environmental Quality: A Tool in Shaping National Policy* 6–9 (CED-81–66 1981).

13. *Department of Housing and Urban Development—Independent Agencies Appropriations for 1983: Hearings Before a Subcomm. of the House Comm. on Appropriations,* 97th Cong., 2d Sess. 11 (1982) (statement of Thomas Delaney, administrative officer, CEQ).

14. *See* 42 U.S.C. § 4374 (Supp. V 1987) (appropriations for fiscal years ending 1979-1986); *see also* 42 U.S.C. § 4347 (1988).

15. *See CEQ Staggering Under Latest Budget Cut,* 221 Science 529 (1983).

16. *Fiscal Year 1987 Budget Review: Hearings Before the Senate Comm. on Environment and Public Works,* 99th Cong., 2d Sess. 424 (1986).

17. *See CEQ to Work Closely with White House, EPA to Define its Focus, New Chairman Deland Says,* 20 Env't Rep. (BNA) 688 (1989).

18. *See CEQ Will Grow, Have Bigger Policy Role, Nominee for Chairman Tells Senate Panel,* 20 Envt. Rep. (BNA) 598 (1989); *see also* Excerpts from President's Fiscal 1991 Budget Request for Environment, *reprinted in* 20 Envt. Rep. (BNA) 1725, 1726–27 (1990) (requesting near-doubling of CEQ budget and stating that president is committed to strengthening CEQ).

19. 42 U.S.C. § 4344 (1988).

20. *Id.* § 4346b.

21. Exec. Order No. 12,114, *reprinted in* 42 U.S.C. § 4321 note (1988).

22. Council on Environmental Quality, Fact Sheet (undated); *see* 40 C.F.R. § 1515.2 (1989).

23. *See Federal Agencies Begin to Consider Global Warming in Impact Statements,* 20 Envt. Rep. (BNA) 1271 (1989).

24. H.R. 1113, 101st Cong., 1st Sess. (1989); *see* H. Rep. No. 219, 101st Cong., 1st Sess. (1989); H.R. 3847, 101st Cong., 2d Sess. (1990); S. 1089, 101st Cong., 1st Sess. (1989).

25. H.R. 1113 § 2, 101st Cong., 1st Sess. (1989); H.R. 3847 § 502, 101st Cong., 2d Sess. (1990); S. 1089 § 2, 101st Cong., 1st Sess. (1989).

26. 42 U.S.C. § 7609(a) (1988); *see* 40 C.F.R. § 1504.1(b) (1989).

27. 42 U.S.C. § 4332(2)(C) (1988); *see* 40 C.F.R. § 1504.1(c) (1989).

28. 16 U.S.C. § 1536(l)(2) (1988); *see* 55 Fed. Reg. 13,821 (1990); 53 Fed. Reg. 7960 (1988).

29. 3 C.F.R. 793, 795 (1971–1975 compilation).

30. *See* H.R. 1113 § 3, 101st Cong., 1st Sess. (1989) (providing the CEQ with regulatory authority); H.R. 3847 § 503, 101st Cong., 2d Sess. (1990) (same); S. 1089 § 3, 101st Cong., 1st Sess. 1989) (same).

31. 42 U.S.C. § 4344(3) (1988).

32. *Id.* § 4344(4).

33. 3 C.F.R. 902 (1970), *as amended by,* Exec. Order 11,991, 3 C.F.R. 123 (1978), *reprinted in* 42 U.S.C. § 4321 note (1988).

34. Council on Environmental Quality, *Environmental Quality 1970: First Annual Report* 21.

35. Council on Environmental Quality, Statements on Proposed Federal Actions Affecting the Environment: Interim Guidelines, 35 Fed. Reg. 7390 (1970).

36. *See* Liroff, *The Council on Environmental Quality,* 3 Envtl. L. Rep. (Envtl. L. Inst.) 50,051, 50,052 (1973) (staffs of Senator Henry Jackson and Representative John Dingell consulted with CEQ in preparing guidelines).

37. Council on Environmental Quality, Statements on Proposed Federal Actions Affecting the Environment: Interim Guidelines, 35 Fed. Reg. 7390, 7391–92 (1970).

38. *Id.* at 7391. *See generally* R. Andrews, *Environmental Policy and Administrative Change* 30 (Lexington Books 1976).

39. Conf. Rep. No. 765, 91st Cong., 1st Sess., *reprinted in* 1969 U.S. Code Cong. & Admin. News 2767, 2771; *see* 115 Cong. Rec. 40,422 (1969) (remarks of Sen. Henry Jackson).

40. R. Andrews, *Environmental Policy and Administrative Change* 31 (Lexington Books 1976).

41. Council on Environmental Quality, Statements on Proposed Federal Actions Affecting the Environment: Interim Guidelines, 35 Fed. Reg. 7390, 7391 (1970).

42. *See* R. Andrews, *Environmental Policy and Administrative Change* 31–32 (Lexington Books 1976).

43. *See, e.g.,* Chelsea Neighborhood Ass'ns v. United States Postal Serv., 516 F.2d 378, 382 (2d Cir. 1975) (Post Office); Kalur v. Resor, 335 F. Supp. 1, 12 (D.D.C. 1971) (Corps of Engineers).

44. *See* Comment, *CEQ Proposes New Guidelines for NEPA,* 3 Envtl. L. Rep. (Envtl. L. Inst.) 10,056 (1973) (citing 36 Fed. Reg. 23,665 (1971) and 37 Fed. Reg. 22,667 (1972)); *Agencies' Revised NEPA Procedural Compliance Guidelines Near Completion, Months After Deadline for Submission to CEQ,* 1 Envtl. L. Rep. (Envtl. L. Inst.) 10,167, 10,171 (1971).

45. Council on Environmental Quality, Statements on Proposed Federal Actions Affecting the Environment: Guidelines, 36 Fed. Reg. 7724 (1971).

46. *Id.* at 7726. *See generally* R. Andrews, *Environmental Policy and Administrative Change* 33 (Lexington Books 1976).

47. Council on Environmental Quality, Statements on Proposed Federal Actions Affecting the Environment: Guidelines, 36 Fed. Reg. 7724, 7726 (1971).

48. *See generally* R. Andrews, *Environmental Policy and Administrative Change* 32–33 (Lexington Books 1976); Liroff, *The Council on Environmental Quality*, 3 Envtl. L. Rep. (Envtl. L. Inst.) 50,051, 50,057 (1973) (citing *Hearings on Federal Agency Compliance with Section 102(2)(C) and Section 103 of the National Environmental Policy Act of 1969 Before the Subcomm. on Fisheries and Wildlife Conservation of the House Comm. on Merchant Marine and Fisheries*, 91st Cong., 2d Sess. (Dec. 1970)).

49. Council on Environmental Quality, Statements on Proposed Federal. Actions Affecting the Environment: Guidelines, 36 Fed. Reg. 7724, 7725–26 (1971).

50. *Id.* at 7724.

51. 449 F.2d 1109, 1117 (D.C. Cir. 1971).

52. *Id.* at 1118 n.19; *see id.* at 1129 n.43.

53. *See Agencies' Revised NEPA Procedural Compliance Guidelines Near Completion, Months After Deadline for Submission to CEQ*, 1 Envtl. L. Rep. (Envtl. L. Inst.) 10,167, 10,168–71 (1971).

54. *See* Hiram Clarke Civic Club, Inc. v. Lynn, 476 F.2d 421, 424 (5th Cir. 1973); Greene County Planning Bd. v. FPC, 455 F.2d 412, 421 (2d Cir.), *cert. denied*, 409 U.S. 849 (1972); *see also* Baltimore Gas & Elec. Co. v. Natural Resources Defense Council, Inc., 462 U.S. 87, 99 n.12 (1983) (declining to decide whether CEQ guidelines bound independent agencies).

55. *E.g.*, Warm Springs Dam Task Force v. Gribble, 417 U.S. 1301, 1309-10 (1974) (Douglas, Circuit Justice). *See generally* Comment, *Supreme Court Ushers in New Era for CEQ in* Warm Springs *Case*, 4 Envtl. L. Rep. (Envtl. L. Inst.) 10,130 (1974).

56. *See generally* Comment, *The Council on Environmental Quality's Guidelines and Their Influence on the National Environmental Policy Act*, 23 Catholic Univ. L. Rev. 547, 561–71 (1974). *See also* 42 Fed. Reg. 61,066 (1977) (CEQ memorandum interpreting NEPA).

57. *See generally* Comment, *The Council on Environmental Quality's Guidelines and Their Influence on the National Environmental Policy Act*, 23 Catholic Univ. L. Rev. 547, 565–66 (1974).

58. Council on Environmental Quality, Preparation of Environmental Impact Statements: Guidelines, 38 Fed. Reg. 20,550 (1973).

59. *Id.* at 20,550–57. *See generally* R. Andrews, *Environmental Policy and Administrative Change* 36–38 (Lexington Books 1976).

60. *See* Harlem Valley Transp. Ass'n v. Stafford, 500 F.2d 328, 332 (2d Cir. 1974) (ICC petitioned CEQ for amendment of 1973 guidelines; CEQ's chairman denied the requested amendment).

61. *See* Druley, *Federal Agency NEPA Procedures*, Env't Rep. (BNA) Monograph No. 23, at 1–2 (1976).

62. *See, e.g.*, Maine Central RR. v. ICC, 410 F. Supp. 657, 658–59 (D.D.C. 1976).

63. 3 C.F.R. 123 (1978) (amending Exec. Order 11,514, 3 C.F.R. 902 (1970)), *reprinted in* 42 U.S.C. § 4321 note (1988).

64. *See* General Accounting Office, *The Council on Environmental Quality: A Tool in Shaping National Policy* 16 (CED-81–66 1981).

65. *See* Comment, *Reinvigorating the NEPA Process: CEQ's Draft Compliance Regulations Stir Controversy,* 8 Envtl. L. Rep. (Envtl. L. Inst.) 10,045, 10,045 (1978).

66. Council on Environmental Quality, National Environmental Policy Act Regulations; Implementation of Procedural Provisions, 43 Fed. Reg. 55,978 (1978).

67. 43 Fed. Reg. 55,978 (1978).

68. *Id.*

69. *See* General Accounting Office, *The Council on Environmental Quality: A Tool in Shaping National Policy* 16 (CED-81–66 1981).

70. 43 Fed. Reg. 55,978, 55,980 (1978).

71. *See* Karp, *The NEPA Regulations,* 19 Am. Bus. L.J. 295, 317 (1981).

72. 40 C.F.R. part 1504 (1989); *see* 42 U.S.C. § 7609 (1988).

73. 40 C.F.R. part 1507 (1989).

74. *Id.* part 1501.

75. *Id.* part 1503.

76. *Id.* § 1501.5.

77. *Id.* § 1505.2.

78. Council on Environmental Quality, The National Environmental Policy Act—Final Regulations, 43 Fed. Reg. 55,978, 55,985 (1978).

79. *Id.; see also* Liebesman, *The Council on Environmental Quality's Regulations to Implement the National Environmental Policy Act—Will They Further NEPA's Substantive Mandate,* 10 Envtl. L. Rep. (Envtl. L. Inst.) 50,039, 50,050–51 (1980) (quoting and describing CEQ review of records of decision prepared since 1978).

80. *See* section 2.10.2.

81. *See* section 1.8.

82. 40 C.F.R. § 1502.22 (1985) (superseded).

83. *See* Save Our Ecosystems v. Clark, 747 F.2d 1240 (9th Cir. 1984); Southern Or. Citizens Against Toxic Sprays, Inc. v. Clark, 720 F.2d 1475 (9th Cir. 1983), *cert. denied,* 469 U.S. 1028 (1984); *see also* Sierra Club v. Sigler, 695 F.2d 957 (5th Cir. 1983).

84. *See* Council on Environmental Quality, Notice of Proposed Guidance and Request for Comments, 48 Fed. Reg. 36,486 (1983); Council on Environmental Quality, Notice—Withdrawal of Proposed Guidance Memorandum for Federal Agency NEPA Liaisons, 49 Fed. Reg. 4803 (1984); Council on Environmental Quality, Advance Notice of Proposed Rulemaking, 49 Fed. Reg. 50,744 (1984); Council on Environmental Quality, Proposed Amendment to 40 C.F.R. 1502.22, 50 Fed. Reg. 32,234 (1985).

85. Council on Environmental Quality, National Environmental Policy Act Regulations; Incomplete or Unavailable Information, Final Rule, 51 Fed. Reg. 15,618 (1986).

86. Robertson v. Methow Valley Citizens Council, 109 S. Ct. 1835, 1848 (1989).

87. *See generally* 20 Env't Rep. (BNA) 1059, 1059-60 (1989).

88. *Federal Agencies Begin to Consider Global Warming in Impact Statements,* 20 Envt. Rep. (BNA) 1271 (1989).

89. Andrus v. Sierra Club, 442 U.S. 347, 357 (1979) (citing Exec. Order 11,991, 3 C.F.R. 124 (1978)). *Cf.* Baltimore Gas & Elec. Co. v. Natural Resources Defense Council, Inc., 462 U.S. 87, 99 n.12 (1983) (declining to decide whether CEQ guidelines bound independent agencies).

90. 40 C.F.R. § 1506.11 (1989); *see* Crosby v. Young, 512 F. Supp. 1363, 1380 (E.D. Mich. 1981); *see also* National Audubon Soc'y v. Hester, 801 F.2d 405, 408 n.3 (D.C. Cir. 1986) (CEQ certified that due to urgent nature of agency action, agency need not immediately record reasons why it preferred alternative course of action discussed in EIS).

91. *See CEQ Proposes Ambitious NEPA Regulations for Comment, Stands Ground Despite Agency Criticism,* 8 Envtl. L. Rep. (Envtl. L. Inst.) 10,129, 10,130 (1978).

92. *See id.;* Council on Environmental Quality, Forty Most Asked Questions Concerning CEQ's National Environmental Policy Act Regulations, 46 Fed. Reg. 18,026, 18,036 (1981).

93. *See* 10 C.F.R. § 51.10 (1989) (Nuclear Regulatory Commission).

94. Steamboaters v. FERC, 759 F.2d 1382, 1392–93 & 1393 n.4 (9th Cir. 1985).

95. Limerick Ecology Action, Inc. v. NRC, 869 F.2d 719, 743 (3d Cir. 1989).

96. *Id.* at 728, 743.

97. *Id.* at 743 & n.29.

98. *See* Andrus v. Sierra Club, 442 U.S. 347, 357 (1979).

99. *See id.* at 358.

100. *See* Township of Lower Alloways Creek v. Public Serv. Elec. & Gas Co., 687 F.2d 732, 740 n.16 (3d Cir. 1982).

101. *See* S. 1089 § 3, 101st Cong., 1st Sess. (1989); H.R. 1113 § 3, 101st Cong., 1st Sess. (1989); H.R. 3847 § 503, 101st Cong., 2d Sess. (1990).

102. Andrus v. Sierra Club, 442 U.S. 347, 358 (1979); *see also* Warm Springs Dam Task Force v. Gribble, 417 U.S. 1301, 1310 (1974) (Douglas, Circuit Justice) (CEQ's determination of an agency's compliance with NEPA is entitled to great weight).

103. *See* Morris County Trust for Historic Preservation v. Pierce, 714 F.2d 271, 276 (3d Cir. 1983).

104. *See, e.g.,* 42 Fed. Reg. 61,066 (1977). *See generally* Liroff, *The Council on Environmental Quality,* 3 Envtl. L. Rep. (Envtl. L. Inst.) 50,051, 50,053–55 (1973) (describing CEQ memoranda).

105. 46 Fed. Reg. 18,026 (1981).

106. 48 Fed. Reg. 34,263 (1983).

107. 49 Fed. Reg. 49,750 (1984).

108. *See* Friends of the Earth v. Hintz, 800 F.2d 822, 837 n.15 (9th Cir. 1986); Louisiana v. Lee, 758 F.2d 1081, 1083 (5th Cir. 1985) ("Forty Questions" is not controlling authority), *cert. denied,* 475 U.S. 1044 (1986).

109. *See* Friends of the Earth v. Hintz, 800 F.2d 822, 837 n.15 (9th Cir. 1986) ("Forty Questions" is not entitled to substantial deference); Deukmejian v. NRC, 751 F.2d 1287, 1302 n.77 (D.C. Cir. 1984) (citing Cabinet Mountain Wilderness/Scotchman's Peak Grizzly Bears v. Peterson, 685 F.2d 678, 682 (D.C. Cir. 1982) (declining to accord substantial deference to "Forty Questions")), *vacated in part,* 760 F.2d 1320 (D.C. Cir. 1985), *cert. denied,* 479 U.S. 923 (1986). *But see* Warm Springs Dam Task Force v. Gribble, 417 U.S. 1301, 1310 (1974) (Douglas, Circuit Justice) (according great weight to CEQ's opinion that EIS was inadequate). *Cf.*

Warm Springs Dam Task Force v. Gribble, 565 F.2d 549, 553–54 (9th Cir. 1977) (letter from CEQ did not state that EIS was inadequate).

110. Trustees for Alaska v. Hodel, 806 F.2d 1378, 1384 n.10 (9th Cir. 1986).

111. 40 C.F.R. § 1507.3 (1989).

112. *See* 54 Fed. Reg. 46,459 (1989) (objecting to categorical exclusions proposed by Navy and recommending exclusions' deletion).

113. 40 C.F.R. § 1505.1(a) (1989).

114. *Id.* § 1505.1(b).

115. *See* 22 C.F.R. § 161.5(c) (1989).

116. *See* 14 C.F.R. § 1216.304 (1989); *see also* 36 C.F.R. § 907.6 (1989) (Pennsylvania Avenue Development Corporation; similar phases).

117. 18 C.F.R. § 380.11(a) (1989).

118. 40 C.F.R. §§ 6.600–.905 (1989).

119. 40 C.F.R. § 1505.1(c) (1989).

120. *See, e.g.,* 44 C.F.R. §§ 10.5(a)(8), 10.5(c)(2) (1989) (Federal Emergency Management Agency); 18 C.F.R. § 380.11(b) (1989) (Federal Energy Regulatory Commission).

121. *See* 40 C.F.R. § 1508.18(a) (1989). *See, e.g.,* 28 C.F.R. § 61.4 (1989) (Department of Justice); 16 C.F.R. § 1021.7(e) (1989) (Consumer Product Safety Commision). *Cf.* Mobil Oil Corp. v. FTC, 562 F.2d 170, 173 (2d Cir. 1977) (reserving issue of whether EIS must precede final order under Federal Trade Commission's adjudicatory proceeding).

122. 40 C.F.R. § 1505.1(d) (1989).

123. *Id.* § 1505.1(e).

124. *See, e.g.,* 50 C.F.R. § 530.2(b) (1989) (Marine Mammal Commission); 12 C.F.R. § 408.5 (1989) (Export-Import Bank of the United States); 41 C.F.R. § 51–6.13 (1989) (Committee for Purchase from the Blind and Other Severely Handicapped).

125. *See* sections 5.7 (timing of EISs), 5.10.1 (alternatives).

126. 28 C.F.R. § 61.3 (1989).

127. 29 C.F.R. § 11.2 (1989) (regulations are primarily designed for Occupational Safety and Health Administration, Mine Safety and Health Administration, and Employment and Training Administration).

128. *See generally* Andrews, *NEPA in Practice: Environmental Policy or Administrative Reform?,* 6 Envtl. L. Rep. (Envtl. L. Inst.) 50,001, 50,003 (1976).

129. Department of the Interior, Departmental Manual part 516; *see* 45 Fed. Reg. 27,541 (1980) (revising Departmental Manual).

130. *See, e.g.,* National Park Service, NEPA Compliance Guideline (NPS-12, Oct. 1984) (amending, inter alia, Appendix 7—National Park Service).

131. *See Implementation of the National Environmental Policy Act by the Council on Environmental Quality; Hearing Before the Subcomm. on Toxic Substances and Environmental Oversight of the Senate Comm. on Environment and Public Works,* 97th Cong., 2d Sess. 19-23 (1982) (listing agencies' final procedures implementing NEPA). *See, e.g.,* 49 Fed. Reg. 29,644 (1984) (revisions to National Oceanic and Atmospheric Administration directives manual); 50 Fed. Reg. 26,078 (1985) (revisions to Forest Service manual and handbook).

132. *See, e.g.,* 51 Fed. Reg. 1855 (1986) (notice of instructions for Minerals Management Service); 46 Fed. Reg. 56,998 (1981) (Forest Service's notice of final policy); 46 Fed. Reg. 7485 (1981) (notice of final revised instructions for the United States Geological Survey).

133. 40 C.F.R. § 1501.4(a) (1989).

134. *Id.* § 1508.4.

135. *Id.*

136. *See, e.g.,* 28 C.F.R. part 61 app. B (1989) (Department of Justice); 29 C.F.R. § 11.10 (1989) (Department of Labor); 52 Fed. Reg. 47,662, 47,668–70 (1987) (Department of Energy).

137. *See, e.g.,* 44 C.F.R. § 10.8 (1989) (Federal Emergency Management Agency); 46 C.F.R. § 504.4 (1989) (Federal Maritime Commission); 38 C.F.R. § 26.6 (1989) (Department of Veterans Affairs).

138. *See, e.g.,* 54 Fed. Reg. 34,796, 34,797 (1989) (United States Postal Service; proposed amendments to 39 C.F.R. part 775).

139. *See, e.g.,* Department of Interior, Departmental Manual part 516.

140. *See, e.g.,* 50 C.F.R. § 530.3 (1989) ("[a]s a general matter, the [Marine Mammal] Commission activities do not include actions for which EIS's or [EAs] are required"); 21 C.F.R. § 25.21(a) (1989) (no actions of Food and Drug Administration ordinarily require preparation of EIS).

141. Sylvester v. Corps of Eng'rs, 884 F.2d 394, 398–401 (9th Cir. 1989).

142. *See* 10 C.F.R. § 51.23 (1989); *see also* 54 Fed. Reg. 39,765 (1989) (proposing to amend another part of rule in light of review of supporting findings).

143. Baltimore Gas & Elec. Co. v. Natural Resources Defense Council, Inc., 462 U.S. 87, 103–04 (1983). *Cf.* Limerick Ecology Action, Inc. v. NRC, 869 F.2d 719, 723 (3d Cir. 1989) (policy statement issued by NRC did not represent careful consideration of environmental effects).

144. *See, e.g.,* 14 C.F.R. § 1216.321 (1989) (National Aeronautics and Space Administration); 49 Fed. Reg. 29,653 (1984) (National Oceanic and Atmospheric Administration); 40 C.F.R. § 6.1001 (1989) (Environmental Protection Agency); 22 C.F.R. § 216.1(a) (1989) (Agency for International Development); 22 C.F.R. §§ 161.3, 161.12 (1989) (Department of State); 12 C.F.R. § 408.3 (1989) (Export-Import Bank of the United States); 32 C.F.R. part 197 (1989) (Office of Secretary of Defense).

145. 44 Fed. Reg. 1957 (1979), *reprinted in* 42 U.S.C. § 4321 note (1988).

146. *See, e.g.,* 18 C.F.R. § 380.3 (1989) (Federal Energy Regulatory Commission); 10 C.F.R. § 51.50 (1989) (Nuclear Regulatory Commission); 49 C.F.R. § 1105.7 (1989) (Interstate Commerce Commission).

147. 40 C.F.R. §§ 1506.9, 1506.10 (1989).

148. *Id.* § 1506.10(a); 54 Fed. Reg. 9592, 9593–94 (1989) (EPA Filing System Guidance).

149. 54 Fed. Reg. 9593 (1989).

150. 42 U.S.C. § 7609 (1988). *See generally* Andreen, *In Pursuit of NEPA's Promise: The Role of Executive Oversight in the Implementation of Environmental Policy,* 64 Ind. L.J. 205, 223 (1989).

151. 42 U.S.C. § 7609(a) (1988).

152. *Id.* § 7609(b).

153. *See* section 1.8.

154. *See* section 2.10.2.

155. *See* 54 Fed. Reg. 9592, 9593–94 (1989).

156. *See* 40 C.F.R. § 1504.1(b) (1989).

157. *See, e.g.,* 50 Fed. Reg. 36,481 (1989); *id.* at 36,388.

158. *See* Letter to Dinah Bear, general counsel, CEQ, from Allan Hirsch, director, Office of Federal Activities, EPA (Sept. 23, 1985).

159. Council on Environmental Quality, Forty Most Asked Questions Concerning CEQ's National Environmental Policy Act Regulations, 46 Fed. Reg. 18,026, 18,031 (1981); *see* section 5.3.

160. *See* 54 Fed. Reg. 41,340 (1989) (commenting on final EISs; review of final EIS not deemed necessary).

161. Environmental Protection Agency, Summary of Rating Definitions, 54 Fed. Reg. 15,006 (1989).

162. *Id.*

163. Environmental Protection Agency, Policy and Procedures for the Review of Federal Actions Impacting the Environment ch. 7 (1984), *as cited in* Andreen, *In Pursuit of NEPA's Promise: The Role of Executive Oversight in the Implementation of Environmental Policy,* 64 Ind. L.J. 205, 241–42 & nn.262–64 (1989).

164. Robertson v. Methow Valley Citizens Council, 109 S. Ct. 1835, 1850 (1989).

165. *See* section 2.10.2.

166. *See* section 6.12.6.

167. Andreen, *In Pursuit of NEPA's Promise: The Role of Executive Oversight in the Implementation of Environmental Policy,* 64 Ind. L.J. 205, 241–42 (1989).

168. *See id.* at 241 n.257 (citing 40 C.F.R. § 1504.3(b) (1989)).

169. *See, e.g.,* 54 Fed. Reg. 36,387 (1989).

170. *See, e.g., id.* at 24,747.

171. *See, e.g., id.* 27,923; *id.* at 26,416; *id.* at 19,612.

172. *See, e.g., id.* at 23,714.

173. *See, e.g., id.* at 6448.

174. *See, e.g.,* 55 Fed. Reg. 7558 (1990).

175. *See, e.g.,* 54 Fed. Reg. 5547 (1989).

176. *See, e.g., id.* at 41,340.

177. *See, e.g., id.* at 10,420; *see* Sylvester v. Corps of Eng'rs, 884 F.2d 394, 398 (9th Cir. 1989) (EPA referred Corps of Engineers' NEPA regulations to CEQ).

178. *See, e.g.,* 54 Fed. Reg. 19,612 (1989); *id.* at 12,479.

179. *See, e.g., id.* at 27,923.

180. *See, e.g., id.* at 63.

181. *See, e.g., id.* at 13,232; *id.* at 10,420.

182. *See* County of Bergen v. Dole, 620 F. Supp. 1009, 1066 (D.N.J. 1985), *aff'd,* 800 F.2d 1130 (3d Cir. 1986).

183. *See, e.g.,* 54 Fed. Reg. 5547 (1989).

184. *See, e.g., id.* at 10,420.

185. *See, e.g., id.* at 5547.

186. *See* Sierra Club v. Adams, 578 F.2d 389, 394 (D.C. Cir. 1978).

187. *See* Sylvester v. Corps of Eng'rs, 884 F.2d 394, 398–99 (9th Cir. 1989).

188. *See* National Forest Preservation Group v. Butz, 485 F.2d 408, 412 (9th Cir. 1973).

189. Council on Environmental Quality, *Environmental Quality 1984: Fifteenth Annual Report* 525.

190. 40 C.F.R. § 1504.2 (1989).

191. *Id.* § 1504.1(c) (reviews to be made available to president, CEQ, and public); *see* 42 U.S.C. § 4332(2)(C) (1988).

192. 40 C.F.R. § 1504.3 (1989).

193. *Id.* § 1504.3(b).

194. *Id.* § 1504.3(d).

195. *Id.* § 1504.3(f).

196. *Id.* § 1504.3(g).

197. *Id.* § 1504.3(c).

198. *Id.* § 1504.3(d).

199. *Id.* § 1504.3(e).

200. *Id.* § 1504.3(f). *See, e.g.,* 54 Fed. Reg. 28,477 (1989) (CEQ findings and recommendations on EPA referral concerning Department of Interior's Bureau of Reclamation proposal to renew long-term water contracts); 53 Fed. Reg. 36,357 (1988) (CEQ findings and recommendations on Department of Interior referral concerning Marine Corps' proposal to fly low-level, high-speed combat training missions over national seashore); 52 Fed. Reg. 22,517 (1987) (CEQ findings and recommendations on EPA referral concerning Corps of Engineers' regulations implementing NEPA).

201. Andreen, *In Pursuit of NEPA's Promise: The Role of Executive Oversight in the Implementation of Environmental Policy,* 64 Ind. L.J. 205, 239 (1989).

202. *See* National Wildlife Fed'n v. Goldschmidt, 504 F. Supp. 314, 320–21 & n.27 (D. Conn. 1980); *see also* National Wildlife Fed'n v. Goldschmidt, 677 F.2d 259, 263 (2d Cir. 1982) (agreeing with district court's opinion).

203. *See* Sierra Club v. United States Dep't of Transp., 753 F.2d 120, 124 (D.C. Cir. 1985); Nader v. Schlesinger, 609 F.2d 494, 495 (Temp. Emer. Ct. App. 1979).

204. Sylvester v. Corps of Eng'rs, 884 F.2d 394, 398 (9th Cir. 1989).

205. *See OEQ Authorization, Fiscal Years 1989-1993; Hearing on H.R. 1113 Before the Subcomm. on Fisheries and Wildlife Conservation and the Environment of the House Comm. on Merchant Marine and Fisheries,* 101st Cong., 1st Sess. 30 (1989) (statement of A. Alan Hill, chairman, CEQ).

206. *See* Alaska v. Andrus, 580 F.2d 465, 474–75 & n.44 (D.C. Cir.), *vacated in nonpertinent part sub nom.* Western Oil & Gas Ass'n v. Alaska, 439 U.S. 922 (1978).

207. Sylvester v. Corps of Eng'rs, 884 F.2d 394, 398–99 (9th Cir. 1989); *see also* Nader v. Schlesinger, 609 F.2d 494, 495–96 (Temp. Emer. Ct. App. 1979) (considering agreement between EPA and Department of Energy subsequent to EPA referring department's action to CEQ).

208. Council on Environmental Quality, *Environmental Quality 1984: Fifteenth Annual Report* 527–28.

209. *Id.*

Threshold Determinations

3.1 INTRODUCTION

NEPA requires federal agencies to prepare detailed statements for "major Federal actions significantly affecting the quality of the human environment."[1] Before commencing any project, therefore, a federal agency must determine whether the proposed project is major, federal, an action, and whether it may affect the quality of the human environment. If an agency project meets all of these criteria, the agency must determine whether the environmental effects of the proposed action may be significant. Conversely, if even one of the criteria is not met, NEPA does not apply.

The courts, the CEQ, and the federal agencies have formulated a framework for complying with NEPA. Unless an action is categorically excluded from NEPA because an agency has determined that that type of action does not have significant environmental effects, the agency must either prepare an environmental assessment (EA) or an environmental impact statement (EIS). The EIS is the "detailed statement" referred to in NEPA.

An agency prepares an EA to aid it in making the significance or threshold determination. An EA must be followed either by a finding of no significant impact (FONSI) or an EIS. Alternatively, the agency may determine, without preparing an EA, that the environmental effects of a proposed action may be significant. In that instance, the agency directly prepares the EIS.

This chapter examines and analyzes the case law and regulations construing the term "major Federal actions significantly affecting the quality of the human environment." The term was not defined in NEPA or its legislative history.

3.2 MAJOR

NEPA case law is split on determining Congress' intent in including the word "major" in NEPA. Some courts read the term independently; other courts read it in conjunction with the term "significantly." Courts that read "major" independently from "significantly" reason that doing so gives full effect to both terms.[2] These cases generally determine whether an action is major by focusing on the amount of planning, resources, time, or expenditure involved in the action.[3] Decisions frequently depend on other factors, however, such as the action's effect on the environment[4] or the extent of federal involvement in the action.[5]

Most courts read "major" in conjunction with "significantly."[6] The rationale behind this interpretation is that if an action has a significant effect on the environment, the action must necessarily be major.[7] This approach, which in effect reads the word "major" out of NEPA, was adopted by the CEQ, which defined "major" in its regulations as reinforcing but not having a meaning independent of "significantly."[8]

3.3 FEDERAL

In order for an action to be federal, there must obviously be a nexus between a federal agency and an action.[9] If a federal agency engages in rule making or similar actions, the agency's involvement in the action is direct and the action is, therefore, federal.

If an agency's action enables a private party to significantly affect the human environment, the private action may be subject to NEPA.[10] The degree of federal involvement required to transform a nonfederal action into an action subject to NEPA is unclear. There are three main ways in which a nonfederal action may become federal: if the nonfederal action is federally funded, federally controlled, or federally permitted or approved.

3.3.1 Federal Funding

The presence of federal funding is not determinative of whether the underlying action is federal, but it is one factor in the analysis of whether a federal agency has sufficient control over, responsibility for, or involvement in an action for the action to be characterized as federal.[11]

The acceptance of federal funding by a nonfederal entity may result in an action becoming federal.[12] The funding must be substantial;

actions with de minimis federal funding are not subject to NEPA.[13] Similarly, not all federal actions are so closely interwoven with non-federal actions to federalize the nonfederal actions.[14] There must be a nexus between the federal funding and a proposed action. The receipt of such nonspecific funding as general revenue sharing funds is generally held not to federalize the actions conducted with the funds.[15]

If the federal funding of an action has not commenced, the action is not necessarily characterized as federal even though it may possibly become federal in the future.[16] A tentative nonbinding allocation of funds is generally insufficient to federalize the underlying action.[17] Likewise, a nonfederal entity's adoption of federal standards to make it eligible for a federal grant may not federalize an action at that time.[18] Filing documents with a federal agency has been held to be federal action, however, when the filing was a necessary part of the process for eventually gaining eligibility for federal funds.[19]

Once an action becomes federal, the withdrawal of federal funding from a part of it may not defederalize the action. The purpose behind this rule is to prevent entities from shifting funds from one project to another to avoid complying with NEPA.[20]

3.3.2 Federal Control

An action may become federal if a federal agency has the right to exercise control over it. The federal agency must have the power to decide whether to approve or deny an action,[21] or whether to impose conditions on it.[22] If a federal agency has no discretion as to whether to act, the action is not a federal action for the purposes of NEPA[23] because NEPA's purpose of ensuring that decision makers are fully informed about the consequences of an action prior to a decision whether to proceed would not be served.[24]

If the federal agency merely has authority to make nonbinding recommendations[25] or to give nonbinding advice[26] to the nonfederal action, the action is not characterized as federal. The right of a federal agency to object to violations of a federal-nonfederal agreement does not federalize the action.[27] Federal monitoring of a nonfederal action and the right to issue noncompliance notices and to commence enforcement proceedings[28] or to require the nonfederal entity to comply with the terms of its federal permit[29] are also not characterized as federal actions.

Action that is peripheral or incidental to a federal action may be characterized as federal or nonfederal depending on the relationship between the federal and the peripheral or incidental action[30] and the extent of control exercised by the federal agency over the nonfederal action.[31] A federal agency's acquiescence in an action may make the action federal in certain situations.[32] The federal agency may not avoid compliance with NEPA by abdicating control of the action to a nonfederal agency.[33]

3.3.3 Federal Permits and Approvals

If a federal agency has discretion to permit or approve an activity, it is usually undisputed that the agency controls the action. Thus, even if the funds to be used for an action are wholly private, the action may be federal if it cannot commence or continue until a federal agency gives its approval.[34] Limited permitting by a federal agency may not be sufficient to federalize the action.[35] The extent of the action that is federalized depends on the facts of each case. A large-scale nonfederal action is not necessarily federal simply because one portion of it requires a federal permit or approval.[36]

Generally the permitted or approved action is not characterized as federal action until the permit or approval is actually applied for.[37] However, if federal permitting or approval is inevitable, the entire action may be characterized as federal even before the approval or permit is requested.[38]

3.4 ACTION

The CEQ regulations define the following federal activities as "actions" under NEPA: adoption of official policy including rules, regulations, and interpretations adopted under the Administrative Procedure Act; treaties and international conventions or agreements; publication of formal documents establishing agency programs or substantially altering them; adoption of formal plans including "official documents, prepared or approved by federal agencies that guide or prescribe alternative uses of federal resources, upon which future agency actions will be based"; adoption of programs including groups of concerted actions to implement specific policies or plans; adoption of systematic and connected agency decisions allocating agency resources to implement specific statutory programs or executive directives; and approval of specific projects including construction and management activities located in defined geographic areas.[39] Thus, an agency may be required to comply with NEPA when it, inter alia, promulgates substantive or procedural regulations,[40] proposes legislation[41] other than appropriation requests,[42] and provides the impetus for private actions by funding, controlling, approving, or permitting nonfederal projects. The funding of projects that are already proposed by an agency is not covered by NEPA because NEPA already applies to the actions to be funded.[43]

Actions may be positive or negative.[44] Generally NEPA case law construing the term "action" focuses on the federal agency's discretion in conducting an activity. If an agency decision maker has an option to act but declines to do so, the failure to act may not be an "action" under NEPA.[45] However, if the agency decision maker has a mandatory duty to act but fails to do so, the failure to act may be an "action" under NEPA.[46] Similarly, inaction by a federal agency after transferring control of a project from the federal agency to a nonfederal entity may be characterized as an action under NEPA.[47] An action is not required to be irreversible in order to require preparation of an EIS.[48]

It has not been finally settled whether NEPA applies only to actions conducted in the United States. The extraterritorial application of NEPA is discussed in section 1.6.

3.5 AFFECTING/EFFECTS

An action has environmental effects if it impacts the physical environment. "Effects," which is thus synonymous with "impacts,"[49] includes direct and indirect effects. Direct effects occur at the same time and place as a proposed action and are caused by it.[50]

Indirect effects are also caused by an action but occur at a later time and greater distance. Examples of indirect effects include "growth inducing effects and other effects related to induced changes in the pattern of land use, population density or growth rate, and related effects on air and water and other natural systems, including ecosystems."[51] The public's loss of knowledge that a resource exists has been considered to be an indirect effect.[52]

Effects should be considered if they are reasonably foreseeable,[53] but not if they are highly speculative or indefinite.[54] The distinction between a reasonably foreseeable action and a remote and indefinite action is amorphous. Criteria to distinguish which actions are speculative include: the agency's degree of confidence in predicting the effects' occurrence; the available knowledge with which to describe the impacts in a manner useful to the decision maker; and the feasibility of the decision maker's meaningfully considering an analysis of environmental effects later in the action without being obligated to continue the action because of past commitments.[55]

Applying the above criteria, the effects of an action would not be overly speculative if the action necessarily resulted in the development of an area and the development pattern may be described based on existing plans or trends.[56] If an agency action is a stepping stone to an area's development,[57] or necessarily accelerates development,[58] the action's indirect effects may be reasonably foreseeable. Effects may be overly speculative if they involve an additional step, however, even if that step is reasonably foreseeable. For example, an increase in Hawaii's permanent population resulting from an increase in tourism was too speculative to be an indirect effect of enlarging an airport, even though the increase in tourism was reasonably foreseeable.[59]

A further analysis of environmental effects as they pertain to EAs is contained in chapter 4. Section 5.10.2 analyzes environmental effects as they pertain to EISs.

3.6 THE QUALITY OF THE HUMAN ENVIRONMENT

An action afffects the physical environment if it changes the physical environment.[60] There must be a reasonably close causal relationship between the change in the physical environment and the environmental effects of the proposed agency action.[61]

3.6.1 Changes in the Physical Environment

If the physical environment is not affected, NEPA is not triggered.[62] An action is subject to NEPA, however, if it commits the agency to future actions that inevitably affect the physical environment[63] or otherwise irretrievably commit a natural resource.[64] As a general rule, however, the proposed action must affect the environmental status quo in order to trigger NEPA.[65]

It is crucial, therefore, to determine the status quo. This determination has led the courts to differing results and reasoning. In the case of a bridge that had existed for twenty-four years before it was destroyed by a hurricane, the Fifth Circuit hesitatingly determined that the status quo for purposes of building a new bridge included the environment with the old bridge in place.[66] If a proposed action will continue the environmental degradation of an area, will not permit a degraded area to recover, or will affect an area beyond that already degraded, however, the action may affect the status quo.[67]

There is no bright line between actions that affect the status quo and actions that do not. As a general rule, proposed actions directly affecting natural resources are more likely to be found to change the status quo than proposed actions affecting the urban environment.[68] The courts are less inclined to find that a proposed action will change the status quo when the area in which the action will occur will continue to be affected by actions similar to the proposed agency action,[69] or when the proposed action does not increase the intensity of the use of an area.[70]

Mitigation of an action's environmental effects by other influences may be enough to reduce the effects to an insignificant level. Thus, if an agency can show that its proposed action's environmental effects will be mitigated because of conditions already existing or occurring at the same time as the action,[71] or events that are likely to take place,[72] the change in the environment from the agency action may not be sufficient to be termed significant. Alternatively, if the agency's action will stabilize an area's environment by relieving pressure on animals or plants, the action may be considered to be insignificant.[73]

3.6.2 The Human Environment

Effects on the human environment from changes in the physical environment include impacts on human health and welfare.[74] As discussed at the beginning of section 3.6, the intermediary effect on the physical environment is critical for NEPA to apply.

The quality of urban life is within NEPA's scope.[75] However, because environmental effects interact with socio-economic effects in an urban setting,[76] there is no bright line between effects on the quality of urban life and socio-economic effects.[77] The CEQ regulations state that preparation of an EIS is not required if the only effects of a proposed action are socio-economic.[78]

The criteria considered by courts in determining if a proposed action significantly affects the quality of urban life (noise, traffic, crime, congestion, overburdened mass transportation systems, crime, congestion, and availability of drugs)[79] include criteria that are sometimes regarded by other courts as having only a socio-economic effect.[80]

Some socio-economic effects should be covered by NEPA because they are caused by an impact on the physical environment. Examples of such effects include increases in noise, odors, congestion,[81] and possibly urban blight caused by the abandonment of an inner city area if a causal link could be shown.[82] Other socio-economic effects that do not impact on the physical environment should not be covered by

NEPA. Such effects include local unemployment,[83] reduction in jobs,[84] and unrealized risks of crime.[85]

The above differentiation is not made in many cases considering socio-economic effects. Some courts have held that consideration of socio-economic effects in an EIS is optional and not mandatory[86] whereas, arguably, consideration of significant socio-economic effects caused by an impact on the physical environment is mandatory,[87] and consideration of socio-economic effects not caused by an impact on the physical environment is not required at all because such effects are outside NEPA's scope.

The CEQ regulations also require agencies to consider socio-economic effects in an EIS when the socio-economic effects are inter-related with natural or physical effects.[88] Arguably, this consideration is only mandated by NEPA if the socio-economic effect is caused by an impact on the human environment, not simply interrelated with it.[89]

Effects on historic and cultural resources are covered by NEPA.[89] Thus, if an agency action may significantly affect an historic or cultural resource, the agency must comply with NEPA. It is not clear, however, whether NEPA is triggered if the cultural resource is a group of people whose culture may be affected by an agency action. In one case, the Ninth Circuit held that the agency need not prepare an EIS to examine the effects of the proposed redevelopment of a building on local artists who inhabited the building. The plaintiffs claimed that the agency action would irreparably damage the area's cultural character.[90] The court did not discuss or determine whether NEPA in fact covered the proposed action.

Because NEPA does not apply to purely socio-economic effects, an argument could be made that NEPA does not apply to an action's effects on people when the physical environment is not also affected. Such an interpretation, however, strains NEPA's use of the term "human environment," and NEPA's express declaration regarding preservation of important cultural aspects of the United States heritage. Indeed, if NEPA was not triggered by an agency action having a significant effect on an important cultural characteristic of some of its people, the physical environment protected by NEPA would include all species except humans.

It is unclear whether aesthetic values are cognizable under NEPA. NEPA apparently includes aesthetic values because an objective of NEPA's policy is to "assure for all Americans safe, healthful, productive, and esthetically and culturally pleasing surroundings."[91] Aesthetic values rarely trigger the need to prepare an EIS, however, unless they are combined with other potentially sigificant effects.[92] When aesthetic effects are considered, agencies are not required to prepare statistical analyses because of the effects' subjective nature.[93]

3.7 PROCEDURES FOR DETERMINING THE SIGNIFICANCE OF ENVIRONMENTAL EFFECTS

Agencies make preliminary determinations of whether an action has significant environmental effects by classifying actions into three general categories: actions with significant effects that automatically require preparation of an EIS; actions with no significant effects that are thus "categorically excluded" from compliance with NEPA; and all other actions for which a determination of the significance of environmental effects must be made on a case-by-case basis.

3.7.1 Actions Automatically Requiring Environmental Impact Statements

Agencies typically include lists of actions that normally have a significant environmental effect, and thus require preparation of an EIS, in their guidelines or regulations for implementing NEPA.[94] The fact that a proposed action meets the description of an action in the list is not dispositive of whether an EIS must be prepared, however. The agency still has discretion to determine whether a particular action may have significant environmental effects and may thus require an EIS.[95]

3.7.2 Categorical Exclusions

At the other end of the spectrum from actions that automatically require EISs are actions that normally do not significantly affect the environment, either individually or cumulatively. These actions are known as categorical exclusions.[96] Agencies generally adopt broad criteria to characterize the type of actions that normally do not cause environmental effects.[97] The agencies then list, in their regulations or guidelines for implementing NEPA, examples of frequently conducted activities that usually are encompassed by that criteria. These lists should be submitted to the CEQ for review.[98]

Categorical exclusions are generally exempt from the NEPA process.[99] If an agency determines that an action is categorically excluded, it does not prepare an EA or an EIS.[100] Thus, categorical exclusions are the only proposed federal actions affecting the human environment for which an EA or an EIS need not be prepared.[101] Challenges to actions treated by an agency as categorical exclusions generally arise when an agency determines that an action of a type normally requiring an EA is a categorical exclusion,[102] when a proposed action awkwardly fits the description of a categorical exclusion,[103] or when "extraordinary" circumstances are considered to exist.

If "extraordinary" circumstances exist such that an action normally described as a categorical exclusion may have significant environmental effects, the action is subject to NEPA.[104] The triggering mechanism for an exemption to a categorical exclusion varies with each agency.[105] In general, however, actions are "extraordinary" if they are substantially controversial on environmental grounds.[106]

To become substantially controversial, an action must be opposed on environmental grounds by a federal, state, or local agency with environmental responsibilities or "a substantial number of the persons affected by such action."[107] Opposition by a small percentage of people in an affected area has been held not to be extraordinary when the only public entities opposing the action did not have environmental responsibilities.[108] On the other hand, opposition by experts including experts from environmental agencies is more likely to show that a controversy exists that the environmental effects may be significant.[109]

If extraordinary conditions exist that may exempt a proposed action from being a categorical exclusion, an agency must address the conditions and the public controversy concerning the environmental consequences of its proposed action.[110] Agency compliance with its categorical exclusion regulations is accorded deference.[111]

To successfully challenge an agency's determination that an action is categorically excluded, a plaintiff must show that the action may have significant environmental effects.[112] This requirement is roughly the same as the requirement for judicial challenges to negative declarations of significance discussed in section 3.7.3. The District of Columbia Circuit uses a less stringent test in reviewing an agency's determination that an action is categorically excluded than it uses in its review of a negative declaration.[113]

3.7.3 Environmental Assessments

Between the two extremes of significance and insignificance lies a large gray area in which threshold determinations are made on a case-by-case basis. Environmental Assessments (EAs) aid decision makers in determining whether the threshold of significance has been passed by a proposed action.[114] EAs must be prepared for all actions that are not categorical exclusions or for which an EIS is not prepared.[115] As with actions requiring EISs and categorical exclusions, agencies frequently list actions requiring the preparation of an EA in their regulations or guidelines for implementing NEPA.[116] As with the other categories of actions, categorization of an action as one requiring an EA is not dispositive; proposed actions may be reclassified.[117]

The purpose, format, scope, and judicial review of EAs are discussed in detail in chapter 4.

NOTES

1. 42 U.S.C. § 4332(2)(C) (1988).

2. NAACP v. Medical Center, Inc., 584 F.2d 619, 626–27, 634 (3d Cir. 1978); Hanly v. Mitchell, 460 F.2d 640, 644 (2d Cir.), cert. denied, 409 U.S. 990 (1972).

3. See, e.g., New Hope Community Ass'n v. HUD, 509 F. Supp. 525, 530 (E.D.N.C. 1981); Cobble Hill Ass'n v. Adams, 470 F. Supp. 1077, 1086 (E.D.N.Y. 1979); Rysavy v. Harris, 457 F. Supp. 796, 802 (D.S.D. 1978); Maryland-Nat'l Capital Park & Planning Comm'n v. Martin, 447 F. Supp. 350, 352 (D.D.C. 1978); Township of Ridley v. Blanchette, 421 F. Supp. 435, 446 (E.D. Pa. 1976); Citizens Organized to Defend the Environment, Inc. v. Volpe, 353 F. Supp. 520, 540 (S.D. Ohio 1972); Natural Resources Defense Council, Inc. v. Grant, 341 F. Supp. 356, 366–67 (E.D.N.C. 1972); see also Sierra Club v. Hodel, 848 F.2d 1068, 1092 (10th Cir. 1988) (describing federal action and commenting: "Surely that much work is a major project"); Kisner v. Butz, 350 F. Supp. 310, 322 (N.D.W. Va. 1972) (noting physical size of action); Julis v. City of Cedar Rapids, 349 F. Supp. 88, 90 (N.D. Iowa 1972) (same).

4. See City of Alexandria v. FHWA, 756 F.2d 1014, 1020 n.5 (4th Cir. 1985). See generally Note, The CEQ Regulations: New Stage in the Evolution of NEPA, 3 Harv. Envtl. L. Rev. 347, 359 (1979).

5. Sierra Club v. Penfold, 857 F.2d 1307, 1314 (9th Cir. 1988).

6. E.g., Sierra Club v. Hodel, 848 F.2d 1068, 1091–92 (10th Cir. 1988); River Road Alliance, Inc. v. Corps of Eng'rs, 764 F.2d 445, 450 (7th Cir. 1985), cert. denied, 475 U.S. 1055 (1986); Minnesota Pub. Interest Research Group v. Butz, 498 F.2d 1314, 1321–22 (8th Cir. 1974); Colorado River Indian Tribes v. Marsh, 605 F. Supp. 1425, 1431–32 (C.D. Cal. 1985).

7. See City of Davis v. Coleman, 521 F.2d 661, 673 n.15 (9th Cir. 1975); Minnesota Pub. Interest Research Group v. Butz, 498 F.2d 1314, 1321–22 (8th Cir. 1974); Patterson v. Exon, 415 F. Supp. 1276, 1281 (D. Neb. 1976).

8. 40 C.F.R. § 1508.18 (1989) ("[m]ajor reinforces but does not have a meaning independent of significantly").

9. See Bradford Township v. Illinois State Toll Highway Auth., 463 F.2d 537, 540 (7th Cir.), cert. denied, 409 U.S. 1047 (1972).

10. See South Dakota v. Andrus, 614 F.2d 1190, 1194 (8th Cir.), cert. denied, 449 U.S. 822 (1980).

11. Atlanta Coalition on Transp. Crisis, Inc. v. Atlanta Regional Comm'n, 599 F.2d 1333, 1347 (5th Cir. 1979); see also Bradley v. HUD, 658 F.2d 290, 294 (5th Cir. 1981) (creating rehabilitation and redevelopment plan with federal funds did not

federalize action when federal government had no substantive control over plan's creation); 40 C.F.R. § 1508.18(b)(4) (1989) (federally assisted activities may be federal actions).

12. *E.g.*, Homeowners Emergency Life Protection Comm. v. Lynn, 541 F.2d 814, 817 (9th Cir. 1976) (federally funded dam and reservoir to be constructed by city); National Forest Preservation Group v. Butz, 485 F.2d 408, 411 (9th Cir. 1973) (federal-nonfederal land exchange was analogous to granting federal funds to nonfederal entity to enable it to act).

13. Scottsdale Mall v. Indiana, 418 F. Supp. 296, 301 (S.D. Ind. 1976), *vacated on other grounds*, 549 F.2d 484 (7th Cir. 1977), *cert. denied*, 434 U.S. 1008 (1978).

14. *See* Friends of the Earth, Inc. v. Coleman, 518 F.2d 323, 327–29 (9th Cir. 1975); *see also* Enos v. Marsh, 769 F.2d 1363, 1372 (9th Cir. 1985) (action that lacked federal funding and federal supervision was not federal); Citizens for Responsible Area Growth v. Adams, 680 F.2d 835, 839-40 (1st Cir. 1982) (use of federally funded utilities by privately funded hangar does not federalize construction of hangar).

15. *See* Citizens for a Better St. Clair County v. James, 648 F.2d 246, 250 (5th Cir. 1981); Carolina Action v. Simon, 522 F.2d 295, 296 (4th Cir. 1975) (per curiam); 40 C.F.R. § 1508.18(a) (1989). *But see* Ely v. Velde, 497 F.2d 252, 256 (4th Cir. 1974) (NEPA applied to action conducted by identified recipient of block grant funding).

16. *See* Atlanta Coalition on Transp. Crisis, Inc. v. Atlanta Regional Comm'n, 599 F.2d 1333, 1347 (5th Cir. 1979); City of Highland Park v. Train, 519 F.2d 681, 695 (7th Cir. 1975), *cert. denied*, 424 U.S. 927 (1976). *But see* No East-West Highway Comm., Inc. v. Whitaker, 403 F. Supp. 260, 277–79 (D.N.H. 1975) (federal agency cannot permit state to complete highway skeleton while only using federal funding for portions that pose no environmental threat).

17. *See* City of Boston v. Volpe, 464 F.2d 254, 258–59 (1st Cir. 1972).

18. *See* Friends of the Earth, Inc. v. Coleman, 518 F.2d 323, 328 (9th Cir. 1975).

19. *See* Scenic Rivers Ass'n v. Lynn, 520 F.2d 240, 243–44 (10th Cir. 1975), *rev'd on other grounds sub nom.* Flint Ridge Dev. Co. v. Scenic Rivers Ass'n, 426 U.S. 776 (1976).

20. *See* Scottsdale Mall v. Indiana, 549 F.2d 484, 489 (7th Cir. 1977), *cert. denied*, 434 U.S. 1008 (1978); Highland Cooperative v. City of Lansing, 492 F. Supp. 1372, 1378 (W.D. Mich. 1980). *But see* City of Boston v. Volpe, 464 F.2d 254, 258 (1st Cir. 1972) (declining to accept "general proposition that once the federal government has participated in a development, that development is necessarily forever federal").

21. City & County of Denver v. Bergland, 695 F.2d 465, 481–82 (10th Cir. 1982).

22. *See* Sierra Club v. Hodel, 848 F.2d 1068, 1089-90 (10th Cir. 1988); Forelaws on Board v. Johnson, 743 F.2d 677, 681 (9th Cir. 1984), *cert. denied*, 478 U.S. 1004 (1986).

23. *See* Pacific Legal Found'n v. Andrus, 657 F.2d 829, 840 (6th Cir. 1981) (mandatory act); South Dakota v. Andrus, 614 F.2d 1190, 1193 (8th Cir.) (nondiscretionary acts), *cert. denied*, 449 U.S. 822 (1980); Kings County Economic Community Dev. Ass'n v. Hardin, 478 F.2d 478, 480 (9th Cir. 1973) (nondiscretionary farm subsidy); Buda v. Saxbe, 406 F. Supp. 399, 402 n.3 (E.D. Tenn. 1975)

(nondiscretionary correctional facility construction grant). *Cf.* Upper Snake River Chapter of Trout Unlimited v. Hodel, 706 F. Supp. 737, 740–41 (D. Idaho 1989) (reduction of river flows was routine or ministerial act); NAACP v. Medical Center, Inc., 584 F.2d 619, 634 (3d Cir. 1978) (when federal agency substantially assisted action, action may be federal even though agency has no discretion in awarding grant).

24. Minnesota v. Block, 660 F.2d 1240, 1259 (8th Cir. 1981).

25. Metropolitan Washington Coalition for Clean Air v. Department of Economic Dev., 373 F. Supp. 1096, 1100–01 (D.D.C. 1973).

26. *See* Almond Hill School v. United States Dep't of Agric., 768 F.2d 1030, 1039 (9th Cir. 1985); McLean Gardens Residents Ass'n, Inc. v. National Capital Planning Comm'n, 390 F. Supp. 165, 174–75 (D.D.C. 1974).

27. Molokai Homesteaders Cooperative Ass'n v. Morton, 506 F.2d 572, 580 (9th Cir. 1974).

28. Sierra Club v. Penfold, 857 F.2d 1307, 1314 (9th Cir. 1988) (quoting 40 C.F.R. § 1508.18(a) (1989) ("judicial or administrative civil or criminal enforcement actions" are not "actions" under NEPA)).

29. *See* Sierra Club v. Hodel, 848 F.2d 1068, 1089-90 (10th Cir. 1988).

30. *See* Friends of Yosemite v. Frizzell, 420 F. Supp. 390, 396 (N.D. Cal. 1976) (nonfederal entity's campaign publicizing construction of facilities in national park was not federal action).

31. *See* Ringsred v. City of Duluth, 828 F.2d 1305, 1308 (8th Cir. 1987) (parking ramp constructed for building was incidental action when ramp was not subject to federal licensing, was not federally funded, and federal agency was not involved in its design or construction); National Org. for Reform of Marijuana Laws v. DEA, 545 F. Supp. 981, 985–86 (D.D.C. 1982) (herbicidal eradication program was not federal action when program lacked federal funding and control).

32. *See* Virginians for Dulles v. Volpe, 541 F.2d 442, 445 (4th Cir. 1976) (FAA acquiesced in vastly expanded use of airport for which it also requested funds from Congress).

33. *See* Bunch v. Hodel, 793 F.2d 129, 135 (6th Cir. 1986).

34. Foundation on Economic Trends v. Heckler, 756 F.2d 143, 155 (D.C. Cir. 1985); Dalsis v. Hills, 424 F. Supp. 784, 787 (W.D.N.Y. 1976); 40 C.F.R. § 1508.18(b)(4) (1989); *see also* Davis v. Morton, 469 F.2d 593, 596–97 (10th Cir. 1972) (agency's approval of lease by Indian tribe to nonfederal lessees); Biderman v. Morton, 497 F.2d 1141, 1147 (2d Cir. 1974) (actions of nonfederal parties may be enjoined under NEPA pending agency's compliance with NEPA for action's approval). *But see* Ringsred v. City of Duluth, 828 F.2d 1305, 1308 (8th Cir. 1987) (agency's approval of contracts for parking ramp did not federalize action when agency had no input into design and construction of ramp).

35. *See* Save Our Wetlands, Inc. v. Sands, 711 F.2d 634, 644 n.9 (5th Cir. 1983).

36. *See* Sylvester v. Corps of Eng'rs, 884 F.2d 394, 400–01 (9th Cir. 1989); Winnebago Tribe v. Ray, 621 F.2d 269, 273 (8th Cir.), *cert. denied*, 449 U.S. 836 (1980); Save the Bay, Inc. v. Corps of Eng'rs, 610 F.2d 322, 326–27 (5th Cir.), *cert. denied*, 449 U.S. 900 (1980).

37. *See* Natural Resources Defense Council, Inc. v. EPA, 822 F.2d 104, 128 (D.C. Cir. 1987); Citizens for a Better St. Clair County v. James, 648 F.2d 246, 251 (5th Cir. 1981); B.R.S. Land Investors v. United States, 596 F.2d 353, 355–56 (9th Cir. 1979).

38. *See, e.g.*, Maryland Conservation Council, Inc. v. Gilchrist, 808 F.2d 1039, 1042 (4th Cir. 1986) (highway is federal action because it will eventually require federal approval for conversion of parkland, probably a dredge and fill permit, and possibly approval for use of parkland).

39. 40 C.F.R. § 1508.18(b) (1989).

40. *See* Illinois Commerce Comm'n v. ICC, 848 F.2d 1246, 1257 (D.C. Cir. 1988), *cert. denied*, 109 S. Ct. 783 (1989).

41. 42 U.S.C. § 4332(2)(C) (1988); *see* North Dakota v. Andrus, 483 F. Supp. 255, 257 (D.N.D. 1980).

42. Andrus v. Sierra Club, 442 U.S. 347, 361 (1979); 40 C.F.R. § 1508.17 (1989).

43. National Wildlife Fed'n v. Coston, 773 F.2d 1513, 1518 (9th Cir. 1985).

44. *See* Arizona Pub. Serv. Co. v. FPC, 483 F.2d 1275, 1283 (D.C. Cir. 1973) (describing agency action as negative because examiner denied, rather than approved, construction of natural gas facilities).

45. *See* Defenders of Wildlife v. Andrus, 627 F.2d 1238, 1245 (D.C. Cir. 1980) (requiring an overt act by federal decision maker); Alaska v. Andrus, 591 F.2d 537, 541 (9th Cir. 1979) (decision maker's decision not to act does not trigger NEPA); District of Columbia v. Schramm, 631 F.2d 854, 862 (D.C. Cir. 1980) (determination not to object to issuance of permit by nonfederal entity was not an action); *see also* Maryland *ex rel.* Burch v. Costle, 452 F. Supp. 1154, 1160 (D.D.C. 1978) (Administrator made no proposal for federal action when he stated that application would not be processed until it was revised).

46. Sierra Club v. Hodel, 848 F.2d 1068, 1091 (10th Cir. 1988).

47. Bunch v. Hodel, 793 F.2d 129, 135–36 (6th Cir. 1986). *But see* District of Columbia v. Schramm, 631 F.2d 854, 862 (D.C. Cir. 1980) (federal agency's decision not to object to issuance of permit by state agency after transferring authority to state to issue permit was not federal action).

48. Alaska v. Andrus, 580 F.2d 465, 478 n.52 (D.C. Cir.), *vacated in nonpertinent part sub nom.* Western Oil & Gas Ass'n v. Alaska, 439 U.S. 922 (1978).

49. 40 C.F.R. §. 1508.8 (1989).

50. *Id.* § 1508.8(a).

51. *Id.* § 1508.8(b).

52. Minnesota Public Interest Research Group v. Butz, 498 F.2d 1314, 1322 & n.27 (8th Cir. 1974).

53. *See* Council on Environmental Quality, Forty Most Asked Questions Concerning CEQ's National Environmental Policy Act Regulations, 46 Fed. Reg. 18,026, 18,031 (1981).

54. *See* Sierra Club v. Marsh, 769 F.2d 868, 878 (1st Cir. 1985).

55. *Id.* at 878–80. *Cf.* Trout Unlimited v. Morton, 509 F.2d 1276, 1284 (9th Cir. 1974) (no significant change in land use patterns or population trends shown when no plan existed and no probability of change was demonstrated).

56. Sierra Club v. Marsh, 769 F.2d at 878–80.

57. *See* City of Davis v. Coleman, 521 F.2d 661, 675 (9th Cir. 1975); Colorado River Indian Tribes v. Marsh, 605 F. Supp. 1425, 1433 (C.D. Cal. 1985).

58. Conservation Council of N. Carolina v. Costanzo, 398 F. Supp. 653, 672 (E.D.N.C.), *aff'd*, 528 F.2d 250 (4th Cir. 1975); *see also* National Forest Preservation Group v. Butz, 485 F.2d 408, 411 (9th Cir. 1973) (effects of planned recreational development on land to be exchanged by Forest Service must be considered under NEPA).

59. Life of the Land v. Brinegar, 485 F.2d 460, 469 (9th Cir. 1973) (EIS), *cert. denied*, 416 U.S. 961 (1974); *see also* Glass Packaging Inst. v. Regan, 737 F.2d 1083, 1091 (D.C. Cir.) (possibility that deranged criminal would dangerously affect human health by injecting poison through walls of plastic bottles was not significant environmental effect of permitting use of bottles), *cert. denied*, 469 U.S. 1035 (1984).

60. Metropolitan Edison Co. v. People Against Nuclear Energy, 460 U.S. 766, 774 (1983).

61. *Id.*; *see* Glass Packaging Inst. v. Regan, 737 F.2d 1083, 1091 (D.C. Cir.) (agency need not consider environmental effect that is merely foreseeable), *cert. denied*, 469 U.S. 1035 (1984).

62. *Metropolitan Edison*, 460 U.S. at 772. *See, e.g.*, Park County Resources Council, Inc. v. United States Dep't of Agric., 817 F.2d 609, 622 (10th Cir. 1987) (issuance of oil and gas lease does not cause a change in the physical environment when lessee must subsequently submit site-specific proposals subject to modification by the agency); Glass Packaging Inst. v. Regan, 737 F.2d 1083, 1091 (D.C. Cir.) (introduction of new plastic container into marketplace), *cert. denied*, 469 U.S. 1035 (1984); Concord Township v. United States, 625 F.2d 1068, 1074 (3d Cir. 1980) (action granting railway company right to operate in area but not to engage in construction activities did not affect physical environment); New England Naturist Ass'n, Inc. v. Larsen, 692 F. Supp. 75, 82 (D.R.I. 1988) (action would affect people's activities in physical environment but not physical environment itself); Ono v. Harper, 592 F. Supp. 698, 701 (D. Hawaii 1983) (transfer of title to land did not harm physical environment); Pacific Northwest Bell Tel. Co. v. Dole, 633 F. Supp. 725, 727 (W.D. Wash. 1986) (no allegation that potential disruption of telephone service would change physical environment).

63. *See* Forelaws on Board v. Johnson, 743 F.2d 677, 682 (9th Cir. 1985), *cert. denied*, 478 U.S. 1004 (1986).

64. Confederated Tribes & Bands of Yakima Nation v. FERC, 746 F.2d 466, 476–77 (9th Cir. 1984), *cert. denied*, 471 U.S. 1116 (1985).

65. Assure Competitive Transp., Inc. v. United States, 635 F.2d 1301, 1309 (7th Cir. 1980); *see also* Sierra Club v. FERC, 754 F.2d 1506, 1510 (9th Cir. 1985) (issuance of preliminary permit for hydroelectric project did not change status quo when permit did not allow entry onto federal land or groundbreaking activities); Environmental Defense Fund, Inc. v. Johnson, 629 F.2d 239, 242 (2d Cir. 1980) (proposal for legislation that would only authorize further study of contemplated project does not significantly affect environment).

66. Sierra Club v. Hassell, 636 F.2d 1095, 1099 (5th Cir. 1981).

67. Louisiana v. Lee, 758 F.2d 1081, 1086 (5th Cir. 1985), *cert. denied*, 475 U.S. 1044 (1986); *see also* Hanly v. Kleindienst, 471 F.2d 823, 831 (2d Cir. 1972) (effect of action may be significant when area's pollution problems are so severe that another pollution source "may represent the straw that breaks the back of the environmental camel"), *cert. denied*, 412 U.S. 908 (1973); Natural Resources Defense Council, Inc. v. Vaughn, 566 F. Supp. 1472, 1475 (D.D.C. 1983) (restart of nuclear reactor after fifteen-year period of inoperation significantly affected recovering environment). *Cf.* Burbank Anti-Noise Group v. Goldschmidt, 623 F.2d 115, 116–17 (9th Cir. 1980) (federal funding for acquisition of operating airport did not affect status quo), *cert. denied*, 450 U.S. 965 (1981); Quinonez-Lopez v. Coco Lagoon Dev. Corp., 733 F.2d 1, 3–4 (1st Cir. 1984) (upholding agency's determination that destruction of wetlands did not significantly affect environment when wetlands were damaged by pre-NEPA actions).

68. *Compare* Confederated Tribes & Bands of Yakima Nation v. FERC, 746 F.2d 466, 476–77 (9th Cir. 1984) *cert. denied*, 471 U.S. 1116 (1985) (relicensing hydropower dam for forty years changed status quo because action irretrievably committed natural resources) *with* Assure Competitive Transp., Inc. v. United States, 635 F.2d 1301, 1309 (7th Cir. 1980) (policy would increase competition for existing traffic but not amount of traffic).

69. *See, e.g.*, Durnford v. Ruckelshaus, 5 Env't Rep. Cases (BNA) 1007, 1010 (N.D. Cal. 1972) (construction of new pier in area already used for fishing would not significantly affect environment).

70. *See, e.g.*, Alaska Factory Trawler Ass'n v. Baldridge, 831 F.2d 1456, 1460 (9th Cir. 1987) (agency action allocated established optimum yield for sablefish among existing gear fleets); Northwest Airlines, Inc. v. Goldschmidt, 645 F.2d 1309, 1321–22 (8th Cir. 1981) (agency action changed scheduling of airline slots but did not increase potential number of reserved carrier operations); Illinois v. United States, 604 F.2d 519, 528 (7th Cir. 1979) (existing operation would continue with change of management), *cert. denied*, 445 U.S. 951 (1980); Committee for Auto Responsibility v. Solomon, 603 F.2d 992, 1002–03 (D.C. Cir. 1979) (change in lessee of agency's parking lot did not change status quo when agency's parking policy was unchanged), *cert. denied*, 445 U.S. 915 (1980).

71. *See* Coalition on Sensible Transp., Inc. v. Dole, 826 F.2d 60, 67–68 (D.C. Cir. 1987) (development triggering potential of highway project was offset by constraining effect of infrastructure servicing highway); Brandon v. Pierce, 725 F.2d 555, 563 (10th Cir. 1984) (high unemployment in area would offset potential pressure on services caused by creation of new jobs); Town of Orangetown v. Gorsuch, 718 F.2d 29, 38 (2d Cir. 1983) (potential increase in development pressure caused by expanding county's sewage treatment system may be offset by overburdening of existing system), *cert. denied*, 465 U.S. 1099 (1984); Mont Vernon Preservation Soc'y v. Clements, 415 F. Supp. 141, 148 (D.N.H. 1976) (effect of road salt entering streams may be offset by high water flows of spring runoff).

72. *See* Rhone-Poulenc, Inc. v. FDA, 636 F.2d 750, 755 (D.C. Cir. 1980) (effects of banning growth-promoting drug will be offset by use of other available

growth promotants); section 4.10 (measures to mitigate significant environmental effects).

73. American Horse Protection Ass'n, Inc. v. Frizzell, 403 F. Supp. 1206, 1219 (D. Nev. 1975).

74. Baltimore Gas & Elec. Co. v. Natural Resources Defense Council, Inc., 462 U.S. 87, 106–07 (1983); Metropolitan Edison Co. v. People Against Nuclear Energy, 460 U.S. 766, 774 (1983); *see id.* at 779 (Brennan, J., concurring) (NEPA covers psychological injuries); *see also* National Pork Producers Council v. Bergland, 631 F.2d 1353, 1363 (8th Cir. 1980) (mentioning but not deciding that effect on human health affects human environment), *cert. denied*, 450 U.S. 912 (1981); City of Irving v. FAA, 539 F. Supp. 17, 28 (N.D. Tex. 1981) (considering without deciding that action affecting human hearing affects human environment).

75. WATCH (Waterbury Action to Conserve Our Heritage, Inc.) v. Harris, 603 F.2d 310, 327 (2d Cir.), *cert. denied*, 444 U.S. 995 (1979); Nucleus of Chicago Homeowners Ass'n v. Lynn, 524 F.2d 225, 229 (7th Cir. 1975), *cert. denied*, 424 U.S. 967 (1976); First Nat'l Bank of Chicago v. Richardson, 484 F.2d 1369, 1377 (7th Cir. 1973); Hanly v. Kleindienst, 471 F.2d 823, 827 (2d Cir. 1972), *cert. denied*, 412 U.S. 908 (1973); Hanly v. Mitchell, 460 F.2d 640, 647 (2d Cir.), *cert. denied*, 409 U.S. 990 (1972); *see also* Davison v. Department of Defense, 560 F. Supp. 1019, 1033 (S.D. Ohio 1982) (requiring more extensive discussion in EIS on sleep disturbance by night flights); Highland Cooperative v. City of Lansing, 492 F. Supp. 1372, 1379 (W.D. Mich. 1980) (highway construction would potentially affect community's quality of life).

76. *See* Council on Environmental Quality, *Environmental Quality 1971: Second Annual Report* 189–91, *quoted in* First Nat'l Bank v. Richardson, 484 F.2d 1369, 1377–78 (7th Cir. 1973).

77. *See* Olmsted Citizens for a Better Community v. United States, 793 F.2d 201, 205 (8th Cir. 1986).

78. 40 C.F.R. § 1508.14 (1989); *see* Como-Falcon Community Coalition, Inc. v. United States Dep't of Labor, 609 F.2d 342, 346 (8th Cir. 1979), *cert. denied*, 446 U.S. 936 (1980); Concerned Citizens for 442nd T.A.W. v. Bodycombe, 538 F. Supp. 184, 190 (W.D. Mo. 1982); Birmingham Realty Co. v. GSA, 497 F. Supp. 1377, 1384 (N.D. Ala. 1980). *But see* Limerick Ecology Action, Inc. v. NRC, 869 F.2d 719, 746–47 (3d Cir. 1989) (requiring consideration of short-term socio-economic effects in EIS); Township of Springfield v. Lewis, 702 F.2d 426, 449 (3d Cir. 1983) (holding that "NEPA's scope can comprehend a substantial adverse impact upon a municipal tax base").

79. Hanly v. Mitchell, 460 F.2d 640, 647 (2d Cir.), *cert. denied*, 409 U.S. 990 (1972).

80. *See* Como-Falcon Coalition, Inc. v. United States Dep't of Labor, 609 F.2d 342, 344 (8th Cir. 1979) (action would affect, inter alia, socio-economic effects such as vehicular and pedestrian congestion; impact on commerce, social services, and local utilities; and contribute to criminal activity), *cert. denied*, 446 U.S. 936 (1980); Federation for Am. Immigration Reform v. Meese, 643 F. Supp. 983, 989 (S.D. Fla. 1986) ("impact of Cuban immigration on South Florida's water supply, sewage, and traffic congestion [was] at best, socioeconomic"); Property Owners Ass'n of

Deep Creek Lake, Inc. v. Gorsuch, 601 F. Supp. 220, 224 (D. Md. 1983) (economic effects of action do not trigger EIS requirement); National Ass'n of Government Employees v. Rumsfeld, 418 F. Supp. 1302, 1307 (E.D. Pa. 1976) (effects of action on crime and on need for additional fire protection are social impacts).

81. See Olmsted Citizens for a Better Community v. United States, 793 F.2d 201, 205 (8th Cir. 1986); see also Vieux Carre Property Owners, Residents & Assocs., Inc. v. Pierce, 719 F.2d 1272, 1275, 1279 (5th Cir. 1983) (evaluating agency consideration of action's impacts on urban historic district including effects on soil, archaeological remains, water, air, socio-economic conditions, visual effects, and traffic).

82. See City of Rochester v. United States Postal Serv., 541 F.2d 967, 973 (2d Cir. 1976); Township of Dover v. United States Postal Serv., 429 F. Supp. 295, 297 (D.N.J. 1977).

83. Image of Greater San Antonio v. Brown, 570 F.2d 517, 522 (5th Cir. 1978); see also Panhandle Producers & Royalty Owners Ass'n v. Economic Regulatory Admin., 847 F.2d 1168, 1179 (5th Cir. 1988) (upholding agency conclusion that importation of natural gas not requiring construction of new pipelines only had socio-economic effects); Committee to Save the Fox Bldg. v. Birmingham Branch of Federal Reserve Bank, 497 F. Supp. 504, 511 (N.D. Ala. 1980) (proposed demolition of architecturally and historically significant building was a "social concern" with no impact on the physical environment); Nucleus of Chicago Homeowner's Ass'n v. Lynn, 372 F. Supp. 147, 149–50 (N.D. Ill. 1973) (socio-economic characteristics of occupants of proposed low-income housing project are not an environmental effect of construction of project), aff'd, 524 F.2d 225 (7th Cir. 1975), cert. denied, 424 U.S. 967 (1976).

84. See Breckinridge v. Rumsfeld, 537 F.2d 864, 865 (6th Cir. 1976) (reduction in jobs and transfer of personnel from army depot), cert. denied, 429 U.S. 1061 (1977).

85. See Metropolitan Edison Co. v. People Against Nuclear Energy, 460 U.S. 766, 777–78 (1983).

86. See Image of Greater San Antonio v. Brown, 570 F.2d 517, 522 (5th Cir. 1978); see also Goodman Group, Inc. v. Dishroom, 679 F.2d 182, 185 (9th Cir. 1982) (consideration of social, cultural, economic, and aesthetic effects is appropriate when primary effect on environment generates an EIS).

The Eighth Circuit has suggested that the United States Supreme Court may have read the requirement to consider socio-economic effects out of existence. Olmsted Citizens for a Better Community v. United States, 793 F.2d 201, 206 (8th Cir. 1986) (citing Metropolitan Edison Co. v. People Against Nuclear Energy, 460 U.S. 766 (1983)). However, this suggestion does not take into account the Supreme Court's subsequent recognition that an EIS must disclose the significant socio-economic effects of the environmental impact of a proposed action. See Baltimore Gas & Elec. Co. v. Natural Resources Defense Council, Inc., 462 U.S. 87, 106–07 (1983).

87. See Baltimore Gas & Elec. Co. v. Natural Resources Defense Council, Inc., 462 U.S. 87, 106–07 (1983) (agreeing with District of Columbia Circuit that "NEPA

requires an EIS to disclose the significant health, socioeconomic, and cumulative consequences of the environmental impact of a proposed action").

88. 40 C.F.R. § 1508.14 (1989); see Dardar v. LaFourche Realty Co., 639 F. Supp. 1525, 1530 (E.D. La. 1986).

89. 42 U.S.C. §§ 4331(b)(2), 4331(b)(4) (1988); see Preservation Coalition, Inc. v. Pierce, 667 F.2d 851, 858 (9th Cir. 1982); WATCH (Waterbury Action to Conserve Our Heritage, Inc.) v. Harris, 603 F.2d 310, 318, 326 (2d Cir.), cert denied, 444 U.S. 995 (1979); Citizen Advocates for Responsible Expansion, Inc. v. Dole, 770 F.2d 423, 436, 439 n.20 (5th Cir. 1985).

90. Goodman Group, Inc. v. Dishroom, 679 F.2d 182, 185–86 (9th Cir. 1982).

91. 42 U.S.C. § 4331(b)(2) (1988); see Maryland-Nat'l Capital Park & Planning Comm'n v. United States Postal Serv., 487 F.2d 1029, 1038 (D.C. Cir. 1973) (considering aesthetic effects of post office); Mahelona v. Hawaiian Elec. Co., 418 F. Supp. 1328, 1334 (D. Hawaii 1976) (recognizing "undeniably significant aesthetic consequences" of construction of wall of 7–10 foot above sea level, 150 feet out to sea for discharge facility).

92. River Road Alliance, Inc. v. Corps of Eng'rs, 764 F.2d 445, 451 (7th Cir.), cert. denied, 475 U.S. 1055 (1985); see also Olmsted Citizens for a Better Community v. United States, 793 F.2d 201, 206 (8th Cir. 1986) (aesthetic effects may be considered in EA rather than lengthier and more costly EIS); Goodman Group, Inc. v. Dishroom, 679 F.2d 182, 185 (9th Cir. 1982) (aesthetic effects are difficult to define in NEPA context).

93. See City of New Haven v. Chandler, 446 F. Supp. 925, 930 (D. Conn. 1978).

94. See, e.g., Corps of Engineers, Policy and Procedures for Implementing NEPA, 33 C.F.R. § 230.6 (1989); Department of Interior, Notice of Instructions for the Minerals Management Service, 51 Fed. Reg. 1855, 1856 (1986); National Oceanic and Atmospheric Administration, Revised NOAA Directive Implementing the National Environmental Policy Act, 49 Fed. Reg. 29,644, 29,651 (1984).

95. See National Ass'n of Government Employees v. Rumsfeld, 418 F. Supp. 1302, 1307 (E.D. Pa. 1976).

96. 40 C.F.R. §§ 1501.4(a)(2), 1508.4 (1989).

97. See, e.g., 23 C.F.R. § 771.117(a) (1989) (Federal Highway Administration regulations define categorical exclusions as "actions which: do not induce significant impacts to planned growth or land use for the area; do not require the relocation of significant numbers of people; do not have a significant impact on any natural, cultural, recreational, historic or other resource; do not involve significant air, noise, or water quality impacts; do not have significant impacts on travel patterns; or do not otherwise, either individually or cumulatively, have any significant environmental impacts").

98. Council on Environmental Quality, Guidance Regarding NEPA Regulations, 48 Fed. Reg. 34,263, 34,265 (1983).

In 1983, the CEQ criticized the federal agencies' widespread use of lists of categorical exclusions as potentially inflexible and recommended the use of broadly defined criteria to characterize categorically excluded actions. The CEQ suggested that the criteria should be supplemented with examples of frequently conducted activities that were normally included within the specified criteria. *Id.* at 34,264–65.

99. 40 C.F.R. § 1508.4 (1989). *See, e.g.,* Corps of Engineers, Policy and Procedures for Implementing NEPA, 33 C.F.R. § 230.9 (1989); Federal Highway Administration, Environmental Impact and Related Procedures, 23 C.F.R. § 771.117 (1989); National Oceanic and Atmospheric Administration, Revised NOAA Directive Implementing the National Environmental Policy Act, 49 Fed. Reg. 29,644, 29,652 (1984).

100. *E.g.,* Sierra Club v. United States Forest Serv., 843 F.2d 1190, 1191–92 (9th Cir. 1988) (Forest Service categorically excluded timber sale).

101. Foundation on Economic Trends v. Weinberger, 610 F. Supp. 829, 840 (D.D.C. 1985).

102. *See* Panhandle Producers & Royalty Owners Ass'n v. Economic Regulatory Admin., 847 F.2d 1168, 1179 (5th Cir. 1988).

In *Panhandle Producers*, the Economic Regulatory Commission treated a natural gas import proposal as a categorical exclusion because the agency determined that its only effects were socio-economic. The action was listed in the Department of Energy guidelines as an action normally requiring an EA. After the Fifth Circuit decision, the Department of Energy proposed a new guideline to list the action as a categorical exclusion. *See* 53 Fed. Reg. 29,934 (1988).

103. *See* Runway 27 Coalition, Inc. v. Engen, 679 F. Supp. 95, 102 (D. Mass. 1987). *Cf.* National Trust for Historic Preservation v. Dole, 828 F.2d 776, 782–83 (D.C. Cir. 1987) (Buckley, J., concurring in part and dissenting in part) (arguing that agency made forced application of its categorical exclusion regulation).

104. 40 C.F.R. § 1508.4 (1989).

105. *See, e.g.,* 23 C.F.R. § 771.117(b) (1989) (listing unusual circumstances that could cause agency and applicant to conduct environmental studies to determine if categorical exclusion classification is proper).

106. *See, e.g.,* 23 C.F.R. § 771.117(b)(2) (1989); FAA Order No. 5050.4, para. 23n, *cited in* West Houston Air Comm. v. FAA, 784 F.2d 702, 705 (5th Cir. 1986).

107. FAA Order No. 5050.4, para. 23n, 45 Fed. Reg. 56,620 (1980).

108. West Houston Air Comm. v. FAA, 784 F.2d 702, 705 & n.3 (5th Cir. 1986).

109. *See* Greenpeace, U.S.A. v. Evans, 688 F. Supp. 579, 582–83 (W.D. Wash. 1987); *see also* Mississippi *ex rel.* Moore v. Marsh, 710 F. Supp. 1488, 1507 (S.D. Miss. 1989) (designation of proposed action as categorical exclusion was clearly contrary to law; agency clearly erred in not treating action as exceptional case).

110. Jones v. Gordon, 792 F.2d 821, 827–29 (9th Cir. 1986).

111. *See* National Trust for Historic Preservation v. Dole, 828 F.2d 776, 782 (D.C. Cir. 1987); City of Alexandria v. FHWA, 756 F.2d 1014, 1019–20 (4th Cir. 1985).

112. *See* Greenpeace, U.S.A. v. Evans, 688 F. Supp. 579, 582 (W.D. Wash. 1987).

113. National Trust for Historic Preservation v. Dole, 828 F.2d 776, 780–81 (D.C. Cir. 1987); *see also* City of Alexandria v. FHWA, 756 F.2d 1014, 1017 (4th Cir. 1985) (citing Citizens to Preserve Overton Park, Inc. v. Volpe, 401 U.S. 402, 416 (1971)).

114. 40 C.F.R. § 1501.4(b) (1989).

115. *See* LaFlamme v. FERC, 852 F.2d 389, 399 (9th Cir. 1988); Steamboaters v. FERC, 759 F.2d 1382, 1392–93 (9th Cir. 1985); Country Club Bank v. Smith, 399 F. Supp. 1097, 1102–03 (W.D. Mo. 1975).

116. *See, e.g.,* Corps of Engineers, Policy and Procedures for Implementing NEPA, 33 C.F.R. § 230.7 (1989); National Oceanic and Atmospheric Administration, Revised NOAA Directive Implementing the National Environmental Policy Act, 49 Fed. Reg. 29,644, 29,651 (1984).

117. Panhandle Producers & Royalty Owners Ass'n v. Economic Regulatory Admin., 847 F.2d 1168, 1179 (5th Cir. 1988) (action normally requiring EA was considered as categorical exclusion).

Environmental Assessments

4.1 INTRODUCTION

The use of environmental assessments (EAs) by agencies has greatly increased since the 1970s. By the late 1980s, ten thousand to twenty thousand EAs were prepared annually compared to about 425 draft and final EISs prepared annually.[1] This chapter discusses the purpose of an EA, how to prepare an EA and who should do so, and the scope of an EA. If an agency determines, based on an EA, that a proposed action will not have significant environmental effects, the agency must prepare and publish a finding of no significant impact (FONSI) before it may proceed with the action.

Public participation in the EA process is discussed in this chapter. Public participation in agency procedures for preparing EAs is more limited than in EIS preparation, but it serves a valuable purpose. Not only does the public become more likely to support an action it is involved in, but reviewing courts give greater weight to agency determinations in which the public was actively involved. The judicial review of EAs and FONSIs is also examined, including the burden of proof to be shown by a plaintiff and the standard of review applied to agency determinations.

Actions may often be mitigated to reduce their environmental effects below the significance threshold. An agency may then prepare an EA instead of an EIS. The incorporation of mitigation measures into an EA is also discussed in this chapter. Finally, the criteria considered by courts in determining whether environmental effects are significant is examined.

4.2 PURPOSE

The purpose of an EA is to identify potential effects on the human environment of a proposed action and to determine whether those effects may be significant.[2] The Seventh Circuit has described an EA's purpose as a determination "whether there is enough likelihood of significant environmental consequences to justify the time and expense of preparing an [EIS]."[3] Although the Seventh Circuit may simply be stating that preparing EAs in actions with less than significant effects allows the agency to spend more time and money on actions with significant effects, for which it prepares EISs[4] the Seventh Circuit's statement is troublesome. The statement implies that the amount of time and expense involved in determining whether the significant environmental effects probably will occur is a determining factor in deciding whether to prepare an EIS.

The Seventh Circuit's statement is contrary to NEPA's requirement that section 102 of NEPA be complied with "to the fullest extent possible."[5] That phrase has been interpreted by the Supreme Court as "a deliberate command that the duty NEPA imposes upon the agencies to consider environmental factors not be shunted aside in the bureaucratic shuffle."[6] Thus, although an agency's decision not to prepare an EIS is upheld unless it is arbitrary and capricious,[7] if the duty to prepare an EIS is triggered, an agency may not refuse to prepare one simply because it believes that preparation is not justified by the time and expense involved. In the Seventh Circuit's opinion, the implication that in certain cases an EA fulfills the purpose of an EIS[8] overlooks this mandate and also overlooks the "very different purposes" of the two documents.[9]

4.3 FORMAT

An EA is a "concise public document" briefly providing the evidence and analysis necessary to make a threshold determination of significance.[10] An EA must include brief discussions of the need for the proposal, alternatives, environmental impacts of the proposed action and alternatives, and a list of agencies and private parties consulted.[11] The EA is less formal and rigorous than an EIS.[12] Therefore, the analysis in it need not be as detailed as that in an EIS, but it must not be conclusory or perfunctory.[13]

Although the CEQ regulations do not specify the appropriate length for an EA, the CEQ informally recommends ten to fifteen pages, with background data incorporated by reference.[14] EAs frequently contain many more pages.[15] Lengthy EAs are not necessarily determined to be adequate, however, and a court may still require an agency to prepare an EIS in addition to the EA.[16] If an EIS is required because an action may have significant environmental effects, an alternate document will not necessarily substitute for an EIS, especially if the agency has not fulfilled all the requirements for preparing an EIS, such as the participation of other agencies and the public.[17] Therefore, if an agency considers that an action may significantly affect the environment, it should prepare an EIS rather than a lengthy EA in the hope that a court would declare it to be a substitute for an EIS.

An agency is not obligated to follow any particular methodology in preparing an EA, but its choice of methodology must be justifiable in light of current scientific thought.[18] Agencies are not required to involve specific disciplines in their assessment of an action's effects or to consider all documents that could possibly be relevant as long as the analysis conducted by the agency is interdisciplinary.[19]

4.4 DELEGATION

The applicant for a federal permit, funding, or approval, or a consultant, may gather the data used in an EA, and may prepare the EA.[20] An agency may not rubber stamp an EA prepared by others, however.[21] Instead, the agency must review the prepared information and analysis and independently verify and assess it.[22] The agency is responsible for the EA, including the accuracy of information contained in it, its scope and the content and evaluation of the environmental issues.[23] A statutory exception to the above rule exists for applicants for community block grants from the Department of Housing and Urban Welfare.[24]

If another agency has already prepared an EA for an action relating to the same project, the agency proposing the action may adopt the other agency's EA instead of preparing a separate one. However, the adopting agency should independently evaluate the information in the EA and assume full responsibility for the information's scope and content.[25]

4.5 SCOPE

In determining the scope of an EA, an agency must assess the significant direct, indirect, and cumulative impacts of the proposed action.[26] The CEQ recommends the use of scoping—a pluralistic decision-making process used to identify the range of actions, alternatives, and impacts dealt with in an EIS—to identify alternatives or potentially significant environmental impacts that may have been overlooked by the agency in preparing an EA.[27]

Direct and indirect effects must be considered in an EA although it is not essential that they be categorized as such.[28] Indirect effects that are highly speculative or indefinite need not be considered.[29] The EA's consideration of indirect environmental effects may not need to be as detailed as that for direct effects.[30] Speculative effects that are considered do not require extensive analysis.[31]

If the proposed action is connected to other actions, the EA must contain an analysis of the connected actions in order to determine whether the joint effects of the connected actions may be significant. The connected actions analysis is required even if the environmental effects of the proposed action are not significant. That is, the analysis is required in any EA in which the action under consideration is connected to any other action. The connected actions analysis is prepared in addition to an analysis of the effects of the proposed action.[32] Actions are connected when there is a clear nexus between them, that is, when the actions justify and depend on each other.[33]

Cumulative actions, which must be considered in an EIS, may require consideration in an EA, according to some courts. A cumulative action is an action "which when viewed with other proposed actions [has] cumulatively significant impacts."[34] The CEQ regulations do not require consideration of cumulative actions in an EA, but some courts have, nevertheless, considered them in determining whether an EA is adequate.[35]

Cumulative effects must also be considered in an EA.[36] This requirement and its confusion with the cumulative actions analysis is discussed in section 5.9.3. The cumulative effects analysis need not be repeated in an EA if it is included in another environmental document for the same area and the EA specifically refers to and incorporates the other document.[37]

NEPA requires agencies to "study, develop, and describe appropriate alternatives to recommended courses of action in any proposal which involves unresolved conflicts concerning alternative uses of available resources."[38] This requirement, which is independent of NEPA's requirement that alternatives must be considered in an EIS, means that an agency must consider alternatives in an EA.[39] The alternatives to be considered differ from those to be considered in an EIS in that alternative uses of the resources at issue must be examined not alternatives to the proposed action.[40] Thus, the scope of alternatives to be considered in an EA is broader than the requirement for consideration of alternatives in an EIS.[41]

An agency must "actively seek out and develop alternatives as opposed to merely writing out options that reasonable speculation suggests might exist."[42] The search for alternatives may decrease as the impact of an action decreases.[43] If plaintiffs can show the feasibility of an alternative, however, the agency should consider it.[44]

Alternatives to be considered in an EA include the "no action" alternative.[45] As in EISs, an agency is not required to consider remote and speculative alternatives.[46] An agency also need not consider alternate means by which an individual applicant can reach his goal, only alternate means by which the goals of the action may be attained.[47]

4.6 FINDINGS OF NO SIGNIFICANT IMPACT

After an agency has prepared an EA, it must either prepare an EIS if the agency determines that its action may have significant environmental effects,[48] or it must prepare a finding of no significant impact (FONSI) if it determines that the action will not have significant environmental effects. The FONSI must set out the reasons for the agency's negative determination.[49] If certain factors are given greater weight than others in making the determination, the agency must explain the reasons for these background decisions.[50] The EA may be attached to the FONSI and incorporated by reference or it may be summarized in the FONSI. Other relevant environmental documents must be noted.[51]

EAs and FONSIs must be made available to the public.[52] Agencies may choose the best method of accomplishing this goal as long as they ensure that all interested or affected parties are notified.[53] The CEQ recommends mailing notices of the documents' availability to interested national groups as well as publication in the *Federal Register* and national publications for actions with a national scope.[54] Notice of availability of EAs and FONSIs for regional or site-specific proposals may be provided by publication in local newspapers.[55]

Under certain circumstances the CEQ recommends that FONSIs be published thirty days before an agency's final decision not to prepare an EIS. The CEQ provides the following examples: borderline cases where a reasonable argument exists for preparation of an EIS; unusual cases (for example, new types of actions or precedent-setting cases such as minor development in a pristine area); cases involving public or scientific controversy; cases similar to those that normally require preparation of an EIS; cases in which the proposed action has been redefined during scoping to include mitigation measures;[56] and cases in which an agency has adopted another agency's EA.[57] The Ninth Circuit requires forty-five day comment periods for certain EAs.[58]

In order for a plaintiff to gain relief for an agency's violation of the publication period, plaintiffs must show that they were injured by the violation.[59] If the agency nevertheless considered the plaintiffs' comments, harm will probably not be shown.[60]

4.7 PUBLIC AND AGENCY PARTICIPATION

The courts are split on whether an agency is required to permit public participation *before* making a threshold determination of significance and if public participation is required, the type of participation that is required.[61] As discussed above, an agency must permit public participation in certain EAs and FONSIs in advance of its decision not to prepare an EIS.

Because public participation is such an integral part of the NEPA process,[62] it is advisable for an agency to invite public comments and comments from other agencies (national, state, and local where appropriate) to its proposed action. If an agency's threshold determination is challenged, a critical factor in judicial review is the degree to which other agencies and the public participated in the determination. For example, courts accord greater weight to an agency's determination of insignificance if the agency held public hearings,[63] or if environmental agencies did not consider that the action's effects were potentially significant.[64] Lack of public comments on a proposal, however, does not demonstrate that a proposed action is unlikely to have significant environmental effects.[65]

If an agency ignores negative comments made by the public and other agencies, especially agencies with environmental expertise, the agency's determination is unlikely to survive judicial review.[66] Although the comments are not determinative,[67] agencies must show that they were considered.[68] If the comments are adequately considered, the agency does not violate NEPA by rejecting them.[69]

4.8 SUPPLEMENTATION

The CEQ regulations do not require supplementation of EAs. However, if new circumstances occur or if information relevant to the environmental concerns of an action arise before the action is conducted, an agency may be required to supplement an EA[70] or to reassess its prior determination.[71]

4.9 JUDICIAL REVIEW

EAs and FONSIs are subject to judicial review. To meet its initial burden of proof in challenging an EA and FONSI, a plaintiff must present evidence to show that the proposed action significantly affects the human environment,[72] an environmental factor may be significantly degraded,[73] or the agency could not have determined that no environmental effect was significant because its analysis was flawed.[74]

Plaintiffs' burden in showing that an action significantly affects the quality of the human environment appears to vary according to the circuit. In the First, Fifth and Ninth Circuits, plaintiffs must show that an action may significantly affect the environment.[75] In other circuits, the standard may be higher,[76] especially in the Second Circuit.[77] In order to challenge an agency's inadequate consideration of alternatives, plaintiffs must show that feasible alternatives exist.[78]

Evidence must be introduced by plaintiffs to support an allegation that an effect may be significant.[79] The evidence must be site-specific and not generalized.[80] Plaintiffs may not rely on a common sense argument that a certain action will necessarily affect the environment; they must present evidence showing why the environment may be affected.[81] Evidence must be presented that shows more than a disagreement of experts. In such a case, reviewing courts defer to the agency[82] as long as the agency has addressed the conflicting opinion.[83] The same level of deference may not be accorded to an agency's expertise in complying with NEPA. Because NEPA imposes duties on all federal agencies rather than authorizing one agency to enforce a statute, no regulatory agency has expertise in NEPA compliance.[84]

If the plaintiff meets the initial burden of proof, the agency must show that its negative determination was not arbitrary or capricious.[85] The agency must show that it took a hard look at the environmental concerns raised by its proposed action,[86] identified relevant environmental concerns, and made a convincing argument that the impact of each concern would be insignificant.[87] It must show that its determination that its action would not have a significant environmental effect was convincingly documented.[88] If an agency fully considers an unsupported concern about a proposed action's environmental effects and concludes that the action will not significantly affect the environment, the agency's determination will be upheld.[89]

Plaintiffs may show that an agency inadequately considered environmental effects by proving that the agency relied on incorrect or misleading information,[90] that its conclusions ignored the differing views of other expert agencies,[91] that it omitted material information,[92] or that it merely concluded that an environmental effect was insignificant without assessing the effect.[93]

The agency's consideration of environmental factors must be documented in the administrative record in existence at the time the determination of no significant impact is made. Courts generally do not go outside an agency's record to see if the research or analysis adequately supports the agency's conclusions.[94] However, a court may go outside the agency's record to determine whether an agency adequately considered factors relevant to the environmental effects of its proposed action.[95] Plaintiffs may introduce evidence of significant effects or realistic alternatives that an agency failed to consider in its significance decision.[96] Evidence of the mental processes of the decision makers in making a significance decision is not subject to discovery unless the plaintiff makes a strong showing of bad faith or improper behavior in the agency's decision-making process.[97]

If an agency's inquiry into the potential environmental effects of a proposed action is adequate, courts examine the agency's determination of insignificance[98] according to fairly deferential standards of review. For many years, the standard varied between the different circuits, with some circuits applying the arbitrary and capricious standard[99] while others applied the more searching reasonableness standard.[100]

The Supreme Court settled the controversy in 1989 by ruling that the correct standard for judicial review of an agency's determination not to supplement an EIS is the arbitrary and capricious standard of the Administrative Procedure Act.[101] The arbitrary and capricious standard will thus probably be applied to all agency determinations under NEPA. The Supreme Court stated that the difference between the standards was "not of great pragmatic consequence."[102]

Under the arbitrary and capricious standard, a reviewing court must determine whether the agency's decision was based upon a consideration of relevant factors and whether a clear error of judgment has been made.[103] The court's inquiry into the facts "must 'be searching and careful' but 'the ultimate standard of review is a narrow one.'"[104] The court may not substitute its judgment for that of the agency.[105]

The District of Columbia Circuit applies the arbitrary and capricious test to a negative declaration by inquiring:

(1) whether the agency took a 'hard look' at the problem;
(2) whether the agency identified the relevant areas of environmental concern;
(3) as to the problems studied and identified, whether the agency made a convincing case that the impact was insignificant; and
(4) if there was an impact of true significance, whether the agency convincingly established that changes in the project sufficiently reduced it to a minimum.[106]

Appellate courts review the decisions of trial courts reviewing agency determinations by determining questions of law de novo and findings of fact by whether they were clearly erroneous. This traditional standard of review may be influenced by the type of review at the trial court level. If the trial court heard factual matters such as witnesses or attorneys describing in detail the agency's decision-making process, the appellate court may apply the clearly erroneous standard. If the trial court has not heard witnesses or found facts but has merely reviewed agency documents to reach legal conclusions, the appellate court has greater freedom to differ with the trial court's conclusions.[107]

4.10 MEASURES TO MITIGATE SIGNIFICANT ENVIRONMENTAL EFFECTS

Agency actions may often be mitigated to reduce otherwise significant environmental effects to an insignificant level. Thus, if an agency can show that its action will be mitigated so that no significant environmental effects will occur, it may prepare a mitigated FONSI supported by an EA instead of an EIS.[108] If an agency is depending on mitigation measures in not preparing an EIS, the mitigation measures must be fully considered before its proposed action proceeds,[109] and the action must be conditioned on them.[110] Contractual obligations,[111] including conditions precedent,[112] design modifications,[113] and measures planned in close cooperation with the local community[114] may be used to mitigate significant effects below the level of significance. Mitigation measures based on good intentions may not be considered.[115] All the significant effects of an action probably do not need to be mitigated if the environmental effect of the action is mitigated below the level of significance.[116]

The CEQ defines mitigation to include a decision not to take all or part of a proposed action; to limit the action's implementation and either its degree or magnitude; to repair, rehabilitate, and restore an affected environment; to preserve and maintain operations conducted during an action's implementation to reduce or eliminate its effects over time; and to replace or provide substitute resources or environments in order to compensate for an action's impact.[117] Compensatory mitigation can be conducted on site or off site.[118]

The CEQ has stated in informal advice that if mitigation measures are used to reduce the environmental effects of an action below the significance level, an agency may rely on those measures in not preparing an EIS only if the measures are imposed by statute or regulation, or if they were contained in the original proposal.[119] Thus, according to the CEQ, mitigation measures added to a proposal during the EA process or scoping do not obviate the need to prepare an EIS unless the entire proposal is resubmitted and the EA and FONSI made publicly available for thirty days.[120] Courts do not necessarily follow the CEQ's informal advice regarding the type of mitigation measures that may be considered in a threshold determination, however.[121]

It is probably not possible to mitigate all actions below the significance level.[122] Therefore, if there is a substantial question whether mitigation measures would render insignificant the environmental effects of an agency action, an EIS must be prepared, especially when an agency will no longer have the right to absolutely control the action.[123]

The informational purpose of NEPA requires mitigation measures to be subject to public comment. Thus, measures based on planned scientific studies alone are inadequate because they preclude involvement by other agencies and the public.[124] Analysis of the measures and explanations of their effectiveness must be provided; a listing is inadequate.[125] The explanation must be site specific.[126] Conclusory statements regarding the effects of mitigation measures are inadequate,[127] as is the adoption of a mitigation plan by an agency without independent analysis.[128]

4.11 CRITERIA FOR DETERMINING THE SIGNIFICANCE OF ENVIRONMENTAL EFFECTS

"Significance" is an amorphous term that is not defined in either NEPA or its legislative history.[129] Judicial definitions have been attempted[130] but no generally accepted definition exists.[131] Thus, courts determine on a case-by-case basis whether a plaintiff challenging an agency's decision not to prepare an EIS had met its burden of showing that an action's environmental effects significantly affect the human environment.[132]

To aid agencies in identifying actions that may have significant environmental effects, the CEQ regulations contain a list of criteria based on CEQ's interpretation of the case law of the 1970s minus marginal decisions.[133] The criteria have two divisions—context and intensity—both of which must be considered in threshold determinations.[134] Agencies determine the context of an action by analyzing its relationship to its setting—local, regional, and/or national—and the interests it affects. The context of an action is also influenced by the short- and long-term nature of its effects.[135]

The intensity of an action is measured by the severity of its impact on the environment. The CEQ lists ten criteria to aid agencies in determining whether an action's potential environmental effects are severe enough to be significant. The criteria are an action's beneficial or adverse effects; effect on public health and safety; effect on a unique geographic area; controversial effects on the human environment; highly uncertain, unique, or unknown risks; precedential effects; cumulative effects; effect on historic, scientific, or cultural resources; effect on endangered species; and compliance with federal, state, or local law.[136] The criteria are supplemented by further criteria contained in the guidelines or regulations of individual agencies.[137]

The criteria are, in fact, a potpourri of factors to be considered in determining whether an action has environmental effects and whether those effects are significant. For example, whether an action has beneficial or adverse effects is a determination of the types of environmental effects that must be considered under NEPA. Whether an action affects the public health and safety is part of a determination of whether the action affects the human environment. Whether the proposed action has cumulative effects is a determination of the scope of effects to be considered in a threshold determination.

Courts use the criteria as examples of factors requiring consideration in a threshold determination.[138] Inclusion of the criteria in the environmental effects of an action does not necessarily mean that the action is significant,[139] but, rather, guides agency decision makers in their determinations.

4.11.1 Local or Regional Effects

NEPA must be complied with on a site-specific basis. That is, the effects of proposed agency actions on individual locales must be investigated; agencies cannot assume that because a project has certain effects in one area it will have those effects in another area.[140] For example, an action may not significantly affect an urban environment, but an identical action could have a significant effect on a rural locale.[141] Locale is determined by the geography of an area and the nature of an action.[142] The locale for a site-specific action is the area directly affected by the action plus its immediate surroundings.[143] It is not settled whether the environmental effects of an action should be determined by examining one part of the total area affected by the action or whether the effects should be evaluated in terms of the total affected area.[144]

4.11.2 Short- or Long-Term Effects

The fact that an agency's action is temporary or that it has short-term effects is insufficient, standing alone, to make those effects insignificant.[145] These factors may be persuasive, however, in upholding an agency's determination of insignificance.[146]

4.11.3 Beneficial or Adverse Effects

NEPA and, in turn, the CEQ regulations require consideration of beneficial as well as adverse effects in threshold determinations, even if an agency believes that the overall effect of the action is more beneficial than adverse.[147] Beneficial economic effects of an action cannot be balanced against adverse environmental effects at the threshold determination stage.[148] If a beneficial effect may be significant, it must be discussed in an EIS.[149]

4.11.4 Effect on Public Health and Safety

The CEQ regulations require consideration of the degree to which a proposed action affects the public health or safety.[150] Public health was identified in NEPA's legislative history as the primary reason for NEPA's enactment[151] and has been referred to as the most important subject dealt with by the act.[152]

Although physical health is definitely within NEPA's ambit, it is not as clear whether psychological health is also included. The problem lies not with a distinction between physical and psychological health, but with the causal chain between a physical effect on the environment and its effect on psychological health. If the chain is too attenuated, NEPA does not apply. For example, the Supreme Court ruled that the causal chain between restarting a nuclear reactor at Three Mile Island and the effect on residents' psychological health posed by the risk of an accident was too attenuated to be covered by NEPA because the risk did not affect the physical environment.[153] Similarly, the effect on residents' psychological health of constructing a jail or low-income housing in a neighborhood is too attentuated to be within the scope of NEPA.[154]

Based on the above examples, it would be difficult to link damage to psychological health to the requisite change in the physical environment. Thus, although psychological health may technically be within NEPA's ambit, it may be excluded as a practical matter.

4.11.5 Unique Character of an Affected Area

In making a threshold determination, the CEQ regulations require consideration of a geographic area's unique characteristics.[155] Unique characteristics include the area's historic or cultural resources, prime farmlands, parklands, wild and scenic rivers, wetlands, or ecologically critical areas.[156]

All effects on an area's unique characteristics are not necessarily significant. The agency's action must significantly affect the unique characteristic.[157] If the action continues an existing use, the effect may be adjudged to be insignificant. For example, when the major change between old and new roads through parkland was increased traffic capacity, the reviewing court upheld the agency's determination that the proposed road construction did not have a significant effect on the environment.[158]

4.11.6 Controversiality of an Environmental Effect

In making threshold determinations, agencies must consider the degree to which the environmental effects of their proposed actions are likely to be highly controversial.[159] The term "controversial" applies to the environmental effects, nature, and size of a proposed action, not opposition to the proposed action itself.[160] Thus, if opposition to a proposed action exists but the nature of the action's effects is not disputed, the proposed action is not controversial for purposes of NEPA.[161]

Opponents of a proposed action must present evidence showing the existence of a scientific controversy about the action's environmental effects; mere speculation is insufficient to make a showing that an action's effects are controversial.[162] Such evidence may consist of disagreements with an insignificance determination by other agencies, experts, or knowledgeable members of the public.[163] If the only opponents of an action are the plaintiffs and their experts, the plaintiffs may not be deemed to have shown that the action is controversial.[164]

If opposition to a project does not occur, an agency may not conclude that the action lacks significance; lack of opposition does not necessarily indicate lack of significance.[165] If substantial questions are raised regarding whether an action has significant environmental effects, the agency must address the issue.[166] If a court finds controversy over the effects of an action, the potential uncertainty of the effects may trigger the need to consider the action's uncertain, unique, or unknown risks.[167]

4.11.7 Uncertain, Unique or Unknown Risks

The CEQ regulations require agencies to consider the degree to which the environmental effects of their actions are highly uncertain or involve unique or unknown risks.[168] Stating in an EA that the environmental effects are unknown is insufficient without analysis even when the action in question is an experiment designed to discover the environmental effects of the action.[169] If the nature of an action makes its effects uncertain and speculative, the agency cannot approve the action unless an EIS is prepared to evaluate the environmental effects.[170] If an action does not increase a risk that already exists, however, assessment of the risk is not required.[171]

The courts have established a framework for considering scientific uncertainty in threshold determinations. This framework weighs the probability of an adverse environmental effect or a risk against its severity. For example, the Second Circuit upheld the Department of Transportation's decision not to prepare an EIS for transporting radioactive materials by highway through urban areas.[172] The agency had concluded, and the court agreed, that the environmental consequences of the action were insignificant.[173] The court stated that agencies must consider possible environmental effects of their actions, but because the effects involved scientific uncertainty, it deferred to the agency's determination that the risk of accidentally releasing radioactive materials in an urban area was too remote to require preparation of an EIS.[174] Because the issue involved a threshold decision, the court stated that it was precluded from imposing its choice of risk analysis on the agency.[175] The agency could select its own methodology for risk assessment as long as it was justified in light of current scientific opinion.[176]

The District of Columbia has adopted a similar test. The court requires agencies to determine the sum of all reasonably foreseeable effects that can be feasibly determined.[177] The probability of the effects occurring is then discounted from the determination to calculate whether the effects are significant.[178] The detail accompanying consideration of each effect is based on the remoteness of the effect and the severity of its potential environmental effects.[179]

Although an agency may not be obligated to prepare an EIS if there is only a remote risk of a significant environmental effect, the agency must fully discuss the basis for its determination of insignificance in the EA. Failure to address environmental concerns because of their speculative nature,[180] or because they are unknown,[181] is inadequate because a potential environmental effect cannot be determined to be insignificant unless it is known.[182] An agency need not discuss the environmental effects of a speculative occurrence, however, if the causal connection between the agency action and any environmental effects is too attenuated.[183]

If the environmental effects of an agency's proposed action are uncertain, unique, or unknown, the agency may not determine that the action will not significantly affect the environment by relying on obtaining future information.[184] Similarly, an agency may not establish a monitoring program to take the place of an informed decision regarding an action's environmental effects. An agency's proposal to discontinue an action if a certain result is evidenced by a monitoring program may be interpreted as a determination to proceed with an action without knowing the action's full environmental effects.[185]

4.11.8 Precedential Nature of an Environmental Effect

The effects of actions that may establish a precedent for future actions with significant effects or that represent "a decision in principle about a future consideration" must be evaluated in determining an effect's intensity.[186] This type of effect may occur when construction of a facility—such as a port—ensures that an area will continue to be developed in lieu of other areas.[187] Once the plans are initiated and begun, it is probable that decision makers will order the project continued.[188]

4.11.9 Cumulative Environmental Effects

There is considerable confusion in the courts regarding cumulative impacts or effects and cumulative actions. This confusion has resulted in a split in the circuits as to the type of analysis required in an EA. The CEQ regulations require that an agency proposing an action with cumulative impacts or effects analyze those effects in an EA (if one is prepared) and/or an EIS (if one is prepared).[189] The CEQ regulations require agencies to prepare a cumulative actions analysis in an EIS.[190] The regulations do not contain a requirement for an agency to prepare a cumulative actions analysis in an EA. Courts occasionally discuss the cumulative actions analysis in connection with an EA, however.[191] In addition, consideration of cumulative effects in an EA has been rejected.[192]

A cumulative actions analysis includes only related actions proposed by the federal agency proposing the action under consideration.[193] The analysis does not focus on the resource affected by the action as the cumulative effects analysis does, but on whether the actions are so interrelated that they comprise a local, regional, or national program.[194] The cumulative effects analysis is discussed in section 5.10.2 as a requirement of appropriate EISs.

A cumulative impacts or effects analysis, on the other hand, considers whether a proposed "action is related to other actions with individually insignificant but cumulatively significant impacts,"[195] that is, whether the environmental effects of the action under consideration may be significant when the effects are considered together with the environmental effects of other actions.[196] The other actions whose environmental effects must be considered are "past, present, and reasonably foreseeable future actions regardless of what agency (Federal or non-Federal) or person undertakes such other actions."[197] The environment that is impacted may be a geographical area[198] or a wildlife population.[199]

The size of the area to be considered in a cumulative effects analysis may be determined by such factors as the character of the landscape, identified ecosystems within the area, proposals to expand the proposed project or to conduct other projects in the same area, and the type of pollution problems caused by other actions in relation to those caused by the proposed action.[200] A cumulative effects analysis of actions in one area of an identified natural resource may not be substituted for a cumulative effects analysis of all actions in another area of the identified resource.[201]

In making a cumulative effects analysis in an EA, an agency must identify the area affected by the proposed project; impacts anticipated in the area by the proposed project; other past, proposed, and reasonably foreseeable actions affecting the area; actual and anticipated impacts caused by other actions; and the overall impact that would probably result from the cumulation of the individual impacts.[202] Cumulative effects include indirect as well as direct effects.[203]

The inclusion of other actions in a cumulative effects analysis is not determined by the public or private nature of those actions, or whether the parties conducting them are subject to NEPA.[204] The effect of an action on an identified natural resource determines whether an action's effects must be considered in the analysis.[205] An agency need not consider the potential environmental effects of actions that are not reasonably foreseeable[206] or the environmental effects of actions that are forbidden by its proposal.[207]

It is not clear how much time must be involved before an action is no longer reasonably foreseeable. One court upheld a decision of the Federal Aviation Administration not to include analysis of an action with cumulative impacts that was contemplated to occur ten years after a first action. The court stated, however, that the agency's procedure stating that the agency could not meaningfully evaluate the environmental effects of actions begun more than three years in the future may provide "an unreasonably brief time in some circumstances."[208]

Once the cumulative impacts are identified, they must be considered. The effects of actions other than the proposed agency action do not necessarily have to be considered or analyzed extensively. The extent of the analysis is dependent on the nature and scope of the affected area and the extent of activity in the area.[209] The extent to which actions in a cumulative effects analysis have been discussed in other NEPA documents is also relevant to the extent of the analysis required in a subsequent action.[210]

If a threshold determination identifies cumulatively significant effects involving the proposed action, the effects must be analyzed.[211] If the cumulative effects analysis reveals related federal proposals, a comprehensive EIS may be required.[212]

4.11.10 Effects on Historic, Scientific, or Cultural Resources

The CEQ regulations require measurement of an effect's intensity by the degree to which an action may cause the loss or destruction of significant scientific, historical, or cultural resources or the degree to which it may affect structures, sites, districts, highways, or objects listed in or eligible for listing in the National Register of Historic Places.[213] For example, an action that seriously impairs the natural beauty of an ecologically rich area and adversely affects resident wildlife significantly affects the environment.[214]

NEPA's policy statement refers to "culturally pleasing surroundings," and to the preservation of "important historic, cultural, and natural aspects of our natural heritage."[215] Thus, the environment protected by NEPA includes historic and cultural resources in addition to natural resources. If an agency's proposed action affects historic and cultural resources, the action is subject to NEPA and the agency must prepare an EIS if the action's effect on the resource is significant.[216] Where better examples of a building's features exist in other retained historic buildings, or where features integral to the building's historic, cultural, or architectural significance would not be affected, the environmental effects may be determined to be insignificant.[217]

If an agency action affects the cultural character of an area but not the physical environment, it is not clear whether the action is subject to NEPA. The Ninth Circuit upheld an agency's decision not to prepare an EIS in such a case but did not discuss whether NEPA was in fact triggered.[218]

4.11.11 Effect on Endangered Species

The CEQ regulations require agencies to evaluate the degree to which actions may adversely affect endangered or threatened species or critical habitat identified under the Endangered Species Act.[219]

The existence of an endangered species in an area or the possibility that an endangered species may be present does not necessarily mean that the environmental effects of an action will be significant.[220] If an agency shows on the basis of an adequate EA that the existence of the endangered or threatened species will not be seriously threatened by the agency's action, the duty to prepare an EIS is not triggered.[221] As with all analyses required by NEPA, an agency may not simply conclude that no endangered species will be affected by its action; it must provide a basis, such as an investigation of the area, for its conclusion.[222]

4.11.12 Compliance with Federal, State, or Local Law

A final CEQ criterion for determining the significance of an action's environmental effects is whether the action has the potential to violate federal, state, or local environmental protection laws.[223] If an action may violate an environmental law or standard, the potential violation must be addressed.[224] However, an action is not necessarily insignificant if it does not violate standards promulgated under an environmental law; environmental effects of actions within legal limits have the potential to be significant.[225] An agency's compliance with other environmental laws does not ensure compliance with NEPA, but that compliance is relevant to a court's review of the agency's threshold determination.[226]

An agency's compliance with local zoning ordinances is especially relevant to threshold determinations. By complying with local ordinances, an agency demonstrates that it is acting in accordance with the demands of the community's residents regarding such factors as land use, construction safeguards, aesthetics, population density, crime control, and neighborhood cohesiveness.[227] Under these circumstances, courts are more likely to uphold an agency's determination of insignificance.[228] Violation of zoning ordinances, however, does not necessarily mean that an environmental effect is significant.[229] If the violated zoning ordinance addressed social and economic concerns rather than ecological concerns, its violation would not be relevant to a NEPA determination.[230]

NOTES

1. *OEQ Authorization, Fiscal Years 1989-1992; Hearing on H.R. 1113 Before the Subcomm. on Fisheries and Wildlife Conservation and the Environment of the House Comm. on Merchant Marine and Fisheries*, 101st Cong., 1st Sess. 59-60 (1989) (statement of Jennifer Wilson, assistant administrator for external affairs, EPA).

2. *See* Sierra Club v. Marsh, 769 F.2d 868, 875 (1st Cir. 1985); *see also* Save the Yaak Comm. v. Block, 840 F.2d 714, 718 (9th Cir. 1988) (EA must evaluate action's environmental consequences).

3. River Road Alliance, Inc. v. Corps of Eng'rs, 764 F.2d 445, 449 (7th Cir. 1985), *cert. denied*, 475 U.S. 1055 (1986).

4. *See* Preservation Coalition, Inc. v. Pierce, 667 F.2d 851, 858 (9th Cir. 1982).

5. 42 U.S.C. § 4332 (1988).

6. Flint Ridge Dev. Co. v. Scenic Rivers Ass'n, 426 U.S. 776, 787–88 (1976); *see* Calvert Cliffs' Coordinating Comm. v. AEC, 449 F.2d 1109, 1114–15 (D.C. Cir. 1971) ("[c]onsiderations of administrative difficulty, delay or economic cost will not suffice to strip the section of its fundamental importance").

7. *See* Marsh v. Oregon Natural Resources Council, 109 S. Ct. 1851, 1861 (1989).

8. *Cf.* Board of Educ. v. City of West Chicago, 701 F. Supp. 662, 664 (N.D. Ill. 1988) (preparation of exhaustive EA satisfied duty to prepare EIS; EA had characteristics of an EIS).

9. Sierra Club v. Marsh, 769 F.2d 868, 875 (1st Cir. 1985); *see* section 5.2 (purpose of EIS).

10. 40 C.F.R. § 1508.9(a) (1989).

11. *Id.* § 1508.9(b).

12. *See* Conner v. Burford, 848 F.2d 1441, 1446 (9th Cir. 1988) (app. pending).

13. Citizen Advocates for Responsible Expansion, Inc. v. Dole, 770 F.2d 423, 434 (5th Cir. 1985).

14. Council on Environmental Quality, Forty Most Asked Questions Concerning CEQ's National Environmental Policy Act Regulations, 46 Fed. Reg. 18,026, 18,037 (1981).

15. *See, e.g.,* Park County Resource Council, Inc. v. United States Dep't of Agric., 817 F.2d 609, 612 (10th Cir. 1987) (over 100 pages); Sierra Club v. Marsh, 769 F.2d 868, 874 (1st Cir. 1985) (over 350 pages).

16. *See* Sierra Club v. Marsh, 769 F.2d 868, 875 (1st Cir. 1985); Florida Wildlife Fed'n v. Goldschmidt, 611 F.2d 547, 549 n.3 (5th Cir. 1980).

17. *See* Scherr v. Volpe, 466 F.2d 1027, 1033 (7th Cir. 1972); Sierra Club v. Coleman, 405 F. Supp. 53, 56 (D.D.C. 1975), *vacated on other grounds sub nom.* Sierra Club v. Adams, 578 F.2d 389 (D.C. Cir. 1978).

18. *See* City of New York v. United States Dep't of Transp., 715 F.2d 732, 751 (2d Cir. 1983), *cert. denied*, 465 U.S. 1055 (1984).

19. *See* Nucleus of Chicago Homeowners Ass'n v. Lynn, 524 F.2d 225, 232 (7th Cir. 1975), *cert. denied*, 424 U.S. 967 (1976); *see also* section 5.5 (methodology in EISs).

20. Friends of the Earth v. Hintz, 800 F.2d 822, 834–35 (9th Cir. 1986) (construing Corps of Engineers regulations regarding permitting); Save Our Wetlands, Inc.

v. Sands, 711 F.2d 634, 643 (5th Cir. 1983) (same). *Cf.* Brandon v. Pierce, 725 F.2d 555, 563–64 (10th Cir. 1984) (when project consultant is involved with the proposed action, the agency is responsible for the EA and must make the ultimate decision).

21. Save Our Wetlands, Inc. v. Sands, 711 F.2d 634, 642 (5th Cir. 1983).

22. *See* Van Abbema v. Fornell, 807 F.2d 633, 639 (7th Cir. 1986) (agency is responsible for independent verification of specifically challenged information); Steamboaters v. FERC, 759 F.2d 1382, 1394 (9th Cir. 1985) (agency cannot rely on another's analysis but must independently assess environmental consequences); Save Our Wetlands, Inc. v. Sands, 711 F.2d 634, 642 (5th Cir. 1983) (agency must independently verify reports); North Carolina v. Hudson, 665 F. Supp. 428, 442 (E.D.N.C. 1987) (agency did not independently verify information supplied by applicant); Sierra Club v. Alexander, 484 F. Supp. 455, 467 (N.D.N.Y. 1980) (agency independently considered information in EA); 40 C.F.R. § 1506.5(b) (1989) (agency must independently evaluate applicant's EA).

23. Life of the Land v. Brinegar, 485 F.2d 460, 467 (9th Cir. 1973), *cert. denied,* 416 U.S. 961 (1974); Stephens v. Adams, 469 F. Supp. 1222, 1227 (E.D. Wis. 1979); *see* section 5.6 (delegation of EISs).

24. 42 U.S.C. § 5304(g) (1988); *see* section 5.6 (statutory exception from EIS nondelegation requirement). *Cf.* Young v. Harris, 599 F.2d 870, 878–79 (8th Cir.) (city-applicant reasonably excluded activities in EA prepared for block grant), *cert. denied,* 444 U.S. 993 (1979).

25. Council on Environmental Quality, Guidance Regarding NEPA Regulations, 48 Fed. Reg. 34,263, 34,265–66 (1983).

26. *See* City of Davis v. Coleman, 521 F.2d 661, 676–77 (9th Cir. 1975); Colorado River Indian Tribes v. Marsh, 605 F. Supp. 1425, 1433 (C.D. Cal. 1985).

27. Council on Environmental Quality, Forty Most Asked Questions Concerning CEQ's National Environmental Policy Act Regulations, 46 Fed. Reg. 18,026, 18,030 (1981); *see also* 40 C.F.R. § 1501.7 (1989); section 5.8.1 (scoping for EIS preparation).

28. Trout Unlimited v. Morton, 509 F.2d 1276, 1283 & n.9 (9th Cir. 1974).

29. Sierra Club v. Marsh, 769 F.2d 868, 878 (1st Cir. 1985); *see* section 5.10.2 (indirect effects in EIS).

30. *See* Enos v. Marsh, 769 F.2d 1363, 1373 (9th Cir. 1985) (EIS).

31. *Id.*

32. Save the Yaak Comm. v. Block, 840 F.2d 714, 720 (9th Cir. 1988).

33. *Id.; see* Thomas v. Peterson, 753 F.2d 754, 759 (9th Cir. 1985); 40 C.F.R. § 1508.25(a)(1) (1989). *Cf.* Sylvester v. Corps of Eng'rs, 884 F.2d 394, 400 (9th Cir. 1989) (resort complex and golf course did not depend on each other); *see also* section 5.9.2 (connected actions in EIS).

34. 40 C.F.R. § 1508.25(a)(2) (1989).

35. *See* People *ex rel.* Van de Kamp v. Marsh, 687 F. Supp. 495, 500 (N.D. Cal. 1988); *see also* Neighbors Organized to Insure a Sound Environment v. Engen, 665 F. Supp. 537, 545 (M.D. Tenn. 1987), *vacated sub nom.* Neighbors Organized to Insure a Sound Env't, Inc. v. McArtor, 878 F.2d 174 (6th Cir. 1989).

36. 40 C.F.R. §§ 1508.7, 1508.27(b)(7) (1989).

37. *See* Sierra Club v. United States Forest Serv., 843 F.2d 1190, 1195 (9th Cir. 1988) (court declined to consider cumulative impacts analysis contained in draft EIS because EAs did not refer to analysis).

38. 42 U.S.C. § 4332(2)(E) (1988).

39. *See* City of New York v. United States Dep't of Transp., 715 F.2d 732, 742 & n.10 (2d Cir. 1983), *cert. denied,* 465 U.S. 1055 (1984); Richland Park Homeowners Ass'n, Inc. v. Pierce, 671 F.2d 935, 944 (5th Cir. 1982).

40. *See* Wicker Park Historic Dist. Preservation Fund v. Pierce, 565 F. Supp. 1066, 1079-81 (N.D. Ill. 1982).

41. Bob Marshall Alliance v. Hodel, 852 F.2d 1223, 1228-29 (9th Cir. 1988), *cert. denied,* 109 S. Ct. 1340 (1989); *see* Environmental Defense Fund, Inc. v. Corps of Eng'rs, 492 F.2d 1123, 1135 (5th Cir. 1974).

42. Olmsted Citizens for a Better Community v. United States, 793 F.2d 201, 208 (8th Cir. 1986).

43. River Road Alliance, Inc. v. Corps of Eng'rs, 764 F.2d 445, 452 (7th Cir. 1985), *cert. denied,* 475 U.S. 1055 (1986); *see* City of New York v. United States Dep't of Transp., 715 F.2d 732, 744 (2d Cir. 1983), *cert. denied,* 465 U.S. 1055 (1984).

44. *See River Road Alliance,* 764 F.2d at 452-53; *see also* Neighbors Organized to Insure a Sound Env't, Inc. v. McArtor, 878 F.2d 174, 178-79 (6th Cir. 1989) (plaintiffs did not demonstrate that agency had overlooked plausible alternatives).

45. *See* Bob Marshall Alliance v. Hodel, 852 F.2d 1223, 1229 (9th Cir. 1988), *cert. denied,* 109 S. Ct. 1340 (1989); *see* section 5.10.1 (alternatives in EIS).

46. Olmsted Citizens for a Better Community v. United States, 793 F.2d 201, 209 (8th Cir. 1986).

47. Van Abbema v. Fornell, 807 F.2d 633, 638 (7th Cir. 1986).

48. 40 C.F.R. 1508.9(a)(1) (1989).

49. *Id.* § 1508.13.

50. Council on Environmental Quality, Forty Most Asked Questions Concerning CEQ's National Environmental Policy Act Regulations, 46 Fed. Reg. 18,026, 18,037 (1981).

51. 40 C.F.R. § 1508.13 (1989).

52. *Id.* § 1501.4(e)(1); Council on Environmental Quality, Forty Most Asked Questions Concerning CEQ's National Environmental Policy Act Regulations, 46 Fed. Reg. 18,026, 18,037 (1981).

To facilitate public and agency involvement in the NEPA process, appendices to the CEQ regulations list federal and federal-state agencies with jurisdiction over, or special expertise in, environmental issues. Council on Environmental Quality, Appendices to Regulations, 49 Fed. Reg. 49,750 (1984). The appendices also list federal and federal-state agency NEPA contacts, and federal and federal-state agency offices for receiving and commenting on other agencies' environmental documents. *Id.*

53. Council on Environmental Quality, Forty Most Asked Questions Concerning CEQ's National Environmental Policy Act Regulations, 46 Fed. Reg. 18,026, 18,037 (1981).

54. *Id.*

55. *Id.*

56. 40 C.F.R. § 1501.4(e)(2) (1989); Council on Environmental Quality, Forty Most Asked Questions Concerning CEQ's National Environmental Policy Act Regulations, 46 Fed. Reg. 18,026, 18,037–38 (1981).

57. Council on Environmental Quality, Guidance Regarding NEPA Regulations, 48 Fed. Reg. 34,263, 34,266 (1983).

58. Save Our Ecosystems v. Clark, 747 F.2d 1240, 1244–47 (9th Cir. 1984) (EAs that supplemented a programmatic EIS were functional equivalents of EISs).

59. Oklahoma Wildlife Fed'n v. Corps of Eng'rs, 681 F. Supp. 1470, 1490 (N.D. Okla. 1988).

60. See Providence Road Community Ass'n v. EPA, 683 F.2d 80, 82 (4th Cir. 1982); see also section 5.8.7 (violations of the EIS process).

61. Compare Hanly v. Kleindienst, 471 F.2d 823, 836 (2d Cir. 1972) (requiring notice and comment procedures), cert. denied, 412 U.S. 908 (1973) with Richland Park Homeowners Ass'n v. Pierce, 671 F.2d 935, 943 (5th Cir. 1982) ("although NEPA and its implementing regulations do indeed encourage agencies to obtain public input regarding agency decisions, agencies are under no obligation to hold public hearings or give any particular form of public notice") and Como-Falcon Community Coalition, Inc. v. United States Dep't of Labor, 609 F.2d 342, 345 (8th Cir. 1979) (public hearings may be advisable but are not statutorily required), cert. denied, 446 U.S. 936 (1980) and National Ass'n of Government Employees v. Rumsfeld, 418 F. Supp. 1302, 1307 n.2 (E.D. Pa. 1976) (declining to require public participation in threshold determination conducted in secret; considered Second Circuit to have wrongly required participation). See also City of West Chicago v. NRC, 701 F.2d 632, 648 n.15 (7th Cir. 1983) (Seventh Circuit has not squarely confronted public participation issue).

62. Illinois Commerce Comm'n v. ICC, 848 F.2d 1246, 1260 (D.C. Cir. 1988), cert. denied, 109 S. Ct. 783 (1989); 40 C.F.R. § 1501.4(b) (1989); see also Progressive Animal Welfare Soc'y v. Department of Navy, 725 F. Supp. 475, 477–79 (W.D. Wash. 1989) (agency must consider environmental effects on dolphins taken and used in agency action).

63. See River Road Alliance, Inc. v. Corps of Eng'rs, 764 F.2d 445, 451 (7th Cir. 1985), cert. denied, 475 U.S. 1055 (1986).

64. Quinones Lopez v. Coco Lagoon Dev. Corp., 733 F.2d 1, 4 (1st Cir. 1984); see Rucker v. Willis, 484 F.2d 158, 162 (4th Cir. 1973) (planning board did not oppose action). See generally Blumm & Brown, Pluralism and the Environment: The Role of Comment Agencies in NEPA Litigation, 14 Harv. Envtl. L. Rev. no. 2 (1990).

65. See Mahelona v. Hawaiian Elec. Co., 418 F. Supp. 1328, 1333 (D. Hawaii 1976).

66. See Thomas v. Peterson, 753 F.2d 754, 759 (9th Cir. 1985); Sierra Club v. Corps of Eng'rs, 701 F.2d 1011, 1030 (2d Cir. 1983).

67. See Save the Bay, Inc. v. Corps of Eng'rs, 610 F.2d 322, 325 (5th Cir.), cert. denied, 449 U.S. 900 (1980).

68. Cf. City of Aurora v. Hunt, 749 F.2d 1457, 1465 (10th Cir. 1984) (agency adequately considered agency comments to its proposed action even though comments were not considered in FONSI).

69. See Hart & Miller Islands Area Envtl. Group, Inc. v. Corps of Eng'rs, 505 F. Supp. 732, 758 (D. Md. 1980); see also River Road Alliance v. Corps of Eng'rs, 764

F.2d 445, 452 (7th Cir. 1985) (agency preparing EA was entitled to disagree with opposition of commenting agency), *cert. denied,* 475 U.S. 1055 (1986); *see also* section 5.8.6 (agency commenting in EIS process).

70. Preservation Coalition, Inc. v. Pierce, 667 F.2d 851, 857 n.1 (9th Cir. 1982); *see also* Central Oklahoma Preservation Alliance, Inc. v. Oklahoma City Urban Renewal Auth., 471 F. Supp. 68, 84 (W.D. Okla. 1979) (not necessary to supplement EA to include designation to the National Register of historic buildings in the project area).

71. See Manasota-88, Inc. v. Thomas, 799 F.2d 687, 694 (11th Cir. 1986).

72. See Fritiofson v. Alexander, 772 F.2d 1225, 1238 n.7 (5th Cir. 1985); Kentucky *ex rel.* Beshear v. Alexander, 655 F.2d 714, 720 (6th Cir. 1981); Sierra Club v. Marsh, 769 F.2d 868, 870 (1st Cir. 1985); Greenwood Utilities Comm'n v. Hodel, 764 F.2d 1459, 1465 (11th Cir. 1985); International Detective Service, Inc. v. ICC, 595 F.2d 862, 865 (D.C. Cir. 1979); Plaza Bank v. Board of Governors of Federal Reserve System, 575 F.2d 1248, 1251 (8th Cir. 1978).

73. See City of Davis v. Coleman, 521 F.2d 661, 673 (9th Cir. 1975); Save Our Ten Acres v. Kreger, 472 F.2d 463, 467 (5th Cir. 1973).

74. See Fritiofson v. Alexander, 772 F.2d 1225, 1238 (5th Cir. 1985); Foundation on Economic Trends v. Heckler, 756 F.2d 143, 154 (D.C. Cir. 1985).

75. Fritiofson v. Alexander, 772 F.2d 1225, 1238 n.7 (5th Cir. 1985) ("test is whether there is a possibility not a certainty, of significant impacts"); Sierra Club v. Marsh, 769 F.2d 868, 870 (1st Cir. 1985) (plaintiffs must show "substantial possibility" that action could significantly affect quality of human environment); Steamboaters v. FERC, 759 F.2d 1382, 1392 (9th Cir. 1985) ("plaintiff need not show that significant effects *will in fact occur*" (emphasis original)).

76. See Kentucky *ex rel.* Beshear v. Alexander, 655 F.2d 714, 720 (6th Cir. 1981) (plaintiffs presented no evidence that action had a significant environmental effect); Greenwood Utilities Comm'n v. Hodel, 764 F.2d 1459, 1465 (11th Cir. 1985) (no evidence that action would significantly affect environment); International Detective Service, Inc. v. ICC, 595 F.2d 862, 865 n.5 (D.C. Cir. 1979) (same); Plaza Bank v. Board of Governors of Federal Reserve System, 575 F.2d 1248, 1251 (8th Cir. 1978) (same).

77. Town of Huntington v. Marsh, 884 F.2d 648, 653 (2d Cir. 1989) (requiring showing of irrepearable environmental injury for injunction), *cert. denied,* 110 S. Ct. 1296 (1990).

78. See Olmsted Citizens for a Better Community v. United States, 793 F.2d 201, 209 (8th Cir. 1986).

79. See Township of Lower Alloways Creek v. Public Serv. Elec. & Gas Co., 687 F.2d 732, 747 (3d Cir. 1982).

80. See Coalition on Sensible Transp., Inc. v. Dole, 826 F.2d 60, 68 (D.C. Cir. 1987).

81. Township of Lower Alloways Creek v. Public Serv. Elec. & Gas Co., 687 F.2d 732, 747 (3d Cir. 1982) (action was "near-quadrupling of nuclear waste storage at a reactor site").

82. Marsh v. Oregon Natural Resources Council, 109 S. Ct. 1851, 1861 (1989).

83. North Carolina v. Hudson, 665 F. Supp. 428, 443 (E.D.N.C. 1987); *see* Webb v. Gorsuch, 699 F.2d 157, 160 (4th Cir. 1983).

84. Park County Resource Council, Inc. v. United States Dep't of Agric., 817 F.2d 609, 620 (10th Cir. 1987); Jette v. Bergland, 579 F.2d 59, 62 (10th Cir. 1978).

85. See Missouri Coalition for the Environment v. Corps of Eng'rs, 866 F.2d 1025, 1033 (8th Cir.), cert. denied, 110 S. Ct. 76 (1989).

86. Fritiofson v. Alexander, 772 F.2d 1225, 1238 (5th Cir. 1985); see also Natural Resources Defense Council, Inc. v. Hodel, 618 F. Supp. 848, 873 (E.D. Cal. 1985) (agency did not take hard look at action's environmental effects by stating that its lenient review process could lead to abuses resulting in serious environmental consequences but abuses were "highly unlikely").

87. Mid-Tex Elec. Co-op, Inc. v. FERC, 773 F.2d 327, 339 (D.C. Cir. 1985); Maryland-Nat'l Capital Park & Planning Comm'n v. United States Postal Serv., 487 F.2d 1029, 1040 (D.C. Cir. 1973); see also Nader v. Butterfield, 373 F. Supp. 1175, 1180 (D.D.C. 1974) (requiring agency to present "more thorough analysis and rationale" why X-ray detection system for baggage would not significantly affect environment).

88. Town of Orangetown v. Gorsuch, 718 F.2d 29, 35 (2d Cir. 1983), cert. denied, 465 U.S. 1099 (1984); American Pub. Transit Ass'n v. Goldschmidt, 485 F. Supp. 811, 835 (D.D.C. 1980); McDowell v. Schlesinger, 404 F. Supp. 221, 250 (W.D. Mo. 1975); see also Foundation on Economic Trends v. Lyng, 680 F. Supp. 10, 16 (D.D.C. 1988) (deferring to agency's discussion of action's effects when technology was new).

89. See National Pork Producers Council v. Bergland, 631 F.2d 1353, 1363 (8th Cir. 1980), cert. denied, 450 U.S. 912 (1981).

90. See Sierra Club v. Corps of Eng'rs, 701 F.2d 1011, 1030 (2d Cir. 1983) (adequacy of EIS).

91. Id.

92. See Missouri Coalition for the Env't v. Corps of Eng'rs, 866 F.2d 1025, 1032 (8th Cir.), cert. denied, 110 S. Ct. 76 (1989); see also People ex rel. Van de Kamp v. Marsh, 687 F. Supp. 495, 499 (N.D. Cal. 1988) (agency's information on environmental effects of action was inadequate).

93. See Citizen Advocates for Responsible Expansion, Inc. v. Dole, 770 F.2d 423, 435 (5th Cir. 1985); Foundation on Economic Trends v. Heckler, 756 F.2d 143, 153 (D.C. Cir. 1985); Sierra Club v. Mason, 351 F. Supp. 419, 426 (D. Conn. 1972); see also Natural Resources Defense Council, Inc. v. Herrington, 768 F.2d 1355, 1432 (D.C. Cir. 1985) (agency's assumption that equal increases and decreases in energy consumption had equal impact was a bald assertion without basis); City of Davis v. Coleman, 521 F.2d 661, 674 (9th Cir. 1975) (describing agency's negative declaration as "nothing more than bureaucratic doubletalk").

94. See Citizen Advocates for Responsible Expansion, Inc. v. Dole, 770 F.2d 423, 434 (5th Cir. 1985). But see Save Our Wetlands, Inc. v. Witherspoon, 638 F. Supp. 1158, 1164–66 (E.D. La. 1986) (EA was inadequate but agency supplemented administrative records with evidence at trial).

The holding in Save Our Wetlands, Inc. v. Witherspoon was contrary to Fifth Circuit precendent. In Citizen Advocates for Responsible Expansion, Inc. v. Dole,

770 F.2d 423 (5th Cir. 1985), the Fifth Circuit stated that supplementation of an agency's record at trial creates an incentive to an agency to prepare an inadequate administrative record initially so as to benefit from the lack of obstacles that may arise if informed public participation were allowed. *Id.* at 437 n.18.

95. Greenpeace U.S.A. v. Evans, 688 F. Supp. 579, 584–85 (W.D. Wash. 1987) (categorical exclusion).

96. Coalition on Sensible Transp., Inc. v. Dole, 826 F.2d 60, 72 (D.C. Cir. 1987).

97. *Id.*

98. An agency's determination of whether an action may have significant environmental effects is a fact issue. *See* Fritiofson v. Alexander, 772 F.2d 1225, 1248 (5th Cir. 1985).

99. *See* Hanly v. Kleindienst, 471 F.2d 823, 829 (2d Cir. 1972), *cert. denied*, 412 U.S. 908 (1973); First Nat'l Bank of Chicago v. Richardson, 484 F.2d 1369, 1373 (7th Cir. 1973); Maryland-Nat'l Capital Park & Planning Comm'n v. U.S. Postal Serv., 487 F.2d 1029, 1035 (D.C. Cir. 1973).

100. *See* Save Our Ten Acres v. Kreger, 472 F.2d 463, 465 (5th Cir. 1973); Minnesota Public Interest Research Group v. Butz, 498 F.2d 1314, 1320 (8th Cir. 1974); Wyoming Outdoor Coordinating Council v. Butz, 484 F.2d 1244, 1249 (10th Cir. 1973).

101. Marsh v. Oregon Natural Resources Council, 109 S. Ct. 1851, 1860 (1989); *see* 5 U.S.C. § 706(2)(A) (1988).

102. Marsh v. Oregon Natural Resources Council, 109 S. Ct. 1851, 1861 n.23 (1989) (citing Manasota-88, Inc. v. Thomas, 799 F.2d 687, 692 n.8 (11th Cir. 1986); River Road Alliance, Inc. v. Corps of Eng'rs, 764 F.2d 445, 449 (7th Cir. 1985), *cert. denied*, 475 U.S. 1055 (1986)).

103. Citizens to Preserve Overton Park, Inc. v. Volpe, 401 U.S. 402, 416 (1971); *see* Ryder Truck Lines, Inc. v. United States, 716 F.2d 1369, 1370 (11th Cir. 1983) (agency "is accorded a large amount of discretion in determining either the necessity for preparing the [EIS] or the scope of the inquiry it will perform"), *cert. denied*, 466 U.S. 927 (1984).

104. *Marsh,* 109 S. Ct. at 1861 (quoting Citizens to Preserve Overton Park, Inc. v. Volpe, 401 U.S. 402, 416 (1971).

105. Citizens to Preserve Overton Park, Inc. v. Volpe, 401 U.S. 402, 416 (1971).

106. Natural Resources Defense Council, Inc. v. Herrington, 768 F.2d 1355, 1430 (D.C. Cir. 1985).

107. *See* Sierra Club v. Marsh, 769 F.2d 868, 872 (1st Cir. 1985).

108. *See* Oklahoma Wildlife Fed'n v. Corps of Eng'rs, 681 F. Supp. 1470, 1489 (N.D. Okla. 1988) (citing cases approving use of mitigated FONSIs).

109. Cabinet Mountains Wilderness/Scotchman's Peak Grizzly Bears v. Peterson, 685 F.2d 678, 683 (D.C. Cir. 1982); *see also* Mardis v. Big Nance Creek Water Mgmt. Dist., 578 F. Supp. 770, 787 (N.D. Ala. 1983) (interagency team aided agency in designing mitigation measures), *aff'd*, 749 F.2d 732 (11th Cir. 1984). *Cf.* Jones v. Gordon, 792 F.2d 821, 829 (9th Cir. 1986) (conditions in permit did not mitigate environmental effects of proposed action but, rather, deferred important agency decisions until after more information was obtained).

110. *Cabinet Mountains,* 685 F.2d at 684; Louisiana v. Lee, 758 F.2d 1081, 1083 (5th Cir. 1985), *cert. denied*, 475 U.S. 1044 (1986); 40 C.F.R. § 1505.3(a)-(b) (1989).

111. Louisiana v. Lee, 758 F.2d at 1083; Preservation Coalition, Inc. v. Pierce, 667 F.2d 851, 861 (9th Cir. 1982); *see also* Van Abbema v. Fornell, 807 F.2d 633, 637 (7th Cir. 1986) (agency attached 23 special conditions to permit).

112. C.A.R.E. NOW, Inc. v. FAA, 844 F.2d 1569, 1575 (11th Cir. 1988).

113. Town of Orangetown v. Gorsuch, 718 F.2d 29, 37 (2d Cir. 1983), *cert. denied*, 465 U.S. 1099 (1984); Bosco v. Beck, 475 F. Supp. 1029, 1037 (D.N.J.), *aff'd*, 614 F.2d 769 (3d Cir. 1979), *cert. denied*, 449 U.S. 822 (1980).

114. City & County of San Francisco v. United States, 615 F.2d 498, 501 (9th Cir. 1980).

115. Preservation Coalition, Inc. v. Pierce, 667 F.2d 851, 860 (9th Cir. 1982); *see also* Sierra Club v. Peterson, 717 F.2d 1409, 1414 (D.C. Cir. 1983) (even if agency would have authority to mitigate, it could not prevent potentially significant environmental facts from occurring); Sierra Club v. Marsh, 769 F.2d 868, 877 (1st Cir. 1985) (noting critically that agency only promised to mitigate impacts).

116. Friends of Endangered Species, Inc. v. Jantzen, 760 F.2d 976, 987 (9th Cir. 1985). *But see Cabinet Mountains*, 685 F.2d at 682 (mitigation measures should "completely compensate for any possible adverse environmental impacts").

117. 40 C.F.R. § 1508.20 (1989).

118. *See* Friends of the Earth v. Hintz, 800 F.2d 822, 837–38 (9th Cir. 1986) (off-site mitigation is proper under appropriate circumstances); *see also* Friends of Endangered Species, Inc. v. Jantzen, 760 F.2d 976, 980 (9th Cir. 1985) (in exchange for permission to develop, developers agreed to dedicate open space and to preserve area as undisturbed habitat of endangered species).

119. Council on Environmental Quality, Forty Most Asked Questions Concerning CEQ's National Environmental Policy Act Regulations, 46 Fed. Reg. 18,026, 18,038 (1981).

120. *Id.*

121. *See* Friends of the Earth v. Hintz, 800 F.2d 822, 837 n.15 (9th Cir. 1986); Louisiana v. Lee, 758 F.2d 1081, 1083 (5th Cir. 1985), *cert. denied*, 475 U.S. 1044 (1986); Cabinet Mountains Wilderness/Scotchman's Peak Grizzly Bears v. Peterson, 685 F.2d 678, 682 (D.C. Cir. 1982). *But see* Sierra Club v. Marsh, 769 F.2d 868, 877, 880 (1st Cir. 1985) (following CEQ Forty Questions).

122. *See* Conner v. Burford, 848 F.2d 1441, 1450 (9th Cir. 1988) (doubting whether effects of oil exploration, development, and production in national forest could be mitigated) (app. pending).

123. *Id.* (when agency would not have power to absolutely control mitigation of environmental effects of oil and gas exploration, development, and production in national forest, agency could not rely on mitigation to reduce environmental effects below significance level).

124. Jones v. Gordon, 621 F. Supp. 7, 12–13 (D. Alaska 1985), *aff'd in part and rev'd in nonpertinent part*, 792 F.2d 821 (9th Cir. 1986).

125. *See* Northwest Indian Cemetery Protective Ass'n v. Peterson, 795 F.2d 688, 697 (9th Cir. 1986), *rev'd on other grounds sub nom.* Lyng v. Northwest Indian Cemetery Protective Ass'n, 485 U.S. 439 (1988).

126. Steamboaters v. FERC, 759 F.2d 1382, 1394 (9th Cir. 1985).

127. LaFlamme v. FERC, 852 F.2d 389, 399–400 (9th Cir. 1988); Foundation for N. Am. Wild Sheep v. United States Dep't of Agric., 681 F.2d 1172, 1180–81 (9th Cir. 1982); Joseph v. Adams, 467 F. Supp. 141, 156 (E.D. Mich. 1978).

128. *See* LaFlamme v. FERC, 852 F.2d 389, 400 (9th Cir. 1988); *see* 5.10.3 (mitigation in EISs).

129. *See* Hanly v. Kleindienst, 471 F.2d 823, 830 (2d Cir. 1972), *cert. denied*, 412 U.S. 908 (1973); Council on Environmental Quality, *Environmental Quality 1972: Third Annual Report* 231.

130. *See, e.g.*, Gifford-Hill & Co. v. FTC, 389 F. Supp. 167, 174 (D.D.C. 1974) (interpreting "significantly affecting" as "having a reasonably substantial relationship to the quality of the environment"), *aff'd*, 523 F.2d 730 (D.C. Cir. 1975); Natural Resources Defense Council, Inc. v. Grant, 341 F. Supp. 356, 367 (E.D.N.C. 1972) ("[a]ny action that substantially affects, beneficially or detrimentally, the depth or course of streams, plant life, wildlife habitats, fish and wildlife, and the soil and air" as well as actions that have "an important or meaningful effect, direct or indirect, upon a broad range of aspects of the human environment").

131. *See* River Road Alliance, Inc. v. Corps of Eng'rs, 764 F.2d 445, 450 (7th Cir. 1985), *cert. denied*, 475 U.S. 1055 (1986); Vieux Carre Property Owners, Residents & Assocs., Inc. v. Pierce, 719 F.2d 1272, 1279 (5th Cir. 1983).

132. *See, e.g.*, Louisiana Wildlife Fed'n, Inc. v. York, 761 F.2d 1044, 1053 (5th Cir. 1985) ("we have no doubt that the potential effect of the [action] is 'significant'"); City of West Chicago v. NRC, 701 F.2d 632, 650 (7th Cir. 1983) (agreeing with parties that EIS was required because action "clearly will have a significant impact on the environment"); City of Davis v. Coleman, 521 F.2d 661, 674–75 (9th Cir. 1975) (regardless of weight accorded plaintiff's evidence, "it is obvious that constructing [a highway in an undeveloped area] will have a substantial impact on a number of environmental factors"); Wyoming Outdoor Coordinating Council v. Butz, 484 F.2d 1244, 1250 (10th Cir. 1973) ("[w]e are convinced that a major federal action significantly affecting the human environment is involved"). *Cf.* Natural Resources Defense Council, Inc. v. Vaughn, 566 F. Supp. 1472, 1475 (D.D.C. 1983) (noting that start-ups of nuclear reactors generally require EISs).

133. 40 C.F.R. § 1508.27 (1989); *see* Note, *The CEQ Regulations: New Stage in the Evolution of NEPA*, 3 Harv. Envtl. L. Rev. 347, 362 (1979).

134. 40 C.F.R. § 1508.27 (1989).

135. *Id.* § 1508.27(a).

136. *Id.* § 1508.27(b).

137. *See, e.g.*, National Oceanic and Atmospheric Administration, Revised NOAA Directive Implementing the National Environmental Policy Act, 49 Fed. Reg. 29,644, 29,656 (1984) (consideration in fishery management plans of long-term productive capability of species and potential substantial damage to ocean and coastal habitats); Department of Interior, National Environmental Policy Act, Revised Implementing Procedures, 49 Fed. Reg. 21,437, 21,439 (1984) (consideration of wilderness areas, sole or principal drinking water aquifers, and ecologically significant areas).

138. *See* Foundation on Economic Trends v. Weinberger, 610 F. Supp. 829, 841–42 (D.D.C. 1985).

139. *See* Puna Speaks v. Hodel, 562 F. Supp. 82, 85 (D. Hawaii 1983).

140. *See* Mont Vernon Preservation Soc'y v. Clements, 415 F. Supp. 141, 147 (D.N.H. 1976).

141. 40 C.F.R. § 1508.27(a) (1989); *see* Goose Hollow Foothills League v. Romney, 334 F. Supp. 877, 879-80 (D. Or. 1971) (change in character of community neighborhood).

142. *See* Sierra Club v. Marsh, 769 F.2d 868, 881 (1st Cir. 1985).

143. *Id.*

144. *Compare* Township of Springfield v. Lewis, 702 F.2d 426, 449 n.48 (3d Cir. 1983) (considering effects of action on one area) *with* City of Santa Clara v. Andrus, 572 F.2d 660, 680 (9th Cir.) ("we think it highly improbable that [one action] will have a more deleterious impact than any other when the total geographic area . . . is considered"), *cert. denied*, 439 U.S. 859 (1978).

145. *See* Louisiana *ex rel.* Guste v. Lee, 635 F. Supp. 1107, 1121 (E.D. La. 1986).

146. *See* River Road Alliance, Inc. v. Corps of Eng'rs, 764 F.2d 445, 451 (7th Cir. 1985) (action's effects on scenic qualities of river were temporary), *cert. denied*, 475 U.S. 1055 (1986).

147. Hiram Clarke Civic Club, Inc. v. Lynn, 476 F.2d 421, 426–27 (5th Cir. 1973); 40 C.F.R. § 1508.27(b)(1) (1989).

148. Sierra Club v. Marsh, 769 F.2d 868, 880 (1st Cir. 1985).

149. Environmental Defense Fund v. Marsh, 651 F.2d 983, 993 (5th Cir. 1981). *Cf.* Township of Springfield v. Lewis, 702 F.2d 426, 437–38 & n.19 (3d Cir. 1983) (distinguishing *Marsh* for improvements to mitigation techniques).

150. 40 C.F.R. § 1508.27(b)(2) (1989).

151. 115 Cong. Rec. 19,009 (1969) (statement of Sen. Jackson) ("What is involved is a congressional declaration that we do not intend, as a government or as a people, to initiate actions which endanger the continued existence or the health of mankind. . . . An environmental policy is a policy for people. Its primary concern is with man and his future").

152. Citizens Against Toxic Sprays, Inc. v. Bergland, 428 F. Supp. 908, 927 (D. Or. 1977).

153. Metropolitan Edison Co. v. People Against Nuclear Energy, 460 U.S. 766, 774–75 (1983).

154. *Id.* at 776–77.

155. 40 C.F.R. § 1508.27(b)(3) (1989). *Cf.* Louisiana *ex rel.* Guste v. Lee, 635 F. Supp. 1107, 1121–22 (E.D. La. 1986) (when natural resource is prevalent over large area outside area of proposed action impacts on resources in affected area may not be significant); Smith v. Soil Conservation Serv., 563 F. Supp. 843, 846 (W.D. Okla. 1982) (upholding agency's determination that action did not significantly affect environment when action eliminated small area by flooding but area's overall natural habitat for wildlife was not irreparably harmed).

156. 40 C.F.R. § 1508.27(b)(3) (1989); *see* Citizen Advocates for Responsible Expansion, Inc. v. Dole, 770 F.2d 423, 435–36 (5th Cir. 1985) (agency must consider proposed action's effect on popular city park and historic properties).

157. *See* Town of Orangetown v. Gorsuch, 718 F.2d 29, 36–37 (2d Cir. 1983) (effect on wetlands of expansion of sewage treatment system was not significant), *cert. denied*, 465 U.S. 1099 (1984).

158. *See* Falls Road Impact Comm., Inc. v. Dole, 581 F. Supp. 678, 696 (E.D. Wis.), *aff'd*, 737 F.2d 1476 (7th Cir. 1984).

159. 40 C.F.R. § 1508.27(b)(4) (1989).

160. Hanly v. Kleindienst, 471 F.2d 823, 830 (2d Cir. 1972), *cert. denied*, 412 U.S. 908 (1973); Rucker v. Willis, 484 F.2d 158, 162 (4th Cir. 1973); *see also* National Oceanic and Atmospheric Administration, Revised NOAA Directive Implementing the National Environmental Policy Act, 49 Fed. Reg. 29,644, 29,647 (1984) (controversial does not refer to propriety of proposed action).

161. *See* North Dakota v. Andrus, 483 F. Supp. 255, 260–61 (D.N.D. 1980); Bosco v. Beck, 475 F. Supp. 1029, 1038 (D.N.J.), *aff'd*, 614 F.2d 769 (3d Cir. 1979), *cert. denied*, 449 U.S. 822 (1980).

162. *See* Town of Orangetown v. Gorsuch, 718 F.2d 29, 39 (2d Cir. 1983), *cert. denied*, 465 U.S. 1099 (1984).

163. *See* Sierra Club v. United States Forest Serv., 843 F.2d 1190, 1193 (9th Cir. 1988); Foundation for N. Am. Wild Sheep v. United States Dep't of Agric., 681 F.2d 1172, 1182 (9th Cir. 1982). *But see* Bosco v. Beck, 475 F. Supp. 1029, 1038 (D.N.J.) (parties agreed about probable nature of proposed action; dispute regarded whether environmental effects were significant; court determined that EIS was not required under EPA regulation implementing NEPA), *aff'd*, 614 F.2d 769 (3d Cir. 1979), *cert. denied*, 449 U.S. 822 (1980).

164. *See* Friends of Endangered Species, Inc. v. Jantzen, 760 F.2d 976, 986 (9th Cir. 1985); *see also* Maryland-Nat'l Capital Park & Planning Comm'n v. Martin, 447 F. Supp. 350, 353 (D.D.C. 1978) (neighborhood opposition to local effects of action did not make action "highly controversial").

165. *See* Mahelona v. Hawaiian Elec. Co., 418 F. Supp. 1328, 1333 (D. Hawaii 1976).

166. *See* LaFlamme v. FERC, 852 F.2d 389, 401 (9th Cir. 1988).

167. *See* Jones v. Gordon, 621 F. Supp. 7, 12 (D. Alaska 1985), *aff'd in part and rev'd in nonpertinent part*, 792 F.2d 821 (9th Cir. 1986).

168. 40 C.F.R. § 1508.27(b)(5) (1989).

169. *See* Foundation on Economic Trends v. Heckler, 756 F.2d 143, 155 (D.C. Cir. 1985); *see also* Foundation on Economic Trends v. Bowen, 722 F. Supp. 787, 792 (D.D.C. 1989) (agency should consider the possible environmental effects of experiment as well as the expected environmental effects).

170. *See* Sierra Club v. United States Forest Serv., 843 F.2d 1190, 1194 (9th Cir. 1988) (effect of modified clear-cutting on giant sequoia regeneration involved highly uncertain, unique, or unknown risks); Conner v. Burford, 848 F.2d 1441, 1450–51 (9th Cir. 1988) (rejecting argument that because of uncertain and speculative nature of oil exploration, agency should approve action after precise extent of effects were known, that is, after agency was irrevocably committed to action) (app. pending).

171. City of Aurora v. Hunt, 749 F.2d 1457, 1468 n.8 (10th Cir. 1984).

172. City of New York v. United States Dep't of Transp., 715 F.2d 732, 746 (2d Cir. 1983), *appeal dismissed and cert. denied*, 465 U.S. 1055 (1984).

173. *Id.* at 752.

174. *Id.* at 746 n.14, 752.

175. *Id.* at 751.

176. *Id.*

177. Potomac Alliance v. NRC, 682 F.2d 1030, 1037 (D.C. Cir. 1982); *see also* Carolina Envtl. Study Group v. United States, 510 F.2d 796, 799 (D.C. Cir. 1975) (probabilities as well as consequences should be considered).

178. *Potomac Alliance,* 682 F.2d at 1037.

179. *Id.* at 1037 n.36.

180. American Public Transit Ass'n v. Goldschmidt, 485 F. Supp. 811, 833 (D.D.C. 1980).

181. Foundation on Economic Trends v. Heckler, 756 F.2d 143, 155 (D.C. Cir. 1985).

182. *See* Foundation for N. Am. Wild Sheep v. United States Dep't of Agric., 681 F.2d 1172, 1178–82 (9th Cir. 1982).

183. *See* No Gwen Alliance of Lane County, Inc. v. Aldridge, 855 F.2d 1380, 1386 (9th Cir. 1988); *see also* National Citizens Comm. for Broadcasting v. FCC, 567 F.2d 1095, 1098 n.3 (D.C. Cir. 1977) (agency was not required to prepare EIS when possibilities of occurrence were remote and speculative), *cert. denied,* 436 U.S. 926 (1978).

184. Jones v. Gordon, 792 F.2d 821, 829 (9th Cir. 1986); *see also* Save the Niobrara River Ass'n, Inc. v. Andrus, 483 F. Supp. 844, 860–61 (D. Neb. 1979) (requiring inclusion in EIS of inventory of wildlife and wildlife habitat in area affected by proposed dam).

185. *See* Foundation for N. Am. Wild Sheep v. United States Dep't of Agric., 681 F.2d 1172, 1181 (9th Cir. 1982) (basing future of decisions on results of monitoring program "represents an agency decision to act now and deal with the environmental consequences later"); Natural Resources Defense Council, Inc. v. Callaway, 524 F.2d 79, 90 (2d Cir. 1975) (agency's argument that it would suspend action if monitoring program uncovered adverse impacts offered "too little . . . too late"); Sierra Club v. Bergland, 451 F. Supp. 120, 131 (N.D. Miss. 1978) (basing continuation of action on results of monitoring program "is a virtual confession [that the project] was being projected without the responsible federal officials knowing the pluses and minuses of the pertinent environmental factors"). *But see* Citizens Against 2,4–D v. Watt, 527 F. Supp. 465, 469 (W.D. Okla. 1981) (effects of spraying reservoir with 2,4–D were not significant; by monitoring concentration levels near intake structures, agency could shut down intake structures if tolerance level for drinking water was exceeded). *Cf.* City of Des Plaines v. Metropolitan Sanitary Dist., 552 F.2d 736, 739 (7th Cir. 1977) (monitoring plan did not vitiate adequacy of EIS when scientific knowledge at time EIS was prepared did not permit fuller assessment of proposed action's environmental effects); 40 C.F.R. §§ 1505.2(c), 1505.3 (1989) (monitoring plans to ensure enforcement of mitigation measures).

186. 40 C.F.R. § 1508.27(b)(6) (1989).

187. *See* Sierra Club v. Marsh, 769 F.2d 868, 879 (1st Cir. 1985).

188. *See id.;* Massachusetts v. Watt, 716 F.2d 946, 952–53 (1st Cir. 1983).

189. 40 C.F.R. §§ 1508.7, 1508.25(c), 1508.27(b)(7) (1989).

190. *Id.* § 1508.25(a)(2).

191. *E.g.,* Crounse Corp. v. ICC, 781 F.2d 1176, 1194–95 (6th Cir.) (applying cumulative actions analysis to EA), *cert. denied,* 479 U.S. 890 (1986); River Road Alliance, Inc. v. Corps of Eng'rs, 764 F.2d 445, 452 (7th Cir. 1985) (stating that agency would have to consider proposed actions in considering cumulative effects), *cert. denied,* 475 U.S. 1055 (1986).

192. *See* Ringsred v. City of Duluth, 828 F.2d 1305, 1309 (8th Cir. 1987) ("[a] requirement that every [EA] must speculate as to the environmental effects of privately proposed developments that are outside the control of the federal government would create burdens in the [EA] 'screening process' that are equally significant to those placed on an agency required to file an EIS"). *But see* Fritiofson v. Alexander, 772 F.2d 1225, 1246 (5th Cir. 1985) ("actions should be considered in the threshold cumulative-impacts analysis without regard to whether they have themselves required a permit or will in the future be the subject of NEPA review").

193. 40 C.F.R. § 1508.25(a)(2) (1989); *see* Kleppe v. Sierra Club, 427 U.S. 390, 409-10 (1976).

194. Kleppe v. Sierra Club, 427 U.S. 390, 409-10 (1976).

195. 40 C.F.R. § 1508.27(b)(7) (1989); *see id.* § 1508.7.

196. Fritiofson v. Alexander, 772 F.2d 1225, 1246 (5th Cir. 1985).

197. 40 C.F.R. § 1508.7 (1989).

198. *See* Sierra Club v. United States Forest Serv., 843 F.2d 1190, 1195 (9th Cir. 1988) (agency must consider cumulative impacts on watersheds); Natural Resources Defense Council, Inc. v. Callaway, 524 F.2d 79, 89 (2d Cir. 1975) (cumulative impacts on area of ocean).

199. *See* Greenpeace, U.S.A. v. Evans, 688 F. Supp. 579, 586 (W.D. Wash. 1987) (agency must consider cumulative impacts on whale population in Puget Sound).

200. *See Fritiofson,* 772 F.2d at 1246–47; National Wildlife Fed'n v. United States Forest Serv., 592 F. Supp. 931, 942 (D. Or. 1984), *vacated in part and appeal dismissed,* 801 F.2d 360 (9th Cir. 1986).

201. LaFlamme v. FERC, 852 F.2d 389, 401 (9th Cir. 1988).

202. *Fritiofson,* 772 F.2d at 1245.

203. *See* Louisiana *ex rel.* Guste v. Lee, 635 F. Supp. 1107, 1122 n.34 (E.D. La. 1986) (loss of benthic organisms caused by shell dredging affected organisms such as shrimp, crab, and bottom-feeding fish which fed on the benthos).

204. *See National Wildlife Fed'n,* 592 F. Supp. at 942; *see also* Save the Yaak Comm. v. Block, 840 F.2d 714, 721 (9th Cir. 1988) (requiring agency to consider cumulative effects of road construction and timber harvesting); Natural Resources Defense Council, Inc. v. Callaway, 524 F.2d 79, 87 (2d Cir. 1975) (requiring agency to consider cumulative effects of ocean dumping).

205. *See* Sierra Club v. United States Forest Serv., 843 F.2d 1190, 1194–95 (9th Cir. 1988) (cumulative effects on watershed); Northwestern Indian Cemetery Protective Ass'n v. Peterson, 795 F.2d 688, 696 (9th Cir. 1986) (cumulative effects on water quality in national forest), *rev'd on other grounds sub nom.* Lyng v. Northwest Indian Cemetery Protective Ass'n, 485 U.S. 439 (1988).

206. *See* North Carolina v. Hudson, 665 F. Supp. 428, 439-40 (E.D.N.C. 1987).

207. C.A.R.E. NOW, Inc. v. FAA, 844 F.2d 1569, 1575 (11th Cir. 1988).

208. Neighbors Organized to Insure a Sound Env't, Inc. v. Engen, 665 F. Supp. 537, 545 (M.D. Tenn. 1987), *vacated sub nom.* Neighbors Organized to Insure a Sound Env't, Inc. v. McArtor, 878 F.2d 174 (6th Cir. 1989).

209. Fritiofson v. Alexander, 772 F.2d 1225, 1245 n.15, 1246 (5th Cir. 1985).

210. *See* Coalition on Sensible Transp., Inc. v. Dole, 826 F.2d 60, 70–71 (D.C. Cir. 1987); *see also* National Wildlife Fed'n v. Benn, 491 F. Supp. 1234, 1251–52 (S.D.N.Y. 1980) (when EAs rather than site-specific EISs were sometimes prepared for individual agency actions, court required preparation of comprehensive EIS).

211. *National Wildlife Fed'n*, 592 F. Supp. at 942.

212. Fritiofson v. Alexander, 772 F.2d 1225, 1249 (5th Cir. 1985).

213. 40 C.F.R. § 1508.27(b)(8) (1989).

214. *See* Patterson v. Exon, 415 F. Supp. 1276, 1281–82 (D. Neb. 1976).

215. 42 U.S.C. §§ 4331(b)(2), 4331(b)(4) (1988).

216. *See* Preservation Coalition, Inc. v. Pierce, 667 F.2d 851, 859–60 (9th Cir. 1982); WATCH (Waterbury Action to Conserve Our Heritage, Inc.) v. Harris, 603 F.2d 310, 318, 326 (2d Cir.) (approving district court's determination that if historic property eligible for National Register would be affected by agency action, EIS was required), *cert. denied*, 444 U.S. 995 (1979); *see also* Citizen Advocates for Responsible Expansion, Inc. v. Dole, 770 F.2d 423, 436, 439 n.20 (5th Cir. 1985) (agency must consider effects of action on historic buildings); Boston Waterfront Residents Ass'n, Inc. v. Romney, 343 F. Supp. 89, 91 (D. Mass. 1972) (enjoining demolition of historic building pending consideration of alternatives). *But see* Committee to Save the Fox Bldg. v. Birmingham Branch of Federal Reserve Bank, 497 F. Supp. 504, 511 (N.D. Ala. 1980) (agency need not consider effects of demolition of historic building because architectural and historic effects are social).

217. Preservation Coalition, Inc. v. Pierce, 667 F.2d 851, 860 (9th Cir. 1982).

218. Goodman Group, Inc. v. Dishroom, 679 F.2d 182, 185–86 (9th Cir. 1982); *see* section 3.6.2 (discussing the human environment).

219. 40 C.F.R. § 1508.27(b)(9) (1989); *see also* 16 U.S.C. § 1536(c)(1) (1988).

220. *See* Friends of Endangered Species, Inc. v. Jantzen, 596 F. Supp. 518, 525 (N.D. Cal. 1984), *aff'd*, 760 F.2d 976 (9th Cir. 1985); Falls Road Impact Comm., Inc. v. Dole, 581 F. Supp. 678, 696 (E.D. Wis.) *aff'd*, 737 F.2d 1476 (7th Cir. 1984).

221. Cabinet Mountains Wilderness/Scotchman's Peak Grizzly Bears v. Peterson, 685 F.2d 678, 684 (D.C. Cir. 1982); *Friends of Endangered Species*, 596 F. Supp. at 524.

222. *See* Sierra Club v. Hodel, 848 F.2d 1068, 1094 (10th Cir. 1988).

223. 40 C.F.R. § 1508.27(b)(10) (1989); James v. TVA, 538 F. Supp. 704, 708 (E.D. Tenn. 1982) (proposed action would comply with federal, state, and local pollution control standards and requirements).

224. *See* Sierra Club v. United States Forest Serv., 843 F.2d 1190, 1195 (9th Cir. 1988) (agency must consider effects of action on state water quality standards).

225. *See* Public Citizen v. National Highway Traffic Safety Admin., 848 F.2d 256, 268 (D.C. Cir. 1988) (upholding agency determination of insignificance but criticizing failure to consider increases of air emissions within legal limits).

226. *See* Goodman Group, Inc. v. Dishroom, 679 F.2d 182, 186 (9th Cir. 1982) (agency complied with National Historic Preservation Act); Preservation Coalition, Inc. v. Pierce, 667 F.2d 851, 859–60 (9th Cir. 1982) (considering agency's compliance with National Historic Preservation Act and NEPA); Conservation Law Found'n of New England, Inc. v. Clark, 590 F. Supp. 1467, 1476–77 (D. Mass. 1984) (compliance with Cape Cod National Seashore Act added weight to agency's decision not to prepare EIS).

227. Maryland-Nat'l Capital Park & Planning Comm'n v. United States Postal Serv., 487 F.2d 1029, 1036–37 (D.C. Cir. 1973); *see also* Sierra Club v. Cavanaugh, 447 F. Supp. 427, 432 (D.S.D. 1978) (zoning regulations required proposed agency action to comply with local standards).

228. *Maryland-Nat'l*, 487 F.2d at 1036–37; Goodman Group, Inc. v. Dishroom, 679 F.2d 182, 186 (9th Cir. 1982); *see also* United Neighbors Civic Ass'n of Jamaica, Inc. v. Pierce, 563 F. Supp. 200, 206 (E.D.N.Y. 1983) (upholding agency's negative determination because, inter alia, project was in compliance with local standards); New Hope Community Ass'n v. HUD, 509 F. Supp. 525, 529–30 (E.D.N.C. 1981) (compliance with zoning ordinance is some evidence that the action does not significantly affect the environment).

229. *See* Stewart v. United States Postal Serv., 508 F. Supp. 112, 116 (N.D. Cal. 1980).

230. Missouri Coalition for the Env't v. Corps of Eng'rs, 866 F.2d 1025, 1033–34 (8th Cir.), *cert. denied*, 110 S. Ct. 76 (1989); Olmsted Citizens for a Better Community v. United States, 793 F.2d 201, 207 (8th Cir. 1986).

Environmental Impact Statements

5.1 INTRODUCTION

Chapter 5 discusses what has become the focal point of NEPA: the EIS and the EIS process. EISs must be prepared for all major federal actions significantly affecting the quality of the human environment. EISs are more formal than EAs and contain consideration of the environmental effects of the proposed action including adverse effects that cannot be avoided, alternatives, the relationship between the short-term and long-term uses of the environment, and irreversible and irretrievable commitments of resources.[1]

Chapter 5 examines how agencies determine which agency prepares an EIS and what the responsibilities of the lead agency and other agencies are. The format of an EIS and the agency's choice of methodology in preparing the EIS are also discussed.

EISs are often prepared by contractors and data for EISs are often provided by applicants for federal funding or permits. The agency's responsibilities are discussed in such cases. Chapter 5 also discusses the timing of an EIS, that is, the time at which an EIS must be prepared for a proposed action. The EIS process from scoping to the record of decision is examined, as is the role of supplemental EISs when significant new information is discovered or an agency makes substantial changes to its proposed action. A discussion of the judicial review of supplemental EISs is included. Public participation and agency commenting, which play a critical role in the EIS process, are discussed, as well as the agency's duty to respond to comments.

The scope and contents of an EIS are analyzed. These issues are critical because the failure by the agency to analyze the required environmental effects or an omission of alternatives may result in a court declaring the EIS to be inadequate.

The discussion on judicial review of EISs deals with such issues as the standard of review used by courts in reviewing agency determinations and the adequacy of EISs, the burden of proof, and the extent of evidence considered by courts in reviewing agency compliance with NEPA. The cost of preparing EISs can amount to thousands, even millions of dollars. The seldom litigated issue of who is liable for the agency's costs is briefly discussed as well.

Finally, chapter 5 discusses two types of EISs that differ from the traditional site-specific EIS. A comprehensive EIS is prepared for joint actions with cumulative environmental effects or for a broad agency program. Analyses contained in EAs and site-specific EISs may be tiered to comprehensive EISs when appropriate.

Agencies prepare legislative EISs when they propose legislation. Because the decision maker in this regard is Congress, and because the timetable for consideration of such EISs is shorter than for other EISs, abbreviated procedures for legislative EISs have been established by the CEQ. These procedures are briefly discussed.

5.2 PURPOSE

NEPA has two major purposes or aims. First, it "places upon an agency the obligation to consider every significant aspect of the environmental impact of a proposed action."[2] Second, NEPA "ensures that the agency will inform the public that it has indeed considered environmental concerns in its decision-making process."[3] The primary mechanism for achieving these aims is the EIS.

The EIS serves NEPA's purposes by ensuring "that the agency, in reaching its decision, will have available and will carefully consider detailed information concerning significant environmental impacts [and by guaranteeing] that the relevant information will be made available to the larger audience that may also play a role in both the decision making process and the implementation of that decision."[4] Thus, the EIS requirement makes NEPA "'an environmental full disclosure law.'"[5] The EIS also provides a record which a court may review to determine whether the agency has made a good faith effort to take environmental values into account in making its decision.[6]

About 425 draft and final EISs were prepared annually in the late 1980s compared with about 10,000 to 20,000 EAs annually. The number of EISs is greatly reduced from the annual average of 1800 in the early 1970s,[7] reflecting the trend towards the preparation of EAs.

5.3 LEAD AND COOPERATING AGENCIES

The CEQ regulations outline a process whereby two or more agencies involved in proposed actions requiring preparation of an EIS determine which agency is the lead agency and which agency is the cooperating agency.[8] A lead agency is the federal agency that prepares or has primary responsibility for preparing an EIS.[9] State or local agencies may be joint lead agencies with a federal agency when an action must comply with state and local laws, including mini-NEPAs.[10]

A cooperating agency is a federal agency with either jurisdiction by law over a proposed federal action or with special expertise regarding environmental effects involved in the proposed action.[11] An agency with jurisdiction by law has independent legal responsibilities with respect to the proposed action.[12] A state or local agency or an Indian tribe may be a cooperating agency upon agreement of the lead agency.[13]

If there is disagreement between the federal agencies as to which agency is the lead agency and which is the cooperating agency, the agencies use the following CEQ factors in making that determination. The factors, which are listed in descending order of importance, follow:

(1) Magnitude of the agency's involvement;
(2) Project approval/disapproval authority;
(3) Expertise concerning the action's environmental effects;
(4) Duration of the agency's involvement; and
(5) Sequence of the agency's involvement.[14]

If the agencies do not reach agreement within forty-five days, the agencies or persons concerned may request the CEQ to determine which agency shall be the lead agency.[15] In effect, the CEQ process places the issue of which agency shall be the lead agency out of the jurisdiction of the courts and within the discretion of the agencies subject to the decision of the CEQ in the event of a dispute.[16]

After the lead agency has been determined, the lead agency requests all cooperating agencies to participate in the NEPA process. The lead agency may request a cooperating agency to participate in the scoping process and to assume responsibility for developing information and preparing part of the EIS in which the cooperating agency has special expertise.[17]

Cooperating agencies with expertise regarding environmental effects involved in the proposed action satisfy their NEPA obligations in regard to the proposed action by commenting. Cooperating agencies with jurisdiction by law must comply with NEPA regarding their independent legal obligations. The cooperating agencies with jurisdiction by law may subsequently rely on the EIS prepared by the lead agency in conducting their individual actions by accepting, rejecting, or modifying the lead agency's analysis in the EIS.[18] The cooperating agency must still consider the environmental effects of its proposed actions.[19] If the cooperating agency accepts and adopts the EIS after independently evaluating it, and the proposed action and the action for which the EIS was prepared are substantially the same, the cooperating agency need not recirculate the EIS if it concludes that its suggestions and comments were satisfied.[20]

The adopted EIS must be legally adequate. If it is not adequate, the cooperating agency can not properly adopt it.[21] The CEQ recommends that cooperating agencies with decisions to make should include all information necessary for their decisions in the lead agency's EIS.[22] The cooperating agency issues its own record of decision.[23]

5.4 FORMAT

The CEQ regulations recommend the following format for EISs unless the agency preparing the EIS has compelling reasons to adopt another format.

Cover sheet. The cover sheet includes a list of the lead and any cooperating agencies; the title of the proposed action, the proposed action's location; the name, address, and telephone number of an agency employee who can supply additional information; the EIS's designation as a draft or final EIS or draft or final supplement; a one-paragraph abstract of the EIS; and the date by which comments must be received.[24]

Summary. The summary, which should not normally exceed fifteen pages, emphasizes the major conclusions in the EIS, controversial areas (including issues raised by the public or agencies), and the issues to be resolved, such as choosing between alternatives.[25]

Purpose of and need for action. The purpose and need statement specifies "the underlying purpose and need to which the agency is responding in proposing the alternatives including the proposed action."[26]

Alternatives. The alternatives section is discussed in section 5.10.1. If, at the draft EIS stage, the agency has a "preferred alternative," that is, an alternative that fulfills its statutory mandate while giving consideration to economic, environmental, technical, and other factors,[27] the agency should identify it. The preferred alternative must be identified in the final EIS unless another law forbids a preference to be expressed.[28] The preferred alternative may be the proposed action, but it need not necessarily be so.[29]

Affected Environment. The affected environment is the area affected or created by the alternatives considered in the EIS. The description of the affected environment must be sufficient for a reader to understand the alternatives' environmental effects.[30] The CEQ regulations recommend keeping this section brief, with less important material being summarized, consolidated, or referenced.[31]

Environmental Effects. The environmental effects section, including mitigation measures, is discussed in sections 5.10.2 and 5.10.3.

List of preparers. The names and qualifications of people who were primarily responsible for preparing the EIS or "significant background papers" should be included in the EIS.[32] The list should include individual members of consulting firms.[33] A "preparer" includes contractors who were primarily responsible for preparing significant background papers as well as those who prepared the EIS.[34]

Appendices (if any). The appendices should not contain analyses and information on environmental effects and alternatives. These must be contained in the body of the EIS. The appendices' purpose is to supplement information when appropriate. Thus, an agency may use an appendix to substantiate fundamental analyses in the EIS or to append technical versions of relevant analytic information contained in the body of the EIS, the results of research, explanations of methodologies used in the body of the EIS, and so on. Specific responses by the agency to comments should be included in an appendix in addition to incorporating the references into the body of the EIS.[35] The CEQ regulations specify that if an appendix is prepared, it should either be circulated with the EIS or be available upon request.[36]

In addition, the EIS should include a table of contents; a list of agencies, organizations, and persons to whom the agency sent a copy of the EIS; and an index.[37] EISs frequently include maps, diagrams, tables, glossaries, and other reader aids.

The final EIS must include comments and responses to the draft EIS[38] including responsible opposing views.[39] Responses to views the agency disagrees with need not be lengthy, but the views must be identified and discussed.[40] If the comments are "especially voluminous," summaries of them and responses to them may be included in the final EIS in lieu of including the entire text.[41]

The CEQ regulations state that the text of an EIS shall normally be less than 150 pages, with a maximum of 300 pages for a proposal of "unusual scope or complexity."[42] EISs frequently exceed this length,

however, and occasionally result in multi-volume publications especially when several separate geographic areas are being considered as
the site of a national project.

5.5 METHODOLOGY

NEPA does not require an EIS to be based on the best scientific
methodology available. Therefore, a court is not required to resolve
disagreements between experts concerning methodology.[43] As long as
the methodology used in an EIS is not arbitrary or capricious, it is
adequate.[44] When better information for projections is not available,
when the EIS discloses this fact and the problems in using the projections, and when the agency uses accepted methodologies in making
projections, the use of the methodology does not violate NEPA.[45]

5.6 DELEGATION

NEPA provides that "the responsible Federal official" shall make an
EIS after following specified procedures.[46] Early in NEPA's history, the
issue arose of whether the responsible federal official could delegate
some or all of that task to persons outside the agency. Delegation
issues generally arise in two contexts: preparation of EISs by applicants for federal funding or permits and preparation of EISs by
contractors with no interest in the proposed action.

A corollary issue occasionally arises of whether an agency may adopt
another federal agency's analysis regarding the environmental effects of
its actions. If the other agency's environmental analysis is site specific,
it may be adopted into the EIS.[47] If the environmental analysis is not site
specific, the agency preparing the EIS must consider any necessary
additional information and must independently analyze the environmental effects.[48] All material included in an EIS must be independently
evaluated by the lead agency, which is responsible for the entire EIS.

5.6.1 Applicants

In the early 1970s, the issue of whether an applicant for federal
funding or an entity with a financial interest in an agency's proposed
action could assist in preparing an EIS for the federal agency was
litigated extensively. The circuits differed on whether NEPA permitted
the practice.[49] The CEQ regulations provide that an agency may direct
an applicant to submit required types of environmental information to

be used in preparing the EIS as long as the agency independently evaluates the information and is responsible for its accuracy.[50] Only the agency or a contractor selected by it may directly prepare the EIS.[51] When the agency delegates the gathering of information to the applicant, the CEQ regulations provide that the agency must list the names of agency personnel who independently evaluated the applicant's information.[52]

There are two statutory exceptions to the above rule. Congress amended NEPA in 1975 to provide an exception for EISs prepared by state agencies or officials with statewide jurisdiction when the federal action is funding.[53] Under this exception, a state agency or official with statewide jurisdiction may prepare an EIS in lieu of the federal agency when "the responsible federal official furnishes guidance and participates" in preparation of the EIS and independently evaluates the statement prior to its approval and adoption by the federal agency. The federal agency must notify any affected state or federal land management entities of the action and must solicit their comments.[54]

The amendment was designed to overrule a Second Circuit case that had held that the Federal Highway Administration (FHWA) was required to prepare EISs for projects funded by it. The FHWA had been delegating preparation of the EISs to states applying for highway funding.[55] As a practical matter, the exception applies mainly to FHWA funding for state highways. The exception does not apply to federal permitting decisions.[56]

A second statutory exception exists for applicants for community development block grants from the Department of Housing and Urban Development (HUD). If an applicant consents to assume the status of a responsible federal official, it may assume the agency's NEPA obligations regarding the block grant.[57] HUD is responsible for ensuring that the applicant complies with the CEQ regulations and HUD regulations implementing the congressional power to delegate NEPA obligations. HUD is not required to independently evaluate the substance of the applicant's environmental analysis.[58] Thus, under this exception, the applicant is responsible for the substantive content of the EIS.

5.6.2 Contractors

The CEQ regulations provide that a federal agency may select a contractor to prepare an EIS for it.[59] The federal agency selecting the contractor must participate in the EIS's preparation, provide guidance, independently evaluate and verify the EIS before approving it, and be responsible for the EIS's scope and contents.[60]

The practice of hiring contractors to prepare EISs is widespread and longstanding. The CEQ regulation has been interpreted to mean that, although the lead agency must select a contractor who prepares the EIS, it need not directly select a contractor who prepares significant background reports. The applicant has been permitted to select such contractors.[61] A contractor must disclose in the EIS that it "has no financial or other interest in the outcome of the project."[62] The CEQ interprets this term broadly.[63] A contractor's failure to disclose may not necessarily be considered as harm by a reviewing court unless the plaintiff can also show that the decision maker's opportunity to adequately review environmental factors was affected by the failure.[64]

5.7 TIMING

NEPA requires an EIS to be "include[d] in every recommendation or report on proposals for legislation and other major Federal actions significantly affecting the quality of the human environment."[65] Thus, until a proposal for an action exists, an agency is not required to comply with NEPA in regard to that action.[66] An agency's contemplation of a proposal does not trigger NEPA.[67] The proposed action must be capable of affecting the human environment. A proposal that does not affect the human environment does not require an EIS[68] unless it commits the agency to an irreversible and irretrievable commitment of resources.[69] At the other end of the spectrum, an agency may not recommend a proposal or proceed with a major federal action significantly affecting the environment until an EIS and a record of decision have been prepared.[70]

By having the power to decide when a proposal exists, an agency controls the point before which a court may not intervene in its decision-making process.[71] This does not mean, however, that an agency need not consider environmental factors before it makes a report or recommendation on a proposal. NEPA requires agencies to engage in certain procedures, such as consulting with and obtaining the comments of federal agencies with environmental expertise, during the report or recommendation's evolution.[72] The CEQ regulations require agencies to commence preparation of an EIS early in the proposal process.[73] Once the proposal is made, the EIS must accompany the proposal through the decision making process.[74]

5.8 EIS PROCESS

An agency's determination that a proposed action may have significant environmental effects begins the EIS process. The EIS process is often referred to as the NEPA process due to the EIS's focal role under NEPA. Agencies generally follow the process outlined in the CEQ regulations, described below, as supplemented by procedures of individual agencies.[75]

5.8.1 Scoping

Shortly after the decision to prepare an EIS is made, the agency must publish in the *Federal Register* a notice of intent to prepare the EIS.[76] As a general rule, notices of intent briefly describe an agency's proposed action, provide a tentative timetable for the deadline for receipt of public comments and for preparation of the draft and final EISs, occasionally announce scoping meetings, and occasionally identify alternatives under consideration as well as anticipated environmental effects.

After the notice of intent is published, the agency generally begins the scoping process.[77] Scoping is the public process whereby an agency determines the scope of issues to be addressed in an EIS and identifies the significant issues.[78] Scoping consists of the agency's inviting participation by the public and affected agencies; determining the scope of the EIS; determining which issues are significant and should be examined in depth and which do not need to be discussed in detail because they have been dealt with in prior environmental reviews or because they are insignificant; determining whether the lead agency will prepare the entire EIS or allocate assignments to any cooperating agencies; coordinating the NEPA process with other required processes; indicating the relationship between preparation of the environmental analyses and the agency's tentative planning and decision-making schedule;[79] setting page and time limits for the EIS; and, if appropriate, holding a scoping meeting.[80]

5.8.2 Draft and Final EISs

As a general rule, agencies are required to prepare EISs in two stages: a draft EIS and a final EIS.[81] Both statements may be supplemented if the agency makes substantial changes in its proposed action or if significant new circumstances or information exist that are relevant to the environmental concerns of the proposed action.[82]

The agency files the draft EIS with the EPA and the EIS's availability is announced in the *Federal Register*.[83] The EPA evaluates and comments on the adequacy of the EIS and the proposed action.[84] At the same time that the draft EIS's availability is published, the agency circulates the draft EIS to appropriate federal, state, and local agencies, and the applicant. Copies of the draft EIS are subsequently sent to any person, organization, or agency requesting the EIS.[85] A copy of the final EIS is subsequently circulated to the above entities and to any person, organization, or agency that submitted substantive comments on the draft EIS.[86] Unless an EIS is circulated and made publicly available, an agency has not complied with NEPA as to preparation of the EIS.[87]

An agency may not make a decision on the proposed action until the later of ninety days following EPA's publication of the notice of availability of the draft EIS in the *Federal Register*, or thirty days following the EPA's publication of the notice of availability of the final EIS in the *Federal Register*.[88] These waiting periods allow interested persons, organizations, and agencies to comment on the agency's compliance with NEPA and give the agency time to consider the comments. The bulk of comments are submitted when the agency circulates the draft EIS. The failure of persons or organizations to comment during this stage may affect their subsequent ability to effectively challenge a final EIS.[89]

The agency's final act in the EIS process, if supplementation is not required,[90] if the EPA does not refer the action to the CEQ,[91] or if a subsequent agency decision maker does not reverse the agency's position,[92] is preparation of the record of decision. The record of decision is discussed in section 5.8.4.

5.8.3 Supplemental EISs

Agencies may be required to supplement their EISs if decisions on major federal actions significantly affecting the quality of the human environment remain to be made,[93] and the "agency makes substantial changes to a proposed action that are relevant to environmental concerns," or if "[t]here are significant new circumstances or information relevant to environmental concerns and bearing on the proposed action or its impacts."[94] An agency is not necessarily required to supplement an EIS prepared years before,[95] but the CEQ advises that if an EIS is more than five years old, the agency should carefully re-examine it to determine whether to supplement it.[96]

Substantial changes to an agency's action are necessarily generated by the agency itself. New information becomes available to an agency in two ways. First, the agency "has a continuing duty to gather and evaluate new information relevant to the environmental impact of its actions."[97] Second, outside interests may make the agency aware of new information.

In accordance with the standards outlined above, courts have frequently been faced with the issues of whether changes to proposed actions were "substantial," whether new information was significant, and whether an agency acted either unreasonably, or arbitrarily or capriciously in deciding not to prepare a supplemental EIS. In 1989, the United States Supreme Court held that the correct standard of review was whether the agency decision maker acted arbitrarily or capriciously in deciding not to prepare a supplemental EIS.[98]

The Supreme Court's holding casts some doubt on the continued validity of prior opinions that used the less deferential reasonableness standard. The Court stated, however, that the change in these jurisdictions' standard was "not of great pragmatic consequence."[99]

The following discussion of the case law interpreting "substantial changes" and "new information" should be read in light of the changed standard and the analysis contained in the 1989 Supreme Court opinion, which is described following the discussion of substantial changes and new information.

The Fifth and Seventh Circuits consider that a "new circumstance must present a *seriously* different picture of the environmental impact of the proposed project from what was previously envisioned" in order to require preparation of a supplemental EIS.[100] If the program and the circumstances are different, a supplemental EIS is required.[101] A supplemental EIS has not been required for such actions as the imposition of continuing controls on mining activities[102] and changes to an alternative that had been rejected by the agency.[103]

Adoption of a mitigation plan may trigger supplementation of an EIS.[104] However, modification of mitigation measures described in an EIS does not necessarily require supplementation of the EIS.[105] As a general rule, revision of an agency estimate included in the final EIS does not require the agency to prepare a supplemental EIS.[106] An exception exists, however, when knowledge of the revised estimate prior to preparation of the final EIS would have resulted in the agency's preparing "a very different document" from the final EIS prepared by it.[107]

In determining whether an agency action in not preparing a supplemental EIS was arbitrary and capricious, reviewing courts apply the rule of reason that applies to all NEPA requirements.[108] The reviewing court must carefully review the record and ensure that the agency took a hard look at the new information[109] and that it "made a reasoned decision based on its evaluation of the significance—or lack of significance—of the new information."[110] The agency's decision must stand, even if it is disputable, as long as the agency based its decision upon a "consideration of the relevant factors" and did not make a clear error of judgment.[111]

A plaintiff has the burden of showing that the information requiring an agency to prepare a supplemental EIS was significant and accurate.[112] If the plaintiff meets this burden, the agency is required to prepare a supplemental EIS.[113] The agency's decision not to prepare a supplemental EIS is entitled to substantial deference particularly when scientific determinations are involved. The agency is entitled to rely on "the reasonable opinions of its own qualified experts."[114] Thus, a conflict in expert opinions as to whether new information is significant will not result in the plaintiffs' prevailing.

It is not clear whether the agency is accorded deference on a finding that the information is not accurate. Because an opinion on accuracy should be verifiable, there is no reason for a court to defer to the agency. Arguably, therefore, a finding of accuracy should be treated in the same manner as an agency's determination that the information was not new. That is, the court should decide the issue. It is recognized, however, that in some cases, it may be difficult to segregate issues of verifiable accuracy and scientific opinions that the data is accurate or inaccurate.[115]

The most frequently litigated issue concerning significant new information is whether the information is new. If the agency shows that the subject matter of the information was discussed in the EIS, the information is not new.[116] The period during which the new information must be available to the agency is before the agency makes its decision; information generated after that date may not be considered.[117] The adequacy of a supplemental EIS is determined by a similar standard for determining the adequacy of an EIS.[118]

As well as being prepared to respond to new information and substantial changes, a supplemental EIS may be prepared to correct deficiencies in a prior draft or final EIS. The supplemental EIS corrects the deficiencies as long as it is legally adequate and the agency complies with the requirements for public participation and agency circulation.[119] The EPA sometimes suggests preparation of supplemental draft EISs to correct deficiencies in draft EISs reviewed by the EPA under section 309 of the Clean Air Act.[120]

A corollary issue may arise when an agency has made the decision for which it prepared a final EIS and subsequently conducts other actions in the same area. If this occurs and significant new circumstances do not exist, the agency is not required to prepare a supplemental EIS but may prepare an EA if it considers the subsequent action's effects not to be significant.[121] In such a case, the agency's decision not to prepare an EIS and the adequacy of the EA are subject to review under the standards described in chapter 4.

5.8.4 Record of Decision

The record of decision identifies the agency's decision and explains why the decision maker made his determination. The record of decision identifies the alternatives considered by the agency and specifies which alternatives were environmentally preferable.[122] The "environmentally preferable alternative" is the alternative that promotes the national environmental policy declared in section 101 of NEPA.[123]

The record must disclose and discuss why the agency preferred one alternative over another and why the agency decision maker balanced the factors in a certain manner. Finally, the record must state whether the agency has taken "all practicable means to avoid or minimize environmental harm" from the selected alternative.[124]

Records of decision are occasionally published in the *Federal Register* and are available from agencies on request. The CEQ has no specific requirement that records of decision be published.[125] Their publication is not widespread.

The CEQ has stated that "the terms of a Record of Decision are enforceable by agencies and private parties" and that "[a] Record of Decision can be used to compel compliance with or execution of the mitigation measures identified therein."[126] As a practical matter, however, post-EIS remedies have not been generally recognized by the courts.[127] In addition, the United States Supreme Court has held that NEPA does not require an agency to carry out a mitigation plan.[128] Thus, an agency may simply not adopt mitigation plans included in its final EIS in its record of decision. Legislation pending in Congress in 1990 would require agencies to include in an EIS, mitigation measures that it will implement.[129]

5.8.5 Public Participation

The public comment procedures mandated by NEPA have been described as being "at the heart of the NEPA review process" in that they "reflect the paramount Congressional desire to internalize opposing viewpoints into the decision making process to ensure that an agency is cognizant of all the environmental trade-offs that are implicit in a decision."[130] The procedures permit other agencies and the public to monitor and criticize the agency's proposed action.[131]

NEPA itself does not specify the manner in which the public should participate in the NEPA process.[132] The process is established by the CEQ regulations, which provide that agencies must "[m]ake diligent efforts to involve the public in . . . NEPA procedures."[133] More specifically, the agency must notify the public of any NEPA hearings or public meetings and must also provide notice of the availability of environmental documents through national, state, or local media, mailing, or posting, as appropriate.[134] A proposed amendment to NEPA would require agencies to consult with and obtain comments from the public thus statutorily requiring what the CEQ regulations currently require.[135]

There is no requirement in NEPA for administrative hearings every time an agency prepares an EIS.[136] However, public hearings or meetings are required in some instances. The CEQ regulations state that public hearings and meetings should be sponsored or held by the agency when the hearings or meetings are requested or when they are appropriate because of substantial controversy or interest in a proposed action.[137]

The CEQ regulations require agencies to solicit appropriate information from the public.[138] The regulations also require an agency to explain in its procedures how the public may receive information on the NEPA process and require the agency to make EISs, comments, and underlying documents available to the public at either no charge or at a charge no more than the actual cost of reproducing the copies for other federal agencies, including the CEQ.[139] As a practical matter, agencies generally mail copies of EAs and EISs without charge to people and entities requesting them until the agency has exhausted its supply of copies for public distribution. When the agency must make a copy in order to respond to a request, it generally charges for the cost of the copy.

If an agency receives responsible opposing views, it must disclose and discuss these views in the final EIS.[140] Responsible opposing views originate either from the public or another agency.[141] The agency has discretion to determine which opposing views are responsible but the agency's determination is subject to judicial review.[142] The agency's responses to responsible opposing views need not be lengthy as long as the agency identifies and addresses the opposing views.[143] The agency's response is subject to a rule of reason.[144] Comments to the draft EIS and responses to the comments must be included in the final EIS but may be summarized if the comments are voluminous.[145]

Obviously, the agency must be able to reconsider its proposed action in light of comments made during the NEPA process. Indeed, the agency should make changes to its proposed action in response to comments. Thus inclusion of new material in a final EIS does not necessarily require the agency to supplement its draft EIS.[146]

The inclusion of a new alternative in a final EIS may violate NEPA in certain circumstances. If the alternative was within the range of alternatives that the public could reasonably anticipate the agency to be considering, the agency need not prepare a supplemental draft EIS.[147] The no action alternative, required to be in the final EIS, should be included in the draft EIS.[148]

5.8.6 Agency Commenting

Cooperating agencies, that is, agencies with jurisdiction by law over a proposed action or agencies with relevant special expertise, must comment on relevant EISs.[149] The agency requesting the comments need not adopt the agency comments but must disclose and adequately respond to them.[150] The extent of the response varies depending on many factors, including the commenting agency's agreement or disagreement with the analysis in the EIS.[151] In certain cases, the lead agency may be required to pursue further data or conduct further study in response to critical comments.[152]

Reviewing courts, while recognizing that a commenting agency may not veto the agency action, generally consider the comments of cooperating agencies in their review of the lead agency's action.[153] The courts often find the comments persuasive in determining whether the agency complied with NEPA.[154] Accordingly, EISs have a stronger likelihood of being found adequate by a reviewing court when the lead agency takes cooperating agency comments into consideration. Comments by individual agency employees need not be individually disclosed and discussed.[155]

5.8.7 Violations of the EIS Process

Occasionally an agency violates a procedure mandated by the CEQ for preparing, circulating, or inviting public participation in an EIS. Litigated violations include a declaration by an agency official that an EIS had been circulated and was publicly available when it was not,[156] failure to give notice to all required persons,[157] and failure to include in an EIS disclosure of interest statements by contractors.[158]

The CEQ regulations provide that trivial violations do not support an independent cause of action.[159] Although the courts have generally not stated that the above violations were trivial, the end result is substantially the same. Courts have examined whether a plaintiff has been prejudiced by the agency action. If the plaintiff is not prejudiced, the tendency is for a reviewing court to find the error harmless.[160]

5.9 SCOPE

Most EISs are site specific. That is, the EISs cover one agency action at one site. Occasionally, however, the appropriate scope of an EIS is disputed, particularly when an agency conducts many actions over a period of time, with each action having individually insignificant effects but cumulatively significant effects. Another problem arises when an agency prepares an EIS for only one action even though future actions are dependent on the first action. For example, in an egregious case of segmentation, an agency planned two segments of a highway that terminated at opposite ends of a park. Because the segment through the park was obviously planned, a reviewing court required the agency to consider the three segments together.[161]

Agencies have broad discretion to determine the scope of their proposed actions,[162] but as a result of problems such as those outlined above, the courts and the CEQ have developed criteria to aid in determining the scope of an EIS in order to "prevent the policies of NEPA from being nibbled away by multiple increments no one of which may in and of itself be important enough to compel preparation of a full EIS."[163]

5.9.1 Judicial Tests for Joint Actions

One of the earliest tests for considering the environmental effects of joint actions was introduced in Scientists' Institute for Public Information, Inc. v. Atomic Energy Commission.[164] The "irretrievable commitment" test created in that opinion is derived from NEPA's language requiring EISs to include discussion of "any irreversible and irretrievable commitments of resources which would be involved in the proposed action should it be implemented."[165] In *Scientists' Institute*, the District of Columbia Circuit ordered the Atomic Energy Commission to prepare an EIS for its liquid metal fast breeder reactor research and development program.[166] The court reasoned that the long-term commitment of resources to the program had the effect of foreclosing later alternative energy options.[167] The test focuses on whether completion of one action by the agency inevitably involves an "irreversible and irretrievable commitment of resources" to a following action or actions.[168] If an agency irretrievably commits federal funds for closely related actions, the actions must be considered together in one EIS.[169]

Another test, the "irrational or unwise" test, is similar to the "irretrievable commitment" test. The purpose of the "irrational and unwise" test is to determine if a proposed action is so dependent on subsequent phases "that it would be irrational, or at least unwise, to undertake the first phase if subsequent phases were not also undertaken."[170]

The Ninth Circuit has used the "irrational or unwise" test to find that it was not irrational for an agency to consider the first phase of a dam and reservoir project separately from the second phase.[171] The court determined that the first phase, consisting of constructing the dam and reservoir and filling it to a capacity of 100,000 acre feet, did not depend on the second phase in which an additional 100,000 acre feet of water was to be added.[172] In a subsequent case, the Ninth Circuit determined that it would be irrational for the environmental effects of mining in one area to be considered separately when contractual obligations also required vast areas of surrounding land to be mined.[173] In another case, the court required the United States Forest Service to consider the environmental effects of a road construction project and a timber sale in one EIS.[174] The court considered it irrational for the Forest Service to construct a road to access timber and then not to sell the timber accessed by the road.[175]

A third judicial test is the "independent utility" test under which the environmental effects of proposed actions must be considered together if the actions are functionally related to other actions.[176] The test, which is widely used in connection with highway projects, has several criteria that are used independently as well as together. To have independent utility, a segment should have logical termini;[177] be large enough to have viable alternatives[178] and to permit a broad scope of environmental consequences to be considered;[179] or have an independent purpose even if other segments are not constructed.[180] The focus of the test has been described as "whether one project will serve a significant purpose even if a second related project is not built."[181]

The above discussion of judicial tests includes the most widely used judicial tests in existence for determining which actions must be considered together for NEPA purposes. The tests have similarities,[182] but they occasionally conflict, resulting in situations in which the outcome of a case is determined by the test being applied.[183] The determination of whether an agency is segmenting its actions also differs depending on the determination of the action's scope.[184]

It is common for courts to apply more than one test to the same fact situation[185] or even to create hybrid tests.[186] Compliance with one test, however, does not necessarily mean compliance with other tests. To comply with NEPA, agencies must follow their jurisdiction's judicial test as well as the tests outlined in the CEQ regulations.[187] Some of the CEQ tests mirror the judicial tests.[188] If an agency meets the relevant tests, one court has held that segmentation was not improper despite the purposeful action of conducting state before federal action in order to avoid compliance with NEPA.[189]

5.9.2 CEQ Tests

The CEQ tests for determining which actions to consider together in one EIS are designed for use in the scoping process—the pluralistic decision-making process held to determine the range of alternatives, effects, and actions to be considered in the EIS.[190] The CEQ regulations require federal agencies to consider three types of actions in determining the scope of EISs: connected, cumulative, and similar.[191] A fourth category of unconnected single actions is necessarily considered.

Connected Actions. The CEQ regulations define connected actions as closely related actions that automatically trigger other actions with a potentially significant effect on the environment, are unable to or do not proceed without prior or simultaneous actions, or are an interdependent part of a larger action justifying them.[192]

The connected actions test has been applied to varying actions, including proposed timber sales in national forests.[193] If the agency constructs or improves a road and a clear nexus exists between that action and a timber sale, the actions are connected.[194] The Ninth Circuit determined that proposals to construct a road and to hold a timber sale fulfilled the second and third criteria of the test because each action justified the other: the timber sale could not proceed without the road construction; justification for the road depended on timber sales. The court, therefore, required the Forest Service to examine together the potential environmental effects of the connected actions.[195]

In other actions, the construction of a terminal and a runway were not connected when construction of a new terminal did not depend on the subsequent construction of a new runway,[196] and construction of housing for a home port was not connected to construction of the home port's operational aspects.[197] The designation of a disposal site was held to be connected to the issuance of permits to dispose of waste materials because the first action had no utility except for the subsequent actions.[198]

Cumulative Actions. Under the CEQ regulations, a proposed action is cumulative if it has cumulatively sigificant impacts when it is viewed with other proposed actions.[199] The leading case, and the basis for the CEQ regulation on cumulative actions, is Kleppe v. Sierra Club.[200]

Kleppe involved the issue of whether a comprehensive EIS was required for the Department of the Interior's coal mining activities on the Northern Great Plains.[201] The department had prepared a comprehensive EIS for its nationwide coal-leasing program,[202] as well as site-specific EISs for individual actions such as approval of mining plans and right-of-way permits.[203] The Sierra Club challenged the Department of the Interior's failure to prepare a programmatic EIS for the Northern Great Plains region on the basis that coal-related activity in the area was environmentally, geographically, and programmatically related.[204]

The Supreme Court rejected the Sierra Club's argument and upheld the trial court's finding that existing and proposed coal development projects in the region were not interrelated.[205] The Court stated that if the department proposed a regional program with a cumulative or synergistic environmental impact, the department must consider the environmental consequences of the program in one EIS, but that a comprehensive EIS was not required for contemplated actions.[206] The Court reasoned that requiring EISs for contemplated actions would result in the unnecessary preparation of a large number of EISs, as well as unwarranted judicial intrusion into day-to-day agency activities.[207] Although the Court noted the department's use of drainage areas and basins in defining the geographic area to be included in individual EISs, it affirmed the broad discretion accorded agencies in defining the scope of their EISs.[208]

The cumulative actions test differs from the connected actions test by focusing on the environment affected by an action rather than the type of action causing the impact. An action, therefore, may be cumulative even though it has independent utility.[209]

Courts apply the cumulative actions test to two types of determinations: the scope of EISs (as in *Kleppe*) and threshold determinations. As detailed in the CEQ regulations,[210] the test is designed for determining whether to consider more than one proposed action in an EIS. If an agency proposed various actions that are so interrelated that they comprise a local,[211] regional, or national program,[212] the agency must consider the effects of the cumulative actions in a comprehensive EIS. Because a central issue is whether a program in fact exists, cases often turn on that issue[213] or on whether actions are proposed or contemplated.[214]

A determination of whether actions are cumulative focuses on the proposed actions, whereas a determination of whether impacts are cumulative focuses on the resource affected by the actions. If a court determines that an agency's action may have cumulatively significant effects, the agency must prepare an EIS analyzing those effects in lieu of preparing EAs and FONSIs for individual actions.[215] In addition to not permitting agencies to segment programmatic actions,[216] courts do not permit agencies to segment repetitive actions that do not have significant environmental effects when examined individually but which have cumulatively significant effects.[217]

Similar Actions. The CEQ defines similar actions as proposed or reasonably foreseeable agency actions with a common feature, such as timing or geography.[218] If an agency determines that it is advantageous to consider the combined impacts of similar actions or reasonable alternatives together, it may do so at its discretion.[219] Because the regulation is precatory, case law defining the regulation is scarce. Courts that have considered similar actions seem to use the similarity as an additional factor in decisions ruling that the cumulative effects of several proposed actions must be considered together.[220]

Unconnected Single Actions. Unconnected single actions, or individual actions, are not defined by the CEQ. Their definition, however, can be determined by reversing the CEQ's definition of connected actions. Unconnected single actions, therefore, are actions that do not automatically trigger other actions potentially requiring EISs, are not interdependent parts of larger actions on which they depend for their justification, and do not require prior or simultaneous actions to be taken in order for them to proceed.[221] Such actions are examined individually. In fact, unconnected single actions encompass most of the proposed federal actions subject to NEPA.

5.10 CONTENTS

5.10.1 Alternatives

NEPA requires agencies to consider and discuss two types of alternatives in an EIS. First, an agency must consider "alternatives to the proposed action."[222] Second, an agency must "study, develop, and describe appropriate alternatives to recommended courses of action in any proposal which involves unresolved conflicts concerning alternative uses of available resources."[223] By placing the discussion of all alternatives together, the environmental effects of the alternatives can be compared.[224]

The alternatives section of the EIS has been described as its "heart"[225] and as its "linchpin."[226] The section provides the agency decision maker with information on which to make a decision. It also informs Congress, other agencies, and the public about the proposed action,[227] thus according them an opportunity to participate meaningfully in the decision-making process.[228]

Legislation pending in Congress in 1990 would require agencies to consider "alternatives to the proposed action that achieve the same or similar public purposes, including alternatives that avoid the adverse environmental effects [which cannot be avoided should the proposal be implemented] and alternatives that otherwise mitigate those adverse environmental effects."[229] The amendment is far-reaching because the word "significant" does not qualify "adverse environmental effects." This provision, if enacted, would greatly strengthen the current requirement for agencies to consider "appropriate mitigation measures."[230]

A Senate bill would go even further and require agencies to include discussion of measures that "will" be taken as well as requiring a description of how a proposed action or chosen alternative and selected mitigation measure conformed to NEPA.[231] The Senate bill would thus provide a much needed bridge between section 101 and section 102.

Range of Alternatives. An agency must consider reasonable alternatives.[232] The range of alternatives is thus subject to a rule of reason.[233] The extent of the range depends on the nature and timing of the proposed action.[234] An agency need not consider every variation of every alternative, but the range must be reasonably comprehensive[235] so that the agency may make a "reasoned choice" among them.[236] An EIS will not be adjudged inadequate because "the agency failed to ferret out every possible alternative, regardless of how uncommon or unknown that alternative may have been at the time the project was approved."[237]

NEPA does not require "crystal ball inquiry."[238] Thus, an agency is not required to consider "every extreme possibility which might be conjectured."[239] If implementation of an alternative is remote and speculative and its environmental effects cannot be reasonably ascertained, it does not require consideration.[240] If an agency does discuss a remote and speculative alternative, the discussion need not be lengthy.[241] NEPA does not require consideration of an alternative that would result in similar or greater environmental harm than another alternative,[242] or an alternative that is as defective as an alternative explicitly rejected by the agency.[243] An alternative that is dependent on technological advances when the agency action must achieve short-term results need only be discussed briefly.[244] Alternatives that are not considered to be feasible, either because they would not be consistent with the purpose of the agency action[245] or for some other reason,[246] need not be discussed. The agency should, however, briefly address in the EIS the reasons why the action is not feasible.[247]

An alternative requiring legislation to make the alternative available needs to be discussed in certain limited circumstances.[248] An agency need not discuss an alternative requiring legislation when Congress enacted legislation declaring the type of action in the alternative illegal shortly before the agency proposed the action.[249]

There is no bright line between alternatives that do not need to be discussed and those that require only brief discussion. Therefore, if an agency considers that an alternative falls just outside the limit of reasonableness, the cautious course for the agency is to briefly discuss the alternative's environmental effects and to set out the reasons why a more detailed discussion was not made. The brief discussion should be in the EIS, although courts may look outside the EIS to other parts of the administrative record to support a determination of infeasibility.[250]

As a general rule, an agency must discuss the no action, or status quo, alternative in an EIS.[251] Consideration of the no action alternative provides a standard for comparing the environmental effects of the other alternatives.[252] The CEQ interprets the no action alternative to apply to two types of actions. First, if an agency is conducting an ongoing action and is developing new plans, the no action alternative is the continuance of the unchanged ongoing plan. When the agency is considering conducting a new action, the no action alternative is the agency not acting at all.[253] The detail to be included in the discussion depends on the circumstances.[254]

Partial as well as complete alternatives to a proposed action must be discussed. Thus, if adoption of an alternative means that the proposed action may be reduced in scale, the partial alternative should be considered.[255] The alternative of deferring the agency action may need to be considered in certain circumstances.[256]

To successfully challenge an agency's failure to discuss a reasonable alternative in an EIS, a plaintiff has the burden of showing that the alternative that was not considered is reasonable. The plaintiff must, therefore, adequately delineate the reasons why the alternative is reasonable.[257] The reasoning must be supported by evidence.[258] During the decision-making process, if a plaintiff does not participate in a meaningful manner, the agency must still comply with NEPA, but the limits to which the agency must investigate alternatives may be restricted.[259]

Consideration of Alternatives. The CEQ regulations state that the discussion of alternatives in the EIS should be based on analysis of the affected environment and the environmental effects of an agency action.[260] If the environmental effects of alternatives are not discussed, the EIS is inadequate.[261]

The extent of detail required in discussion of an alternative is related to the complexity of the alternative's environmental effects.[262] An agency has reasonable discretion to determine when it has sufficient information to make an intelligent choice between alternatives.[263] If an agency, based on its study of an alternative, determines that the alternative is not feasible,[264] or that it is remote and speculative,[265] the agency is not required to continue analyzing or studying the alternative.

Discussion of the alternatives in the EIS is subject to a rule of reason.[266] The discussion must include sufficient information "to permit a reasoned choice of alternatives so far as environmental aspects are concerned."[267] The agency must state the facts supporting its conclusions[268] and comparatively evaluate "'the environmental benefits, costs, and risks of the proposed action and each reasonable alternative.'"[269] The discussion need not be repetitive.[270]

5.10.2 Environmental Effects

The environmental effects section provides "the analytic basis for the concise comparison in the 'alternatives' section" of the EIS.[271] NEPA requires federal agencies to discuss in an EIS "the environmental impact of the proposed action,"[272] "any adverse environmental effects which cannot be avoided should the proposal be implemented,"[273] "the relationship between local short-term uses of man's environment and the maintenance and enhancement of long-term productivity,"[274] and "any irreversible and irretrievable commitments of resources which would be involved in the proposed action should it be implemented."[275]

The CEQ regulations require agencies to consolidate discussion of the above in an environmental consequences analysis in the EIS. The discussion must include the following types of environmental effects and consideration of them: any direct, indirect, and cumulative effects of the proposed action and its alternatives, and the effects' significance; possible conflicts between the proposed action and federal, state, regional, local, or Indian land use plans, policies, and controls; the potential of alternatives and mitigation measures regarding energy requirements and conservation, natural or depletable resource requirements and conservation, and urban quality, historic, and cultural resources including reuse and conservation. Finally, the means to mitigate adverse environmental effects must be discussed if the mitigation measures are not fully discussed in the alternatives section.[276] Only significant environmental effects need to be discussed.[277] The CEQ regulations state that if an EIS is prepared and if socio-economic effects are interrelated with natural physical effects, the socio-economic effects should be discussed.[278]

Types. All significant environmental effects, beneficial as well as adverse,[279] and direct as well as indirect,[280] must be considered in an EIS. A direct effect is caused by an agency action and occurs at the same time and place.[281] An indirect, or secondary, effect is caused by an agency action but occurs later in time or is further removed in distance than a direct effect. An indirect effect must be reasonably foreseeable.[282] Specific as well as aggregate indirect effects must be considered.[283] Indirect effects include the growth-inducing potential of an action,[284] the loss of a resource,[285] a change in an area's character[286] and the opportunity to classify land as wilderness if a decision is made to manage the land as nonwilderness.[287]

NEPA does not require agencies to consider remote or speculative environmental effects.[288] However, NEPA implies that an agency must engage in reasonable forecasting and speculation in preparing an EIS.[289] The line between reasonable forecasting and speculation and remote and speculative effects has proven to be elusive and depends on the circumstances. Even if an environmental effect will be latent for many years following an agency action, it must still be considered in an EIS.[290]

Cumulative effects must be considered in an EIS.[291] A cumulative effect "results from the incremental impact of the action when added to other past, present, and reasonably foreseeable future actions regardless of what agency (Federal or non-Federal) or person undertakes such other actions. Cumulative [effects] can result from individually minor but collectively significant actions taking place over a period of time."[292]

In identifying a cumulative effect, an agency focuses on the affected resource and the environmental effect on it of various actions. The resource is traditionally an ecosystem[293] but may also be a species.[294] A cumulative effect that is speculative when the EIS is prepared may not need to be considered.[295] If the actions are cumulative, analysis of their cumulative environmental effects may not be deferred until after the initial action is taken.[296]

Consideration. In reviewing an agency's consideration of environmental effects, a court determines whether the agency took a "hard look" at the environmental effects of its proposed action[297] and whether the EIS was "sufficiently detailed to aid in the substantive decision whether to proceed."[298] In order to evaluate the environmental risks of a proposed action, an agency must weigh environmental considerations against economic considerations. The agency must, therefore, fully disclose economic considerations.[299] A nondisclosure or distortion of the considerations prevents the decision maker from fairly weighing the environmental against the economic considerations.[300]

The EIS must provide a "reasonably thorough discussion of the significant aspects of the probable environmental consequences,"[301] not a "complete evaluation" of them.[302] The depth of discussion of environmental effects, whether they are direct, indirect, or cumulative, depends on the circumstances.[303] The discussion of environmental effects must be in the EIS. A reviewing court may look outside the record, however, to determine if the agency ignored the environmental effects of its proposed action.[304]

Uncertain Effects. The CEQ regulations formerly mandated preparation of a worst case analysis when scientific uncertainty existed.[305] If scientific uncertainty or gaps in relevant information were discovered by an agency when it was "evaluating significant adverse effects on the human environment" the uncertainty and/or gaps had to be disclosed.[306] If the relevant unavailable information was "essential to a reasoned choice among alternatives and . . . the overall costs of obtaining it [were] not exorbitant," the information had to be included in the EIS.[307]

If the costs were exorbitant, or if important information was unavailable because it was beyond the state-of-the-art, the agency was to "weigh the need for the action against the risk and severity of possible adverse impacts were the action to proceed in the face of uncertainty."[308] A decision to proceed obligated the agency to include a worst case analysis in the EIS, together with an indication of the probability of the adverse impacts occurring.[309] In essence, the worst case analysis regulation addressed agency actions with the potential for low probability but catastrophic environmental consequences, where important information regarding such consequences was unknown or conflicting. If an agency's actions involved a leap into the unknown, the worst environmental consequences of that leap had to be analyzed.[310]

The CEQ withdrew the worst case analysis regulation in 1986.[311] The new regulation provides that if unavailable information is "essential to a reasoned choice among alternatives and . . . the overall costs of obtaining it are not exorbitant," the information must be included in the EIS.[312] This requirement, which was contained in the superseded regulation, is unchanged. Thus the new regulation implies, as did the superseded regulation, that if the costs of obtaining essential available information are not exorbitant, the agency must obtain the information before it proceeds.[313]

The new regulation also provides that if the costs of obtaining the information are exorbitant, or if important information is unavailable because it is beyond the state-of-the-art, the agency must disclose the fact that information is incomplete or unavailable, state the relevance of such information to the evaluation of reasonably foreseeable adverse environmental effects, summarize "credible scientific evidence" relevant to an evaluation of reasonably foreseeable significant adverse impacts, and evaluate the impacts by the use of "theoretical approaches or research methods generally accepted in the scientific community."[314] "Reasonably foreseeable" is defined to include environmental effects of low probability but catastrophic consequences if an analysis of such effects "is supported by credible scientific evidence, is not based on pure conjecture, and is within the rule of reason."[315]

Beyond not requiring a worst case analysis, it is not clear what the practical difference is between the new and the old regulation. Under the new regulation, federal agencies could conceivably exclude from consideration scientific evidence they believed to be incredible.[316] Scientific evidence that conflicted with an agency's belief may necessarily be considered incredible by the agency. However, although courts traditionally defer to agency expertise involving evidence at the cutting edge of science,[317] agencies must adequately consider the scientific evidence in dispute.[318]

Unaffected by the change in regulation are the following NEPA principles concerning uncertain scientific information. The cost of scientific uncertainty of a proposed action's environmental effects must be disclosed and considered in an EIS so that the cost may be weighed by an agency decision maker.[319] Significant environmental risks must also be disclosed.[320] A good faith effort to describe reasonably foreseeable environmental impacts must be made even if it requires reasonable speculation and forecasting.[321] If significant environmental effects are the subject of scientific conflict, an EIS must disclose the uncertainty by including "responsible opposing views."[322] Courts defer to an agency's decision to rely on the reasonable opinions of its own experts.[323]

5.10.3 Mitigation

The CEQ regulations require agencies to discuss mitigation measures in an EIS.[324] Mitigation measures must also be discussed in the record of decision.[325] The CEQ regulations define mitigation to include avoidance of the environmental effect of the proposed action by not taking part or all of the action; minimizing the environmental effect by limiting the degree of magnitude of the action and its implementation; rectifying the environmental effect by repairing, rehabilitating, or restoring the environment affected by the proposed action; reducing or eliminating the environmental effect by preservation or maintenance operations to be taken during the life of the action; and compensating for the environmental effect by replacing or providing substitute resources or environments.[326]

Mitigation measures must be discussed in an EIS "in sufficient detail to ensure that environmental consequences have been fairly evaluated."[327] In 1989, however, the United States Supreme Court held that NEPA does not require a complete mitigation plan to be formulated and adopted by the agency.[328] Thus, unless an agency commits itself in its record of decision to performing the mitigation measure[329] the agency does not have to adopt mitigation measures considered in the EIS.

A Senate bill pending in Congress in 1990 would require agencies to include mitigation measures they "will" perform in EISs.[330] House bills would require agencies to perform mitigation measures and other conditions of an action only if the agency selects the conditions in its final decision.[331] All the bills provide for review of prior mitigation measures to determine the extent to which they have been implemented and their effectiveness.[332] Whether the review will be a one-time matter or an ongoing requirement is the subject of discussions between individual members of congressional committees and between the agencies and Congress.[333]

5.10.4 Cost-Benefit Analyses

NEPA requires agencies to balance the environmental costs of a proposed action against the action's economic and technological benefits.[334] An EIS must, therefore, contain some form of balancing or informal cost-benefit analysis pertinent to the proposed agency action.[335] As a general rule, the balancing or cost-benefit analysis need not be formal and mathematically expressed.[336] However, the balancing or informal cost-benefit analysis must give the decision maker and the public sufficient information regarding the proposed action's "costs and benefits to permit [a] reasoned evaluation and decision."[337] Dollar figures do not have to be assigned to environmental costs and benefits.[338] The costs used must not be misleading or highly speculative.[339] Environmental costs are not entitled to more weight than other costs and benefits.[340]

If a formal cost-benefit analysis is prepared, it should be incorporated in an EIS by reference or be included as an appendix. The EIS should discuss the relationship between the cost-benefit analysis and any analyses of unquantified environmental effects, values, and amenities.[341]

5.11 JUDICIAL REVIEW

To successfully challenge an agency's decision to proceed with an action for which an EIS has been prepared, a plaintiff must prove by a preponderance of the evidence that the EIS is inadequate and that the agency's decision to proceed is arbitrary and capricious.[342] That is, the court reviews whether the agency took "a 'hard look' at the environmental consequences" of its proposed action before deciding to act.[343]

The trial court does not determine whether an effect was significant or whether an alternative was reasonable.[344] Instead, "[t]he role of the courts is simply to ensure that the agency has adequately considered and disclosed the environmental impact of its actions and that its decision is not arbitrary or capricious."[345]

For many years, the circuits were split on the appropriate standard of review to apply to review an agency's compliance with NEPA. Some circuits adopted the "reasonableness" standard while others adopted the "arbitrary and capricious" standard of the Administrative Procedure Act.[346] In 1989, the United States Supreme Court ruled, in a case involving an agency's decision not to supplement an EIS, that the correct standard for this type of action was the arbitrary and capricious standard.[347]

Under the arbitrary and capricious standard, a reviewing court considers whether the agency's determination is "based on a consideration of the relevant factors and whether there has been a clear error of judgment." The court's "inquiry must 'be searching and careful,' but 'the ultimate standard of review is a narrow one.'"[348] The court may not substitute its judgment for that of the agency.[349]

In reviewing the adequacy of an EIS, courts insure that the agency has taken a "hard look" at the environmental effects of its proposed action.[350] Courts use a rule of reason to determine whether an EIS is adequate.[351] That is, the courts recognize that NEPA "mandates that no agency [may] limit its environmental activity by the use of an artificial framework and on the other that the act does not intend to impose an impossible standard on the agency."[352] In other words, courts do not "fly speck" an EIS for inconsequential, technical deficiencies.[353] Instead, the courts determine if the agency has in good faith considered the environmental consequences of its action. The agency's good faith is reviewed objectively.[354]

An EIS need not be perfect.[355] The amount of detail to be included varies with the circumstances.[356] If future EISs will be prepared for an action, the amount and specificity of information required decreases.[357]

The criteria considered by reviewing courts to determine an EIS's or supplemental EIS's adequacy varies somewhat between the circuits[358] but, in general, courts consider the following criteria. The EIS must provide sufficient detail so that persons who did not participate in the proposed action may understand and consider relevant environmental effects.[359] Thus, an EIS must not be composed of vague, general, or conclusory statements.[360] The agency "must explicate fully its course of inquiry, its analysis and its reasoning."[361] The EIS must be capable of being understood by nontechnical people and must contain "'enough scientific reasoning to alert specialists to particular problems within the field of their expertise.'"[362] The EIS must be "concise, clear, and to the point,"[363] and "be written in plain language."[364] A trial court's conclusion as to the understandability of an EIS is reviewed by an appellate court under the clearly erroneous standard.[365]

A final EIS must contain responsible opposing views.[366] The opposing views need not be discussed in detail but must adequately disclose and address the disagreement with the agency view[367] in "a good faith, reasoned analysis."[368] In this way, the agency decision maker can factor the opposing views into his decision. NEPA does not require a court to resolve disagreements between experts. An agency has the "discretion to rely on the reasonable opinions of its own qualified experts" even when a court may be persuaded by contrary views.[369]

The consideration of alternatives must be sufficient to permit a reasoned choice among the various courses of action.[370] The EIS must fully disclose the environmental costs[371] and the economic and technological benefits of a proposed action[372] in order to permit the balancing of such benefits against a proposed action's environmental costs.

In determining the EIS's adequacy, the reviewing court may consider evidence outside the EIS but in the administrative record to assess the extent of discussion required for a given alternative or environmental consequence.[373] The evidence may not be used to substitute for the discussion required to be in the EIS.[374] To permit such evidence to be considered as a part of the EIS would not comply with NEPA's full disclosure purpose.[375]

This does not mean that the EIS may not incorporate certain data by reference.[376] Material incorporated by reference is generally composed of data that is indirectly related to the EIS.[377] As a general rule, material incorporated by reference does not need to accompany the EIS.[378] Information that is generally available does not need to be repeated in an EIS if it is adequately cited in the EIS.[379] Other information, including supporting studies and technical references, also need not be included in an EIS as long as it is identified, available, and accessible.[380]

The court may also consider evidence outside the administrative record and may permit discovery to determine if the agency considered all relevant factors and explained its decision or conduct, to determine if the agency relied on documents or materials not in the record, or to explain technical terms or complex subject matter involved in the agency action.[381] A plaintiff is generally not entitled to discover evidence, and a reviewing court is generally not entitled to extend review beyond the administrative record if the administrative record, including the EIS, contains sufficient information to respond to the plaintiff's allegations.[382]

The above discussion of the judicial review of EISs has focused on whether an EIS is legally adequate. If the EIS is legally inadequate, an agency's decision to proceed with its proposed action is arbitrary and capricious. The United States Supreme Court has declared that if an agency proceeds with an action after having prepared an adequate EIS, regardless of whether the action is environmentally destructive, the agency has complied with NEPA.[383] For a discussion of the Supreme Court's interpretation of NEPA as probably having no substantive effect, see section 1.8.

5.12 PREPARATION COST OF AN EIS

NEPA does not address the issue of whether an applicant for a federal permit must pay for the cost of preparing an EIS if one is required. Because EISs are expensive,[384] litigation occasionally arises as to whether an agency or an applicant for a permit should bear the agency's cost of preparing an EIS.

Most litigation has concerned right-of-way permits over federal land. Congress provided in the Federal Land Policy Management Act that the cost of preparing an EIS was a "reasonable cost" that the Bureau of Land Management (BLM) was entitled to recover from applicants for rights-of-way.[385] Congress further provided that in determining whether costs were reasonable, the Secretary should consider costs incurred for the benefit of the general public but not costs incurred for the exclusive benefit of the applicant.[386] This provision raised the issue of whether the BLM could seek reimbursement of the total cost of EIS preparation from the applicant. The BLM determined that it could and, under authority of the Federal Land Policy Management Act, the Mineral Leasing Act,[387] and the Independent Offices Appropriation Act,[388] promulgated regulations requiring reimbursement before the BLM would issue the right-of-way permit.[389]

The Tenth Circuit held that only a portion of the costs had to be reimbursed by the applicant because some of the benefits of the EIS inured to the applicant. The court left to the BLM the task of determining how much of the cost should be borne by the applicant.[390]

The BLM's authority to require reimbursement only became effective when the regulation requiring reimbursement was promulgated. Until that time, the agency could not require reimbursement of the cost of preparing an EIS.[391] The current version of the regulation provides for reimbursement of the costs of preparing reports and statements pursuant to NEPA.[392] Thus, reimbursement for EAs prepared by the agency is also covered.

The Federal Land Policy Management Act does not contain the sole grant of authority for an agency to charge a permit applicant for an EIS. The Independent Offices Appropriation Act provides a general grant of authority to federal agencies to seek reimbursement of EIS costs.[393] The Nuclear Regulatory Commission has used this authority to charge a fee for the full cost of conducting NEPA reviews as a prerequisite to issuing a license.[394] An applicant who is required to pay the agency's cost of complying with NEPA for processing its license or permit may be able to challenge the fee charged if the fee is excessive.[395]

5.13 COMPREHENSIVE EISs

A comprehensive, or programmatic, EIS differs from the traditional site-specific EIS required by NEPA in that it deals with either joint actions or a broad program in one EIS. Agencies have discretion in determining whether to prepare a comprehensive EIS.[396] A comprehensive EIS for joint actions is apropriate when it is "the best way" to assess the environmental effects of connected, cumulative, or sufficiently similar actions.[397] A comprehensive EIS is required if an agency has several proposed actions pending at the same time and those actions will have cumulative or synergistic environmental effects.[398]

The individual related actions may not be segmented to avoid considering their cumulative environmental effects.[399] The area affected by the proposed actions may be regional or even national.[400] Legislation pending in Congress in 1990 would require agencies to consider the effects of their actions on the global environment.[401] If passed, this legislation could trigger the need for more comprehensive EISs.

Comprehensive or programmatic EISs for broad agency programs permit agency decision makers to look ahead at broad issues.[402] Thus, if a comprehensive EIS is unable to be forward-looking, its preparation may not be required.[403] When an agency proposes a broad program, for example, the introduction of a new technology,[404] it must consider the advisability of preparing a comprehensive EIS. If the agency decides not to prepare a comprehensive EIS for a proposed broad program, it should specify and explain the reasons for its decision.[405] Site-specific EISs for individual actions that are part of a broad program or policy may not substitute for a comprehensive EIS if one is required.[406]

5.14 TIERING

When an agency prepares a comprehensive EIS for a broad program, it may prepare site-specific EISs for a second tier of EISs under the comprehensive EIS. Alternatively, depending on the circumstances, the agency may prepare EAs as a second tier.

Site-specific EISs under a comprehensive EIS are prepared when an agency makes a "critical decision" leading to the development of a site.[407] Such a decision occurs when the agency proposes a major federal action that may significantly affect the environment. Thus, site-specific EISs are not necessarily required for all agency actions taken under a comprehensive EIS.[408]

The CEQ regulations permit agencies to tier analyses of environmental effects. Thus, an agency does not need to repeat analyses contained in a comprehensive EIS but may summarize the analyses or make narrower statements in a comprehensive EIS of narrower scope, a site-specific EIS or an EA and incorporate the broader analysis by reference.[409] Site-specific analyses may also be contained in comprehensive EISs or in tiered EAs as long as the analysis is incorporated into a site-specific EIS by reference or is adequately evaluated in the comprehensive EIS if no site-specific EIS is prepared.[410]

5.15 LEGISLATIVE EISs

A legislative EIS must be prepared for any recommendation or report to Congress on a legislative proposal significantly affecting the human environment.[411] Legislative proposals do not include appropriation requests,[412] authorizations for further study of a contemplated action,[413] and agency responses to congressional inquiries.[414] The legislative EIS must be available within thirty days of the transmittal to Congress of the proposed legislation and before congressional hearings and deliberations occur.[415]

The EIS process is usually abbreviated for legislative EISs. The agency need not engage in scoping, nor must it prepare a draft as well as a final EIS except for specified exceptions.[416] Comments received on the legislative EIS are given to the lead agency, which responds to the comments and forwards the comments and responses to the congressional committees with jurisdiction over the proposed legislation.[417]

Once a proposal for legislation is transmitted to Congress, judicial review of the legislative EIS is not possible for several reasons including problems involving the separation of powers, standing,[418] and Congress' power to declare an EIS adequate,[419] or to declare an action exempt from NEPA.

NOTES

1. 42 U.S.C. § 4332(2)(C) (1988); see Township of Lower Alloways Creek v. Public Serv. Elec. & Gas Co., 687 F.2d 732, 741 (3d Cir. 1982).

2. Baltimore Gas & Elec. Co. v. Natural Resources Defense Council, Inc., 462 U.S. 87, 97 (1983) (quoting Vermont Yankee Nuclear Power Corp. v. Natural Resources Defense Council, Inc., 435 U.S. 519, 553 (1978)); see Robertson v. Methow Valley Citizens Council, 109 S. Ct. 1835, 1845 (1989).

3. Baltimore Gas & Elec. Co. v. Natural Resources Defense Council, Inc., 462 U.S. 87, 97 (1983) (citing Weinberger v. Catholic Action of Hawaii/Peace Educ. Project, 454 U.S. 139, 143 (1981)).

4. Robertson v. Methow Valley Citizens Council, 109 S. Ct. 1835, 1845 (1989); see 40 C.F.R. § 1502.1 (1989).

5. Sierra Club v. Morton, 510 F.2d 813, 820 (5th Cir. 1975) (quoting Silva v. Lynn, 482 F.2d 1282, 1285 (1st Cir. 1973)).

6. Id.

7. OEQ Authorization, Fiscal Years 1989–1993; Hearing on H.R. 1113 Before the Subcomm. on Fisheries and Wildlife Conservation and the Environment of the House Comm. on Merchant Marine and Fisheries, 101st Cong., 1st Sess. 59–60 (1989) (statement of Jennifer Wilson, assistant administrator for external affairs, EPA).

8. 40 C.F.R. §§ 1501.5, 1501.6 (1989). Cf. Save Our Ecosystems v. Clark, 747 F.2d 1240, 1249–50 (9th Cir. 1984) (trial court did not err in not requiring agencies with similar programs in separate but close areas to prepare joint EIS).

9. 40 C.F.R. § 1508.16 (1989).

10. Id. § 1506.2(c); see Council on Environmental Quality, Forty Most Asked Questions Concerning CEQ's National Environmental Policy Act Regulations, 46 Fed. Reg. 18,026, 18,032–33 (1981).

11. 40 C.F.R. § 1508.5 (1989).

12. Council on Environmental Quality, Forty Most Asked Questions Concerning CEQ's National Environmental Policy Act Regulations, 46 Fed. Reg. 18,026, 18,035 (1981).

13. 40 C.F.R. § 1508.5 (1989).

14. *Id.* § 1501.5(c).

15. *Id.* § 1501.5(e).

16. *Compare* Sierra Club v. Corps of Eng'rs, 701 F.2d 1011, 1041 (2d Cir. 1983) (designation of lead agency or joint lead agencies is a matter committed to agency discretion) *with* Upper Pecos Ass'n v. Stans, 452 F.2d 1233, 1236 (10th Cir. 1971) (pre-CEQ regulations: upholding trial court's lead agency determination), *vacated*, 409 U.S. 1021 (1972).

17. 40 C.F.R. § 1501.6 (1989).

18. *See* Henry v. FPC, 513 F.2d 395, 407 (D.C. Cir. 1975).

19. *See* Silentman v. FPC, 566 F.2d 237, 240–41 (D.C. Cir. 1977).

20. 40 C.F.R. § 1506.3(b) (1989).

21. *Id.* § 1506.3(a); *see* Sierra Club v. Marsh, 714 F. Supp. 539, 582 n.62 (D. Me. 1989).

22. Council on Environmental Quality, Forty Most Asked Questions Concerning CEQ's National Environmental Policy Act Regulations, 46 Fed. Reg. 18,026, 18,030 (1981).

23. *Id.* at 18,035.

24. 40 C.F.R. § 1502.11 (1989).

25. *Id.* § 1502.12.

26. *Id.* § 1502.13.

27. Council on Environmental Quality, Forty Most Asked Questions Concerning CEQ's National Environmental Policy Act Regulations, 46 Fed. Reg. 18,026, 18,027 (1981).

28. *Id.*; 40 C.F.R. § 1502.14(e) (1989).

29. Council on Environmental Quality, Forty Most Asked Questions Concerning CEQ's National Environmental Policy Act Regulations, 46 Fed. Reg. 18,026, 18,027–28 (1981).

30. 40 C.F.R. § 1502.15 (1989); *see* Montgomery v. Ellis, 364 F. Supp. 517, 521 (N.D. Ala. 1973) (agency failed to describe physical characteristics of proposed action).

31. 40 C.F.R. § 1502.15 (1989).

32. *Id.* § 1502.17.

33. Council on Environmental Quality, Forty Most Asked Questions Concerning CEQ's National Environmental Policy Act Regulations, 46 Fed. Reg. 18,026, 18,034 (1981).

34. Sierra Club v. Marsh, 714 F. Supp. 539, 551 (D. Me. 1989).

35. 40 C.F.R. § 1502.18 (1989); Council on Environmental Quality, Forty Most Asked Questions Concerning CEQ's National Environmental Policy Act Regulations, 46 Fed. Reg. 18,026, 18,033 (1981).

36. 40 C.F.R. § 1502.18 (1989).

37. *Id.* § 1502.10; *see id.* § 1502.11–.18 (discussing format).

38. *See id.* § 1503.4; *see also* Life of the Land v. Brinegar, 485 F.2d 460, 468 (9th Cir. 1973) (comments to draft EIS must accompany proposal through agency review process), *cert. denied*, 416 U.S. 961 (1974).

39. *See* Environmental Defense Fund, Inc. v. Hoffman, 566 F.2d 1060, 1069–70 (8th Cir. 1977) (citing Committee for Nuclear Responsibility, Inc. v. Seaborg, 463 F.2d 783, 787 (D.C. Cir. 1971); sections 5.8.5, 5.8.6; *see also* California v. Block, 690 F.2d 753, 773 (9th Cir. 1982) (agency must respond to responsible opposing views with good faith reasoned analysis).

40. California v. Block, 690 F.2d 753, 773 (9th Cir. 1982).

41. Council on Environmental Quality, Forty Most Asked Questions Concerning CEQ's National Environmental Policy Act Regulations, 46 Fed. Reg. 18,026, 18,033–36 (1981).

42. 40 C.F.R. § 1502.7 (1989).

43. Oregon Envtl. Council v. Kunzman, 817 F.2d 484, 496 (9th Cir. 1987) (citing Friends of Endangered Species, Inc. v. Jantzen, 760 F.2d 976 (9th Cir. 1985)).

44. *Id.; see* Druid Hills Civic Ass'n, Inc. v. FHWA, 772 F.2d 700, 711 (11th Cir. 1985) (agency's choice of methodology was not unreasonable), *cert. denied*, 109 S. Ct. 60 (1988); Louisiana Envtl. Soc'y, Inc. v. Dole, 707 F.2d 116, 123 (5th Cir. 1983) (agency's choice of methodology had a reasonable basis, consistently applied, that took into account relevant considerations).

45. *See* D.C. Fed'n of Civic Ass'ns v. Adams, 571 F.2d 1310, 1313 (4th Cir. 1978); *see* section 4.3 (methodology in EAs).

46. 42 U.S.C. § 4332(2)(C) (1988); *see* Swain v. Brinegar, 517 F.2d 766, 777 (7th Cir. 1975); *see also* section 4.4 (delegation in EAs).

47. *See* New England Coalition on Nuclear Pollution v. NRC, 582 F.2d 87, 98 (1st Cir. 1978).

48. *See* Northwest Coalition for Alternatives to Pesticides v. Lyng, 844 F.2d 588, 596 (9th Cir. 1988); Save Our Ecosystems v. Clark, 747 F.2d 1240, 1248 (9th Cir. 1984).

49. *Compare* Greene County Planning Bd. v. FPC, 455 F.2d 412, 420 (2d Cir.) (agency "abdicated a significant part of its responsibility by substituting the [EIS of the state agency] for its own"), *cert. denied*, 409 U.S. 849 (1972) *with* Life of the Land v. Brinegar, 485 F.2d 460, 467 (9th Cir. 1973) ("We find nothing . . . in either the wording of NEPA or the case law, which indicates that, as a matter of law, a firm with a financial interest in the project may not assist with the drafting of the EIS"), *cert. denied*, 416 U.S. 961 (1974). *See* Life of the Land v. Brinegar, 414 U.S. 1052, 1053 (1973) (Douglas, J., dissenting from vacation of stay and injunction) ("It seems to me a total frustration of the entire purpose of NEPA to entrust evaluation of the environmental factors to a firm with a multimillion dollar stake in the approval of this project").

50. 40 C.F.R. § 1506.5(a) (1989); *see* City of Des Plaines v. Metropolitan Sanitary Dist., 552 F.2d 736, 738 (7th Cir. 1977).

51. 40 C.F.R. § 1506.5(c) (1989).

52. *Id.* § 1506.5(a).

53. 42 U.S.C. § 4332(2)(D) (1988).

54. *Id.*

55. Conservation Soc'y of Southern Vermont, Inc. v. Secretary of Transp., 508 F.2d 927, 931–32 (2d Cir. 1974), *vacated*, 423 U.S. 809 (1975). *Cf.* Essex County Preservation Ass'n v. Campbell, 536 F.2d 956, 959 (1st Cir. 1976) (applying 1975 amendment); Ecology Center of La., Inc. v. Coleman, 515 F.2d 860, 871 (5th Cir.

1975) (initial responsibility for preparing FHWA EIS may be delegated to the states); Iowa Citizens for Envtl. Quality, Inc. v. Volpe, 487 F.2d 849, 853–54 (8th Cir. 1973) (same).

56. *See* Sierra Club v. Corps of Eng'rs, 701 F.2d 1011, 1037–38 (2d Cir. 1983).

57. 42 U.S.C. § 5304(g) (1988); *see* Brandon v. Pierce, 725 F.2d 555, 560 (10th Cir. 1984); National Center for Preservation Law v. Landrieu, 496 F. Supp. 716, 731 (D.S.C.), *aff'd*, 635 F.2d 324 (4th Cir. 1980).

58. *See* Brandon v. Pierce, 725 F.2d 555, 560 (10th Cir. 1984); Atlantic Terminal Urban Renewal Area Coalition v. New York City Dep't of Envtl. Protection, 705 F. Supp. 988, 995 (S.D.N.Y. 1989); Crosby v. Young, 512 F. Supp. 1363, 1383 (E.D. Mich. 1981); Colony Federal Savings & Loan Ass'n v. Harris, 482 F. Supp. 296, 304 (W.D. Pa. 1980).

59. 40 C.F.R. § 1506.5(c) (1989); *see* Sierra Club v. Lynn, 502 F.2d 43, 59 (5th Cir. 1974), *cert. denied*, 421 U.S. 994 (1975).

60. *See* Natural Resources Defense Council, Inc. v. Callaway, 524 F.2d 79, 86–87 (2d Cir. 1975); Sierra Club v. Marsh, 714 F. Supp. 539, 555–59 (D. Me. 1989); 40 C.F.R. § 1506.5(c) (1989).

61. Sierra Club v. Marsh, 714 F. Supp. 539, 552 (D. Me. 1989).

62. 40 C.F.R. § 1506.5(c) (1989); Council on Environmental Quality, Forty Most Asked Questions Concerning CEQ's National Environmental Policy Act Regulations, 46 Fed. Reg. 18,026, 18,031 (1981). *Cf.* Brandon v. Pierce, 725 F.2d 555, 563 (10th Cir. 1984) (when project consultant prepares EA or EIS, agency must "exercise considerable caution" in making decision; project consultant in case involving EA appeared to have an interest in the project).

63. Council on Environmental Quality, Forty Most Asked Questions Concerning CEQ's National Environmental Policy Act Regulations, 46 Fed. Reg. 18,026, 18,031 (1981).

64. *See* Sierra Club v. Marsh, 714 F. Supp. 539, 583 (D. Me. 1989); *see* section 5.8.7.

65. 42 U.S.C. § 4332(2)(C) (1988).

66. Kleppe v. Sierra Club, 427 U.S. 390, 401 (1976).

67. Weinberger v. Catholic Action of Hawaii/Peace Educ. Project, 454 U.S. 139, 146 (1981); Kleppe v. Sierra Club, 427 U.S. 390, 404 (1976).

68. *See* Park County Resource Council, Inc. v. United States Dep't of Agric., 817 F.2d 609, 622 (10th Cir. 1987); *see also* Committee for Auto Responsibility v. Solomon, 603 F.2d 992, 1003 (D.C. Cir. 1979) (when agency did not alter status quo, it did not make a proposal), *cert. denied*, 445 U.S. 915 (1980); section 3.6.1 (changes in the physical environment).

69. *See* 42 U.S.C. § 4332(2)(C)(v) (1988). *See, e.g.*, Conner v. Burford, 848 F.2d 1441, 1451 (9th Cir. 1988) (app. pending); Sierra Club v. Peterson, 717 F.2d 1409, 1414 (D.C. Cir. 1983); California v. Block, 690 F.2d 753, 761 (9th Cir. 1982); Environmental Defense Fund, Inc. v. Andrus, 596 F.2d 848, 852 (9th Cir. 1979); Sierra Club v. Hathaway, 579 F.2d 1162, 1168 (9th Cir. 1978). *Cf.* City of Oak Creek v. Milwaukee Metropolitan Sewerage Dist., 576 F. Supp. 482, 490 (E.D. Wis. 1983) (landfill, not land acquisition, caused major environmental impact; agency could proceed with land acquisition because, if proposed action was rejected, expenditures on land would not be wasted).

70. *See* Colorado River Water Conservation Dist. v. United States, 593 F.2d 907, 910 (10th Cir. 1977); Council on Environmental Quality, Forty Most Asked Questions Concerning CEQ's National Environmental Policy Act Regulations, 46 Fed. Reg. 18,026, 18,029 (1981).

71. Kleppe v. Sierra Club, 427 U.S. 390, 406 n.15 (1976); *see also* section 6.4.1 (ripeness).

72. Kleppe v. Sierra Club, 427 U.S. 390, 406 n.15 (1976); *see also* Save the Yaak Comm. v. Block, 840 F.2d 714, 718 (9th Cir. 1988) (awarding construction contracts prior to preparation of EAs demonstrated agency's noncompliance with NEPA's timing requirements).

73. 40 C.F.R. §§ 1502.5, 1508.23 (1989).

74. Aberdeen & Rockfish Ry. v. Students Challenging Regulatory Agency Procedures, 422 U.S. 289, 320 (1975); City of Willcox v. FPC, 567 F.2d 394, 415 (D.C. Cir. 1977), *cert. denied*, 434 U.S. 1012 (1978); Cady v. Morton, 527 F.2d 786, 794 (9th Cir. 1975).

75. *See* section 2.8.

76. 40 C.F.R. § 1501.7 (1989).

77. *See* Council on Environmental Quality, Forty Most Asked Questions Concerning CEQ's National Environmental Policy Act Regulations, 46 Fed. Reg. 18,026, 18,030 (1981) (scoping may begin before notice of intent if public participation is permitted; pre-notice scoping generally cannot substitute for post-notice scoping).

78. 40 C.F.R. § 1501.7 (1989).

79. *Id.* § 1501.7(a); *see* Isle of Hope Historical Ass'n, Inc. v. Corps of Eng'rs, 646 F.2d 215, 220 (5th Cir. 1981) (agency preparing "EIS is expected to *cooperate* and *consult* with local government" (emphasis original)); Ventura County v. Gulf Oil Corp., 601 F.2d 1080, 1086 (9th Cir. 1979) (NEPA mandates "extensive federal consideration and federal-local cooperation concerning the local, environmental impact of federal action"), *aff'd*, 445 U.S. 947 (1980).

80. 40 C.F.R. § 1501.7(b) (1989).

81. Legislative EISs are an exception to this general rule. *See* section 5.15.

82. 40 C.F.R. § 1502.9 (1989).

83. *Id.* §§ 1506.9, 1506.10; *see* section 2.9.

84. 40 C.F.R. § 1504.1(b) (1989); *see* section 2.10.

85. 40 C.F.R. § 1502.19 (1989); *see* National Wildlife Fed'n v. Adams, 629 F.2d 587, 593 (9th Cir. 1980) (draft EIS was sufficiently adequate to allow comment by all interested parties).

86. 40 C.F.R. § 1502.19(d) (1989).

87. *See* Massachusetts v. Watt, 716 F.2d 946, 951 (1st Cir. 1983).

88. 40 C.F.R. § 1506.10 (1989).

89. *See* sections 6.8 and 6.10.

90. *See* section 5.8.3.

91. *See* section 2.10.

92. *See* Environmental Defense Fund, Inc. v. Higginson, 655 F.2d 1244, 1247 (D.C. Cir. 1981) (Department of Interior was not prevented from changing its position regarding necessity for preparing comprehensive EIS); Citizens Comm. Against Interstate Route 675 v. Lewis, 542 F. Supp. 496, 572–73 (S.D. Ohio 1982)

(agency decision maker disapproved final EIS; two years later, decision was reconsidered by different decision maker and EIS was approved; court found that reconsideration was not prohibited).

93. *See* Essex County Preservation Ass'n v. Campbell, 536 F.2d 956, 961 (1st Cir. 1976).

94. 40 C.F.R. § 1502.9(c) (1989).

95. *See* Hickory Neighborhood Defense League v. Burnley, 703 F. Supp. 1208, 1227 (W.D.N.C. 1988) (final EIS was prepared more than ten years earlier), *aff'd in part and vacated in part*, 893 F.2d 58, 63 (4th Cir. 1990).

96. Council on Environmental Quality, Forty Most Asked Questions Concerning CEQ's National Environmental Policy Act Regulations, 46 Fed. Reg. 18,026, 18,036 (1981).

97. Warm Springs Dam Task Force v. Gribble, 621 F.2d 1017, 1023 (9th Cir. 1980) (citing 42 U.S.C. §§ 4332(2)(A), (B) (1988)).

98. Marsh v. Oregon Natural Resources Council, 109 S. Ct. 1851, 1860 (1989).

99. *Id.* at 1861 n.23.

100. Sierra Club v. Froehlke, 816 F.2d 205, 210 (5th Cir. 1987) (emphasis original) (citing Wisconsin v. Weinberger, 745 F.2d 412, 420 (7th Cir. 1984)); *see also* Louisiana Wildlife Fed'n, Inc. v. York, 761 F.2d 1044, 1050–51 (5th Cir. 1985) (decided under Corps of Engineers' regulations requiring supplemental EIS for change with significant environmental effect as well as under corps' regulations); Township of Springfield v. Lewis, 702 F.2d 426, 437–38 (3d Cir. 1983) (change in plans for highway was not substantial enough to require supplemental EIS); Piedmont Heights Civic Club, Inc. v. Moreland, 637 F.2d 430, 442–43 (5th Cir. 1981) (changes would not significantly affect project).

101. Sierra Club v. Block, 614 F. Supp. 488, 491 (D.D.C. 1985).

102. National Indian Youth Council v. Watt, 664 F.2d 220, 225 (10th Cir. 1981).

103. Animal Defense Council v. Hodel, 840 F.2d 1432, 1439 (9th Cir. 1988), *modified*, 867 F.2d 1244 (9th Cir. 1989).

104. National Wildlife Fed'n v. Marsh, 721 F.2d 767, 784 (11th Cir. 1983); *see id.* at 784 n.22 ("[i]f there were no significant impact from the plan it would not qualify as a Mitigation Plan at all").

105. *See* Concerned Citizens on I-190 v. Secretary of Transp., 641 F.2d 1, 6 (1st Cir. 1981).

106. *See* Town of Orangetown v. Ruckelshaus, 740 F.2d 185, 190 (2d Cir. 1984) (possible revision of estimated future inflow capacity was not a significant change); Friends of the River v. FERC, 720 F.2d 93, 109 (D.C. Cir. 1983) (supplemental EIS not required for new forecasts); California v. Watt, 683 F.2d 1253, 1268 (9th Cir. 1982) (supplemental EIS not required for increased estimates of oil reserve involved in lease sale), *rev'd on other grounds sub nom.* Secretary of Interior v. California, 464 U.S. 312 (1984).

107. *See* Massachusetts v. Watt, 716 F.2d 946, 948 (1st Cir. 1983) (information that estimate of oil to be recovered was 1/31 amount considered in final EIS required preparation of supplemental EIS).

108. Marsh v. Oregon Natural Resources Council, 109 S. Ct. 1851, 1859 (1989); *see also* Cuomo v. NRC, 772 F.2d 972, 975 (D.C. Cir. 1985) (applying rule of reason to find that agency was not required to prepare supplemental EIS to consider

remote and highly speculative environmental consequences of its action); Deukmejian v. NRC, 751 F.2d 1287, 1300–01 (D.C. Cir. 1984) (same), *vacated in nonpertinent part*, 760 F.2d 1321 (9th Cir. 1985), *cert. denied*, 479 U.S. 923 (1986).

109. Marsh v. Oregon Natural Resources Defense Council, 109 S. Ct. 1851, 1865 (1989).

110. *Id.* at 1861; *see* Cuomo v. NRC, 772 F.2d 972, 975 (D.C. Cir. 1985) (agency "adequately supported its conclusion with a statement of reasons and relevant data").

111. Marsh v. Oregon Natural Resources Defense Council, 109 S. Ct. 1851, 1861, 1865 (1989); *see* Hickory Neighborhood Defense League v. Skinner, 893 F.2d 58, 63 (4th Cir. 1990).

112. *See* Wisconsin v. Weinberger, 745 F.2d 412, 424 (7th Cir. 1984) (evidence presented by plaintiffs "is generally unimpressive and cannot be deemed sufficiently significant"); Stop H-3 Ass'n v. Dole, 740 F.2d 1442, 1465 (9th Cir. 1984) (plaintiffs did not show that census data was significant in terms of environmental effects), *cert. denied*, 471 U.S. 1108 (1985).

113. Marsh v. Oregon Natural Resources Council, 109 S. Ct. 1851, 1865 (1989).

114. *Id.* at 1861.

115. *See* Portland Audubon Soc'y v. Lujan, 712 F. Supp. 1456, 1485 (D. Or.) (agency was required to prepare supplemental EIS "in light of the new, significant, and probably accurate information"; preparation of supplemental EIS was not mandated on other grounds), *aff'd and rev'd in nonpertinent part*, 884 F.2d 1233 (9th Cir. 1989).

116. *See* Natural Resources Defense Council, Inc. v. City of New York, 672 F.2d 292, 298 (2d Cir. 1981) (declaration of eligibility of theater for National Register did not require preparation of supplemental EIS; theater was discussed in EIS), *cert. dismissed*, 456 U.S. 920 (1982); National Indian Youth Council v. Watt, 664 F.2d 220, 226 (10th Cir. 1981) (information confirming number and significance of sites discussed in final EIS was not new information); Environmental Defense Fund, Inc. v. Andrus, 619 F.2d 1368, 1382 (10th Cir. 1980) (plaintiffs provided no evidence of significant environmental effects not identified or described in final EIS); *see also* Louisiana Envtl. Soc'y, Inc. v. Dole, 707 F.2d 116, 124 (5th Cir. 1983) (information was not new nor did it significantly affect environment).

117. *See* Wisconsin v. Weinberger, 745 F.2d 412, 420 (7th Cir. 1984).

118. *See* Texas Comm. on Natural Resources v. Marsh, 736 F.2d 262, 266 (5th Cir. 1984); *see* section 5.11 (judicial review of EISs).

119. *See* Natural Resources Defense Council, Inc. v. Callaway, 524 F.2d 79, 91–92 (2d Cir. 1975).

120. *See* section 2.10.1 (discussing section 309 of Clean Air Act).

121. *See* Oregon Natural Resources Council v. Lyng, 882 F.2d 1417, 1424 (9th Cir. 1989); Sierra Club v. United States Dep't of Transp., 753 F.2d 120, 126–29 (D.C. Cir. 1985); Michigan Dep't of Transp. v. ICC, 698 F.2d 277, 280 (6th Cir. 1983).

122. 40 C.F.R. § 1505.2 (1989); *see* section 2.4 (discussing record of decision).

123. Council on Environmental Quality, Forty Most Asked Questions Concerning CEQ's National Environmental Policy Act Regulations, 46 Fed. Reg. 18,026, 18,028 (1981); *see* section 1.3.2 (discussing section 101 of NEPA).

124. 40 C.F.R. s. 1505.2 (1989).

125. *See* Council on Environmental Quality, Forty Most Asked Questions Concerning CEQ's National Environmental Policy Act Regulations, 46 Fed. Reg. 18,026, 18,036 (1981).

126. *Id.* at 18,037.

127. *See* section 6.12.6.

128. *See* Robertson v. Methow Valley Citizens Council, 109 S. Ct. 1835, 1847 (1989).

129. S. 1089 § 1(b)(2), 101st Cong., 1st Sess. (1989).

130. Half Moon Bay Fishermans' Marketing Ass'n v. Carlucci, 857 F.2d 505, 508 (9th Cir. 1988) (quoting California v. Block, 690 F.2d 753, 770–71 (9th Cir. 1982)).

131. *See* Grazing Fields Farm v. Goldschmidt, 626 F.2d 1068, 1073 (1st Cir. 1980).

132. 42 U.S.C. § 4332(2)(C) (1988) (copies of EIS and agency comments shall be made available to public); *see* Jicarilla Apache Tribe of Indians v. Morton, 471 F.2d 1275, 1284 (9th Cir. 1973) ("[w]e can find no language in NEPA which would indicate that hearings are a requirement in all instances").

133. 40 C.F.R. § 1506.6(a) (1989).

134. *Id.* § 1506.6(b); *see* I-291 Why? Ass'n v. Burns, 517 F.2d 1077, 1081 (2d Cir. 1975) (agency must circulate environmental analyses for review and comment).

135. *See* S. 1089 § 1(b)(6), 101st Cong., 1st Sess. (1989); H.R. 1113 § 1(b)(2), 101st Cong., 1st Sess. (1989); H.R. 3847 § 501(b)(2), 101st Cong., 2d Sess. (1990). *Cf.* 40 C.F.R. § 1503.1(a)(4) (1989).

136. *See* Jicarilla Apache Tribe of Indians v. Morton, 471 F.2d 1275, 1286 (9th Cir. 1973) (no express requirement under NEPA for administrative hearings).

137. 40 C.F.R. § 1506.6(c) (1989).

138. *Id.* § 1506.6(d).

139. *Id.* §§ 1506.6(e), (f); *see* City of West Chicago v. NRC, 547 F. Supp. 740, 746 (N.D. Ill. 1982) (regulations mean that agency must disclose comments of other agencies to public).

140. *See* Environmental Defense Fund, Inc. v. Hoffman, 566 F.2d 1060, 1069–70 (8th Cir. 1977); Committee for Nuclear Responsibility, Inc. v. Seaborg, 463 F.2d 783, 787 (D.C. Cir. 1971); sections 5.8.5, 5.8.6; *see also* California v. Block, 690 F.2d 753, 773 (9th Cir. 1982) (agency must respond to responsible opposing views with "good faith reasoned analysis") (quoting Silva v. Lynn, 482 F.2d 1282, 1285 (1st Cir. 1973)).

141. Union of Concerned Scientists v. AEC, 499 F.2d 1069, 1083 (D.C. Cir. 1974).

142. Committee for Nuclear Responsibility, Inc. v. Seaborg, 463 F.2d 783, 787 (D.C. Cir. 1971).

143. *Id.*

144. *See* Natural Resources Defense Council, Inc. v. Morton, 458 F.2d 827, 834 (D.C. Cir. 1972).

145. Council on Environmental Quality, Forty Most Asked Questions Concerning CEQ's National Environmental Policy Act Regulations, 46 Fed. Reg. 18,026, 18,033 (1981).

146. *See* Township of Springfield v. Lewis, 702 F.2d 426, 439 (3d Cir. 1983); Environmental Defense Fund, Inc. v. Hoffman, 566 F.2d 1060, 1072 n.19 (8th Cir. 1977).

147. Council on Environmental Quality, Forty Most Asked Questions Concerning CEQ's National Environmental Policy Act Regulations, 46 Fed. Reg. 18,026, 18,035 (1981); *see also* Half Moon Bay Fishermans' Marketing Ass'n v. Carlucci, 857 F.2d 505, 508–09 (9th Cir. 1988) (agency's statement in draft EIS that site was selected, when subsequently different site was chosen, was not fatal); Lake Hefner Open Space Alliance v. Dole, 871 F.2d 943, 947 (10th Cir. 1989) (inclusion of new alternatives in final EIS was not fatal). *Cf.* Council on Environmental Quality, Forty Most Asked Questions Concerning CEQ's National Environmental Policy Act Regulations, 46 Fed. Reg. 18,026, 18,035 (1981) (agency must discuss in supplemental EIS, reasonable alternative that could not reasonably have been raised during the scoping process).

148. *See* Natural Resources Defense Council, Inc. v. Hughes, 437 F. Supp. 981, 990 (D.D.C. 1977), *modified*, 454 F. Supp. 148 (D.D.C. 1978).

149. 40 C.F.R. §§ 1503.2, 1508.5 (1989); Council on Environmental Quality, Forty Most Asked Questions Concerning CEQ's National Environmental Policy Act Regulations, 46 Fed. Reg. 18,026, 18,030 (1981).

150. *See* Sierra Club v. Corps of Eng'rs, 772 F.2d 1043, 1054 (2d Cir. 1985); Hickory Neighborhood Defense League v. Burnley, 703 F. Supp. 1208, 1225 (W.D.N.C. 1988), *aff'd in part and vacated in part*, 893 F.2d 58 (4th Cir. 1990); National Wildlife Fed'n v. Andrus, 440 F. Supp. 1245, 1252–55 (D.D.C. 1977); *see also* Massachusetts v. Andrus, 594 F.2d 872, 886 (1st Cir. 1979) (comments to final EIS).

151. Council on Environmental Quality, Forty Most Asked Questions Concerning CEQ's National Environmental Policy Act Regulations, 46 Fed. Reg. 18,026, 18,030 (1981). *Compare* Silva v. Lynn, 482 F.2d 1282, 1285 (1st Cir. 1973) (comments "disclos[ing] new or conflicting data or opinions that cause concern that the agency may not have fully evaluated the project and its alternatives [must be responded to with] good faith, reasoned analysis") *with* Conservation Law Found'n of New England, Inc. v. Andrus, 623 F.2d 712, 718 (1st Cir. 1979) (agency was not required to respond to commenting agency's comment that did not merit individual response beyond general discussion in EIS).

152. *See* Sierra Club v. Corps of Eng'rs, 701 F.2d 1011, 1030 (2d Cir. 1983) (agency comments criticized flaws in draft EIS).

153. Piedmont Heights Civic Club, Inc. v. Moreland, 637 F.2d 430, 436 n.9 (5th Cir. 1981). *See generally* Blumm & Brown, *Pluralism and the Environment; The Role of Comment Agencies in NEPA Litigation*, 14 Harv. Envtl. L. Rev. no. 2 (1990).

154. *See, e.g.*, Township of Huntington v. Marsh, 859 F.2d 1134, 1143 (2d Cir. 1988) (noting agency comments critical of EIS); Sierra Club v. Corps of Eng'rs, 701 F.2d 1011, 1030 (2d Cir. 1983) ("court may properly be skeptical as to whether an EIS's conclusions have a substantial basis in fact if the responsible agency has apparently ignored the conflicting views of other agencies having pertinent expertise"); Environmental Defense Fund, Inc. v. Froehlke, 473 F.2d 346, 351 & n.13 (8th Cir. 1972) (listing agencies critical of proposed action); Mississippi *ex rel.* Moore v. Marsh, 710 F. Supp. 1488, 1497–98 (S.D. Miss. 1989) (agency's preparation of EA was opposed by commenting agencies). *See* section 4.7 (discussing public and agency participation in EA process).

155. *See* Sierra Club v. United States Dep't of Transp., 664 F. Supp. 1324, 1338 (N.D. Cal. 1987); *see also* Union of Concerned Scientists v. AEC, 499 F.2d 1069,

1083 (D.C. Cir. 1974) (agency need not prepare minority report containing opposing comments of some of its personnel); No Oilport! v. Carter, 520 F. Supp. 334, 358–59 (W.D. Wash. 1981) (fact that government employees felt EIS should be more detailed is of very little significance).

156. County of Del Norte v. United States, 732 F.2d 1462, 1465–66 (9th Cir. 1984), *cert. denied*, 469 U.S. 1189 (1985).

157. Northwest Coalition for Alternatives to Pesticides v. Lyng, 844 F.2d 588, 595 (9th Cir. 1988); County of Josephine v. Watt, 539 F. Supp. 696, 705–06 (N.D. Cal. 1982).

158. Sierra Club v. Marsh, 714 F. Supp. 539, 583 (D. Me. 1989).

159. 40 C.F.R. § 1500.3 (1989).

160. Northwest Coalition for Alternatives to Pesticides v. Lyng, 844 F.2d 588, 595–96 (9th Cir. 1988); County of Del Norte v. United States, 732 F.2d 1462, 1467 (9th Cir. 1984), *cert. denied*, 469 U.S. 1189 (1985); County of Josephine v. Watt, 539 F. Supp. 696, 705 (N.D. Cal. 1982); *see* 40 C.F.R. § 1500.3 (1989) (trivial violation of regulations does not give rise to independent cause of action; only substantial violation).

161. Named Individual Members of San Antonio Conservation Soc'y v. Texas Highway Dep't, 446 F.2d 1013, 1022, 1024 (5th Cir. 1971), *cert. denied*, 406 U.S. 933 (1972).

162. Kleppe v. Sierra Club, 427 U.S. 390, 412 (1976).

163. Alpine Lakes Protection Soc'y v. Schlapfer, 518 F.2d 1089, 1090 (9th Cir. 1975).

164. 481 F.2d 1079 (D.C. Cir. 1973)

165. 42 U.S.C. § 4332(2)(C)(v) (1988).

166. 481 F.2d at 1090–91.

167. *Id.* at 1090.

168. Minnesota Public Interest Research Group v. Butz, 541 F.2d 1292, 1306 (8th Cir. 1976), *cert. denied*, 430 U.S. 922 (1977); Friends of the Earth v. Coleman, 513 F.2d 295, 299 (9th Cir. 1975).

169. *See* Piedmont Heights Civic Club, Inc. v. Moreland, 637 F.2d 430, 439 (5th Cir. 1981); *see also* Conservation Soc'y of Southern Vt., Inc. v. Secretary of Transp., 531 F.2d 637, 640 (2d Cir. 1976) (highway had local utility only; no irreversible and irretrievable commitment of federal funding for entire highway corridor).

170. Trout Unlimited v. Morton, 509 F.2d 1276, 1285 (9th Cir. 1974). A variation of this test is the "bandwagon" test, which focuses on whether a proposed project will have the effect of causing future actions to proceed by the project's own momentum. *See* Natural Resources Defense Council, Inc. v. Callaway, 524 F.2d 79, 89 & n.9 (2d Cir. 1975).

171. *Trout Unlimited*, 509 F.2d at 1284–85.

172. *Id.* at 1279 n.2, 1285.

173. Cady v. Morton, 527 F.2d 786, 795 (9th Cir. 1975).

174. Thomas v. Peterson, 753 F.2d 754, 759 (9th Cir. 1985).

175. *Id.*

176. *See* Piedmont Heights Civic Club, Inc. v. Moreland, 637 F.2d 430, 440 (5th Cir. 1981); *see also* Lange v. Brinegar, 625 F.2d 812, 815 (9th Cir. 1980) (highway segment had independent utility); Natural Resources Defense Council, Inc. v.

NRC, 539 F.2d 824, 844 (2d Cir. 1976) (interim activity had no independent utility), *vacated*, 434 U.S. 1030 (1978).

177. Indian Lookout Alliance v. Volpe, 484 F.2d 11, 19 (8th Cir. 1973).

178. Save Our Sycamore v. Metropolitan Atlanta Rapid Transit Auth., 576 F.2d 573, 575 (5th Cir. 1978); Daly v. Volpe, 514 F.2d 1106, 1110 (9th Cir. 1975). *Cf.* Coalition on Sensible Transp., Inc. v. Dole, 826 F.2d 60, 69 (D.C. Cir. 1987) ("'logical terminus' criterion is unusually elusive").

179. *Daly*, 514 F.2d at 1109 (citing Federal Highway Administration criteria); Patterson v. Exon, 415 F. Supp. 1276, 1284 (D. Neb. 1976).

180. *Piedmont Heights*, 637 F.2d at 440–41; *see also* Sierra Club v. Froehlke, 534 F.2d 1289, 1299 (8th Cir. 1976) (reservoirs would operate independently of each other); Swain v. Brinegar, 542 F.2d 364, 369 (7th Cir. 1976) (applying three standards: whether proposed segment had independent utility; whether its construction foreclosed significant alternate routes or locations for an extension from segment; and whether proposed segment was part of larger plan concrete enough to raise high degree of probability that entire plan would be carried out in near future); Thompson v. Fugate, 347 F. Supp. 120, 124 (E.D. Va. 1972) (city's beltway cannot be segmented for NEPA purposes).

181. *See* Coalition on Sensible Transp., Inc. v. Dole, 826 F.2d 60 (D.C. Cir. 1987).

182. *See* Fritiofson v. Alexander, 772 F.2d 1225, 1242 (5th Cir. 1985) (comparing connected actions test of CEQ regulations and independent utility test); Friends of the Earth v. Coleman, 513 F.2d 295, 299 n.4 (9th Cir. 1975) (comparing irrational or unwise test and irretrievable commitment test).

183. *See* Note, *Program Environmental Impact Statements: Review and Remedies*, 75 Mich. L. Rev. 107, 113–15 (1976) (arguing that the same fact situation could fail the irreversible commitment test but pass the independent utility test).

184. *See* Taxpayers Watchdog, Inc. v. Stanley, 819 F.2d 294, 299–300 (D.C. Cir. 1987); Sierra Club v. Callaway, 499 F.2d 982, 987 (5th Cir. 1974).

185. *See* Minnesota Public Interest Research Group v. Butz, 541 F.2d 1292, 1306 (8th Cir. 1976) (applying independent utility test and irretrievable commitment test), *cert. denied*, 430 U.S. 922 (1977).

186. *See* Conner v. Burford, 605 F. Supp. 107, 109 (D. Mont. 1985) (piecemealing could result in "significant and irreversible impact"), *aff'd and rev'd in nonpertinent part*, 848 F.2d 1441 (9th Cir. 1988) (app. pending).

187. *See* Thomas v. Peterson, 753 F.2d 754, 758–60 (9th Cir. 1985) (applying CEQ regulations and Ninth Circuit precedent).

188. *See* Hudson River Sloop Clearwater, Inc. v. Department of Navy, 836 F.2d 760, 764 (2d Cir. 1988).

189. Macht v. Skinner, 715 F. Supp. 1131, 1135 (D.D.C. 1989).

190. 40 C.F.R. §§ 1501.7, 1508.25 (1989).

191. *Id.* § 1508.25(a).

192. *Id.*

193. Save the Yaak Comm. v. Block, 840 F.2d 714, 719–20 (9th Cir. 1988); Thomas v. Peterson, 753 F.2d 754, 758–59 (9th Cir. 1985); *see also* Township of Huntington v. Marsh, 859 F.2d 1134, 1142 (2d Cir. 1988) ("simply untenable to view site designation as distinct from issuing permits to use the [ocean disposal] site").

194. *Save the Yaak Comm.*, 840 F.2d at 720; *see* Big Hole Ranchers Ass'n, Inc. v. United States Forest Serv., 686 F. Supp. 256, 263 (D. Mont. 1988).

195. Thomas v. Peterson, 753 F.2d 754, 758–59 (9th Cir. 1985).

196. Neighbors Organized to Insure a Sound Env't, Inc. v. Engen, 665 F. Supp. 537, 544–45 (M.D. Tenn. 1987), *vacated*, 878 F.2d 174 (6th Cir. 1989).

197. Hudson River Sloop Clearwater, Inc. v. Department of Navy, 836 F.2d 760, 764 (2d Cir. 1988).

198. Town of Huntington v. Marsh, 859 F.2d 1134, 1142 (2d Cir. 1988).

199. 40 C.F.R. § 1508.25(a)(2) (1989).

200. 427 U.S. 390 (1976).

201. *Id.* at 397–98.

202. *Id.*

203. *Id.* at 399–400.

204. *Id.* at 412.

205. *Id.* at 400–01.

206. *Id.* at 410 & n.20. *Cf.* Foundation on Economic Trends v. Lyng, 817 F.2d 882, 884 (D.C. Cir. 1987) (activities were not sufficiently systematic and connected to require programmatic EIS).

207. 427 U.S. 390, 406 (1976).

208. *Id.* at 410–12.

209. *See* Council on Environmental Quality, Memorandum to Heads of Agencies on "Kleppe v. Sierra Club" and "Flint Ridge v. Scenic Rivers," 42 Fed. Reg. 61,069, 61,070 (1977); *see also* Manatee County v. Gorsuch, 554 F. Supp. 778, 793 (M.D. Fla. 1982) (rejecting Corps of Engineers' argument that ocean dumping projects were not interdependent in light of cumulative or synergistic effect of material being dumped at same place).

210. 40 C.F.R. § 1508.25(a)(2) (1989).

211. *See* Citizens for Responsible Area Growth v. Adams, 477 F. Supp. 994, 1002 (D.N.H. 1979) (projects for different areas of complex were part of same action for NEPA purposes), *vacated*, 680 F.2d 835 (1st Cir. 1982).

212. *See* Fritiofson v. Alexander, 772 F.2d 1225, 1249 (5th Cir. 1985); Committee for Auto Responsibility v. Solomon, 603 F.2d 992, 1001 n.37 (D.C. Cir. 1979), *cert. denied*, 445 U.S. 915 (1980); *see also* American Public Transit Ass'n v. Goldschmidt, 485 F. Supp. 811, 833–34 (D.D.C. 1980) (regulations concerning access of handicapped persons to federally assisted mass transit program represent national program as defined by *Kleppe*).

213. *See* Sierra Club v. Hodel, 544 F.2d 1036, 1040–41 (9th Cir. 1976) (no regional plan for supply of hydroelectric power by Bonneville Power Administration exists); Peshlakai v. Duncan, 476 F. Supp. 1247, 1258 (D.D.C. 1979) (no comprehensive plan exists for uranium mining and milling activities in region).

214. *See* Izaak Walton League of Am. v. Marsh, 655 F.2d 346, 374–75 (D.C. Cir.) (no proposal for deep channel), *cert. denied*, 454 U.S. 1092 (1981); Environmental Defense Fund v. Marsh, 651 F.2d 983, 999 (5th Cir. 1981) (one action was proposed; other action was still being studied and designed); South La. Envt'l Council, Inc. v. Sand, 629 F.2d 1005, 1015 (5th Cir. 1980) (levee extension would have cumulative environmental effect as well as direct and significant impact on navigation channel, but does not require consideration because extension was

only one of several flood protection schemes under consideration); Atlanta Coalition on Transp. Crisis, Inc. v. Atlanta Regional Comm'n, 599 F.2d 1333, 1349 (5th Cir. 1979) (many individual transportation projects were not proposed); Watershed Assocs. Rescue v. Alexander, 586 F. Supp. 978, 992 (D. Neb. 1982) (levee system was not a proposal); Hart & Miller Islands Area Envtl. Group, Inc. v. Corps of Eng'rs, 505 F. Supp. 732, 754 (D. Md. 1980) (expansion of proposed dike is contemplated but not proposed). *But see* Natural Resources Defense Council, Inc. v. Callaway, 524 F.2d 79, 89 (2d Cir. 1975) (actions must be considered in EIS because, although they are not approved, they are beyond speculation stage).

215. *See* Thomas v. Peterson, 753 F.2d 754, 759 (9th Cir. 1985).

216. *See* City of Rochester v. United States Postal Serv., 541 F.2d 967, 972 (2d Cir. 1976) (construction of new postal facility and abandonment of old facility are cumulatively significant actions).

217. *See* Manatee County v. Gorsuch, 554 F. Supp. 778, 793 (M.D. Fla. 1982) (repetitive dumping of dredged material on ocean dump site); Sierra Club v. Bergland, 451 F. Supp. 120, 129–30 (N.D. Miss. 1978) (repetitive channelization of watershed).

218. 40 C.F.R. § 1508.25(a)(3) (1989).

219. *Id.*

220. *See, e.g.*, Natural Resources Defense Council, Inc. v. Callaway, 524 F.2d 79, 89 (2d Cir. 1975) (similarity of dredge dumping operation to others using same ocean dump was one factor requiring cumulative environmental effects of actions to be considered together); National Wildlife Fed'n v. United States Forest Serv., 592 F. Supp. 931, 942 (D. Or. 1984) (federal timber sales and private timber harvesting on adjacent land were actions resulting in similar cumulative threats to fish habitat), *vacated in part and appeal dismissed*, 801 F.2d 360 (9th Cir. 1986).

221. *See* 40 C.F.R. § 1508.25(a)(1) (1989).

222. 42 U.S.C. § 4332(2)(C)(iii) (1988).

223. *Id.* § 4332(2)(E); *see* 40 C.F.R. § 1502.10(e) (1989). This latter requirement must be considered in EAs as well as EISs. *See* section 4.5.

224. *See* Environmental Defense Fund, Inc. v. Corps of Eng'rs, 470 F.2d 289, 296 (8th Cir. 1972), *cert. denied*, 412 U.S. 931 (1973).

225. 40 C.F.R. § 1502.14 (1989).

226. Alaska v. Andrus, 580 F.2d 465, 474 (D.C. Cir.) (quoting Monroe County Conservation Council, Inc. v. Volpe, 472 F.2d 693, 697–98 (2d Cir. 1972), *vacated in nonpertinent part sub nom.* Western Oil & Gas Ass'n v. Alaska, 439 U.S. 922 (1978).

227. *See* Natural Resources Defense Council, Inc. v. Hodel, 865 F.2d 288, 296 (D.C. Cir. 1988).

228. *Id.* at 296 & n.5.

229. S. 1089 § 1(b)(2), 101st Cong., 1st Sess. (1989); *see* H.R. 1113 § 1(b)(1), 101st Cong., 1st Sess. (1989) (adding "reasonable" before "alternatives"); H.R. 3847 § 501(b)(1), 101st Cong., 2d Sess. (1990) (same).

230. S. 1089 § 1(b)(2), 101st Cong., 1st Sess. (1989); *see* H.R. 1113 § 1(b)(1), 101st Cong., 1st Sess. (1989); H.R. 3847 § 501(b)(1), 101st Cong., 2d Sess. (1990).

231. S. 1089 § 1(b)(5), 101st Cong., 1st Sess. (1989); *see* H.R. 1113 § 1(d), 101st Cong., 1st Sess. (1989) (requiring agency to implement mitigation measures and other conditions discussed in EIS and selected by agency as part of its final decision); H.R. 3847 § 501(d), 101st Cong., 2d Sess. (1990) (same).

232. *See* Friends of the River v. FERC, 720 F.2d 93, 120 (D.C. Cir. 1983); Citizens for a Better Henderson v. Hodel, 768 F.2d 1051, 1057 (9th Cir. 1985); Coalition for Canyon Preservation v. Bowers, 632 F.2d 774, 784 (9th Cir. 1980); Fayetteville Area Chamber of Commerce v. Volpe, 515 F.2d 1021, 1027 (4th Cir.), *cert. denied*, 423 U.S. 912 (1975); *see also* Lidstone v. Block, 773 F.2d 1135, 1137 (10th Cir. 1985) (EIS discussed all feasible, reasonable alternatives).

233. Life of the Land v. Brinegar, 485 F.2d 460, 472 (9th Cir. 1973), *cert. denied*, 416 U.S. 961 (1974); Natural Resources Defense Council, Inc. v. Morton, 458 F.2d 827, 834 (D.C. Cir. 1972); *see* Natural Resources Defense Council, Inc. v. Hodel, 865 F.2d 288, 294–95 (D.C. Cir. 1988) (rule of reason applies to range and extent of alternatives); Cummington Preservation Comm. v. FAA, 524 F.2d 241, 244 (1st Cir. 1975) (agency's consideration of alternatives met rule of reason).

234. Natural Resources Defense Council, Inc. v. Morton, 458 F.2d 827, 835 (D.C. Cir. 1972); *see* Natural Resources Defense Council, Inc. v. Hodel, 865 F.2d 288, 296 (D.C. Cir. 1988).

235. *See* Monroe County Conservation Council, Inc. v. Adams, 566 F.2d 419, 425 (2d Cir. 1977), *cert. denied*, 435 U.S. 1006 (1978); Council on Environmental Quality, Forty Most Asked Questions Concerning CEQ's National Environmental Policy Act Regulations, 46 Fed. Reg. 18,026, 18,026–27 (1981).

236. *See* California v. Block, 690 F.2d 753, 767 (9th Cir. 1982); *see also* Seacoast Anti-Pollution League v. NRC, 598 F.2d 1221, 1232 (1st Cir. 1979) (agency is not required to discuss alternative sites ad infinitum); Porter City Chapter of Izaak Walton League of Am., Inc. v. AEC, 533 F.2d 1011, 1017 (7th Cir.) (adequate consideration was given to alternate sites), *cert. denied*, 429 U.S. 945 (1976).

237. Vermont Yankee Nuclear Power Corp. v. Natural Resources Defense Council, Inc., 435 U.S. 519, 551 (1978).

238. Natural Resources Defense Council, Inc. v. Morton, 458 F.2d 827, 837 (D.C. Cir. 1972).

239. Carolina Envtl. Study Group v. United States, 510 F.2d 796, 801 (D.C. Cir. 1975).

240. *See* California v. Block, 690 F.2d 753, 767 (9th Cir. 1982) (citing Life of the Land v. Brinegar, 485 F.2d 460, 472 (9th Cir. 1973), *cert. denied*, 416 U.S. 961 (1974)); Miller v. United States, 654 F.2d 513, 514 (8th Cir. 1981); Farmland Preservation Ass'n v. Goldschmidt, 611 F.2d 233, 240 (8th Cir. 1979); Coalition for Responsible Regional Dev. v. Coleman, 555 F.2d 398, 402 (4th Cir. 1977); Sierra Club v. Lynn, 502 F.2d 43, 62 (5th Cir. 1974), *cert. denied*, 421 U.S. 994 (1975).

241. Natural Resources Defense Council, Inc. v. Morton, 458 F.2d 827, 837–38 (D.C. Cir. 1972).

242. Northern Plains Resource Council v. Lujan, 874 F.2d 661, 666 (9th Cir. 1989); Sierra Club v. Morton, 510 F.2d 813, 825 (5th Cir. 1975); *see* Iowa Citizens for Envtl. Quality, Inc. v. Volpe, 487 F.2d 849, 852–53 (8th Cir. 1973) (discussion of alternative with similar environmental effects as other alternative need not "be as exhaustive as otherwise").

243. Natural Resources Defense Council, Inc. v. SEC, 606 F.2d 1031, 1054 (D.C. Cir. 1979).

244. Natural Resources Defense Council, Inc. v. Morton, 458 F.2d 827, 837 (D.C. Cir. 1972).

245. *See* Maryland Wildlife Fed'n v. Dole, 747 F.2d 229, 242 (4th Cir. 1984).

246. *See* City of Angoon v. Hodel, 803 F.2d 1016, 1021 (9th Cir. 1986) (when "purpose [of action] is to accomplish one thing, it makes no sense to consider the alternative ways by which another thing might be achieved"), *cert. denied,* 484 U.S. 870 (1987).

247. 40 C.F.R. § 1502.14(a) (1989); *see* Jackson County v. Jones, 571 F.2d 1004, 1010 (8th Cir. 1978); Valley Citizens for a Safe Env't v. Aldridge, 695 F. Supp. 605, 611 (D. Mass. 1988), *aff'd,* 886 F.2d 458 (1st Cir. 1989); Ashwood Manor Civic Ass'n v. Dole, 619 F. Supp. 52, 83 (E.D. Pa.), *aff'd,* 779 F.2d 41 (3d Cir. 1985), *cert. denied,* 475 U.S. 1082 (1986); Gloucester County Concerned Citizens v. Goldschmidt, 533 F. Supp. 1222, 1233 (D.N.J. 1982).

248. Natural Resources Defense Council, Inc. v. Morton, 458 F.2d 827, 837 (D.C. Cir. 1972); Council on Environmental Quality, Forty Most Asked Questions Concerning CEQ's National Environmental Policy Act Regulations, 46 Fed. Reg. 18,026, 18,027 (1981). *Cf.* City of Angoon v. Hodel, 803 F.2d 1016, 1021–22 n.2 (9th Cir. 1986) (alternative requiring congressional action "will qualify for inclusion in an EIS only in very rare circumstances"), *cert. denied,* 484 U.S. 870 (1987); County of Suffolk v. Secretary of Interior, 562 F.2d 1368, 1387 (2d Cir. 1977), *cert. denied,* 434 U.S. 1064 (1978).

249. Pacific Legal Found'n v. Clark, 738 F.2d 1449, 1454 (9th Cir. 1984).

250. *See* Kentucky *ex rel.* Beshear v. Alexander, 655 F.2d 714, 719 (6th Cir. 1981); *see also* North Slope Borough v. Andrus, 642 F.2d 589, 603 (D.C. Cir. 1980) (court looked outside EIS to other parts of administrative record to find that extent of primary discussion of alternatives and mitigation measures was adequate); Citizens Comm. Against Interstate Route 675 v. Lewis, 542 F. Supp. 496, 544 (S.D. Ohio 1982) (court looked outside EIS to other parts of administrative record to evaluate degree of discussion potential alternatives deserved in EIS); Nashvillians Against I-440 v. Lewis, 524 F. Supp. 962, 988–89 (M.D. Tenn. 1981) (court looked outside EIS to find that no action alternative was not reasonable).

251. 40 C.F.R. § 1502.14(d) (1989); *see* Bob Marshall Alliance v. Hodel, 852 F.2d 1223, 1228 (9th Cir. 1988) (EA), *cert. denied,* 109 S. Ct. 1340 (1989). *Cf.* Kilroy v. Ruckelshaus, 738 F.2d 1448, 1453–54 (9th Cir. 1984) (agency need not discuss no action alternative when Congress prohibited continuation of status quo which was discharge of sludge through ocean outfalls).

252. Council on Environmental Quality, Forty Most Asked Questions Concerning CEQ's National Environmental Policy Act Regulations, 46 Fed. Reg. 18,026, 18,027 (1981); *see* Kilroy v. Ruckelshaus, 738 F.2d 1448, 1453 (9th Cir. 1984).

253. Council on Environmental Quality, Forty Most Asked Questions Concerning CEQ's National Environmental Policy Act Regulations, 46 Fed. Reg. 18,026, 18,027 (1981).

254. *E.g.,* Druid Hills Civic Ass'n, Inc. v. FHWA, 772 F.2d 700, 713 (11th Cir. 1985) (discussion of no action alternative in draft EIS was two sentences long; although discussion in final EIS was not detailed, court of appeals upheld district

court's conclusion that alternatives were analyzed adequately), *cert. denied,* 109 S. Ct. 60 (1988); Gloucester County Concerned Citizens v. Goldschmidt, 533 F. Supp. 1222, 1223 (D.N.J. 1982) (discussion of no action alternative was adequate). *Cf.* Natural Resources Defense Council v. Hughes, 437 F. Supp. 961, 990 (D.D.C. 1977) (discussion of no action alternative was perfunctory and inadequate).

255. Natural Resources Defense Council, Inc. v. Hodel, 865 F.2d 288, 296 & n.4 (D.C. Cir. 1988); Natural Resources Defense Council, Inc. v. Callaway, 524 F.2d 79, 93 (2d Cir. 1975); Natural Resources Defense Council, Inc. v. Morton, 458 F.2d 827, 836 (D.C. Cir. 1972).

256. *See* Environmental Defense Fund, Inc. v. Froehlke, 473 F.2d 346, 351–52 (8th Cir. 1972); Natural Resources Defense Council, Inc. v. Grant, 355 F. Supp. 280, 289 (E.D.N.C. 1973); *see also* National Indian Youth Council v. Watt, 664 F.2d 220, 226 (10th Cir. 1981) (alternative of delay does not necessarily have to be specifically discussed); South La. Envtl. Council, Inc. v. Sand, 629 F.2d 1005, 1017 (5th Cir. 1980) (alternative of delay was not viable because agency was not required to wait for other agencies to complete studies of area; pendency of study was fully disclosed in EIS). *Cf.* Swinomish Tribal Community v. FERC, 627 F.2d 499, 514 (D.C. Cir. 1980) (alternative of delay was not valid due to circumstances).

257. *See* City of Angoon v. Hodel, 803 F.2d 1016, 1022 (9th Cir. 1986), *cert. denied,* 484 U.S. 870 (1987); *see also* North Carolina v. FPC, 533 F.2d 702, 707 (D.C. Cir. 1976) (plaintiffs' concern was too generalized), *vacated,* 429 U.S. 891 (1976); Upper West Fork River Watershed Assoc. v. Corps of Eng'rs, 414 F. Supp. 908, 920 (N.D.W. Va. 1976) (plaintiff did not support conclusion that alternative was reasonable), *aff'd,* 556 F.2d 576 (4th Cir. 1977), *cert. denied,* 436 U.S. 1010 (1978); *see also* Vermont Yankee Nuclear Power Corp. v. Natural Resources Defense Council, Inc., 435 U.S. 519, 553 (1978) (intervenors to agency action must make participation meaningful); Natural Resources Defense Council, Inc. v. NRC, 606 F.2d 1261, 1270 (D.C. Cir. 1979) (plaintiffs fairly presented alternatives to agency).

258. *See* Roosevelt Campobello International Park Comm'n v. EPA, 684 F.2d 1041, 1047 (1st Cir. 1982); Environmental Defense Fund, Inc. v. Stamm, 430 F. Supp. 664, 667 (N.D. Cal. 1977).

259. Seacoast Anti-Pollution League v. NRC, 598 F.2d 1221, 1231 (1st Cir. 1979); *see* section 6.8 (exhaustion of administrative remedies).

260. 40 C.F.R. § 1502.14 (1989).

261. *See* Natural Resources Defense Council, Inc. v. Grant, 355 F. Supp. 280, 289 (E.D.N.C. 1973).

262. *See* Robinson v. Knebel, 550 F.2d 422, 425–26 (8th Cir. 1977).

263. Alaska v. Andrus, 580 F.2d 465, 476 (D.C. Cir.), *vacated in nonpertinent part sub nom.* Western Oil & Gas Ass'n v. Alaska, 439 U.S. 922 (1978); *see* Natural Resources Defense Council, Inc. v. NRC, 606 F.2d 1261, 1272 (D.C. Cir. 1979) (agency's treatment and rejection of alternative was within range of reasonableness).

264. *See* Cape Henry Bird Club v. Laird, 359 F. Supp. 404, 421–22 (W.D. Va. 1973).

265. *See* Seacoast Anti-Pollution League v. NRC, 598 F.2d 1221, 1230 (1st Cir. 1979).

266. Natural Resources Defense Council, Inc. v. Morton, 458 F.2d 827, 834 (D.C. Cir. 1972).

267. *Id.* at 836; *see* Britt v. Corps of Eng'rs, 769 F.2d 84, 91 (2d Cir. 1985); Friends of the Earth v. Hall, 693 F. Supp. 904, 942–43 (W.D. Wash. 1988); Minnesota Public Interest Research Group v. Adams, 482 F. Supp. 170, 177 (D. Minn. 1979). *Cf.* National Center for Preservation Law v. Landrieu, 496 F. Supp. 716, 735 (D.S.C.) ("discussion of alternatives, although not exhaustive, is highly reasonable and certainly adequate"), *aff'd*, 635 F.2d 324 (4th Cir. 1980).

268. *See* Silva v. Lynn, 482 F.2d 1282, 1287 (1st Cir. 1973); Town of Matthews v. United States Dep't of Transp., 527 F. Supp. 1055, 1058 (W.D.N.C. 1981).

269. Alaska v. Andrus, 580 F.2d 465, 475 (D.C. Cir.) (quoting 40 C.F.R. § 1500.8(4) (superseded)), *vacated in nonpertinent part sub nom.* Western Oil & Gas Ass'n v. Alaska, 439 U.S. 922 (1978); *see* Natural Resources Defense Council, Inc. v. Callaway, 524 F.2d 79, 94 (2d Cir. 1975).

270. *See* Citizens for Mass Transit, Inc. v. Adams, 630 F.2d 309, 316 (5th Cir. 1980).

271. Council on Environmental Quality, Forty Most Asked Questions Concerning CEQ's National Environmental Policy Act Regulations, 46 Fed. Reg. 18,026, 18,028 (1981).

272. 42 U.S.C. § 4332(2)(C)(i) (1988).

273. *Id.* § 4332(2)(C)(ii).

274. *Id.* § 4332(2)(C)(iv).

275. *Id.* § 4332(2)(C)(v); *see* section 3.5 (environmental effects).

276. 40 C.F.R. § 1502.16 (1989).

277. *See* South La. Envtl. Council, Inc. v. Sand, 629 F.2d 1005, 1016 (5th Cir. 1980) (secondary effects).

278. 40 C.F.R. § 1508.14 (1989); *see* section 3.6.2.

279. Environmental Defense Fund v. Marsh, 651 F.2d 983, 997 (5th Cir. 1981); 40 C.F.R. § 1508.8 (1989).

280. *See* Trout Unlimited v. Morton, 509 F.2d 1276, 1283 n.9 (9th Cir. 1974); Sierra Club v. Marsh, 714 F. Supp. 539, 584–85 (D. Me. 1989).

281. 40 C.F.R. § 1508.8(a) (1989).

282. *Id.* § 1508.8(b); *see* Winnebago Tribe of Nebraska v. Ray, 621 F.2d 269, 273 (8th Cir.) (construction of nonfederal portions of agency action was not a secondary effect of agency action), *cert. denied*, 449 U.S. 836 (1980); Pennsylvania Protect Our Water & Envtl. Resources, Inc. v. Appalachian Regional Comm'n, 574 F. Supp. 1203, 1236 (M.D. Pa. 1982) (secondary growth was remote and speculative when only planned development was motel, civic arena, and ski area).

283. Greenspon v. FHWA, 488 F. Supp. 1374, 1381 (D. Md. 1980).

284. *See* City of Davis v. Coleman, 521 F.2d 661, 676 (9th Cir. 1975); *see also* Concerned Citizens on I-190 v. Secretary of Transp., 641 F.2d 1, 5–6 (1st Cir. 1981) (disclosure of projected growth in EIS was adequate; growth was highly speculative).

285. *See* National Helium Corp. v. Morton, 486 F.2d 995, 1003 (10th Cir. 1973), *cert. denied*, 416 U.S. 993 (1974).

286. *See* Coalition for Canyon Preservation v. Bowers, 632 F.2d 774, 783 (9th Cir. 1980).

287. California v. Block, 690 F.2d 753, 764 (9th Cir. 1982).

288. *See* Limerick Ecology Action, Inc. v. NRC, 869 F.2d 719, 739, 747 (3d Cir. 1989) (because of uncertainty of estimating socio-economic consequences more

than a year following a severe nuclear accident, agency was not required to consider such effects in EIS); Save Lake Washington v. Frank, 641 F.2d 1330, 1335 (9th Cir. 1981) (agency was not required to discuss chance of remote major oil spill from reduced passage of ships); Warm Springs Dam Task Force v. Gribble, 621 F.2d 1017, 1026 (9th Cir. 1980) (discussion of total failure of dam following catastrophic earthquake was not required); Trout Unlimited v. Morton, 509 F.2d 1276, 1283–84 (9th Cir. 1974) (agency was not required to discuss improbable, remote and highly speculative consequences and possibilities); Scientists' Inst. for Public Information, Inc. v. AEC, 481 F.2d 1079, 1092 (D.C. Cir. 1973) ("agency need not foresee the unforeseeable"); *see also* Limerick Ecology Action, Inc. v. NRC, 869 F.2d 719, 739 (3d Cir. 1989) (agency may not argue that risk was remote and speculative when agency decision was not based on belief that risk was remote and speculative); Story v. Marsh, 732 F.2d 1375, 1382 (8th Cir. 1984) (EIS need only consider "reasonably expected environmental consequences of the proposed action").

289. *See* Alaska v. Andrus, 580 F.2d 465, 473 (D.C. Cir.), *vacated in nonpertinent part sub nom.* Western Oil & Gas Ass'n v. Alaska, 439 U.S. 922 (1978); Scientists' Inst. for Public Information, Inc. v. AEC, 481 F.2d 1079, 1092 (D.C. Cir. 1973); *see also* California v. Block, 690 F.2d 753, 765 (9th Cir. 1982) (agency is not excused from preparing EIS because forecasting environmental consequences is difficult).

290. Natural Resources Defense Council, Inc. v. NRC, 539 F.2d 824, 841 (2d Cir. 1976), *vacated,* 434 U.S. 1030 (1978); Scientists' Inst. for Public Information, Inc. v. AEC, 481 F.2d 1079, 1089–90 (D.C. Cir. 1973).

291. 40 C.F.R. §§ 1508.7, 1508.25(c) (1989); *see* Natural Resources Defense Council, Inc. v. Callaway, 524 F.2d 79, 87 (2d Cir. 1975); Akers v. Resor, 443 F. Supp. 1355, 1360 (W.D. Tenn. 1978).

292. 40 C.F.R. § 1508.7 (1989); *see* Sierra Club v. Penfold, 664 F. Supp. 1299, 1303 (D. Alaska 1987) (case involving effects of 60 or more placer mines on watershed is "paradigm instance of 'cumulative' or 'synergistic' impacts"), *aff'd,* 857 F.2d 1307, 1321 (9th Cir. 1988).

293. *See* North Slope Borough v. Andrus, 642 F.2d 589, 600 (D.C. Cir. 1980) (effects of energy development actions on Alaska's North Slope).

294. *See* Natural Resources Defense Council, Inc. v. Hodel, 865 F.2d 288, 297 (D.C. Cir. 1988) (considering cumulative effects of simultaneous development on migratory species).

295. *See* Coalition for Canyon Preservation v. Bowers, 632 F.2d 774, 783 (9th Cir. 1980); *see also* Life of the Land v. Brinegar, 485 F.2d 460, 469 (9th Cir. 1973) (increase in city's permanent population from enlargement of airport was speculative), *cert. denied,* 416 U.S. 961 (1974). *Cf.* Natural Resources Defense Council, Inc. v. Callaway, 524 F.2d 79, 87–90 (2d Cir. 1975) (requiring agency to consider proposed projects with cumulative effects).

296. Town of Huntington v. Marsh, 859 F.2d 1134, 1142–43 (2d Cir. 1988).

297. Kleppe v. Sierra Club, 427 U.S. 390, 410 n.21 (1976).

298. Trout Unlimited v. Morton, 509 F.2d 1276, 1283 (9th Cir. 1974).

299. *See* Columbia Basin Land Protection Ass'n v. Schlesinger, 643 F.2d 585, 595 (9th Cir. 1981); South La. Envtl. Council, Inc. v. Sand, 629 F.2d 1005, 1011 (5th Cir. 1980).

300. *See* Columbia Basin Land Protection Ass'n v. Schlesinger, 643 F.2d 585, 595 (9th Cir. 1981); South La. Envtl. Council, Inc. v. Sand, 629 F.2d 1005, 1011 (5th Cir. 1980).

301. Trout Unlimited v. Morton, 509 F.2d 1276, 1283 (9th Cir. 1974); *see* Citizens for a Better Henderson v. Hodel, 768 F.2d 1051, 1058 (9th Cir. 1985) (health hazards were adequately discussed in EIS).

302. Stop H-3 Ass'n v. Dole, 740 F.2d 1442, 1462 (9th Cir. 1984), *cert. denied*, 471 U.S. 1108 (1985).

303. *See* Enos v. Marsh, 769 F.2d 1363, 1373 (9th Cir. 1985) (indirect effects); Concerned Citizens on I-190 v. Secretary of Transp., 641 F.2d 1, 5 (1st Cir. 1981) (indirect effects); Westside Property Owners v. Schlesinger, 597 F.2d 1214, 1217 (9th Cir. 1979) (cumulative effects); Scientists' Inst. for Public Information, Inc. v. AEC, 481 F.2d 1079, 1092 (D.C. Cir. 1973) (effects of new technology); *see also* Sierra Club v. Froehlke, 534 F.2d 1289, 1296 (8th Cir. 1976) (brief discussion was adequate when only limited knowledge of environmental effects was available).

304. County of Suffolk v. Secretary of Interior, 562 F.2d 1368, 1384 (2d Cir. 1977), *cert. denied*, 434 U.S. 1064 (1978); *see* Valley Citizens for a Safe Env't v. Aldridge, 886 F.2d 458, 460 (1st Cir. 1989).

305. 40 C.F.R. § 1502.22 (1985) (superseded).

306. *Id.*

307. *Id.* § 1502.22(a).

308. *Id.* § 1502.22(b).

309. *Id.*

310. *See* Yost, *Don't Gut Worst Case Analysis*, 13 Envtl. L. Rep. (Envt. L. Inst.) 10,394, 10,394 (1983).

311. *See* Council on Environmental Quality, National Environmental Policy Act Regulations; Incomplete or Unavailable Information, 51 Fed. Reg. 15,618 (1986).

312. 40 C.F.R. § 1502.22(a) (1989).

313. *Id.; see* Save the Niobrara River Ass'n, Inc. v. Andrus, 483 F. Supp. 844, 853 (D. Neb. 1979). *Cf.* Izaak Walton League of Am. v. Marsh, 655 F.2d 346, 377 (D.C. Cir.) (agency not required to postpone action until further data was obtained; agency determined that environmental effects of proposed action would be minor), *cert. denied*, 454 U.S. 1092 (1981); Sierra Club v. Froehlke, 534 F.2d 1289, 1296 n.25 (8th Cir. 1976) (study on environmental effects of actions were estimated to take several years; disclosure in EIS of need for study was sufficient).

314. 40 C.F.R. § 1502.22(b) (1989).

315. *Id.*

316. *See id.* (analysis must be "supported by credible scientific evidence").

317. *See, e.g.*, Baltimore Gas & Elec. Co. v. Natural Resources Defense Council, Inc., 462 U.S. 87, 103 (1983); Ethyl Corp. v. EPA, 541 F.2d 1, 28 (D.C. Cir.), *cert. denied*, 426 U.S. 941 (1976); Reserve Mining Co. v. EPA, 514 F.2d 492, 519–20 (8th Cir. 1975), *modified*, 529 F.2d 181 (8th Cir. 1976).

318. Foundation on Economic Trends v. Heckler, 756 F.2d 143, 153–54 (D.C. Cir. 1985).

319. *See* Alaska v. Andrus, 580 F.2d 465, 473 (D.C. Cir.), *vacated in part sub nom.* Western Oil & Gas Ass'n v. Alaska, 439 U.S. 922 (1978); Scientists' Inst. for Public Information, Inc. v. AEC, 481 F.2d 1079, 1092 (D.C. Cir. 1973); Save the Niobrara

River Ass'n, Inc. v. Andrus, 483 F. Supp. 844, 852 (D. Neb. 1979). *Cf.* Animal Defense Council v. Hodel, 840 F.2d 1432, 1440–41 (9th Cir. 1988) (when plaintiffs did not establish that risk was unknown or uncertain; former worst case analysis regulation was not triggered), *modified*, 867 F.2d 1244 (9th Cir. 1989).

320. Baltimore Gas & Elec. Co. v. Natural Resources Defense Council, Inc., 462 U.S. 87, 100 (1983).

321. Scientists Inst. for Public Information, Inc. v. AEC, 481 F.2d at 1092.

322. Committee for Nuclear Responsibility, Inc. v. Seaborg, 463 F.2d 783, 787 (D.C. Cir. 1971); *see* section 5.8.5 (public participation).

323. Marsh v. Oregon Natural Resources Council, 109 S. Ct. 1851, 1861 (1989).

324. 40 C.F.R. §§ 1502.14(f), 1502.16(h), 1508.25(b)(3) (1989).

325. *Id.* § 1505.2(c).

326. *Id.* § 1508.20; *see also* Council on Environmental Quality, Forty Most Asked Questions Concerning CEQ's National Environmental Policy Act Regulations, 46 Fed. Reg. 18,026, 18,031 (1981) (mitigation measures must cover range of environmental effects of proposed action).

327. Robertson v. Methow Valley Citizens Council, 109 S. Ct. 1835, 1847 (1989); *see* Sierra Club v. Clark, 774 F.2d 1406, 1411 (9th Cir. 1985) (agency did not incorporate complete discussion of site-specific mitigation measures in EIS but implemented such measures extensively, thus demonstrating that agency was informed and responsive to need to minimize adverse environmental effects).

328. Robertson v. Methow Valley Citizens Council, 109 S. Ct. 1835, 1847 (1989).

329. *See* 40 C.F.R. § 1505.3 (1989).

330. S. 1089 § 1(b)(2), 101st Cong., 1st Sess. (1989).

331. H.R. 1113 § 1(b), 101st Cong., 1st Sess. (1989); H.R. 3847 § 501(b), 101st Cong., 2d Sess. (1990).

332. S. 1089 § 4(b), 101st Cong., 1st Sess. (1989); H.R. 1113 § 4(b), 101st Cong., 1st Sess. (1989); H.R. 3847 § 504(b), 101st Cong., 2d Sess. (1989).

333. *See* H. Rep. No. 219, 101st Cong., 1st Sess. 7, 16–17 (1989); *OEQ Authorization, Fiscal Years 1989–1993; Hearing on H.R. 1113 Before the Subcomm. on Fisheries and Wildlife Conservation and the Environment of the House Comm. on Merchant Marine and Fisheries*, 101st Cong., 1st Sess. 5 (1989).

334. 42 U.S.C. § 4332(2)(B) (1988); *see* Columbia Basin Land Protection Ass'n v. Schlesinger, 643 F.2d 585, 594 (9th Cir. 1981); Calvert Cliffs' Coordinating Comm., Inc. v. AEC, 449 F.2d 1109, 1113 (D.C. Cir. 1971).

335. *See* Sierra Club v. Sigler, 695 F.2d 957, 978 (5th Cir. 1983) (requiring "at least a broad informal cost-benefit analysis by federal agencies of the economic, technical, and environmental costs and benefits of a particular action").

336. *See* Suburban O'Hare Comm'n v. Dole, 787 F.2d 186, 191 n.8 (7th Cir.), *cert. denied*, 479 U.S. 847 (1986); Sierra Club v. Sigler, 695 F.2d 957, 978 (5th Cir. 1983); Columbia Basin Land Protection Ass'n v. Schlesinger, 643 F.2d 585, 594 (9th Cir. 1981); Robinson v. Knebel, 550 F.2d 422, 426 (8th Cir. 1977); Daly v. Volpe, 514 F.2d 1106, 1112 (9th Cir. 1975); Trout Unlimited v. Morton, 509 F.2d 1276, 1286 & n.14 (9th Cir. 1974); 40 C.F.R. § 1502.23 (1989).

337. South La. Envtl. Council, Inc. v. Sand, 629 F.2d 1005, 1013 n.7 (5th Cir. 1980) (citing Sierra Club v. Morton, 510 F.2d 813, 827 (5th Cir. 1975)); Gloucester City Concerned Citizens v. Goldschmidt, 533 F. Supp. 1222, 1231 (D.N.J. 1982).

338. Sierra Club v. Morton, 510 F.2d 813, 827 (5th Cir. 1975); Sierra Club v. Stamm, 507 F.2d 788, 794 (10th Cir. 1974); 40 C.F.R. § 1502.23 (1989). Cf. Johnston v. Davis, 698 F.2d 1088, 1092 (10th Cir. 1983) (Congress specified discount rate formula for water resource projects).

339. See Burkey v. Ellis, 483 F. Supp. 897, 912–14 (N.D. Ala. 1979) (cost-benefit analysis was wholly misleading); see also Conservation Law Found'n v. Watt, 560 F. Supp. 561, 570 (D. Mass.) (cost-benefit analysis was no longer relevant to agency action), aff'd, 716 F.2d 946 (1st Cir. 1983); Duck River Preservation Ass'n v. TVA, 410 F. Supp. 758, 764 (E.D. Tenn. 1974) (EIS did not reveal all environmental costs), aff'd, 529 F.2d 524 (6th Cir. 1976).

340. See Strycker's Bay Neighborhood Council, Inc. v. Karlen, 444 U.S. 223, 227 (1980) (per curiam).

341. 40 C.F.R. § 1502.23 (1989).

342. Sierra Club v. Froehlke, 534 F.2d 1289, 1300 (8th Cir. 1976); see Grazing Fields Farm v. Goldschmidt, 626 F.2d 1068, 1072 (1st Cir. 1980); Sierra Club v. Morton, 510 F.2d 813, 818 (5th Cir. 1975).

343. See Baltimore Gas & Elec. Co. v. Natural Resources Defense Council, Inc., 462 U.S. 87, 97 (1983).

344. See Citizens for a Better Henderson v. Hodel, 768 F.2d 1051, 1057–58 (9th Cir. 1985).

345. Baltimore Gas & Elec. Co. v. Natural Resources Defense Council, Inc., 462 U.S. 87, 97–98 (1983).

346. See Marsh v. Oregon Natural Resources Council, 109 S. Ct. 1851, 1861 n.23 (1989). See generally Comment, Shall We Be Arbitrary or Reasonable: Standards of Review for Agency Threshold Determinations Under NEPA, 19 Akron L. Rev. 685 (1986).

347. Marsh v. Oregon Natural Resources Council, 109 S. Ct. 1851, 1861 (1989).

348. Id. (quoting Citizens to Preserve Overton Park, Inc. v. Volpe, 401 U.S. 402, 416 (1971)); see Sierra Club v. Marsh, 714 F. Supp. 539, 565 (D. Me. 1989) (record did not indicate that agency action was founded on reasoned evaluation of relevant information).

349. Kleppe v. Sierra Club, 427 U.S. 390, 410 n.21 (1976); see Sierra Club v. Sigler, 695 F.2d 957, 983 (5th Cir. 1983) (inadequate EIS prevents agency decision maker from carefully weighing all relevant factors).

350. See Kleppe v. Sierra Club, 427 U.S. 390, 410 n.21 (1976).

351. See Oregon Envtl. Council v. Kunzman, 817 F.2d 484, 492 (9th Cir. 1987); see also Township of Springfield v. Lewis, 702 F.2d 426, 442 n.29 (3d Cir. 1983) (discussing application to EIS of rule of reason).

352. Sierra Club v. Morton, 510 F.2d 813, 819 (5th Cir. 1975) (quoting Environmental Defense Fund, Inc. v. Corps of Eng'rs, 492 F.2d 1123, 1131 (5th Cir. 1974)).

353. Oregon Envtl. Council v. Kunzman, 817 F.2d 484, 492 (9th Cir. 1987); Lathan v. Brinegar, 506 F.2d 677, 693 (9th Cir. 1974).

354. Oregon Envtl. Council v. Kunzman, 817 F.2d 484, 493 (9th Cir. 1987); Isle of Hope Historical Ass'n, Inc. v. Corps of Eng'rs, 646 F.2d 215, 220 (5th Cir. 1981) (affirming trial court's order).

355. Sierra Club v. Morton, 510 F.2d 813, 820 (5th Cir. 1975).

356. See sections 5.10.1, 5.10.2.

357. *E.g.,* Tribal Village of Akutan v. Hodel, 869 F.2d 1185, 1192 (9th Cir. 1988) (amount of specificity of data required in EIS varies at different stages of multiphase project), *cert. denied,* 110 S. Ct. 204 (1989); Sierra Club v. Morton, 510 F.2d 813, 827–28 (5th Cir. 1975) (agency's future ability to control development of multiphased action may be taken into account by reviewing court in determining EIS's adequacy).

358. *See* Stop H-3 Ass'n v. Dole, 740 F.2d 1442, 1461 (9th Cir. 1984) ("whether the EIS contains 'a reasonably thorough discussion of the significant aspects of the probable environmental consequences'"; and "whether the EIS's 'form, content and preparation foster both informed decision-making and informed public participation'"), *cert. denied,* 471 U.S. 1108 (1985); Isle of Hope Historical Ass'n, Inc. v. Corps of Eng'rs, 646 F.2d 215, 220 (5th Cir. 1981) (affirming trial court's order) (whether an agency in good faith objectively took a hard look at the environmental consequences of its proposed action and alternatives; whether the EIS provided sufficient detail so that persons who did not participate in the proposed action could understand and consider relevant environmental effects; and whether consideration of alternatives was sufficient to permit reasoned choice among the various courses of action); Environmental Defense Fund v. Andrus, 619 F.2d 1368, 1376 (10th Cir. 1980) (whether the EIS discusses the five procedural requirements of 42 U.S.C. § 4332(2)(C); whether the EIS constitutes a good faith compliance with NEPA's demands; and whether the EIS contains a reasonable discussion of the subject matter involved in the five procedural requirements cited above); Minnesota Public Interest Research Group v. Butz, 541 F.2d 1292, 1300 (8th Cir. 1976) ("reviewing court must first determine whether the agency reached its decision after a full, good faith consideration and balancing of environmental factors [and] whether the agency's actual balance of costs and benefits was arbitrary or clearly gave insufficient weight to environmental values"), *cert. denied,* 430 U.S. 922 (1977).

359. Isle of Hope Historical Ass'n, Inc. v. Corps of Eng'rs, 646 F.2d 215, 220 (5th Cir. 1981) (affirming trial court's order); *see* Oregon Envtl. Council v. Kunzman, 817 F.2d 484, 493 (9th Cir. 1987).

360. Sierra Club v. Morton, 510 F.2d 813, 820 (5th Cir. 1975) (citing Silva v. Lynn, 482 F.2d 1282, 1284–85 (1st Cir. 1973)); *see* Association Concerned About Tomorrow, Inc. v. Dole, 610 F. Supp. 1101, 1111 (N.D. Tex. 1985) ("unabashedly justificatory language is cursory, conclusory and inadequate").

361. Sierra Club v. Morton, 510 F.2d 813, 820 (5th Cir. 1975) (citing Silva v. Lynn, 482 F.2d 1282, 1284–85 (1st Cir. 1973)); Environmental Defense Fund, Inc. v. Froehlke, 473 F.2d 346, 351 (8th Cir. 1972) (quoting Ely v. Velde, 451 F.2d 1130, 1139 (4th Cir. 1971)).

362. Sierra Club v. Morton, 510 F.2d 813, 820 (5th Cir. 1975) (quoting Silva v. Lynn, 482 F.2d 1282, 1284–85 (1st Cir. 1973)); *see also* Pack v. Corps of Eng'rs, 428 F. Supp. 460, 466 (M.D. Fla. 1977) (use of scientific terms in EIS alerted agency specialists to problems raised by plaintiffs). *Cf.* Oregon Envtl. Council v. Kunzman, 614 F. Supp. 657, 665 (D. Or. 1985) (analysis contained in appendix of EIS was "hypertechnical, complex and replete with lengthy equations and calculations"), *vacated,* 636 F. Supp. 632 (D. Or.), *aff'd in part, vacated and remanded in part,* 817 F.2d 484 (9th Cir. 1987).

363. 40 C.F.R. §§ 1500.2(b), 1502.1 (1989).

364. *Id.* § 1502.8; *see* Sierra Club v. Corps of Eng'rs, 772 F.2d 1043, 1049 (2d Cir. 1985); *see also* Natural Resources Defense Council, Inc. v. Callaway, 524 F.2d 79, 93 (2d Cir. 1975) ("discussion of alternatives should be presented in a straightforward, compact and comprehensible manner").

365. Oregon Envtl. Council v. Kunzman, 817 F.2d 484, 494 (9th Cir. 1987).

366. *See* Environmental Defense Fund, Inc. v. Hoffman, 566 F.2d 1060, 1069–70 (8th Cir. 1977); Friends of the Earth v. Hall, 693 F. Supp. 904, 934 (W.D. Wash. 1988); section 5.8.5; *see also* Enos v. Marsh, 769 F.2d 1363, 1373 (9th Cir. 1985) (information must be significant enough to require discussion); Citizens for Balanced Envt. & Transp., Inc. v. Volpe, 650 F.2d 455, 461–62 (2d Cir. 1981) (when EIS addressed problem of missing data; agency substantially complied with requirement that it consider all environmental factors).

367. Environmental Defense Fund, Inc. v. Hoffman, 566 F.2d 1060, 1069–70 (8th Cir. 1977) (citing Committee for Nuclear Responsibility, Inc. v. Seaborg, 463 F.2d 783, 787 (D.C. Cir. 1971)); *see* Residents in Protest—I-35E v. Dole, 583 F. Supp. 653, 663 (D. Minn. 1984) (views of plaintiff's expert were included in EIS; therefore, divergent views were made known to decision maker).

368. Silva v. Lynn, 482 F.2d 1282, 1285 (1st Cir. 1973).

369. Marsh v. Oregon Natural Resources Council, 109 S. Ct. 1851, 1861 (1989); *see* Life of the Land v. Brinegar, 485 F.2d 460, 472–73 (9th Cir. 1973) (disagreement between experts does not invalidate EIS), *cert. denied*, 416 U.S. 961 (1974); Kentucky *ex rel.* Beshear v. Alexander, 655 F.2d 714, 720 (6th Cir. 1981) (same); Manygoats v. Kleppe, 558 F.2d 556, 560 (10th Cir. 1977) (declining to enter into controversy between experts); City of N. Miami v. Train, 377 F. Supp. 1264, 1273 (S.D. Fla. 1974) (same).

370. Isle of Hope Historical Ass'n, Inc. v. Corps of Eng'rs, 646 F.2d 215, 220 (5th Cir. 1981) (affirming trial court's order); Minnesota Public Interest Research Group v. Butz, 541 F.2d 1292, 1300 (8th Cir. 1976), *cert. denied*, 430 U.S. 922 (1977); section 5.10.1.

371. Sierra Club v. Sigler, 695 F.2d 957, 979 (5th Cir. 1983).

372. Columbia Basin Land Protection Ass'n v. Schlesinger, 643 F.2d 585, 594 (9th Cir. 1981); Calvert Cliffs' Coordinating Comm. v. AEC, 449 F.2d 1109, 1113 (D.C. Cir. 1971).

373. *See* Kentucky *ex rel.* Beshear v. Alexander, 655 F.2d 714, 719 (6th Cir. 1981) (alternatives); County of Suffolk v. Secretary of Interior, 562 F.2d 1368, 1384–85 (2d Cir. 1977) (alternatives and environmental effects), *cert. denied*, 434 U.S. 1064 (1978); *see also* Silva v. Lynn, 482 F.2d 1282, 1283 (1st Cir. 1973) (advocating full disclosure). *Cf.* Piedmont Heights Civic Club, Inc. v. Moreland, 637 F.2d 430, 438 (5th Cir. 1981) (publicly available studies cited in EIS and referred to in EIS could be used to justify agency's refusal to consider alternative in EIS).

374. *See* Grazing Fields Farm v. Goldschmidt, 626 F.2d 1068, 1074 (1st Cir. 1980) (discussion of adequacy of alternatives); National Wildlife Fed'n v. Marsh, 568 F. Supp. 985, 999 (D.D.C. 1983); Save the Niobrara River Ass'n, Inc. v. Andrus, 483 F. Supp. 844, 849–50 (D. Neb. 1979).

375. Grazing Fields Farm v. Goldschmidt, 626 F.2d 1068, 1073 (1st Cir. 1980); *see* Friends of the River v. FERC, 720 F.2d 93, 105–06 (D.C. Cir. 1983); Save the Niobrara River Ass'n, Inc. v. Andrus, 483 F. Supp. 844, 849–50 (D. Neb. 1979).

376. 40 C.F.R. § 1502.21 (1989). *Cf.* Association Concerned About Tomorrow, Inc. v. Dole, 610 F. Supp. 1101, 1109 (N.D. Tex. 1985) (cursory reference to study that was not attached to EIS and did not accompany EIS did not incorporate study by reference).

377. Council on Environmental Quality, Forty Most Asked Questions Concerning CEQ's National Environmental Policy Act Regulations, 46 Fed. Reg. 18,026, 18,034 (1981).

378. *Id.*

379. Citizens for Mass Transit, Inc. v. Adams, 630 F.2d 309, 315 (5th Cir. 1980).

380. *See* Sierra Club v. Clark, 774 F.2d 1406, 1411 (9th Cir. 1985); Coalition for Canyon Preservation v. Bowers, 632 F.2d 774, 782 (9th Cir. 1980); Life of the Land v. Brinegar, 485 F.2d 460, 468 (9th Cir. 1973); Upper West Fork River Watershed Assoc. v. Corps of Eng'rs, 414 F. Supp. 908, 927 (N.D.W. Va. 1976), *aff'd*, 556 F.2d 576 (4th Cir. 1977), *cert. denied*, 434 U.S. 1010 (1978). *Cf.* California v. Block, 690 F.2d 753, 765 (9th Cir. 1982) (agency work sheets were not available and accessible when they were scattered in various agency offices in the United States).

381. Animal Defense Council v. Hodel, 840 F.2d 1432, 1436 (9th Cir. 1988), *modified*, 867 F.2d 1244 (9th Cir. 1989).

382. *Id.* at 1437. *Cf. id.* (courts may extend review beyond administrative record if plaintiffs make strong showing of bad faith).

383. Robertson v. Methow Valley Citizens Council, 109 S. Ct. 1835, 1846 (1989).

384. *See, e.g.,* Sohio Transp. Co. v. United States, 766 F.2d 499, 501 (Fed. Cir. 1985) (cost of EIS preparation for pipeline right-of-way was $2.5 million); Alyeska Pipeline Serv. Co. v. United States, 624 F.2d 1005, 1008 (Ct. Cl. 1980) (cost of EIS preparation for Alaska pipeline right-of-way was about $9 million).

385. 43 U.S.C. § 1734(b) (1988).

386. *Id.; see also* Beaver v. Andrus, 637 F.2d 749, 756–57 (10th Cir. 1980) (state and local governments and agencies are exempt from reimbursement requirement under 43 C.F.R. § 2808.1(b)(2) (1989)).

387. 30 U.S.C. §§ 181–287 (1988).

388. 31 U.S.C. § 9701 (1988).

389. 43 C.F.R. § 2808.1(a) (1989); *see* Sohio Transp. Co. v. United States, 766 F.2d 499, 501–05 (Fed. Cir. 1985) (upholding validity of regulation).

390. *See* Nevada Power Co. v. Watt, 711 F.2d 913, 930–31 (10th Cir. 1983); *see also* Alumet v. Andrus, 607 F.2d 911, 916 (10th Cir. 1979).

391. Alyeska Pipeline Serv. Co. v. United States, 624 F.2d 1005, 1016 (Ct. Cl. 1980); *see* Nevada Power Co. v. Watt, 711 F.2d 913, 931–32 (10th Cir. 1983) (reimbursement regulation applies to rights-of-way pending at time of statute's enactment for reasonable costs incurred prior to that date).

392. 43 C.F.R. § 2808.1(a) (1989).

393. 31 U.S.C. § 9701 (1988); *see* Sohio Transp. Co. v. United States, 766 F.2d 499, 502 (Fed. Cir. 1985).

394. Mississippi Power & Light Co. v. NRC, 601 F.2d 223, 231 (5th Cir. 1979), *cert. denied*, 444 U.S. 1102 (1980).

395. *See* Sohio Transp. Co. v. United States, 766 F.2d 499, 501 (Fed. Cir. 1985) (issue was not timely raised but court noted that permit was for right-of-way over 17 miles of federal land, whereas EIS, costing $2.5 million, was for environ-

mental effect of crude oil transportation from Alaska to contiguous United States).

396. Kleppe v. Sierra Club, 427 U.S. 390, 412 (1976).

397. Foundation on Economic Trends v. Heckler, 756 F.2d 143, 159 (D.C. Cir. 1985); *see* Coalition on Sensible Transp., Inc. v. Dole, 826 F.2d 60, 70 n.8 (D.C. Cir. 1987).

398. Kleppe v. Sierra Club, 427 U.S. 390, 410 (1976); *see* 40 C.F.R. § 1508.25 (1989).

399. *See* Foundation on Economic Trends v. Heckler, 756 F.2d 143, 159 (D.C. Cir. 1985); National Wildlife Fed'n v. Appalachian Regional Comm'n, 677 F.2d 883, 889 (D.C. Cir. 1981); *see also* Concerned About Trident v. Rumsfeld, 555 F.2d 817, 826 (D.C. Cir. 1977) (upholding agency's decision not to prepare a comprehensive EIS; environmental effects discussed in comprehensive EIS would not be broader than those discussed in site-specific EIS); Minnesota Public Interest Research Group v. Butz, 541 F.2d 1292, 1306 (8th Cir. 1976) (more comprehensive data required to assess environmental effects), *cert. denied*, 430 U.S. 922 (1977); Cady v. Morton, 527 F.2d 786, 795 (9th Cir. 1975) (comprehensive EIS needed in order to inform agency decision maker of entire action's environmental effects).

400. *See* Kleppe v. Sierra Club, 427 U.S. 390, 410 (1976) (regional); American Public Transit Ass'n v. Goldschmidt, 485 F. Supp. 811, 832–33 (D.D.C. 1980) (national).

401. S. 1089 § 3, 101st Cong., 1st Sess. (1989); H.R. 1113 § 5(b), 101st Cong., 1st Sess. (1989); H.R. 3847 § 505(b), 101st Cong., 2d Sess. (1990).

402. *See* National Wildlife Fed'n v. Appalachian Regional Comm'n, 677 F.2d 883, 888 (D.C. Cir. 1981).

403. *See id.* at 889–90.

404. *See* Scientists' Inst. for Public Information v. AEC, 481 F.2d 1079, 1089–90 (D.C. Cir. 1973); 40 C.F.R. § 1502.4(b) (1989).

405. *See* Foundation on Economic Trends v. Heckler, 756 F.2d 143, 160 (D.C. Cir. 1985).

406. Natural Resources Defense Council v. Hughes, 437 F. Supp. 981, 992 (D.D.C. 1977), *modified*, 454 F. Supp. 148 (D.D.C. 1978).

407. California v. Block, 690 F.2d 753, 761 (9th Cir. 1982).

408. *See* Badoni v. Higginson, 638 F.2d 172, 181 (10th Cir. 1980), *cert. denied*, 452 U.S. 954 (1981). *Cf.* City of Tenakee Springs v. Block, 778 F.2d 1402, 1407 (9th Cir. 1985) (comprehensive and site-specific EISs required for regional development).

409. 40 C.F.R. §§ 1502.20, 1508.28 (1989).

410. *See* United States v. 162.20 Acres, 733 F.2d 377, 381 (5th Cir. 1984) (site-specific EIS is not required if analyses are contained in comprehensive EIS), *cert. denied*, 469 U.S. 1158 (1985); Oregon Environmental Council v. Kunzman, 714 F.2d 901, 904–05 (9th Cir. 1983) (required analysis was not contained in comprehensive EIS or EA); Headwaters, Inc. v. BLM, 684 F. Supp. 1053, 1055 (D. Or. 1988) (site-specific analyses not necessary in EA if adequately considered in document incorporated into final EIS); Sierra Club v. Block, 614 F. Supp. 134, 136 (E.D. Tex. 1985) (site-specific issue was analyzed in EA with references to discussions in prior EISs).

411. 40 C.F.R. § 1506.8(a) (1989).

412. Andrus v. Sierra Club, 442 U.S. 347, 361 (1979).

413. Environmental Defense Fund v. Johnson, 629 F.2d 239, 242 (2d Cir. 1980).

414. Citizens for Mgt. of Alaska Lands v. Department of Agriculture, 447 F. Supp. 753, 755 (D. Alaska 1978).

415. 40 C.F.R. § 1506.8 (1989). *Cf.* Realty Income Trust v. Eckerd, 564 F.2d 447, 454 (D.C. Cir. 1977) (pre-CEQ regulations; unreasonable for agency as a policy matter not to release draft EIS until after committee approval).

416. 40 C.F.R. § 1506.8 (1989); *see id.* (requiring draft and final EISs when required by congressional committee, proposal results from statutorily required study process, legislative approval is sought for specified construction and site acquisition; or agency decides to prepare draft and final EISs). *Cf.* Trustees for Alaska v. Hodel, 806 F.2d 1378, 1383 (9th Cir. 1986) (required report was a statutorily-required study process).

417. 40 C.F.R. § 1506.8(c) (1989); *see* Trustees for Alaska v. Hodel, 806 F.2d 1378, 1380–81 (9th Cir. 1986) (agency may not refuse to circulate report and draft LEIS until after report was submitted to Congress).

418. *See* Chamber of Commerce of United States v. Department of Interior, 439 F. Supp. 762, 768 (D.D.C. 1977).

419. *See* sections 1.3.3 and 6.5.

NEPA Litigation

6.1 INTRODUCTION

Chapter 6 discusses issues that frequently arise in NEPA litigation. The first issue to be discussed is jurisdiction. A federal court must have jurisdiction over the subject matter of the lawsuit and over the parties to it in order to be able to review whether the agency complied with NEPA. In addition, there must be a case or controversy for the court to decide.

There are several aspects to a determination whether a case or controversy exists. First, the plaintiff must have standing. That is, the plaintiff must have a personal stake in the cause of action and must have an interest protected by NEPA. Second, the cause of action must have ripened into a case or controversy. Finally, the plaintiff's interest in the cause of action must continue throughout the litigation. If there is no longer a case or controversy, the cause of action becomes moot.

Intervention occurs frequently in NEPA litigation but is rarely litigated. This chapter contains a brief discussion of the few decisions available on the issue. The infrequently litigated issue of necessary or indispensable parties to NEPA litigation is also briefly discussed.

Before plaintiffs may seek a judicial resolution of an agency's alleged noncompliance with NEPA, they must have exhausted any administrative remedies available to them. Plaintiffs may lose the right to judicially challenge an agency's alleged noncompliance with NEPA if they do not participate in the NEPA process and do not alert the agency to reasonable alternatives or environmental consequences needing the agency's consideration under NEPA.

NEPA does not contain a statute of limitations. NEPA lawsuits may be barred by laches, however, if plaintiffs inexcusably delay in bringing an action, thereby unduly prejudicing an agency. The discussion of remedies deals with the types of relief that are available under NEPA as well as those that are not available. The issue of the amount of bonds required in NEPA actions by plaintiffs seeking injunctive relief is also discussed.

NEPA does not contain an attorney fee provision. Since the passage of the Equal Access to Justice Act in the early 1980s, plaintiffs have been able to obtain attorney fees for NEPA actions in which they prevail. The criteria considered by courts in determining whether to award attorney fees in NEPA actions are examined.

Several litigation issues are discussed in other sections of the book rather than in this chapter because they relate to specific NEPA procedures. Judicial review of EAs and FONSIs is discussed in section 4.9, judicial review of EISs is discussed in section 5.11, and judicial review of the decision not to prepare a supplemental EIS is discussed in section 5.8.3.

6.2 JURISDICTION

Judicial review of agency actions is not mentioned in NEPA or its legislative history. In the early 1970s, however, the courts (not quite unanimously) determined that they had jurisdiction to review agency compliance with NEPA based either upon NEPA or upon other acts of Congress. The question of whether NEPA provided a jurisdictional base became academic.[1]

This does not mean, however, that jurisdictional issues ceased to arise. Decisions holding that jurisdiction is available solely under NEPA are rare.[2] The cautious course of action for plaintiffs is to seek to invoke jurisdiction under several statutory bases in case one base fails.[3] A typical base for NEPA actions includes section 10 of the Administrative Procedure Act[4] and the federal question jurisdiction statutory provision.[5] Other jurisdictional bases such as the Federal Declaratory Judgment Act and other sections of the Administrative Procedure Act are often invoked in addition to NEPA in establishing a basis for jurisdiction.

To invoke a federal court's jurisdiction, there must be a case or controversy.[6] This requirement is constitutional. To satisfy the case or controversy requirement, there must be a dispute that is "presented in an adversary context and in a form historically viewed as capable of judicial resolution."[7] If an agency is engaged in the NEPA process, a case or controversy does not arise until the process is completed.[8]

Issues must be justiciable in order for a federal court to have jurisdiction to review them. There are three main exceptions to a federal district court having jurisdiction to review an agency's action for compliance with NEPA. First, if a challenge is brought under the Administrative Procedure Act, decisions that are committed to agency discretion by law are nonreviewable.[9] Agencies rarely succeed in this argument because courts distinguish the underlying action, which may be committed to an agency's discretion by law, from NEPA's requirement that the agency consider the environmental consequences of proceeding with the action.[10] Whereas the underlying action may be nonreviewable, an agency's compliance with NEPA is subject to judicial review.[11]

The second major exception to a federal district court having jurisdiction to review an agency's action for compliance with NEPA is if the plaintiff seeks review of a nonjusticiable political question. The Supreme Court regards a nonjusticiable political question to have arisen if there is "a textually demonstrable constitutional commitment of the issue to a coordinate political department; or a lack of judicially discoverable and manageable standards for resolving it; or the impossibility of deciding without an initial policy determination of a kind clearly for nonjudicial discretion; or the impossibility of a court's undertaking independent resolution without expressing lack of the respect due coordinate branches of government; or an unusual need for unquestioning adherence to a political decision already made; or the potentiality of embarrassment from multifarious pronouncements by various departments on one question."[12]

Whether an agency complied with NEPA regarding an action involving national defense policy is not a nonjusticiable federal question. The Ninth Circuit held that although it had no judicially discoverable and manageable standards to review the merits of actions involving national defense policy, a lawsuit challenging the action on the grounds that the agency failed to discuss the action's environmental effects was justiciable.[13] Similarly, the Eighth Circuit held that review of an EIS prepared for the proposed deployment and peacetime operations of MX missiles in Minuteman silos was justiciable.[14]

The situation differs if trial of a cause of action would inevitably lead to disclosure of confidential national security matters. For example, the navy was prohibited, for national security reasons, from admitting or denying that it intended to store nuclear weapons at one of its facilities. Thus, although the navy was required to comply with NEPA by preparing an EIS if it intended to store nuclear weapons at the facility, the court could not review the navy's compliance with NEPA because to do so would disclose confidential matters.[15]

The third main exception to a federal district court's jurisdiction to review an agency action for compliance with NEPA applies if Congress vested exclusive jurisdiction of the action under review in a court of appeals. In such a case, the federal district court does not have concurrent jurisdiction with the court of appeals to review the agency's alleged noncompliance with NEPA in undertaking the action under review in the court of appeals.[16]

6.3 STANDING

6.3.1 Requirements for Standing

In order to invoke a federal court's jurisdiction, a plaintiff must have standing to sue. The requirements for standing for NEPA actions vary depending on whether a plaintiff brings the cause of action under the Administrative Procedure Act or under a non-specific statute.[17]

When a plaintiff brings a NEPA action based on a nonspecific statute and/or on NEPA, he must allege "'such a personal stake in the outcome of the controversy' as to ensure that "the dispute sought to be adjudicated will be presented in an adversary context and in a form historically viewed as capable of judicial resolution."[18] The plaintiff must also show that he is in a class for whose especial benefit NEPA was enacted.[19] This latter requirement is more stringent than the requirement for NEPA litigation brought under the Administrative Procedure Act in which a plaintiff must show that he is within NEPA's zone of interests.[20]

To establish standing to challenge an agency's alleged violation of a statute such as NEPA under section 10 of the Administrative Procedure Act, a plaintiff must show that it was aggrieved by an agency action, the challenged action caused it an "injury-in-fact," and the "alleged injury was to an interest 'arguably within the zone of interests to be protected or regulated'" by the statute being invoked.[21] A "mere 'interest in a problem'" is insufficient by itself to confer standing.[22]

A plaintiff must allege that "he has been or will in fact be "perceptibly harmed by the challenged agency action."[23] An allegation of imaginary circumstances in which a plaintiff may be affected,[24] an interest in the environment,[25] or a generalized fear of the loss of resources[26] is insufficient.

An injury-in-fact may be economic[27] or noneconomic.[28] Noneconomic injuries include harm to a person's aesthetic and environmental well-being.[29] Thus, plaintiffs do not need to have an economic interest in resources affected by an agency action in order to have standing to challenge the agency's alleged noncompliance with

NEPA.[30] By failing to comply with NEPA, the agency creates a risk that serious environmental effects will be overlooked by the agency decision maker. This injury is sufficient to create standing if the plaintiff can establish "'that he may be expected to suffer whatever environmental consequences the project may have.'"[31] An injury-in-fact need not be large. As long as the interest involved is "an identifiable trifle," it provides a basis for standing.[32]

6.3.2 Interests Protected by NEPA

NEPA protects environmental interests[33] affecting the human environment.[34] Economic interests are not protected by NEPA. Therefore, if a plaintiff is motivated in bringing a lawsuit solely by protecting his own economic interests, he does not have standing.[35] However, a plaintiff may still have standing even though its primary reason for challenging the agency action is economic self-interest.[36] The deciding factor is whether the plaintiffs allege an environmental interest that is not so insignificant that it should be disregarded.[37] The environmental interest is not weighed against an accompanying economic interest.[38]

In effect, the proposition that NEPA does not protect economic interests is equivalent to the proposition that NEPA accords a right of action to protect the public interest to persons with standing.[39] Thus, a person or entity invoking NEPA to protect his or its own economic interests does not state a cause of action under NEPA because NEPA does not authorize a private right of action.[40]

Interests in resources that have been deemed sufficient for standing include: recreational interests in a tract of public land that will be affected by an agency action;[41] aesthetic injuries in no longer being able to view natural environments,[42] or in viewing the despoliation of animals,[43] increased pollution and other environmental consequences of an action affecting people who reside or work near the affected resource,[44] and effects on people who use and study a public tract of land.[45]

Interests must be capable of being affected by an agency action. Thus, recreational use of private land as a trespasser or licensee does not give a plaintiff standing to sue because the plaintiff does not necessarily have an interest capable of being affected by a proposed agency action.[46] The plaintiff's interest in such a case is susceptible to termination by the owner of the private land at any time. Likewise, a potential resident of an area that will be affected by an agency action does not have standing to challenge the action.[47]

When an agency action affects natural resources nationwide, people who use those resources may have standing if they would suffer individualized harm distinct from the interest held by the general public.[48] Similarly, when a broad, integrated long-range action is planned, plaintiffs suffering injury in one location that will be affected by the action may have standing to challenge the agency's compliance with NEPA for another part of the action.[49] The fact that many people would suffer an injury does not defeat standing as long as plaintiffs allege a specific and perceptible harm to distinguish them from the general population that uses the natural resource that will be affected by the agency action.[50]

6.3.3 Associational Standing

An association may have standing in two ways: by alleging individualized harm to the association, or by representing members who would suffer individualized harm.[51] Individual harm to an association with informational and educational purposes may occur when an agency fails to prepare an EIS, circulate it to other agencies, and make it available to the public as required by NEPA. In such a case, the association may suffer an injury because it is unable to fulfill its informational and educational purposes.[52]

An association typically brings a NEPA action as the representative of its members. The typical, and cautious, course is for an association to join at least one member of the association who is personally affected by the agency action.[53] An association has standing to sue on behalf of its members if "its members would otherwise have standing to sue in their own right," the interests sought to be protected are germane to the association's purposes, and neither the asserted claim nor the requested relief require the members' individual participation.[54]

An association satisfies the first prong of the test by alleging that its members' health, aesthetic, environmental, or conservation values will be impaired or adversely affected by an agency action.[55] If the association merely alleges that its members have a general interest in protecting the environment, however strong that interest, it does not have standing.[56] The second prong is satisfied by an association's litigation purposes being pertinent to its organizational purpose and special expertise.[57] An association that is formed solely to bring the NEPA action may not have standing to sue for harm to the association because the association's interests do not sufficiently differentiate it from the general public.[58] The final prong is satisfied by requesting

NEPA's traditional remedy of declaratory and injunctive relief. This remedy does not require the participation of individual members.[59]

6.3.4 Other Entities with Standing

Governmental entities that must be consulted in the NEPA process have standing to challenge the agency's noncompliance with NEPA.[60] A governmental agency that does not have primary responsibility for environmental standards does not have standing, however, because Congress did not intend it to be entitled to comment on the agency action.[61]

Entities that have been found to have standing to sue include a regional planning board when an agency action created a variance from its regional plan;[62] a state suing on behalf of its citizens under its parens patriae power;[63] and a class when its members would be individually harmed by an agency's action.[64] Other entities that have been found to have standing to sue include a corporation,[65] a broadcasting company,[66] and unions.[67]

6.3.5 Characterization of Alleged Injury

As a general rule, standing is determined from the face of a complaint.[68] The plaintiff should articulate the nature of the alleged injury.[69] If the alleged personal harm is not readily apparent, further explanation such as geographic proximity of the plaintiff to the affected resources, prior usage of the resources in question and concern for them, or an explanation of how the plaintiff would be injured by the agency action, is advisable.[70]

6.3.6 Representing the Public Interest

Once a plaintiff has established standing to sue under NEPA, it may argue the public interest in support of its claim.[71] On this basis, a governmental entity with standing has been permitted to represent the environmental interests of its citizens,[72] an association with standing on one ground has been permitted to challenge other alleged acts of noncompliance by the agency in the NEPA process under review,[73] and an association has been permitted to represent the interests of the public as well as its members.[74]

6.4 RIPENESS

A cause of action must be ripe before a court may resolve it. In deciding whether a cause of action is ripe, a reviewing court must consider whether the issue is fit for judicial decision and "the hardship to the parties of withholding court consideration."[75]

Several types of ripeness questions arise under NEPA. In the first type, courts decide whether an agency has conducted a final action in the NEPA process. The second type involves challenges to legislative EISs. Finally, ripeness issues occur in challenges to agency regulations.

6.4.1 Final Agency Actions

Before judicial review may occur, there must be a proposed action by an agency[76] that may significantly affect the human environment.[77] That action does not need to be the final agency action for all purposes as long as it is the final action for purposes of NEPA.[78] In an action brought under the Administrative Procedure Act, a court does not have jurisdiction to review an agency action until the action is final.[79] Thus, whether a plaintiff brings a cause of action under the Administrative Procedure Act or under other federal statutes, the agency action must be final before a court may review it.

If the agency determines that NEPA does not apply to the action or if it acts without following procedures mandated by NEPA, a challenge to the action is ripe.[80] On the other hand, if the agency follows NEPA procedures, a challenge to those procedures is not ripe in most cases until the procedures have been completed and a final EIS has been issued.[81] The agency does not need to proceed with the action before a plaintiff is entitled to judicial review of the alleged NEPA violation.[82] The decision not to prepare a supplemental EIS is a final agency action for NEPA purposes.[83]

6.4.2 Legislative EISs

An exception to the above rule requiring final actions by an agency for a case or controversy to be ripe is judicial review of a refusal by an agency to permit public comments to a draft EIS accompanying a proposal for legislation until the proposal is submitted to Congress. A controversy over whether public comments should be permitted is ripe in this instance because of the limited time to comment at the administrative level once Congress receives the legislative EIS.[84]

6.4.3 Regulations

Agency regulations may be ripe for judicial review after they are promulgated but before they are applied if the regulations implement procedural requirements of NEPA,[85] allegedly evade compliance with NEPA,[86] or if they condition permitted actions under other environmental laws to compliance with NEPA requirements.[87]

6.5 MOOTNESS

Mootness is closely related to standing and ripeness in that it is "'standing set in a time frame'" in which a plaintiff's personal stake in the controversy's outcome must continue throughout the litigation.[88] A NEPA action may become moot by the actions of the agency or by a third party.

Actions can become moot when the agency whose action is being challenged brings itself into compliance with NEPA. Compliance thus remedies the agency's earlier NEPA violation.[89] The agency must fulfill the NEPA obligation at issue, however. Staying litigation until an EIS is prepared does not render an action moot.[90] Neither does a promise by an agency to file an EIS while it proceeds with the challenged action.[91]

If a plaintiff fails to seek injunctive relief, he runs the risk of a court declaring the action moot if the court determines that it is unable to undo what has already occurred[92] or if the action is too far advanced to permit consideration of environmental effects.[93] Mootness does not, of course, cause dismissal of a lawsuit when the agency action is capable of being undone such as the distribution of funds and the transfer of title.[94] However, because NEPA is not triggered unless the human environment is significantly affected, the effect on the environment of the vast majority of agency actions will not be capable of being undone once the action is completed.

Courts have equitable powers to require the removal of all construction or other activities taken by an agency or by a nonfederal entity pursuant to an agency action if the action is taken in violation of NEPA.[95] Thus, commencement of an action that is subject to NEPA involves a risk especially when the action is judicially challenged for alleged noncompliance with NEPA.[96]

If an agency action is capable of repetition yet could evade judicial review, a cause of action challenging it is not moot.[97] An exception exists if review under NEPA is required for future agency actions that follow from the challenged action and if the plaintiffs will be given notice and/or opportunity to challenge the future actions.[98]

Finally, an action may become moot because of the actions of a governmental body. Outside governmental action has mooted NEPA causes of action when new environmental studies are required before the agency action may proceed;[99] the action under review is no longer feasible;[100] or the environmental documentation is reappraised by a reviewing body and considered adequate.[101]

Congress also occasionally moots causes of action by specifically exempting agency actions from compliance with NEPA.[102] Congressional intent must be specific.[103] The appropriation of funds for a project is not clear and convincing evidence that Congress intended the project to be exempt from NEPA.[104]

6.6 INTERVENTION

Intervention occurs frequently in NEPA actions. Whether an applicant has the right to intervene or whether a court may grant the applicant permission to intervene is rarely litigated. Only a few opinions have been published regarding the issue of whether there is a right to intervene in NEPA actions. These opinions have reached different results for different reasons. Even fewer opinions have discussed permissive intervention which is generally permitted and not challenged.

6.6.1 Intervention as of Right

NEPA does not contain a provision permitting intervention. Therefore, to determine whether a right to intervention exists, courts apply the requirements for intervention as of right that are specified in the Federal Rules of Civil Procedure. To have the right to intervene under the federal rules, an applicant must file a timely motion to intervene, claim "an interest relating to the property or transaction which is the subject of the action," be situated so "that the disposition of the action may as a practical matter impair or impede [his] ability to protect that interest," and have an interest that is not adequately represented by existing parties to the action.[105]

The intervention issue that has been litigated most in the NEPA context is whether an applicant for intervention has "an interest relating to the property or transaction which is the subject of the action."[106] The Supreme Court has stated that the interest must be a "significantly protectable interest."[107] The Ninth Circuit has ruled that economic interests are not protectable under NEPA, therefore, persons with only economic interests are not entitled to intervene as of right.[108]

The Ninth Circuit's holding accords with the general rule that persons with only economic interests do not have standing to sue under NEPA.[109] Thus, although the Supreme Court has not decided whether an applicant for intervention as of right must have standing,[110] the Ninth Circuit law on intervention as of right in NEPA actions is consistent with NEPA standing doctrine. In effect, the Ninth Circuit applies NEPA's standing requirement to potential intervening defendants.

The Tenth Circuit, reading the federal rules' requirement that an interest must be protectable, together with the requirement that an applicant show that the resolution of the judicial action may as a practical matter impair that interest, determined that applicants for intervention who operated a uranium mill pursuant to a state license, and who had applied for a renewal of the license, had a protectable interest in a cause of action that could affect the licensing procedure.[111] The court decided that the existing intervenor in the action did not necessarily represent the other applicants' interests. The court, therefore, granted the application for intervention as of right.[112] The court did not consider whether the applicants were adequately represented by the federal agency defending the action.

The Tenth Circuit's holding is contrary to cases decided in the Seventh and Second Circuits. The Seventh Circuit considers that the only defendants in an action challenging a federal agency's compliance with the procedural requirements of a statute are the governmental agencies charged with compliance.[113] Similarly, the Second Circuit denied an application to intervene as of right by the preparer of an allegedly inadequate environmental document because the applicant's interest was not related to the agency's failure to comply with NEPA or to the nature of the proceeding.[114]

Intervention as of right may be granted when the applicant has an interest that is antagonistic to the plaintiffs in the action. The District of Columbia Circuit held that Canadian environmental groups were entitled to intervene in a NEPA action because the interests of the plaintiffs, United States environmental groups, were antagonistic to the applicants. The agency's EIS at issue considered alternative methods of shipping oil to the contiguous United States from Alaska.

The alternatives included methods that would affect the Canadian environment.[115]

6.6.2 Permissive Intervention

Applicants may be permitted to intervene in a lawsuit when their claim or defense has a question of law or fact in common with the question in the lawsuit.[116] Although it can be argued that a private party's defense is necessarily different from that of the agency/defendant,[117] permissive intervention is widespread and rarely challenged. Trial courts have broad discretion to grant or deny applications for permissive intervention.[118] In exercising their discretion, the courts consider whether intervention will unduly delay or prejudice adjudication of the original parties' rights.[119] As a practical matter, the trial court's decision on whether to permit intervention is usually final.

6.7 NECESSARY AND INDISPENSABLE PARTIES

The issue of whether a nonparty is a necessary party to a NEPA lawsuit is similar to the issue of whether a person may intervene in a NEPA lawsuit. Rule 19 of the Federal Rules of Civil Procedure requires joinder of persons subject to service of process when their joinder does not deprive the court of jurisdiction over the subject matter if either of the following two situations exist. First, complete relief must not be able to be accorded among the parties in the absence of the necessary party. Second, the necessary party's interest must relate to the subject of the action and, in addition, either the disposition of the case would, as a practical matter, impair that interest, or the necessary party's claimed interest could leave parties to the action with a substantial risk of incurring inconsistent obligations.

Persons claiming to be necessary parties have been permitted to join a NEPA lawsuit.[120] However, private persons and entities are probably not necessary parties to a NEPA action because the subject of a NEPA lawsuit is agency compliance with NEPA's requirements, and non-federal persons and entities are not entitled to have the agency follow certain procedures.[121]

If a nonparty is a necessary party but cannot be made a party, a court may still permit the cause of action to proceed in the absence of the nonparty if the court determines that the nonparty is not an indispensable party. That is, a case may proceed in the absence of a necessary party when such action may proceed in equity and good conscience.[122]

6.8 EXHAUSTION OF ADMINISTRATIVE REMEDIES

As a general rule, plaintiffs must exhaust any applicable administrative remedies before they may seek judicial review of an agency's alleged noncompliance with NEPA.[123] An exception may arise if a plaintiff challenges an agency action based on a jurisdictional ground that is independent from an available administrative remedy.[124] The doctrine of exhaustion of remedies is applicable to the NEPA process in two major ways.

First, if a plaintiff fails to comment on an agency's proposed action despite public notice of the action, depending on the jurisdiction, the plaintiff may be precluded from judicially challenging the action.[125] The rationale behind this argument, which is sometimes brought under the doctrine of laches,[126] is that the NEPA procedure would be frustrated if plaintiffs were permitted to remain silent during public comment periods but were permitted to object after the NEPA process was complete.[127] This approach, which is favored by the Forest Service[128] has been criticized as not serving the purposes of NEPA because it tends to shift the burden of NEPA compliance to plaintiffs instead of the agency as mandated by NEPA.[129] It is well settled, however, that a plaintiff's burden of persuading a court that the agency failed to comply with NEPA by not considering information suggested by it is increased by a failure to bring those concerns to the agency's attention before the agency finalized the EIS at issue.[130]

Second, if a plaintiff fails to follow an agency's administrative review procedures, or if it maintains silence on NEPA issues at the administrative level and raises the issues for the first time in a court, it may not be entitled to judicial review of the agency's alleged noncompliance with NEPA.[131] Similarly, if a plaintiff challenges agency actions judicially but fails to timely raise NEPA issues in those challenges, a court may bar it from raising the issues[132] or may limit its right to raise the issues.[133] The person must have had an opportunity to participate in the administrative proceedings, however. When a person is affected by a proposed agency action only after the agency has provided the opportunity for review, the doctrine does not bar a direct challenge of the agency action in court.[134]

The doctrine of exhaustion of administrative remedies is flexible. If the interest to the agency in allowing it to pass on an issue first is clearly outweighed by the severity of the burden on the plaintiffs if their request for judicial review is denied, judicial review of the issue is permitted.[135] Judicial review is also permitted despite a plaintiff's failure to exhaust administrative remedies when the administrative remedy is inadequate, when the plaintiff would suffer irreparable harm if judicial review was not permitted, or when it would be futile for plaintiffs to pursue administrative remedies.[136]

In addition, if a court determines that an issue is of great public importance, it may decide that judicial review of the action is appropriate despite the plaintiff's failure to comment on the action when the agency requested public comments.[137] Similarly, a court may determine that the public interest in determining whether an agency complied with NEPA is of greater importance than permitting an agency to avoid judicial review of its alleged noncompliance because plaintiffs did not exhaust their administrative remedies at the correct time.[138]

6.9 STATUTE OF LIMITATIONS

Neither NEPA nor the Administrative Procedure Act have specific statutes of limitations. Thus, the most frequent defense to a tardily filed lawsuit is laches, which is discussed below.

The general statute of limitations of title 28 of the United States Code has been applied to a procedural challenge to agency regulations. The challenge was based on the agency's alleged noncompliance with NEPA.[139] The statute provides that except for a limited exception "every civil action commenced against the United States shall be barred unless the complaint is filed within six years after the right of action first accrues."[140] The Ninth Circuit held that the challenge, which had been added to a lawsuit as a new claim, was barred by the statute of limitations.[141]

6.10 LACHES

A claim may be barred by laches if the defendant can show that the plaintiffs delayed in asserting the claim, the delay was inexcusable, and the defendant asserting the laches defense was unduly prejudiced.[142] Defendants must show all three elements for laches to apply.[143] The applicability of laches to a cause of action depends on the facts and circumstances of each case.[144]

6.10.1 Delay

As a general rule, if an agency files a final EIS, the triggering date to determine delay is the date the final EIS is issued.[145] If an agency files an EA/FONSI, the triggering date is the date the EA/FONSI is issued.[146]

Some courts appear to have considered that the date the draft EIS was issued is relevant to a determination of the triggering date.[147] This view is erroneous, however, because a cause of action is not ripe until the agency makes its final environmental decision.[148] Thus, the adequacy of an agency's draft EIS is ordinarily not subject to judicial review.

The triggering date is more difficult to determine if the agency plans and commences an action without preparing the environmental documentation required by NEPA. Courts have found that the triggering date in such cases is, variously, the date on which: "it became reasonably clear to the plaintiffs that other efforts which might be undertaken . . . would be fruitless,"[149] preparation for construction of the project "began in earnest,"[150] an agency publicly announced a proposed action,[151] and plaintiffs' counsel advised the plaintiffs that it would be necessary to file a lawsuit to deter the agency action.[152]

Although the length of delay is an element in deciding if laches applies,[153] the decisions vary because of the interplay of other factors in applying laches. Thus, unless the length of time is unusually long, for example, seven years,[154] there is no bright line to aid in determining if a given length of time constitutes a delay for purposes of laches. For example, laches barred an action with a delay of seven and one-half months[155] but not an action with a delay of ten months.[156]

Delay may factor into a lawsuit even when laches is not an issue. For example, if an agency shows that the plaintiff delayed in seeking judicial relief,[157] or if the agency action was substantially complete,[158] a court may decide not to grant injunctive relief.

6.10.2 Inexcusable Delay

The most crucial element in determining if the delay in filing suit was inexcusable depends on whether the plaintiff knew of its legal right to challenge the agency action. Knowledge may be actual or constructive.[159] Plaintiffs have successfully shown that they could not have had constructive knowledge of their legal rights by showing that they could not be certain that a legal right existed because of uncertainties in the law at that time.[160]

Courts have found that plaintiffs had constructive knowledge of a legal right to challenge an agency action when the agency acted without filing an EIS and there was judicial precedent holding that actions of that type required EISs;[161] the agency's commencement of the action after filing a final EIS was accompanied by widespread publicity and massive construction activities;[162] and activities on a project for which a dredge and fill permit had been publicly applied for, but for which no EIS was prepared, were highly publicized and visible.[163]

If plaintiffs had actual or constructive knowledge of their legal rights, courts determine if they exercised due diligence in challenging the agency's alleged noncompliance with NEPA. Plaintiffs are not expected to file a lawsuit immediately but are entitled to presume that a federal agency intends to comply with NEPA until the contrary is indicated.[164] This presumption disappears, however, if the plaintiffs know the action may have environmental effects before the agency complies with NEPA[165] or if it becomes apparent to plaintiffs that their attempts to negotiate with the agency do not have a reasonable chance of success.[166]

Courts have found that plaintiffs' delay in filing suit was excusable when the delay was caused by the plaintiffs' attempts to negotiate with the agency,[167] continuance of the decision-making process,[168] and unsuccessful attempts to raise money from other environmental groups to file the lawsuit.[169]

There is a fine line between excusable and inexcusable delay. As mentioned above, negotiation with an agency excuses a potential plaintiff's delay in filing suit, but only to the point at which the negotiations are believed to have a reasonable likelihood of success. Other examples of inexcusable delay include the following. If plaintiffs make their opposition known to the agency but fail to file suit, laches may bar a subsequent suit.[170] In addition, plaintiffs may not be able to rely on another entity's negotiations with the agency to excuse their own delay in waiting to file suit.[171] Similarly, plaintiffs may not rely on a lack of financial resources unless they show they used diligence to overcome that lack.[172] The conscious pursuit of a state court action to attain equivalent relief does not excuse plaintiffs from the application of laches if they forgo filing an action in federal court to do so, especially if the state court action is brought for delay purposes.[173]

The Ninth Circuit has formulated a test to determine whether plaintiffs have constructive knowledge of their rights and whether they exercised due diligence in bringing a NEPA action. Three factors are considered: whether the plaintiffs attempted to make their position known to the agency before filing the cause of action; whether the agency responded to the request; and whether developments such as preparatory construction occurred to motivate citizens to investigate any legal bases for challenging the agency action.[174] In essence, the Ninth Circuit test fulfills a similar purpose to tests by other circuits for determining whether delay was inexcusable.

6.10.3 Undue Prejudice

Laches may be appropriate if an agency has been unduly prejudiced by a plaintiff's delay in filing the lawsuit. The agency's interests are accorded varying weight by the courts. The monetary cost of an agency action, by itself, does not necessarily establish prejudice,[175] especially if the cost is capable of mitigation.[176] The increased cost from delay, by itself, is also not sufficient to establish prejudice because compliance with NEPA necessarily results in a delay in agency actions.[177] A court may decide not to consider agency actions, such as agency actions preparatory to an agency's construction project, in determining if the agency was unduly prejudiced.[178]

The agency may have to have relied on a plaintiff's inaction for undue prejudice to arise. For example, even if an agency shows substantial expenditure on an action, the amount of expenditure may not be relevant to a showing of undue prejudice unless the agency relied on a plaintiff's inaction in spending the money.[179] This principle accords with the court's power to order an agency to undo actions taken by the agency after it had knowledge of the NEPA challenge.[180]

6.10.4 Public Interest

The doctrine of laches is applied sparingly to NEPA actions for several reasons. First, the plaintiffs represent the public interest as well as themselves. Therefore, the plaintiffs would not be the only people adversely affected if their lawsuit was barred.[181] Thus, the public cost of unnecessary environmental harm is balanced against any undue prejudice suffered by the agency.[182]

Second, the agency is a proxy for the public interest in accomplishing its mission while considering the environmental effects of that action.[183] Congress mandated that the agencies were to comply with NEPA; it did not leave compliance to vigilant plaintiffs.[184] Thus, the public interest in the agency complying with NEPA is balanced against any undue prejudice suffered by the agency.[185]

Even if an agency shows that a plaintiff's inexcusable delay has unduly prejudiced the agency, courts do not necessarily bar NEPA actions. The relevant issue in applying laches to NEPA actions has been described as determining whether a plaintiff's lawsuit could result in changes to the agency action.[186] Thus, laches may not apply if some environmental harm is still capable of amelioration.[187] On the other hand, if compliance with NEPA would only result in marginal benefits because an irreversible commitment of resources had already occurred, the public interest in requiring the agency to comply with NEPA may be outweighed.[188]

6.11 UNCLEAN HANDS

This doctrine is rarely used in NEPA actions, but an agency may be able to successfully defend a NEPA challenge if it can show that the plaintiffs had unclean hands. For example, if the plaintiffs attempt to use NEPA solely for their economic gain, their cause of action may be adjudged unjust and inequitable.[189] This principle is consistent with the principle that NEPA does not protect economic interests. The principle appears in NEPA standing and intervention issues.[190]

Whereas a court does not weigh a plaintiff's allegations of economic and noneconomic interests in determining whether it had standing under NEPA, the unclean hands doctrine suggests that if a defendant can subsequently show that the plaintiff's economic interests were the only reason for the plaintiff's bringing the cause of action, or, conversely, that the plaintiff's allegations of environmental interests were false, the defendant may be successful in defending the lawsuit on equitable grounds.

6.12 REMEDIES

NEPA accords "a right of action in adversely affected parties to enforce" the federal agencies' obligation to "give written consideration of environmental issues in connection with certain major federal actions."[191] NEPA does not, however, authorize a private right of action.[192] Thus, a private party with standing has the right to sue under NEPA to enforce NEPA's environmental purposes by requiring an agency to consider the significant environmental effects of its actions. A private party does not have the right, however, to invoke NEPA to gain a purely personal or economic benefit.

6.12.1 Declaratory and Injunctive Relief

Courts grant declaratory and injunctive relief in NEPA actions[193] with some courts relying only on declaratory relief.[194] The purpose of injunctive relief under NEPA is to preserve the status quo, to ensure that when an agency decision maker decides whether to proceed with a proposed action, he has available to him information on the possible adverse consequences of the proposed action. In this way, an injunction preserves the possibility that the decision maker will proceed with an agency action in a more environmentally-beneficial manner.[195]

A timely request for injunctive relief may be crucial to the outcome of a NEPA challenge. If plaintiffs request declaratory relief when they challenge an agency's proposed action but fail to also request injunctive relief, they risk the agency's continuing its action and the cause of action becoming moot.[196] "NEPA does not contemplate post-completion relief."[197] Therefore, absent proof of bad faith on the part of the agency, post-EIS injunctions, and after-the-fact EISs are not available as remedies.[198]

6.12.2 Scope of Injunctive Relief

There is nothing in NEPA to foreclose courts from balancing the equities in considering whether to issue an injunction.[199] Therefore, courts do not automatically grant injunctive relief if they find that an agency may have violated NEPA.[200] Indeed, a court has the equitable power not to order an injunction even if it finds that the agency violated NEPA.[201]

Relief under NEPA is remedial and not punitive.[202] Therefore, relief should not be ordered merely "to teach the agency a lesson"; the relief should benefit the public and advance NEPA policies.[203] An injunction should not be broader than necessary.[204]

NEPA does not prevent an agency from proceeding with an environmentally unwise action. Instead, it requires the agency to consider the environmental effects of its action before the decision maker decides whether to proceed with a proposed action. Thus, injunctive relief that permanently prevents an agency from proceeding with its action is inappropriate.[205]

On the other hand, a court has the power to maintain jurisdiction over a cause of action pending an agency's preparation of an EIS. In this way, the court may review the adequacy of the EIS when the EIS is subsequently submitted to it.[206] A court may not, however, interfere in the agency's preparation of the EIS.[207] Nor may a court enjoin procedures taken by the agency during its preparation of an EIS. The court must wait and review the EIS for adequacy after it is prepared.[208] The court also may not determine on the evidence before it at trial that an agency adequately complied with NEPA when it determines that the agency was required to prepare an EA or EIS and failed to do so. To allow a court to do this would circumvent NEPA's requirement that agencies and the public must be involved in the NEPA process.[209] If an agency delays unreasonably in issuing an EIS, a court may have jurisdiction to compel the agency to issue the EIS in a timely manner.[210]

6.12.3 Preliminary Injunctions

Various types of injunctive relief are requested and granted in NEPA actions, including temporary restraining orders, preliminary and final injunctions, and stays. The following discussion concerns preliminary injunctions. However, the discussion applies to all types of injunctive relief because the equities considered by the courts in all types of injunctive relief are similar.[211]

The judicial test for determining whether a preliminary injunction should be granted varies between the circuits. The judicial test typically includes the following four criteria in some form. The plaintiff must show a substantial likelihood of success on the merits, a substantial threat of irreparable injury to the plaintiff if the injunction is denied, that the threatened injury to the plaintiff outweighs the threatened harm the injunction may cause the defendants, and that granting the injunction does not disserve the public interest.[212] District courts have broad discretion in balancing these factors.[213] An injunction prevents the agency's actions from reaching a stage at which consideration of environmental effects would be meaningless because it would be impractical or impossible to alter or stop the action.[214]

Irreparable Harm. "Harm" has been defined in the NEPA context to mean environmental harm and also to mean, in some circuits, "the failure of decision-makers to take environmental factors into account in the way that NEPA mandates." The latter type of harm matures at the time NEPA is violated.[215] It is harm to the environment consisting of the added risk to the environment that occurs when an agency decision maker does not know the probable environmental effects of his decision.[216]

In a well-reasoned opinion, the First Circuit described why the "irreparable harm" that plaintiffs are required to show in order to attain injunctive relief should be the harm to the environment of an environmentally uninformed decision rather than environmental harm per se. The First Circuit analyzed the procedural nature of NEPA and held that, because an agency could proceed with an action upon completion of the NEPA process, a failure to comply with NEPA in informing the decision maker of environmental risks would be irreparable once the decision was made.[217]

Other courts consider only direct environmental harm and not the harm caused by noncompliance with NEPA to be "irreparable harm."[218] Defining the irreparable harm according to the latter definition has resulted in questionable decisions. For example, the Second Circuit has stated that in order to gain injunctive relief plaintiffs must show that irreparable injury will result during the pendency of the lawsuit if relief is not granted.[219] However, in at least the First, Fifth, and Ninth Circuits, NEPA requires that a plaintiff show that significant environmental effects may occur, not that they will occur.[220] Thus, plaintiffs in the Second Circuit are required to carry a heavier burden to show a likelihood of success on the merits than they would be required to prove at trial in other circuits.

There are other problems with requiring irreparable harm to be direct environmental harm. In determining whether environmental harm has occurred, courts tend to make determinations that are committed by NEPA to the agencies. For example, courts have held that injunctions are inappropriate when an agency action did not involve physical environmental harm,[221] when environmental effects were considered to be too speculative,[222] or when the environmental effects were considered to be minimal.[223] In determining whether to issue an injunction, one court considered the extent and long-term consequences of an action's environmental effects.[224] In effect, such determinations by the courts take into account whether the environmental effect of the agency action will be significant. These determinations should be made by an agency with input from other agencies and the public when appropriate, not by a court.

Threatened Harm to Defendant. Some costs arising from an injunction are not generally considered to substantially harm a defendant. Other costs such as threatened harm to the national security are allowable costs.[225] Costs that are not generally considered include the cost of delay that may result in increased monetary costs, postponement of initial employment and/or interruption of employment of people involved in the agency action.[226] Investments made pursuant to an agency action have been considered in some decisions but not in others.[227] Such investments should not be considered because NEPA anticipates that actions may be delayed until the agency complies with NEPA and that compliance with NEPA may result in changes to the proposed action. Thus expenditures in reliance on an agency action occurring at a given time or in a given manner should not be used to help defeat a judicial challenge to the agency's duty to comply with NEPA.

Public Interest. In determining whether to order a preliminary injunction in which the public interest is affected, a court must consider the public interest.[228] The public interest in an agency's completing an action tends to rise in importance the longer plaintiffs delay in filing the NEPA challenge.[229]

Courts have interpreted the public interest to include various interests. For example, the public interest has been held to include the interests of people who would benefit from the agency action,[230] the public interest in the agency's not continuing to spend public money on any action that may be abandoned or substantially altered,[231] the public interest in scientific information generated by an agency's scientific experiment,[232] and the public interest in irreparable harm to the environment not being permitted to occur.[233]

6.12.4 Permanent Injunctions

The principles and scope of review for permanent injunctions are similar to those for preliminary injunctions.[234] Thus, the above discussion on preliminary injunctions is relevant to permanent injunctions. Because permanent injunctions are issued after a trial on the merits, plaintiffs do not, of course, need to show a substantial likelihood of success on the merits.

6.12.5 Persons and Entities Subject to Injunctions

In addition to reaching an agency, an injunction in a NEPA case may reach nonfederal persons or entities in partnership with an agency. For example, recipients of federal funds[235] and entities whose projects require federal approval[236] may be enjoined until the respective agency complies with NEPA. Entities that have been enjoined under NEPA include a city,[237] a university,[238] and a private developer.[239]

When a private person or entity, or an agency continues to invest in a proposed agency action that is being challenged on the basis of noncompliance with NEPA, the private person or entity acts at its own risk.[240] An agency action taken on the basis of an inadequate EIS is ineffective.[241] Thus, the courts have authority to require an agency or a private person to undo activities taken in reliance on the agency action.[242] Because NEPA is essentially procedural, the agency could not be required to conduct its action in a different manner from that decided by the agency. However, the NEPA process could result in modifications to the agency's proposed action or even in a determination not to conduct the action. Although it appears unlikely that an agency would decide not to conduct an action it had already completed and thus spend funds undoing the action, it is not unforeseeable that an agency could decide not to issue a permit after a private entity had commenced construction of a facility on the faulty assumption that the permit would be issued.

6.12.6 Post-EIS Relief

It is well settled that once an agency action is completed before the action is judicially challenged, a court will not order an agency that

acted in good faith to comply with NEPA's procedural requirements.[243] It is not clear whether there is a right of action against an
agency that conducts an action that does not comply with an EIS.
There is no explicit requirement in NEPA that an agency must conduct
an action in conformity with an EIS.[244] If plaintiffs discover that the
agency is reneging on commitments contained in an EIS or is preventing the plaintiffs from discovering noncompliance with an EIS, the
plaintiffs may be able to challenge the agency's action on the basis that
the agency must comply with NEPA in regard to the new action.[245]
That is, plaintiffs may be able to successfully challenge the action on
the basis that changes in the action necessitate preparation of new
environmental documentation.

Such a challenge would depend upon the provisions in the EIS that
were violated. In an action seeking relief for an agency's failure to
keep within noise limits predicted by an EIS, the court noted that, if
agencies could be sued for failing to stay within predictions in an EIS,
the result could be that agencies would "hedge" estimates, which
could mean that decision makers would not receive the best available
information.[246]

In a case involving the inclusion in an EIS of an agreement by third
parties not to take certain actions at an airport that had been improved
by a federal grant, the Sixth Circuit held that NEPA did not create a
cause of action for an injunction to prevent federal actions that are
contrary to the provisions of an EIS.[247] However, the right to challenge
the post-EIS action may exist if the agency acted in bad faith in not
complying with the EIS.[248] If the agency commits itself to an action by
specifying the action it will take in a record of decision, the agency's
noncompliance with that action may be challenged through administrative law procedures.

If a decision is made to challenge an agency's noncompliance with
statements in an EIS, the plaintiff bringing the action should not be a
person or entity suing for relief to their property or for damages.
NEPA does not create a private right of action.[249] This principle is
similar to the principle that plaintiffs do not have standing if their sole
interest in bringing the action is economic.[250] In summary, to maximize
chances of a court recognizing a post-EIS cause of action, plaintiffs
must be able to allege environmental interests that affect the public as
well as themselves and must also be able to allege bad faith on the part
of the agency. However, even if a plaintiff is able to make both these
allegations, NEPA's procedural nature weighs against a court recognizing a post-EIS cause of action. The situation could change if Congress enacts a substantive amendment to NEPA that was pending in
1990.

6.12.7 Other Relief

Most lawsuits under NEPA involve challenges by plaintiffs against an agency's alleged noncompliance with NEPA. Atypical actions occasionally arise. One such action was a successful challenge by several political subdivisions to a citizens group that had threatened to judicially challenge the adequacy of an EIS prepared for a proposed highway that would benefit the subdivisions.[251] The court declared that the subdivisions had standing to sue the citizens group under the Federal Declaratory Judgment Act to declare the agency's final EIS adequate. In its discussion on standing, the court did not discuss whether the plaintiffs were within the class of people for whose especial benefit NEPA was enacted.[252] A plaintiff is required to allege such an interest before it has standing to bring about the NEPA challenge.[253] Without this interest, the subdivisions should not have had standing to sue. Alternatively, it is difficult to see how a court's decision that an EIS is adequate is binding on nonparties to the lawsuit.

Another unusual NEPA action involved the Forest Service's request for an injunction to prevent a gathering of people in a national forest until the Forest Service complied with NEPA.[254] The court questioned the Forest Service's good faith in raising the NEPA challenge and stated that NEPA should not be used "in a manner designed to suppress First Amendment activity, or out of hostility to a particular group."[255]

In other atypical actions, the courts have rejected arguments that there is a private right of action under NEPA.[256] They have also rejected arguments that damages[257] and restitution[258] are available as relief under NEPA.

Alternate relief to an injunction may be available in certain cases in which the agency action may be "set aside."[259] As in injunctions, however, the setting aside should not be permanent. Upon the agency's compliance with NEPA, the need for the relief ceases.[260]

6.13 BONDS

Federal Rule of Civil Procedure 65(c) provides that "[n]o restraining order or preliminary injunction shall issue except upon the giving of security by the applicant, in such sum as the court deems proper, for the payment of such costs and damages as may be incurred or suffered by any party who is found to have been wrongfully enjoined or restrained."

The general rule in NEPA cases is for a bond not to be required[261] or to be nominal.[262] Courts have occasionally imposed bonds in more than nominal amounts.[263] Arguably, however, bonds reflecting delay costs and costs incurred in reliance on an action that has been challenged for noncompliance with NEPA are improper because such costs should not be considered by a court in determining whether to issue an injunction.[264] Therefore, such costs should not be reflected in any bond that may be required.

The general rule that bonds should be nominal if they are required reflects congressional intent that plaintiffs aid the public in enforcing national environmental policy by seeking judicial review of agency actions.[265] Requiring plaintiffs, who are typically nonprofit organizations, to post large bonds would preclude them from filing suit and would "stifle the intent of [NEPA]."[266] Thus, despite the broad discretion enjoyed by the district court in setting the amount of a bond, a determination that the plaintiff must post a large bond may be viewed as unreasonable by a reviewing court.[267]

6.14 ATTORNEY FEES

Unless Congress specifies otherwise, each party to a lawsuit is generally responsible for its own attorney fees regardless of which party prevails.[268] An exception exists if the losing party acted in bad faith.[269]

Oddly, because NEPA's enforcement depends on citizen suits, NEPA does not contain a provision for awarding attorney fees. The fees and costs of challenging an agency's noncompliance with NEPA have been permitted under attorney fee provisions of interacting statutes.[270] Since the mid-1980s, however, most attorney fee claims in NEPA actions are brought under the Equal Access to Justice Act (EAJA), an act that applies generally to successful claims by certain plaintiffs against the United States.

The EAJA,[271] which was enacted in 1980 and re-enacted in 1985, is being used increasingly by prevailing NEPA plaintiffs to seek attorney fees and other expenses from the United States. Under the EAJA, plaintiffs are entitled to fees and other expenses from the United States if they fit the act's eligibility criteria and prevail in the lawsuit. The United States may avoid payment if it shows that its position was "substantially justified" or that special circumstances exist to make an award unjust.[272] Prevailing *pro se* litigants are entitled to expenses under the EAJA but are not entitled to attorney fees.[273]

Eligibility under the EAJA is restricted to parties with limited resources.[274] The following persons and entities are eligible: individuals with a net worth of not more than two million dollars when the lawsuit was filed; owners of unincorporated businesses, partnerships, corporations, associations, local governmental units, or organizations with a net worth of not more than seven million dollars and not more than five hundred employees when the lawsuit was filed; and certain section 501(c)(3) tax-exempt organizations regardless of net worth.[275]

The plaintiff has the burden of proving that it is the prevailing party.[276] A plaintiff proves that it prevailed by showing that it succeeded on at least one legal theory advanced by it.[277] The plaintiff also does not need to show success after a full trial on the merits; the relief may result from a settlement.[278]

A plaintiff must satisfy the following two criteria to prove that it prevailed. First, it must have achieved some of the benefits it sought.[279] The benefits may be of the same general class of relief sought by the plaintiff; the relief does not have to be the exact relief sought.[280] Second, a plaintiff must show a causal link between the litigation and either a change in the defendant's conduct or a change in the defendant's proposed action.[281] If the agency can show that the benefits obtained could not have resulted from the plaintiff's pursuit of the litigation because the plaintiffs did not introduce evidence on or argue for the type of relief obtained, causation is lacking.[282]

If an eligible plaintiff shows that it has prevailed, the agency has the burden of showing that its position was substantially justified or that special circumstances could make the fee shifting unjust.[283] In determining whether an agency's position is substantially justified, a court does not rely on the fact that the agency did not prevail on its litigation theory. The court conducts an independent inquiry into the agency's position.[284] The agency's position includes at least its litigation position and, in some circuits, the conduct that was the subject of the litigation.[285]

The agency must show that its position was substantially justified in fact and law.[286] That is, the agency must show that its position is "justified to a degree that could satisfy a reasonable person."[287] If an agency relitigates an issue that has previously been determined by a court in the relevant jurisdiction, the relitigation will weigh strongly against the agency's position being substantially justified.[288]

Courts have examined the agency's position over time in determining whether the agency's position was substantially justified in NEPA actions. The agency's position may have been substantially justified at one stage of the litigation but not at a later stage.[289] Thus, if the law was clear that the agency was violating NEPA at the time the agency adopted certain positions, the agency's position was not substantially justified as to the subsequent positions.[290] The comments of commenting agencies are relevant to a consideration of whether the agency's position was substantially justified.[291]

An early victory in the trial court is some evidence that the agency's position was substantially justified, but it is not dispositive.[292] An agency's willingness to enter into settlement proceedings is also not dispositive that the agency promptly abandoned its substantially unjustified litigation position. If the settlement proceedings are protracted, the agency may have to justify the delay.[293]

An agency may show that it falls within the "special circumstances" exception of the EAJA and that an award of attorney fees and costs to a prevailing plaintiff would be unjust.[294] This exception may apply in cases in which one or more of the plaintiffs was an ineligible plaintiff under the EAJA. If the ineligible plaintiff was willing and able to conduct the litigation, the other plaintiffs may not be entitled to attorney fees under the EAJA. Conversely, if the ineligible plaintiff's participation was nominal, attorney fees may be allowed to the eligible plaintiffs.[295]

NOTES

1. Yarrington, *The National Environmental Policy Act*, 4 Env't Rptr. (BNA) Monograph No. 17 at 13 (1974).

2. *See id.* at 11. *Compare* National Helium Corp. v. Morton, 486 F.2d 995, 1000 (10th Cir. 1973) ("NEPA furnishes a jurisdictional base"), *cert. denied*, 416 U.S. 993 (1974) *with* Borough of Morrisville v. Delaware River Basin Comm'n, 382 F. Supp. 543, 545 (E.D. Pa. 1974) (NEPA "does not in itself create jurisdiction"). *Cf.* Sierra Club v. Penfold, 857 F.2d 1307, 1315 (9th Cir. 1988) (NEPA does not authorize a private right of action); Noe v. Metropolitan Atlanta Rapid Transit Auth., 644 F.2d 434, 435 (5th Cir.) (same), *cert. denied*, 454 U.S. 1126 (1981).

3. *E.g.*, Hall County Historical Soc'y, Inc. v. Georgia Dep't of Transp., 447 F. Supp. 741, 748 (N.D. Ga. 1978) (plaintiffs satisfied requirements of 28 U.S.C. § 1331(a) (1988) and 5 U.S.C. § 701 (1988) even if 5 U.S.C. § 702 (1988) was not satisfied because of lack of standing).

4. 5 U.S.C. § 702 (1988); *see* United States v. Students Challenging Regulatory Agency Procedures, 412 U.S. 669, 686 (1973).

5. 28 U.S.C. § 1331 (1988); *see* Sylvester v. Corps of Eng'rs, 871 F.2d 817, 820 (9th Cir. 1989) (action brought under 28 U.S.C. § 1331 (1988) and 5 U.S.C. § 702 (1988)); Joseph v. Adams, 467 F. Supp. 141, 147–48 (E.D. Mich. 1978) (court has jurisdiction under 28 U.S.C. §§ 1331 and 1361 (1988)).

6. U.S. Const. art. III.

7. Flast v. Cohen, 392 U.S. 83, 101 (1968).

8. *See* Committee Against RR. Relocation v. Adams, 471 F. Supp. 142, 145 (E.D. Ark. 1979) (draft EIS was not subject to judicial review); *see also* section 6.4.1.

9. 5 U.S.C. § 701(a)(2) (1988).

10. *See, e.g.,* Shiffler v. Schlesinger, 548 F.2d 96, 101 (3d Cir. 1977) (Defense Department); Krueger v. Morton, 539 F.2d 235, 238–39 (D.C. Cir. 1976) (Secretary of Interior). *Cf.* McQueary v. Laird, 449 F.2d 608, 612 (10th Cir. 1971) (matters within Rocky Mountain Arsenal were wholly committed to agency discretion).

11. *See Krueger,* 539 F.2d at 239; *Shiffler,* 548 F.2d at 101–02.

12. Baker v. Carr, 369 U.S. 186, 217 (1962); *see* Mississippi *ex rel.* Moore v. Marsh, 710 F. Supp. 1488, 1502 (S.D. Miss. 1989) (challenge to agency's compliance with NEPA for action authorized by Congress did not present political question).

13. No Gwen Alliance of Lane County, Inc. v. Aldridge, 855 F.2d 1380, 1383–84 (9th Cir. 1988).

14. Romer v. Carlucci, 847 F.2d 445, 463 (8th Cir. 1988).

15. Weinberger v. Catholic Action of Hawaii/Peace Educ. Project, 454 U.S. 139, 146–47 (1981).

16. *See* Public Utils. Comm'r v. Bonneville Power Admin., 767 F.2d 622, 627 (9th Cir. 1985); City of Alexandria v. Helms, 728 F.2d 643, 646 (4th Cir. 1984); City of West Chicago v. NRC, 701 F.2d 632, 652 n.21 (7th Cir. 1983); Natural Resources Defense Council, Inc. v. Zeller, 688 F.2d 706, 711 (11th Cir. 1982); City of Rochester v. Bond, 603 F.2d 927, 936 (D.C. Cir. 1979); City of Southlake v. FAA, 679 F. Supp. 618, 622 (N.D. Tex. 1986). *See generally* General Public Utilities Corp. v. Susquehanna Valley Alliance, 449 U.S. 1096, 1099-1100 (1981) (Rehnquist, J., dissenting from denial of cert.) (noting that district court was exercising concurrent jurisdiction over action in which exclusive review was committed to courts of appeals); *but see* City of West Chicago v. NRC, 701 F.2d 632, 652 n.21 (7th Cir. 1983) (action in *Susquehanna Valley Alliance* did not come within exclusive review provisions).

17. Sierra Club v. Morton, 405 U.S. 727, 732–33 (1972); *see* No Gwen Alliance of Lane County, Inc. v. Aldridge, 855 F.2d 1380, 1382–83 (9th Cir. 1988).

18. Sierra Club v. Morton, 405 U.S. 727, 732 (1972) (quoting Baker v. Carr, 369 U.S. 186, 204 (1962); Flast v. Cohen, 392 U.S. 83, 101 (1968) (footnotes omitted)); *see* South East Lake View Neighbors v. HUD, 685 F.2d 1027, 1036–40 (7th Cir. 1982) (plaintiff must show injury capable of being redressed by remedy available to court). *Cf.* Rhode Island Comm. on Energy v. General Servs. Admin., 561 F.2d 397, 401 (1st Cir. 1977) (relief sought would cure alleged injury).

19. *See* Association of Data Processing Serv. Orgs., Inc. v. Camp, 397 U.S. 150, 153–55 (1970); *see also* Allen v. Wright, 468 U.S. 737, 751 (1984) (plaintiff must show that its alleged injury is within zone of interests protected by law being invoked).

20. *See* Clarke v. Securities Industry Ass'n, 107 S. Ct. 750, 758 n.16 (1987).

21. Sierra Club v. Morton, 405 U.S. 727, 733 (1972); *see* 5 U.S.C. § 702 (1988). *Cf.* Gifford-Hill & Co. v. FTC, 523 F.2d 730, 732 (D.C. Cir. 1975) (agency's decision to institute adjudicatory proceeding was not agency action reviewable under Administrative Procedure Act).

22. Sierra Club v. Morton, 405 U.S. 727, 739 (1972).

23. United States v. Students Challenging Regulatory Agency Procedures, 412 U.S. 669, 688 (1973).

24. *Id.* at 688–89; *see also* Citizens Comm. Against Interstate Route 675 v. Lewis, 542 F. Supp. 496, 525 (S.D. Ohio 1982) (plaintiffs' speculation as to consequences of agency action on city was insufficient to establish standing).

25. Sierra Club v. Morton, 405 U.S. 727, 734–35 (1972).

26. *See* Cane Creek Conservation Auth. v. Orange Water & Sewer Auth., 590 F. Supp. 1123, 1128 (M.D.N.C. 1984).

27. Association of Data Processing Serv. Orgs., Inc. v. Camp, 397 U.S. 150, 152 (1970).

28. Sierra Club v. Morton, 405 U.S. 727, 734 (1972).

29. *Id.*

30. *See* Neighborhood Dev. Corp. v. Advisory Council on Historic Preservation, 632 F.2d 21, 23–24 & n.1 (6th Cir. 1980); Cady v. Morton, 527 F.2d 786, 791–92 (9th Cir. 1975); Coalition for the Env't v. Volpe, 504 F.2d 156, 167 (8th Cir. 1974).

31. Oregon Envtl. Council v. Kunzman, 817 F.2d 484, 491 (9th Cir. 1987) (quoting City of Davis v. Coleman, 521 F.2d 661, 671 (9th Cir. 1975)); *see also* Sierra Club v. Marsh, 872 F.2d 497, 504 (1st Cir. 1989) ("harm at stake in a NEPA violation *is* a harm to the *environment* . . . the risk implied by a violation of NEPA is that real environmental harm will occur through inadequate foresight and deliberation" (emphasis original)); City of Davis v. Coleman, 521 F.2d 661, 672 (9th Cir. 1975) (a governmental entity authorized to participate in the EIS process suffers an injury-in-fact if an agency does not file an EIS). *Cf.* South East Lake View Neighbors v. HUD, 685 F.2d 1027, 1039 (7th Cir. 1982) (because agency action was in final construction phase, environmental injuries would not be averted by preparation of adequate EIS).

32. United States v. Students Challenging Regulatory Agency Procedures, 412 U.S. at 689 n.14 (quoting Davis, *Standing: Taxpayers and Others*, 35 U. Chi. L. Rev. 601, 613); *see* South East Lake View Neighbors v. HUD, 685 F.2d 1027, 1035 (7th Cir. 1982) (allegations of small increase in severe urban problems satisfied injury-in-fact test).

33. United States v. Students Challenging Regulatory Agency Procedures, 412 U.S. 669, 686 n.13 (1973).

34. *See* Animal Lovers Volunteer Ass'n, Inc. v. Weinberger, 765 F.2d 937, 938–39 (9th Cir. 1985).

35. *See* Port of Astoria v. Hodel, 595 F.2d 467, 475 (9th Cir. 1979); Churchill Truck Lines, Inc. v. United States, 533 F.2d 411, 416 (8th Cir. 1976); Clinton Community Hosp. Corp. v. Southern Md. Medical Center, 510 F.2d 1037, 1038 (4th Cir.), *cert. denied,* 422 U.S. 1048 (1975); Benton County Savings & Loan Ass'n v. Federal Home Loan Bank Bd., 450 F. Supp. 884, 890 (W.D. Ark. 1978).

36. Realty Income Trust v. Eckerd, 564 F.2d 447, 452 (D.C. Cir. 1977); *see also* Pack v. Corps of Eng'rs, 428 F. Supp. 460, 465 (M.D. Fla. 1977) (fishermen had interest in conserving shrimp as well as economic interest in shrimping).

37. *See* Robinson v. Knebel, 550 F.2d 422, 425 (8th Cir. 1977); Gerosa, Inc. v. Dole, 576 F. Supp. 344, 348–49 (S.D.N.Y. 1983); College Gardens Civic Ass'n, Inc. v. United States Dep't of Transp., 522 F. Supp. 377, 382 (D. Md. 1981).

38. National Helium Corp. v. Morton, 455 F.2d 650, 655 (10th Cir. 1971); Greenspon v. FHWA, 488 F. Supp. 1374, 1377 (D. Md. 1980); *see also* section 6.11 (unclean hands doctrine).

39. *Cf.* National Helium Corp. v. Morton, 455 F.2d 650, 654 (10th Cir. 1971) (companies' representation of public interest justified them seeking judicial review of agency action even though public interest was "admittedly less important than their private financial stake").

40. *See* Sierra Club v. Penfold, 857 F.2d 1307, 1315 (9th Cir. 1988) (no private right of action under NEPA); Noe v. Metropolitan Atlanta Rapid Transit Auth., 644 F.2d 434, 435 (5th Cir.) (same), *cert. denied*, 454 U.S. 1126 (1981).

41. *See* National Forest Preservation Group v. Butz, 485 F.2d 408, 410 (9th Cir. 1973).

42. *See* Coalition for the Env't v. Volpe, 504 F.2d 156, 167 (8th Cir. 1974). *Cf.* Protect Our Eagles' Trees v. City of Lawrence, 715 F. Supp. 996, 999 (D. Ks. 1989) (unincorporated association did not have standing when it did not allege that its members suffered any recreational or aesthetic injury; association alleged only that bald eagles would suffer if trees were cut down).

43. *See* Humane Soc'y of the United States v. Hodel, 840 F.2d 45, 52 (D.C. Cir. 1988).

44. *See* Committee for Auto Responsibility v. Solomon, 603 F.2d 992, 998 (D.C. Cir. 1979), *cert. denied*, 445 U.S. 915 (1980); Rhode Island Comm. on Energy v. General Servs. Admin., 561 F.2d 397, 401 (1st Cir. 1977); City of Davis v. Coleman, 521 F.2d 661, 671 (9th Cir. 1975).

45. *See* West Va. Highlands Conservancy v. Island Creek Coal Co., 441 F.2d 232, 235 (4th Cir. 1971).

46. *See* Conservation Council of North Carolina v. Costanzo, 505 F.2d 498, 502 (4th Cir. 1974).

47. *See* South East Lake View Neighbors v. HUD, 685 F.2d 1027, 1034 n.6 (7th Cir. 1982); *see also* Roshan v. Smith, 615 F. Supp. 901, 907 (D.D.C. 1985) (alien detainees did not have standing to challenge agency's action in constructing facility when they were not in sufficient threat of transfer to facility).

48. United States v. Students Challenging Regulatory Agency Procedures, 412 U.S. 669, 687–88 (1973); *see also* Oregon Envtl. Council v. Kunzman, 817 F.2d 484, 491 (9th Cir. 1987) (persons in state with actual gypsy moth problem had standing to challenge nationwide EIS on spraying problem applicable to them); Committee on Auto Responsibility v. Solomon, 603 F.2d 992, 998 n.15 (D.C. Cir. 1979) (small group of people affected by air pollution that affects all people in surrounding area has standing), *cert. denied*, 445 U.S. 915 (1980); Foundation on Economic Trends v. Watkins, 731 F. Supp. 530, 532–33 (D.D.C. 1990) (plaintiffs had standing to challenge actions affecting the global atmosphere).

49. *See* Greene County Planning Bd. v. FPC, 528 F.2d 38, 43–45 (2d Cir. 1975).

50. United States v. Students Challenging Regulatory Agency Procedures, 412 U.S. 669, 687–89 (1973); *see* No Gwen Alliance of Lane County, Inc. v. Aldridge, 855 F.2d 1380, 1383 (9th Cir. 1988); Greene County Planning Bd. v. FPC, 528 F.2d 38, 43–45 (2d Cir. 1975).

51. *See* Sierra Club v. Morton, 405 U.S. 727, 734–36 (1972).

52. *See* Scientists Inst. for Public Information, Inc. v. AEC, 481 F.2d 1079, 1086 n.29 (D.C. Cir. 1973); Foundation on Economic Trends v. Watkins, 731 F. Supp. 530, 532 (D.D.C. 1990); National Org. for Reform of Marijuana Laws v. United States Dep't of State, 452 F. Supp. 1226, 1230–31 (D.D.C. 1978).

53. *Cf.* Humane Soc'y of the United States v. Hodel, 840 F.2d 45, 54 n.13 (D.C. Cir. 1988) ("had the Society taken the trouble to join its members as fellow plaintiffs rather than premising the bulk of this suit on its role as a representative of its members, this lengthy inquiry . . . would perforce be unnecessary"); *see also* Citizens Comm. Against Interstate Route 675 v. Lewis, 542 F. Supp. 496, 524 (S.D. Ohio 1982) (association accorded standing because one of its members had standing).

54. Hunt v. Washington State Apple Advertising Comm'n, 432 U.S. 333, 343 (1977).

55. *See, e.g.,* United States v. Students Challenging Regulatory Agency Procedures, 412 U.S. 669, 678 (1973); Committee for Auto Responsibility v. Solomon, 603 F.2d 992, 998 n.13 (D.C. Cir. 1979).

56. *See* Humane Soc'y of the United States v. Hodel, 840 F.2d 45, 51–52 (D.C. Cir. 1988); Sierra Club v. Andrus, 610 F.2d 581, 593 (9th Cir. 1979); Environmental Defense Fund v. TVA, 468 F.2d 1164, 1171–72 (6th Cir. 1972); *see also* Citizens Comm. Against Interstate Route 675 v. Lewis, 542 F. Supp. 496, 525 (S.D. Ohio 1982) (association did not have standing when members suffered no injury-in-fact).

57. Humane Soc'y of the United States v. Hodel, 840 F.2d 45, 53–60 (D.C. Cir. 1988).

58. *See* Animal Lovers Volunteer Ass'n, Inc. v. Weinberger, 765 F.2d 937, 939 (9th Cir. 1985).

59. *See* Humane Soc'y of the United States v. Hodel, 840 F.2d 45, 53 (D.C. Cir. 1988); Committee on Auto Responsibility v. Solomon, 603 F.2d 992, 998 n.13 (D.C. Cir. 1979).

60. California v. Block, 690 F.2d 753, 776 (9th Cir. 1982); City of Davis v. Coleman, 521 F.2d 661, 672 (9th Cir. 1975); *see* 42 U.S.C. § 4332(2)(C) (1988).

61. *See* Port of Astoria v. Hodel, 595 F.2d 467, 475 (9th Cir. 1979).

62. *See* City of Rochester v. United States Postal Serv., 541 F.2d 967, 972 (2d Cir. 1976).

63. *See* Pennsylvania v. Morton, 381 F. Supp. 293, 300 (D.D.C. 1974).

64. *See* Prince George's County v. Holloway, 404 F. Supp. 1181, 1185 (D.D.C. 1975); Nolop v. Volpe, 333 F. Supp. 1364, 1367 (D.S.D. 1971).

65. *See* National Helium Corp. v. Morton, 455 F.2d 650, 655 (10th Cir. 1971).

66. *See* Port of Astoria v. Hodel, 595 F.2d 467, 476 (9th Cir. 1979).

67. *See* Lake Erie Alliance for Protection of Coastal Corridor v. Corps of Eng'rs, 486 F. Supp. 707, 710–14 (W.D. Pa. 1980).

68. Borelli v. City of Reading, 532 F.2d 950, 951 (3d Cir. 1976).

69. California *ex rel.* Younger v. Andrus, 608 F.2d 1247, 1249 (9th Cir. 1979).

70. *See* City of Evanston v. Regional Transp. Auth., 825 F.2d 1121, 1126 (7th Cir. 1987), *cert. denied,* 484 U.S. 1005 (1988); Save the Courthouse Comm. v. Lynn, 408 F. Supp. 1323, 1332 (S.D.N.Y. 1975).

71. Sierra Club v. Morton, 405 U.S. 727, 737 (1972); *see* Environmental Defense Fund v. TVA, 468 F.2d 1164, 1172 (6th Cir. 1972); *see also* Rhode Island Comm. on Energy v. General Servs. Admin., 561 F.2d 397, 402 n.4 (1st Cir. 1977).

72. City of Davis v. Coleman, 521 F.2d 661, 672 n.14 (9th Cir. 1975).

73. Sierra Club v. Adams, 578 F.2d 389, 391–92 (D.C. Cir. 1978).

74. United Family Farmers, Inc. v. Kleppe, 418 F. Supp. 591, 594 (D.S.D. 1976), *aff'd*, 552 F.2d 823 (8th Cir. 1977).

75. Abbott Laboratories v. Gardner, 387 U.S. 136, 149 (1967).

76. *See* Alabama *ex rel.* Baxley v. Woody, 473 F.2d 10, 14 (5th Cir. 1973); Daingerfield Island Protective Soc'y, Inc. v. Andrus, 458 F. Supp. 961, 963 (D.D.C. 1978); *see also* Grand Canyon Dorries, Inc. v. Walker, 500 F.2d 588, 590–91 (10th Cir. 1974) (agency must first determine extent to which NEPA applies to ongoing action); Wilderness Soc'y v. Morton, 479 F.2d 842, 889 (D.C. Cir.) (NEPA issues were not ripe when Congress must amend statute before agency action could occur), *cert. denied*, 411 U.S. 917 (1973).

77. *See* Rapid Transit Advocates, Inc. v. Southern Cal. Rapid Transit Dist., 752 F.2d 373, 378–79 (9th Cir. 1985); National Wildlife Fed'n v. Goldschmidt, 504 F. Supp. 314, 324–26 (D. Conn. 1980); *see also* Society Hill Civic Ass'n v. Harris, 632 F.2d 1045, 1059-60 (3d Cir. 1980) (challenge to consent decree authorizing agency to construct housing but not expressly requiring agency to comply with NEPA was premature; if noncompliance with NEPA occurred, plaintiffs could challenge agency action at that time).

78. *See* Aberdeen & Rockfish Ry. v. Students Challenging Regulatory Agency Procedures, 422 U.S. 289, 318–19 (1975).

79. 5 U.S.C. § 704 (1988). *But see* Iowa Student Public Interest Research Group v. Callaway, 379 F. Supp. 714, 715, 720 (S.D. Iowa 1974) (in action brought under Administrative Procedure Act, 28 U.S.C. §§ 1331, 1337, 1362, 2201, and 2202 (1988), plaintiffs were barred by laches from seeking injunction to restrain agency action pending release of final EIS).

80. *See* Friedman Bros. Investment Co. v. Lewis, 676 F.2d 1317, 1319 (9th Cir. 1982); Vine Street Concerned Citizens, Inc. v. Dole, 604 F. Supp. 509, 512–13 (E.D. Pa. 1985); Izaak Walton League of Am. v. Schlesinger, 337 F. Supp. 287, 293 (D.D.C. 1971).

81. *See* Oregon Envtl. Council v. Kunzman, 817 F.2d 484, 492 (9th Cir. 1987); Norvell v. Sangre de Cristo Dev. Co., 519 F.2d 370, 375 (10th Cir. 1975); National Wildlife Fed'n v. Clark, 630 F. Supp. 412, 417 (D.D.C. 1985); *see also* Sierra Club v. Penfold, 857 F.2d 1307, 1319 (9th Cir. 1988) (issue of whether agency could be ordered to comply with NEPA in future actions was not ripe in absence of evidence that agency would violate NEPA in those actions).

82. *See* Friedman Bros. Inv. Co. v. Lewis, 676 F.2d 1317, 1319 (9th Cir. 1982); Natural Resources Defense Council v. Hughes, 437 F. Supp. 981, 987 (D.D.C. 1977), *modified*, 454 F. Supp. 148 (D.D.C. 1978).

83. Portland Audubon Soc'y v. Lujan, 712 F. Supp. 1456, 1483 (D. Or. 1989), *aff'd in part and rev'd in nonpertinent part*, 884 F.2d 1233 (9th Cir. 1989).

84. Trustees for Alaska v. Hodel, 806 F.2d 1378, 1381 (9th Cir. 1986); *see* section 5.15.

85. *See* Harlem Valley Transp. Ass'n v. Stafford, 500 F.2d 328, 334–35 (2d Cir. 1974).

86. *See* National Wildlife Fed'n v. Snow, 561 F.2d 227, 236–37 (D.C. Cir. 1976).

87. *See* Natural Resources Defense Council v. EPA, 859 F.2d 156, 168 (D.C. Cir. 1988).

88. United States Parole Comm'n v. Geraghty, 445 U.S. 388, 397 (1980) (quoting Monaghan, *Constitutional Adjudication: The Who and When*, 82 Yale L.J. 1363, 1384 (1973)).

89. *See* Northern Alaska Envtl. Center v. Hodel, 803 F.2d 466, 469 (9th Cir. 1986); City of Newport Beach v. Civil Aeronautics Bd., 665 F.2d 1280, 1284 (D.C. Cir. 1981); Upper Pecos Ass'n v. Stans, 500 F.2d 17, 19 (10th Cir. 1974); Warren County v. North Carolina, 528 F. Supp. 276, 283 (E.D.N.C. 1981); Citizens for Mass Transit Against Freeways v. Brinegar, 357 F. Supp. 1269, 1275 (D. Ariz. 1973); *see also* City of Boston v. Brinegar, 512 F.2d 319, 320 (1st Cir. 1975) (action became moot when agency completed EIS; court dismissed action without prejudice to issues concerning adequacy of NEPA compliance).

90. *See* National Audubon Soc'y v. Andrus, 442 F. Supp. 42, 44 (D.D.C. 1977).

91. *See* Arlington Coalition on Transp. v. Volpe, 458 F.2d 1323, 1332 (4th Cir.), *cert. denied*, 409 U.S. 1000 (1972).

92. *See* Neighbors Organized to Insure a Sound Env't, Inc. v. McArtor, 878 F.2d 174, 178 (6th Cir. 1989) (airport terminal was completed and operational); Sierra Club v. Penfold, 857 F.2d 1307, 1318 (9th Cir. 1988) (mining had occurred); American Horse Protection Ass'n, Inc. v. Watt, 679 F.2d 150, 151 (9th Cir. 1982) (wild horse roundup had occurred); Richland Park Homeowners Ass'n, Inc. v. Pierce, 671 F.2d 935, 941–42 (5th Cir. 1982) (apartment units were complete and fully occupied; therefore, issue was moot except for further subsidies to be paid by agency); City of Romulus v. County of Wayne, 634 F.2d 347, 348 (6th Cir. 1980) (runway was constructed; plaintiffs failed to request injunction pending appeal; injunction prior to completion of EIS had been dissolved); Friends of the Earth, Inc. v. Bergland, 576 F.2d 1377, 1379 (9th Cir. 1978) (exploratory mining activities had ceased and permit had expired).

93. *See* Upper Pecos Ass'n v. Stans, 500 F.2d 17, 19 (10th Cir. 1974) (construction was not too far advanced to permit consideration of environmental factors).

94. *See* Burbank Anti-Noise Group v. Goldschmidt, 623 F.2d 115, 116 (9th Cir. 1980), *cert. denied*, 450 U.S. 965 (1981).

95. *See* Columbia Basin Land Protection Ass'n v. Schlesinger, 643 F.2d 585, 591 n.1 (9th Cir. 1981); Lake Wylie Water Resources Protective Ass'n v. Rodgers Builders, Inc., 621 F. Supp. 305, 306 (D.S.C. 1985); *see also* Northern Cheyenne Tribe v. Hodel, 851 F.2d 1152, 1157 (9th Cir. 1988) (in issuing injunction, court should not consider investments made in reliance on agency action that was challenged for noncompliance with NEPA); Van Abbema v. Fornell, 807 F.2d 633, 636–37 (7th Cir. 1986) (if plaintiffs prevail "we presumably could order that the facility be dismantled, altered or operated differently").

96. *See* South Carolina Dep't of Wildlife & Marine Resources v. Marsh, 866 F.2d 97, 100–01 (4th Cir. 1989); Coalition for Safe Nuclear Power v. AEC, 463 F.2d 954, 956 n.1 (D.C. Cir. 1972); *see also* Allied-General Nuclear Servs. v. United States, 839 F.2d 1572, 1573–74 (Fed. Cir.) (issues raised consequent to NEPA process eventually caused the president to freeze agency action), *cert. denied*, 109 S. Ct. 61 (1988).

97. *See* Missouri Coalition for the Env't v. Corps of Eng'rs, 866 F.2d 1025, 1029-30 (8th Cir.), *cert. denied*, 110 S. Ct. 76 (1989); Oregon Envtl. Council v. Kunzman, 714 F.2d 901, 902–03 (9th Cir. 1983).

98. *See* American Horse Protection Ass'n, Inc. v. Watt, 679 F.2d 150, 151 (9th Cir. 1982); Cedar-Riverside Envtl. Defense Fund v. Hills, 560 F.2d 377, 382 (8th Cir. 1977); Potomac River Ass'n, Inc. v. Lundeberg Md. Seamanship School, Inc., 402 F. Supp. 344, 351–52 (D. Md. 1975); *see also* Natural Resources Defense Council, Inc. v. Morton, 337 F. Supp. 170, 173 (D.D.C. 1972) (no indication that agency would conduct future actions illegally).

99. Cedar-Riverside Envtl. Defense Fund v. Hills, 560 F.2d 377, 382 (8th Cir. 1977).

100. Cartwright Van Lines, Inc. v. United States, 400 F. Supp. 795, 804 (W.D. Mo. 1975), *aff'd*, 423 U.S. 1083 (1976).

101. National Ass'n of Recycling Indus., Inc. v. ICC, 627 F.2d 1341, 1345 (D.C. Cir. 1980).

102. *See, e.g.*, City of Tenakee Springs v. Block, 778 F.2d 1402, 1405 (9th Cir. 1985) (citing Alaska Lands Act § 708(b)(1)); Navajo Tribe of Indians v. Andrus, 644 F.2d 790, 791 (9th Cir. 1981) (citing Navajo and Hopi Indian Relocation Amendments Act of 1980 § 28(a)); Earth Resources Co. v. FERC, 617 F.2d 775, 779-80 (D.C. Cir. 1980) (citing Alaska Natural Gas Transportation Act, 15 U.S.C. § 719h(c)(3)); Named Individual Members of San Antonio Conservation Soc'y v. Texas Highway Dep't, 496 F.2d 1017, 1022 (5th Cir. 1974) (citing Federal-Aid Highway Act of 1973 § 154(a)), *cert. denied*, 420 U.S. 926 (1975).

103. *See* Izaak Walton League of Am. v. Marsh, 655 F.2d 346, 366 (D.C. Cir.) (Congress declared EIS adequate but did not exempt agency action from further compliance with NEPA), *cert. denied*, 454 U.S. 1092 (1981).

104. Committee for Nuclear Responsibility, Inc. v. Seaborg, 463 F.2d 783, 785–86 (D.C. Cir. 1971); National Audubon Soc'y v. Andrus, 442 F. Supp. 42, 45 (D.D.C. 1977); *see also* Sierra Club v. Corps of Eng'rs, 732 F.2d 253, 258 (2d Cir. 1984) ("simple fact that Congress authorized appropriations . . . is totally dispositive"); Environmental Defense Fund v. TVA, 468 F.2d 1164, 1182 (6th Cir. 1972) ("we are unimpressed with appellants' argument that Congress authorized appropriations"); Natural Resources Defense Council v. Hughes, 437 F. Supp. 981, 987 (D.D.C. 1977) (legislative history of amendment did not indicate that Congress intended to exempt agency action from NEPA), *modified*, 454 F. Supp. 148 (D.D.C. 1978). *Cf.* Sierra Club v. Adams, 578 F.2d 389, 395–96 (D.C. Cir. 1978) (discussions of alternatives to Pan American highway in EIS were "somewhat brief" but discussions are reasonable because Congress authorized United States assistance in constructing highway).

105. Fed. R. Civ. P. 24(a)(2).

106. *Id.*

107. Donaldson v. United States, 400 U.S. 517, 531 (1971).

108. Portland Audubon Soc'y v. Hodel, 866 F.2d 302, 309 (9th Cir.) (quoting County of Fresno v. Andrus, 622 F.2d 436, 438 (9th Cir. 1980)), *cert. denied*, 109 S. Ct. 3229 (1989).

109. *See* section 6.3.2.

110. *See* Diamond v. Charles, 476 U.S. 54, 68–69 & n.21 (1986); *see also* Portland Audubon Soc'y v. Hodel, 866 F.2d 302, 308 n.1 (9th Cir.), *cert. denied*, 109 S. Ct. 3229 (1989). *Cf.* United States v. Students Challenging Regulatory Agency Pro-

cedures, 412 U.S. 669, 680 n.9 (1973) (discussing intervenors' allegations of standing).

111. Natural Resources Defense Council, Inc. v. NRC, 578 F.2d 1341, 1344 (10th Cir. 1978); *see also* Organizations United for Ecology v. Bell, 446 F. Supp. 535, 550 (M.D. Pa. 1978) (state and local entities were permitted to intervene as of right).

112. Natural Resources Defense Council, Inc. v. NRC, 578 F.2d 1341, 1345–46 (10th Cir. 1978).

113. Wade v. Goldschmidt, 673 F.2d 182, 185 (7th Cir. 1982).

114. Sierra Club v. Corps of Eng'rs, 709 F.2d 175, 176 (2d Cir. 1983).

115. Wilderness Soc'y v. Morton, 463 F.2d 1261, 1262–63 (D.C. Cir. 1972).

116. Fed. R. Civ. P. 24(b)(2).

117. *See* Wade v. Goldschmidt, 673 F.2d 182, 187 (7th Cir. 1982).

118. *See, e.g.,* Sierra Club v. Corps of Eng'rs, 709 F.2d 175, 177 (2d Cir. 1983) (upholding denial of intervention application); Wade v. Goldschmidt, 673 F.2d 182, 186–87 (7th Cir. 1982) (same); Illinois *ex rel.* Scott v. Butterfield, 396 F. Supp. 632, 636 (N.D. Ill. 1975) (upholding grant of intervention).

119. Fed. R. Civ. P. 24(b)(2).

120. *See* Conner v. Burford, 848 F.2d 1441, 1445 (9th Cir. 1988) (trial court permitted joinder for limited purpose of protecting right to appeal) (app. pending).

121. *See* Northern Alaska Envtl. Center v. Hodel, 803 F.2d 466, 468–69 (9th Cir. 1986).

122. Fed. R. Civ. P. 19(b); *see* Manygoats v. Kleppe, 558 F.2d 556, 559 (10th Cir. 1977).

123. 5 U.S.C. § 704 (1988); *see* General Public Utilities Corp. v. Susquehanna Valley Alliance, 449 U.S. 1096, 1098–99 (1981) (Rehnquist, J., dissenting from denial of certiorari). *Cf.* Potomac River Ass'n, Inc. v. Lundeberg Md. Seamanship School, Inc., 402 F. Supp. 344, 352 (D. Md. 1975) (agency, not court, had primary jurisdiction over agency action).

124. *See* Merrell v. Thomas, 807 F.2d 776, 782 n.3 (9th Cir. 1986), *cert. denied*, 484 U.S. 848 (1987).

125. *See, e.g.,* Foundation on Economic Trends v. Heckler, 756 F.2d 143, 156 (D.C. Cir. 1985) (permitting review of issue of great public importance); Ecology Center of La., Inc. v. Coleman, 515 F.2d 860, 865–66 (5th Cir. 1975) (doctrine is a "flexible concept"); *see also* Valley Citizens for a Safe Env't v. Aldridge, 886 F.2d 458, 469 (1st Cir. 1989) (comments on agency's methodology should be made before the agency not before a reviewing court); Environmental Defense Fund, Inc. v. Callaway, 497 F.2d 1340, 1342 (8th Cir. 1974) (declining to adopt or reject dicta in trial court opinion that plaintiffs' failure to comment during NEPA process may be considered in decision whether EIS is adequate). *Cf.* County of Suffolk v. Secretary of Interior, 562 F.2d 1368, 1385 (2d Cir. 1977) (plaintiffs' failure to present evidence of inadequacy to agency did not bar judicial challenge), *cert. denied*, 434 U.S. 1064 (1978).

126. *See* Michigan v. City of Allen Park, 501 F. Supp. 1007, 1018 (E.D. Mich. 1980).

127. Wisconsin Heritages, Inc. v. Harris, 490 F. Supp. 1334, 1338 (E.D. Wis. 1980).

128. *See, e.g.,* 54 Fed. Reg. 28,081 (1989) (citing *Wisconsin Heritages*); *id.* at 19,423 (same).

129. Atlantic Terminal Urban Renewal Area Coalition v. New York City Dep't of Envtl. Protection, 705 F. Supp. 988, 997–98 (S.D.N.Y. 1989); see County of Suffolk v. Secretary of Interior, 562 F.2d 1368, 1385 (2d Cir. 1977) (responsibility of providing adequate EIS is primary and nondelegable with the agency), cert. denied, 434 U.S. 1064 (1978).

130. See Marsh v. Oregon Natural Resources Council, 109 S. Ct. 1851, 1862 (1989); California v. Watt, 712 F.2d 584, 609-10 (D.C. Cir. 1983).

131. See, e.g., Jette v. Bergland, 579 F.2d 59, 64 (10th Cir. 1978) (administrative remedies were exhausted); Arkansas Power & Light Co. v. FPC, 517 F.2d 1223, 1236–37 (D.C. Cir. 1975) (agency had opportunity to pass on issue sought to be raised), cert. denied, 424 U.S. 933 (1976).

132. See Wisconsin Heritages, Inc. v. Harris, 490 F. Supp. 1334, 1338 (E.D. Wis. 1980) (refusing to grant plaintiff leave to file supplemental pleading); Pennsylvania v. Federal Maritime Comm'n, 392 F. Supp. 795, 803 (D.D.C. 1975) (applying laches to NEPA issue because plaintiffs initiated previous administrative and judicial challenges to agency action without mentioning issue).

133. See Atlantic Terminal Urban Renewal Area Coalition v. New York City Dep't of Envtl. Protection, 705 F. Supp. 988, 999 (S.D.N.Y. 1989).

134. See Greenspon v. FHWA, 488 F. Supp. 1374, 1377 (D. Md. 1980); see also Milo Community Hosp. v. Weinberger, 525 F.2d 144, 147 (1st Cir. 1975) (agency effectively argued at trial that exhaustion was unnecessary).

135. Jette v. Bergland, 579 F.2d 59, 62 (10th Cir. 1978); see Ecology Center of La., Inc. v. Coleman, 515 F.2d 860, 865–66 (5th Cir. 1975).

136. See Southeast Alaska Conservation Council, Inc. v. Watson, 697 F.2d 1305, 1309 (9th Cir. 1983); American Horse Protection Ass'n, Inc. v. Frizzell, 403 F. Supp. 1206, 1215 (D. Nev. 1975).

137. See Foundation on Economic Trends v. Heckler, 756 F.2d 143, 156 (D.C. Cir. 1985) (reviewing agency action despite plaintiff's failure to exhaust administrative remedies because "appropriate environmental review for the first deliberate release of genetically engineered organisms is one of great public importance").

138. See Jette v. Bergland, 579 F.2d 59, 64 (10th Cir. 1978).

139. Sierra Club v. Penfold, 857 F.2d 1307, 1315 (9th Cir. 1988).

140. 28 U.S.C. § 2401(a) (1988).

141. Sierra Club v. Penfold, 857 F.2d 1307, 1315 (9th Cir. 1988).

142. Ecology Center of La., Inc. v. Coleman, 515 F.2d 860, 867 (5th Cir. 1975). Laches has also been applied to bar a counterclaim. Michigan v. City of Allen Park, 501 F. Supp. 1007, 1017 (E.D. Mich. 1980).

143. See Jicarilla Apache Tribe v. Andrus, 687 F.2d 1324, 1338 (10th Cir. 1982); Save Our Wetlands, Inc. v. Corps of Eng'rs, 549 F.2d 1021, 1026 (5th Cir.), cert. denied, 434 U.S. 836 (1977); see also Coalition for Canyon Preservation v. Bowers, 632 F.2d 774, 780 & n.2 (9th Cir. 1980) (declining to determine triggering date of delay because undue prejudice not shown); Ecology Center of La., Inc. v. Coleman, 515 F.2d 860, 868 & n.9 (5th Cir. 1975) (same).

144. See Coalition for Canyon Preservation v. Bowers, 632 F.2d 774, 779 (9th Cir. 1980).

145. See Save Our Wetlands, Inc. v. Rush, 424 F. Supp. 354, 356 (E.D. La. 1976); Essex County Preservation Ass'n v. Campbell, 399 F. Supp. 208, 219 (D. Mass.

1975), *aff'd*, 536 F.2d 956 (1st Cir. 1976); *see also* Cady v. Morton, 527 F.2d 786, 792 (9th Cir. 1975) (plaintiffs did not fail to exercise due diligence by not filing suit until after final EIS was prepared). *But see* Watershed Assocs. Rescue v. Alexander, 586 F. Supp. 978, 985 (D. Neb. 1982) (triggering date was commencement of action not date final EIS was filed with CEQ). *Cf.* Citizens Comm. Against Interstate Route 675 v. Lewis, 542 F. Supp. 496, 527 (S.D. Ohio 1982) (triggering date was not date of approval of EIS when plaintiffs were not directly affected by action at that time).

146. *See* Dalsis v. Hills, 424 F. Supp. 784, 788 (W.D.N.Y. 1976).

147. *See* Woida v. United States, 446 F. Supp. 1377, 1391 (D. Minn. 1978); Iowa Student Public Interest Research Group v. Callaway, 379 F. Supp. 714, 720 (S.D. Iowa 1974).

148. *See* section 6.4.1.

149. Save the Courthouse Comm. v. Lynn, 408 F. Supp. 1323, 1334 (S.D.N.Y. 1975).

150. Steubing v. Brinegar, 511 F.2d 489, 495 (2d Cir. 1975).

151. Shiffler v. Schlesinger, 548 F.2d 96, 104 (3d Cir. 1977).

152. Organizations United for Ecology v. Bell, 446 F. Supp. 535, 546–47 (M.D. Pa. 1978).

153. *See* Peshlaki v. Duncan, 476 F. Supp. 1247, 1256 (D.D.C. 1979) (citing cases listing length of delay).

154. *See id.*

155. Smith v. Schlesinger, 371 F. Supp. 559, 561 (C.D. Cal. 1974).

156. Save Our Wetlands, Inc. v. Rush, 424 F. Supp. 354, 356 (E.D. La. 1976).

157. *See, e.g.,* Fund for Animals v. Frizzell, 530 F.2d 982, 987–88 (D.C. Cir. 1975); Smith v. Schlesinger, 371 F. Supp. 559, 561 (C.D. Cal. 1974).

158. *See, e.g.,* Public Interest Research Group v. Brinegar, 517 F.2d 917, 918 (6th Cir. 1975).

159. *See* Jicarilla Apache Tribe v. Andrus, 687 F.2d 1324, 1338–39 (10th Cir. 1982) (tribe could have learned that agency had not prepared an EIS for an action requiring an EIS).

160. *See* City of Davis v. Coleman, 521 F.2d 661, 677 (9th Cir. 1975).

161. Jicarilla Apache Tribe v. Andrus, 687 F.2d 1324, 1339 (10th Cir. 1982).

162. Mansfield Area Citizens Group v. United States, 413 F. Supp. 810, 824 (M.D. Pa. 1976).

163. Save Our Wetlands v. Corps of Eng'rs, 549 F.2d 1021, 1027 (5th Cir.), *cert. denied*, 434 U.S. 836 (1977).

164. *Id.* at 1027–28; Steubing v. Brinegar, 511 F.2d 489, 495 (2d Cir. 1975).

165. Save Our Wetlands, Inc. v. Corps of Eng'rs, 549 F.2d 1021, 1028 (5th Cir.), *cert. denied*, 434 U.S. 836 (1977).

166. Organizations United for Ecology v. Bell, 446 F. Supp. 535, 549 (M.D. Pa. 1978).

167. *See* Hall County Historical Soc'y, Inc. v. Georgia Dep't of Transp., 447 F. Supp. 741, 748 (N.D. Ga. 1978); Save the Courthouse Comm. v. Lynn, 408 F. Supp. 1323, 1334 (S.D.N.Y. 1975).

168. *See* Save Our Wetlands, Inc. v. Rush, 424 F. Supp. 354, 356 (E.D. La. 1976).

169. *See* Arkansas Community Org. for Reform Now v. Coleman, 531 F.2d 864, 866 (8th Cir. 1976); *see also* Organizations United for Ecology v. Bell, 446 F. Supp. 535, 549 (M.D. Pa. 1978) (threat of personal liability for would-be plaintiffs may excuse delay in filing suit).

170. *See* City of Rochester v. United States Postal Serv., 541 F.2d 967, 977 (2d Cir. 1976); Stow v. United States *ex rel.* Soil Conservation Serv., 696 F. Supp. 857, 863 (W.D.N.Y. 1988); *see also* International Fund for Animal Welfare v. Baldrige, 594 F. Supp. 129, 133 (D.D.C. 1984) (plaintiffs barred by laches from challenging agency's three-year-old EIS for adequacy when agency would be too late to conduct action if it had to revise EIS).

171. *See* Centerview/Glen Avalon Homeowners Ass'n v. Brinegar, 367 F. Supp. 633, 639 (C.D. Cal. 1973).

172. *See* Organizations United for Ecology v. Bell, 446 F. Supp. 535, 548–49 (M.D. Pa. 1978).

173. *See id.* at 548.

174. Coalition for Canyon Preservation v. Bowers, 632 F.2d 774, 779 (9th Cir. 1980); *see* Preservation Coalition, Inc. v. Pierce, 667 F.2d 851, 855 (9th Cir. 1982) (plaintiffs' action was not barred by laches because plaintiffs complained to agency that an EIS was required, and filed suit immediately after being told none was required); Cady v. Morton, 527 F.2d 786, 792 (9th Cir. 1975) (plaintiffs made their opposition known to agency); *see also* Watershed Assocs. Rescue v. Alexander, 586 F. Supp. 978, 984 (D. Neb. 1982) (applying Ninth Circuit test).

175. Watershed Assocs. Rescue v. Alexander, 586 F. Supp. 978, 985–86 (D. Neb. 1982); *see also* Coalition for Canyon Preservation v. Bowers, 632 F.2d 774, 780 (9th Cir. 1980) (expenditure of one million dollars on project is not, by itself, sufficient prejudice for laches to bar cause of action).

176. Ecology Center of La., Inc. v. Coleman, 515 F.2d 860, 869 n.10 (5th Cir. 1975).

177. Preservation Coalition, Inc. v. Pierce, 667 F.2d 851, 855 (9th Cir. 1982); Shiffler v. Schlesinger, 548 F.2d 96, 103 (3d Cir. 1977).

178. *See* Arlington Coalition on Transp. v. Volpe, 458 F.2d 1323, 1328–30 (4th Cir.) (construction had scarcely begun even though 93.9% of residences, 98.5% of businesses, and 84.4% of necessary rights-of-way were acquired and 75.6% of all families were relocated), *cert. denied*, 409 U.S. 1000 (1972); Hall County Historical Soc'y, Inc. v. Georgia Dep't of Transp., 447 F. Supp. 741, 748 (N.D. Ga. 1978) (construction had not begun).

179. *See* Cady v. Morton, 527 F.2d 786, 792 (9th Cir. 1975); *see also* Citizens Comm. Against Interstate Route 675 v. Lewis, 542 F. Supp. 496, 527 (S.D. Ohio 1982) (possibility of environmental harm occurring was not caused by plaintiff's delay); Save Our Wetlands, Inc. v. Rush, 424 F. Supp. 354, 356 (E.D. La. 1976) (agency would have expended money even if plaintiffs had filed suit earlier). *But see* International Fund for Animal Welfare v. Baldrige, 594 F. Supp. 129, 133 (D.D.C. 1984) (plaintiffs barred by laches from challenging adequacy of three-year-old EIS when revising EIS would mean not conducting action).

180. *See* section 6.5.

181. *See* Coalition for Canyon Preservation v. Bowers, 632 F.2d 774, 779 (9th Cir. 1980); Arlington Coalition on Transp. v. Volpe, 458 F.2d 1323, 1329 & n.2 (4th Cir.), *cert. denied*, 409 U.S. 1000 (1972).

206 Guide to the National Environmental Policy Act

182. Ecology Center of La., Inc. v. Coleman, 515 F.2d 860, 868 (5th Cir. 1975); Save Our Wetlands, Inc. v. Corps of Eng'rs, 549 F.2d 1021, 1028 (5th Cir.), *cert. denied*, 434 U.S. 836 (1977).

183. Ecology Center of La., Inc. v. Coleman, 515 F.2d 860, 868 (5th Cir. 1975); *see also* Mansfield Area Citizens Group v. United States, 413 F. Supp. 810, 825 (M.D. Pa. 1976) (recognizing public interest in agency's completion of action).

184. *See* Shiffler v. Schlesinger, 548 F.2d 96, 103 (3d Cir. 1977); *see also* Steubing v. Brinegar, 511 F.2d 489, 495 (2d Cir. 1975) (Congress imposed duties on agencies).

185. Ecology Center of La., Inc. v. Coleman, 515 F.2d 860, 868 (5th Cir. 1975).

186. Watershed Assocs. Rescue, 586 F. Supp. 978, 986 (D. Neb. 1982); *see also* Coalition for Canyon Preservation v. Bowers, 632 F.2d 774, 781 (9th Cir. 1980) (unnecessary environmental damage could be mitigated even though action had already begun); Steubing v. Brinegar, 511 F.2d 489, 496 (2d Cir. 1975) (agency action was only in early construction phase). *Cf.* Marsh v. Oregon Natural Resources Council, 109 S. Ct. 1851, 1858 (1989) (citing TVA v. Hill, 437 U.S. 153, 188 n.34 (1978) ("'it would make sense to hold NEPA inapplicable at some point in the life of a project because the agency would no longer have a meaningful opportunity to *weigh* the benefits of the project versus the detrimental effects on the environment' up to that point" (emphasis original)).

187. *See* Save the Courthouse Comm. v. Lynn, 408 F. Supp. 1323, 1333 (S.D.N.Y. 1975).

188. *See* Save Our Wetlands, Inc. v. Corps of Eng'rs, 549 F.2d 1021, 1028–29 (5th Cir.), *cert. denied*, 434 U.S. 836 (1977); Shiffler v. Schlesinger, 548 F.2d 96, 104 (3d Cir. 1977); *see also* Stow v. United States *ex rel.* Soil Conservation Serv., 696 F. Supp. 857, 863 (W.D.N.Y. 1988) (landscape was irreversibly altered); Dalsis v. Hills, 424 F. Supp. 784, 789 (W.D.N.Y. 1976) (comparing public interest in preserving unspoiled natural environment to construction of commercial structure in predominantly commercial area); Friends of Yosemite v. Frizzell, 420 F. Supp. 390, 398 (N.D. Cal. 1976) (costs of altering or abandoning project outweighed benefits of preparing EIS).

189. Jicarilla Indian Tribe v. Andrus, 687 F.2d 1324, 1340 (10th Cir. 1982); *see* Peshlaki v. Duncan, 476 F. Supp. 1247, 1257 (D.D.C. 1979).

190. *See* sections 6.3.2 (standing) and 6.6.1 (intervention).

191. Aberdeen & Rockfish Ry. v. Students Challenging Regulatory Agency Procedures, 422 U.S. 289, 319 (1975).

192. *See* Noe v. Metropolitan Atlanta Rapid Transit Auth., 644 F.2d 434, 435 (5th Cir.), *cert. denied*, 454 U.S. 1126 (1981).

193. Environmental Defense Fund, Inc. v. Froehlke, 477 F.2d 1033, 1037 (8th Cir. 1973).

194. *See* Atchison, Topeka & Santa Fe Ry. v. Callaway, 431 F. Supp. 722, 730 (D.D.C. 1977).

195. *See* Alaska v. Andrus, 580 F.2d 465, 485 (D.C. Cir.), *vacated in nonpertinent part sub nom.* Western Oil & Gas Ass'n v. Alaska, 439 U.S. 922 (1978).

196. *See* Chick v. Hills, 528 F.2d 445, 447–48 & n.3 (1st Cir. 1976); *see also* Taylor Bay Protective Ass'n v. Ruckelshaus, 687 F. Supp. 1319, 1323 (E.D. Ark. 1988)

(action on agency project completed sixteen years previously was moot), *aff'd*, 884 F.2d 1073 (8th Cir. 1989).

197. Richland Park Homeowners Ass'n v. Pierce, 671 F.2d 935, 941 (5th Cir. 1982).

198. *See id.* at 942; Aertsen v. Landrieu, 637 F.2d 12, 19 (1st Cir. 1980).

199. *See* Northern Cheyenne Tribe v. Hodel, 842 F.2d 224, 230 (9th Cir. 1988).

200. *See* New York v. NRC, 550 F.2d 745, 753 (2d Cir. 1977); Conservation Council of N. Carolina v. Costanzo, 528 F.2d 250, 252 (4th Cir. 1975).

201. *See* Northern Cheyenne Tribe v. Hodel, 851 F.2d 1152, 1157–58 (9th Cir. 1988); *see also* Marquez-Colon v. Reagan, 668 F.2d 611, 616 (1st Cir. 1981) (no bad faith on part of agency); Warm Springs Dam Task Force v. Gribble, 621 F.2d 1017, 1022 (9th Cir. 1980) (agency made good faith effort to comply).

202. Warm Springs Dam Task Force v. Gribble, 621 F.2d 1017, 1022 (9th Cir. 1980); *see also* Realty Income Trust v. Eckerd, 564 F.2d 447, 457 (D.C. Cir. 1977) ("relief would serve no remedial purpose in this case").

203. Friends of the River v. FERC, 720 F.2d 93, 107 (D.C. Cir. 1983).

204. *See* South Carolina Dep't of Wildlife & Marine Resources, 866 F.2d 97, 100 (4th Cir. 1989); *see also* Ohio *ex rel.* Brown v. Callaway, 497 F.2d 1235, 1240–41 (6th Cir. 1974) (partial injunction).

205. *Cf.* Sierra Club v. Hennessy, 695 F.2d 643, 647–48 (2d Cir. 1982) (vacating injunction that permanently enjoined agency paying right-of-way acquisition costs to state); *see also* Sierra Club v. Corps of Eng'rs, 732 F.2d 253, 257 (2d Cir. 1984) (injunction did not permanently enjoin agency action; purpose was to ensure agency's compliance with NEPA); City of Rochester v. United States Postal Serv., 541 F.2d 967, 978 (2d Cir. 1976) (agency should be enjoined from conducting action until NEPA is complied with).

206. *See* Sierra Club v. Penfold, 857 F.2d 1307, 1322 (9th Cir. 1988); *see also* Fayetteville Area Chamber of Commerce v. Volpe, 463 F.2d 402, 405–06 (4th Cir. 1972) (remanding action to district court that was to retain jurisdiction until court was satisfied agency complied with NEPA), *cert. denied*, 423 U.S. 912 (1975).

207. *See* Sierra Club v. Corps of Eng'rs, 701 F.2d 1011, 1043 (2d Cir. 1983); Society for Animal Rights, Inc. v. Schlesinger, 512 F.2d 915, 918 (D.C. Cir. 1975).

208. *See* Bennett Hills Grazing Ass'n v. United States, 600 F.2d 1308, 1309 (9th Cir. 1979) (court may not enjoin preparation of final EIS until plaintiffs had ninety days to comment on draft EIS).

209. *See* Sierra Club v. Hodel, 848 F.2d 1068, 1092–94 (10th Cir. 1988).

210. *See* City of West Chicago v. NRC, 701 F.2d 632, 652 (7th Cir. 1983).

211. *Compare* Canal Auth. v. Callaway, 489 F.2d 567, 572 (5th Cir. 1974) (criteria for preliminary injunction) *with* Texas v. United States Forest Serv., 805 F.2d 524, 525 (5th Cir. 1986) (criteria for stay pending appeal).

212. Canal Auth. v. Callaway, 489 F.2d 567, 572 (5th Cir. 1974); *see* Foundation on Economic Trends v. Heckler, 756 F.2d 143, 157 (D.C. Cir. 1985); Sierra Club v. Hennessy, 695 F.2d 643, 647 (2d Cir. 1982); National Indian Youth Council v. Andrus, 623 F.2d 694, 695 (10th Cir. 1980); Conservation Council of N.C. v. Costanzo, 528 F.2d 250, 252 (4th Cir. 1975); Ohio *ex rel.* Brown v. Callaway, 497 F.2d 1235, 1241 (6th Cir. 1974).

213. Northern Alaska Envtl. Center v. Hodel, 803 F.2d 466, 471 (9th Cir. 1986); Foundation on Economic Trends v. Heckler, 756 F.2d 143, 157 (D.C. Cir. 1985).

214. Steubing v. Brinegar, 511 F.2d 489, 497 (2d Cir. 1975); Arlington Coalition on Transp. v. Volpe, 458 F.2d 1323, 1333 (4th Cir.), *cert. denied*, 409 U.S. 1000 (1972).

215. *See* Jones v. District of Columbia Redevelopment Land Agency, 499 F.2d 502, 512 (D.C. Cir. 1974), *cert. denied*, 423 U.S. 937 (1975); *see also* Proetta v. Dent, 484 F.2d 1146, 1149 (2d Cir. 1973) (injunction denied where irreparable harm was caused by nonfederal act). *But see* Town of Huntington v. Marsh, 884 F.2d 648, 653 (2d Cir. 1989) ("threat of irreparable injury must be proved, not assumed, and may not be postulated *eo ipso* on the basis of procedural violations of NEPA"), *cert. denied*, 110 S. Ct. 1296 (1990).

216. Sierra Club v. Marsh, 872 F.2d 497, 500 (1st Cir. 1989); *see also* New York v. Kleppe, 429 U.S. 1307, 1312 (1976) (Marshall, Circuit J.) ("[i]t is axiomatic that if the Government, without preparing an adequate impact statement were to make an 'irreversible commitment of resources' a citizen's right to have environmental factors taken into account by the decisionmaker would be irreparably impaired" (citation omitted)).

217. Sierra Club v. Marsh, 872 F.2d 497, 502–05 (1st Cir. 1989); *see also* Jones v. District of Columbia Redevelopment Land Agency, 499 F.2d 502, 512 (D.C. Cir. 1974) (harm is "failure of decision-makers to take environmental factors into account in the way that NEPA mandates"), *cert. denied*, 423 U.S. 937 (1975).

218. *See* Town of Huntington v. Marsh, 884 F.2d 648, 653 (2d Cir. 1989), *cert. denied*, 110 S. Ct. 1296 (1990).

219. *E.g.*, New York v. NRC, 550 F.2d 745, 756 (2d Cir. 1977). *But see* Steubing v. Brinegar, 511 F.2d 489, 496 (2d Cir. 1975) (court record contained adequate showing of "probable, irreparable injury").

220. *See* Fritiofson v. Alexander, 772 F.2d 1225, 1238 n.7 (5th Cir. 1985); Sierra Club v. Marsh, 769 F.2d 868, 870 (1st Cir. 1985); Steamboaters v. FERC, 759 F.2d 1382, 1392 (9th Cir. 1985).

221. *See, e.g.*, Stand Together Against Neighborhood Decay, Inc. v. Board of Estimate, 690 F. Supp. 1192, 1196–98 (E.D.N.Y. 1988).

222. *See, e.g.*, Cuomo v. NRC, 772 F.2d 972, 976 (D.C. Cir. 1985); New York v. NRC, 550 F.2d 745, 754–55 (2d Cir. 1977).

223. *See, e.g.*, Fund for Animals v. Frizzell, 530 F.2d 982, 987 (D.C. Cir. 1975); Massachusetts Air Pollution & Noise Abatement Comm. v. Brinegar, 499 F.2d 125, 126 (1st Cir. 1974); Environmental Defense Fund, Inc. v. Froehlke, 477 F.2d 1033, 1037 (8th Cir. 1973). *See also* Adams v. Vance, 570 F.2d 950, 957 (D.C. Cir. 1978) (environmental effects could be mitigated).

224. City of Alexandria v. Helms, 719 F.2d 699, 700 (4th Cir. 1983).

225. *See* Committee for Nuclear Responsibility, Inc. v. Seaborg, 463 F.2d 796, 798 (D.C. Cir. 1971) (considering harm to national security from action not proceeding).

226. *See* Steubing v. Brinegar, 511 F.2d 489, 497 & n.15 (2d Cir. 1975); *see also* Stop 3-H Ass'n v. Volpe, 353 F. Supp. 14, 18 (D. Hawaii 1972). *Cf.* National Indian Youth Council v. Andrus, 623 F.2d 694, 696 (10th Cir. 1980) (considering employment opportunities for Navajo Tribe members in consideration of public interest).

227. *See* Northern Cheyenne Tribe v. Hodel, 851 F.2d 1152, 1157 (9th Cir. 1988) (investments made on basis of defective EIS or by persons with knowledge of NEPA lawsuit should not be considered). *Cf.* Sierra Club v. Hennessy, 695 F.2d 643, 645, 650 (2d Cir. 1982) (considering harm to state in not receiving federal funding; state acquired property for which it expected partial federal reimbursement during pendency of NEPA challenge); National Indian Youth Council v. Andrus, 623 F.2d 694, 696 (10th Cir. 1980) (considering monetary harm to intervenors of investing in action); Lake Wylie Water Resources Protective Ass'n v. Rodgers Builders, Inc., 621 F. Supp. 305, 307 (D.S.C. 1985) (considering harm to permittee).

228. American Motorcyclist Ass'n v. Watt, 714 F.2d 962, 967 (9th Cir. 1983).

229. *See, e.g.*, Smith v. Schlesinger, 371 F. Supp. 559, 561 (C.D. Cal. 1974) (harm to agency and national defense outweighed harm to public interest when plaintiffs unreasonably delayed filing NEPA challenge).

230. *See* National Indian Youth Council v. Andrus, 623 F.2d 694, 696 (10th Cir. 1980); Lake Wylie Water Resources Protective Ass'n v. Rodgers Builders, Inc., 621 F. Supp. 305, 310 (D.S.C. 1985).

231. *See* Stop H-3 Ass'n v. Volpe, 353 F. Supp. 14, 19 (D. Hawaii 1972).

232. *See* Mack v. Califano, 447 F. Supp. 668, 670 (D.D.C. 1978).

233. *See* Sierra Club v. Lujan, 716 F. Supp. 1289, 1293 (D. Ariz. 1989).

234. Sierra Club v. Hennessy, 695 F.2d 643, 647 (2d Cir. 1982); *see also* Sierra Club v. Corps of Eng'rs, 732 F.2d 253, 256 (2d Cir. 1984) (describing preliminary and final injunctions).

235. *See* Silva v. Romney, 473 F.2d 287, 292 (1st Cir. 1973).

236. *See* Foundation on Economic Trends v. Heckler, 756 F.2d 143, 155 (D.C. Cir. 1985).

237. *See* Proetta v. Dent, 484 F.2d 1146, 1148 (2d Cir. 1973).

238. *See* Foundation on Economic Trends v. Heckler, 756 F.2d 143, 155 (D.C. Cir. 1985).

239. *See* Silva v. Romney, 473 F.2d 287, 289-90 (1st Cir. 1973).

240. *See* South Carolina Dep't of Wildlife & Marine Resources v. Marsh, 866 F.2d 97, 100–01 (4th Cir. 1989); Coalition for Safe Nuclear Power v. AEC, 463 F.2d 954, 956 n.1 (D.C. Cir. 1972). *See generally* Allied-General Nuclear Servs. v. United States, 839 F.2d 1572, 1573–74 (Fed. Cir.) (issues raised consequent to NEPA process eventually caused the president to freeze agency action), *cert. denied*, 109 S. Ct. 61 (1988).

241. Northern Cheyenne Tribe v. Hodel, 842 F.2d 224, 229 (9th Cir. 1988).

242. *See* Van Abbema v. Fornell, 807 F.2d 633, 636–37 (7th Cir. 1986).

243. *See* Richland Park Homeowners Ass'n, Inc. v. Pierce, 671 F.2d 935, 941 (5th Cir. 1982). *Cf.* Marsh v. Oregon Natural Resources Council, 109 S. Ct. 1851, 1858 (1989) (citing TVA v. Hill, 437 U.S. 153, 188 n.34 (1978)) (if agency action has produced all significant environmental effects it will produce, agency no longer has a meaningful opportunity to weigh the benefits of the action against the environmental costs).

244. *See* City of Blue Ash v. Lucas, 596 F.2d 709, 712 (6th Cir. 1979); Sierra Club v. Mason, 365 F. Supp. 47, 49-50 (D. Conn. 1973); Mountainbrook Homeowners Ass'n, Inc. v. Adams, 492 F. Supp. 521, 529 (W.D.N.C. 1979).

245. *See* Sierra Club v. Mason, 365 F. Supp. 47, 49-50 (D. Conn. 1973).

246. Noe v. Metropolitan Atlanta Rapid Transit Auth., 644 F.2d 434, 439 (5th Cir.), *cert. denied*, 454 U.S. 1126 (1981).

247. City of Blue Ash v. McLucas, 596 F.2d 709, 712 (6th Cir. 1979); Ogunquit Village Corp. v. Davis, 553 F.2d 243, 246 (1st Cir. 1977).

248. Marquez-Colon v. Reagan, 668 F.2d 611, 616 (1st Cir. 1981).

249. Noe v. Metropolitan Atlanta Rapid Transit Auth., 644 F.2d 434, 435 (5th Cir.), *cert. denied*, 454 U.S. 1126 (1981).

250. *See* section 6.3.2.

251. Collin County v. Homeowners Ass'n for Values Essential to Neighbors, 716 F. Supp. 953 (N.D. Tex. 1989).

252. *See id.* at 964–65.

253. *See* Clarke v. Securities Industry Ass'n, 107 S. Ct. 750, 758 n.16 (1987) (plaintiff must show he was in class for whose especial benefit invoked statute was enacted); section 6.3.1.

254. United States v. Rainbow Family, 695 F. Supp. 314, 323–25 (E.D. Tex. 1988).

255. *Id.* at 325.

256. Sierra Club v. Penfold, 857 F.2d 1307, 1315 (9th Cir. 1988); Noe v. Metropolitan Atlanta Rapid Transit Auth., 644 F.2d 434, 435 (5th Cir.), *cert. denied*, 454 U.S. 1126 (1981); Mountainbrook Homeowners Ass'n, Inc. v. Adams, 492 F. Supp. 521, 526 (W.D.N.C. 1979). *Cf.* Kennedy v. United States, 643 F. Supp. 1072, 1082 (E.D.N.Y. 1986) (there may be private right of action under Environmental Quality Improvement Act).

257. Ogunquit Village Corp. v. Davis, 553 F.2d 243, 245 n.3 (1st Cir. 1977); Pye v. Department of Transp., 513 F.2d 290, 293 (5th Cir. 1975); United States v. 45,149.58 Acres of Land, 455 F. Supp. 192, 203 (E.D.N.C. 1978); Tanner v. Armco Steel Corp., 340 F. Supp. 532, 537 (S.D. Tex. 1972).

258. Pye v. Department of Transp., 513 F.2d 290, 293 (5th Cir. 1975).

259. 5 U.S.C. § 706(2)(D) (1988); *see* Port of Astoria v. Hodel, 595 F.2d 467, 479-80 (9th Cir. 1979).

260. *See* Port of Astoria v. Hodel, 595 F.2d 467, 479-80 (9th Cir. 1979) (agency declared leases unenforceable pending completion of EIS); *see also* Northern Cheyenne Tribe v. Hodel, 851 F.2d 1152, 1156–57 (9th Cir. 1988) (district court did not abuse discretion in suspending rather than voiding leases).

261. *See* Morgan v. Walter, 728 F. Supp. 1483, 1494 (D. Idaho 1989); Story v. Marsh, 563 F. Supp. 679, 684 (E.D. Mo. 1983); Wisconsin Heritages, Inc. v. Harris, 476 F. Supp. 300, 302 (E.D. Wis. 1979); Boston Waterfront Residents Ass'n, Inc. v. Romney, 343 F. Supp. 89, 91 (D. Mass. 1972).

262. *See* Wilderness Soc'y v. Tyrrel, 701 F. Supp. 1473, 1492 (E.D. Cal. 1988); Wisconsin Heritages, Inc. v. Harris, 476 F. Supp. 300, 302 (E.D. Wis. 1979) (listing cases where nominal bonds were required and ordering that no bond be posted); Stop H-3 Ass'n v. Volpe, 349 F. Supp. 1047, 1049, *as amended by*, 353 F. Supp. 14 (D. Hawaii 1972). *Cf.* Kansas *ex rel.* Stephan v. Adams, 705 F.2d 1267, 1269-70 (10th Cir. 1983) (upholding trial court decision that costs and expenses of temporary restraining order imposed by court should not be imposed on plaintiffs).

263. *See* Stockslager v. Carroll Elec. Cooperative Corp., 528 F.2d 949, 951 (8th Cir. 1976) (bond of at least $10,000 should have been required); *see also* River Defense Comm. v. Thierman, 380 F. Supp. 91, 95 (S.D.N.Y. 1974) ($7,500 bond was sufficient); Natural Resources Defense Council, Inc. v. Grant, 341 F. Supp. 356, 370 (E.D.N.C. 1972) (bond of $75,000 reflected costs of delay and costs expended by agency and intervenors).

264. *See* Steubing v. Brinegar, 511 F.2d 489, 497 & n.15 (2d Cir. 1975).

265. Wisconsin Heritages, Inc. v. Harris, 476 F. Supp. 300, 302 (E.D. Wis. 1979); Natural Resources Defense Council, Inc. v. Morton, 337 F. Supp. 167, 168–69 (D.D.C. 1971), *motion for summary reversal denied*, 458 F.2d 827 (D.C. Cir. 1972).

266. Natural Resources Defense Council, Inc. v. Morton, 337 F. Supp. 167, 169 (D.D.C. 1971), *motion for summary reversal denied*, 458 F.2d 827 (D.C. Cir. 1972).

267. *See* Friends of the Earth, Inc. v. Brinegar, 518 F.2d 322, 323 (9th Cir. 1975); *see also* Sylvester v. Corps of Eng'rs, 871 F.2d 817, 824 (9th Cir.) ("district court should reconsider the amount of [plaintiff's] $100,000 bond if it determines that a preliminary injunction should issue"), *as amended*, 884 F.2d 394, 397 n.2, 401 (9th Cir. 1989).

268. Alyeska Pipeline Serv. Co. v. Wilderness Soc'y, 421 U.S. 240, 269 (1975).

269. *Id.* at 258–59; *see* Sierra Club v. Corps of Eng'rs, 776 F.2d 383, 390 (2d Cir. 1985) (court's decision to award fees on basis of bad faith was not an abuse of discretion), *cert. denied*, 475 U.S. 1084 (1986); Robinson v. Ritchie, 646 F.2d 147, 148 (4th Cir. 1981) (no evidence of bad faith); *see also* Rhode Island Comm. on Energy v. GSA, 561 F.2d 397, 404–05 (1st Cir. 1977) (considering that bad faith exception probably did not exist to 28 U.S.C. § 2412 (1988)). *Cf.* Greene County Planning Bd. v. FPC, 559 F.2d 1227, 1235 (2d Cir. 1977) (agency was authorized to pay intervenor's expenses in administrative process), *cert. denied*, 434 U.S. 1086 (1978).

270. *See* Conservation Law Found'n of New England, Inc. v. Secretary of Interior, 790 F.2d 965, 970 (1st Cir. 1986) (claims under Outer Continental Shelf Lands Act and NEPA were interrelated); *see also* Morris County Trust for Historic Preservation v. Pierce, 730 F.2d 94, 95 (3d Cir. 1983) (National Historic Preservation Act provision for attorney fees and costs claim included NEPA claim).

271. 28 U.S.C. § 2412(d) (1988).

272. *Id.* § 2412(d)(1)(A).

273. Merrell v. Block, 809 F.2d 639, 641–42 (9th Cir. 1987).

274. 28 U.S.C. § 2412(d)(2)(B) (1988); *see* Thomas v. Peterson, 841 F.2d 332, 337 (9th Cir. 1988).

275. 28 U.S.C. § 2412(d)(2)(B) (1988).

276. Dunn v. United States, 842 F.2d 1420, 1432–33 (3d Cir. 1988).

277. Southern Or. Citizens Against Toxic Sprays, Inc. v. Clark, 720 F.2d 1475, 1481 (9th Cir. 1983), *cert. denied*, 469 U.S. 1028 (1984).

278. *See* Dunn v. United States, 842 F.2d 1420, 1433 (3d Cir. 1988); *see also* Environmental Defense Fund, Inc. v. Watt, 722 F.2d 1081, 1085–86 (2d Cir. 1983) (examining plaintiff's right to attorney fees in case involving settlement); North Ga. C.O.P.S. v. Reagan, 587 F. Supp. 1506, 1508 (N.D. Ga. 1984) (plaintiffs voluntarily dismissed all claims except NEPA claim; parties stipulated that NEPA claim was moot; court decides EAJA claim).

279. Dunn v. United States, 842 F.2d 1420, 1433 (3d Cir. 1988).

280. *Id.* at 1434.

281. *Id.* at 1433; *see also* Thomas v. Peterson, 841 F.2d 332, 337 (9th Cir. 1988) (change need not result directly from court order as long as it results from litigation); Oregon Envtl. Council v. Kunzman, 817 F.2d 484, 497 (9th Cir. 1987) (plaintiffs must play catalytic role in bringing about desired result).

282. *See* Dunn v. United States, 842 F.2d 1420, 1434–35 (3d Cir. 1988).

283. Sierra Club v. Secretary of Army, 820 F.2d 513, 517 (1st Cir. 1987).

284. Louisiana *ex rel.* Guste v. Lee, 853 F.2d 1219, 1222 (5th Cir. 1988); *see also* Trustees for Alaska v. Hodel, 806 F.2d 1378, 1384 (9th Cir. 1986) (agency "argued forcefully and well for its position. Its position was at all times justified, although erroneous").

285. Citizens Council v. Brinegar, 741 F.2d 584, 592–93 (3d Cir. 1984); *see* Environmental Defense Fund, Inc. v. Watt, 722 F.2d 1081, 1084–85 (2d Cir. 1983) (discussing split in circuits on definition of "position"); *see also* Thomas v. Peterson, 841 F.2d 332, 335 (9th Cir. 1988) (as a matter of law, agency's underlying conduct and litigation position were not substantially justified).

286. Citizens Council v. Brinegar, 741 F.3d 584, 593 (3d Cir. 1984).

287. Pierce v. Underwood, 108 S. Ct. 2541, 2550 (1988); *see* Animal Lovers Volunteer Ass'n, Inc. v. Carlucci, 867 F.2d 1224, 1225 (9th Cir. 1989).

288. *See* Save Our Ecosystems v. Clark, 747 F.2d 1240, 1250 (9th Cir. 1984).

289. *See* Southern Or. Citizens Against Toxic Sprays, Inc. v. Clark, 720 F.2d 1475, 1481 (9th Cir. 1983), *cert. denied*, 469 U.S. 1028 (1984).

290. *See* Thomas v. Peterson, 841 F.2d 332, 336 (9th Cir. 1988); *see also* Louisiana *ex rel.* Guste v. Lee, 853 F.2d 1219, 1223 (5th Cir. 1988) (circuit law may have been unclear but agency regulations were clear); North Ga. C.O.P.S. v. Reagan, 587 F. Supp. 1506, 1509 (N.D. Ga. 1984) (prior case law supported agency's position).

291. *See* Sierra Club v. Secretary of Army, 820 F.2d 513, 520 (1st Cir. 1987).

292. *See id.* at 517–20; *see also* Thomas v. Peterson, 841 F.2d 332, 334 (9th Cir. 1988) (examining totality of circumstances to determine whether agency's position was substantially justified).

293. Environmental Defense Fund, Inc. v. Watt, 722 F.2d 1081, 1086 (2d Cir. 1983).

294. 28 U.S.C. § 2412(d)(1)(A) (1988).

295. Louisiana *ex rel.* Guste v. Lee, 853 F.2d 1219, 1225 (5th Cir. 1988); *see also* Citizens Council v. Brinegar, 741 F.2d 584, 589, 597–98 (3d Cir. 1984) (apportionment of fees may be appropriate when some plaintiffs are ineligible under the EAJA).

7

State Statutes

7.1 INTRODUCTION

Shortly after NEPA was enacted, states began to enact their own environmental policy acts, frequently known as mini-NEPAs. Some states closely followed NEPA's language, applying the mini-NEPAs to the actions of state, and occasionally local, agencies.[1] Twenty-seven states have statutes that are either based on NEPA, have the same purposes as NEPA, or require procedures similar to those of NEPA. Chapter 7 provides an overview of three state environmental policy statutes and contrasts and compares them with NEPA.

The first statute to be examined is the Michigan Environmental Protection Act. Whereas NEPA is essentially procedural, the Michigan statute has no procedural requirements with which agencies must comply. The Michigan statute applies to private as well as public actions and to ongoing as well as proposed actions, thus contrasting with NEPA, which only applies to proposed federal actions.

The second statute to be examined, the California Environmental Quality Act, was modeled on NEPA but has substantive as well as procedural provisions. It is a detailed statute implemented by detailed guidelines. The influence of NEPA case law and the CEQ regulations is evident in the statute, the guidelines implementing it, and its case law.

Finally, the New York State Environmental Quality Review Act, enacted in 1975, is reviewed. The New York statute, which has substantive and procedural provisions, was modeled on NEPA. Regulations and case law under the statute are also influenced by NEPA case law and the CEQ guidelines and regulations.

7.2 THE MICHIGAN ENVIRONMENTAL PROTECTION ACT

7.2.1 Overview

The Michigan Environmental Protection Act (MEPA) became effective on October 1, 1970.[2] The act authorizes any person, agency, corporation, or "other legal entity" to sue any other legal entity "for the protection of the air, water and other natural resources and the public trust therein from pollution, impairment or destruction."[3] That is, MEPA gives people and other legal entities a right to environmental quality that can be protected by the courts through the development of a common law of environmental quality.[4] Conversely, it imposes a duty on people and other legal entities to prevent or minimize environmental degradation caused by their actions.[5] MEPA is broad, extending not only to actions by state and local agencies but also to private actions conducted on property to which the public has no right of access.[6]

MEPA provides "a procedural cause of action for protection of Michigan's natural resources" and prescribes "substantive environmental rights, duties and functions of subject entities."[7] Under MEPA, courts may grant temporary or permanent injunctions or impose conditions on actions.[8] Restoration of natural habitat is also a proper remedy under MEPA.[9] MEPA strongly encourages citizen suits and has provided a model of a citizen suit provision used in other statutes.

The issue of whether a court may impose large bonds against citizens acting in the public interest is avoided by MEPA imposing a cap of $500 on any security bond required to be posted.[10] The Act authorizes costs, which includes attorney's fees, to be apportioned if required by the interests of justice.[11]

If a pollution standard or antipollution device is at issue, a court may determine its validity, applicability, and reasonableness, and the court may direct adoption of a new standard if it finds the existing standard to be deficient.[12] This power to create standards is not necessarily preempted by federal law. Thus, the holder of a federal permit may be judicially required to adopt more stringent standards than those imposed by federal law in certain cases.[13]

To obtain relief under the act, a plaintiff must present a prima facie case that the defendant's conduct "has, or is likely to pollute, impair or destroy the air, water or other natural resources or the public trust therein."[14] The prima facie case may be rebutted by a defendant presenting contrary evidence or by presenting an affirmative defense that no feasible and prudent alternative to the conduct exists and by showing that the "conduct is consistent with the promotion of the public health, safety and welfare in light of the state's paramount concern for the protection of its natural resources from pollution, impairment or destruction."[15] Detailed scientific evidence need not be presented in order to make a prima facie case.[16] Courts do not defer to an agency's expertise regarding whether the agency activity prevents potential pollution, impairment, or destruction but make an independent determination instead.[17] A plaintiff need not exhaust administrative remedies before seeking judicial review of an agency decision under MEPA.[18]

MEPA does not contain procedures that a state or local agency must follow before it can act. Professor Joseph Saxan, author of the act designed by MEPA to reach the merits of cases as quickly as possible without extensive litigation on procedural issues.[19] Sax rejected the creation of a special environmental review board to monitor state environmental decisions. Wary of the board's potential control by economic and political interests, Sax preferred to designate the courts as the overseers of environmental decisions, with the aid of suits brought by citizens.[20]

The Michigan Legislature deliberately excluded an explicit threshold of harm from MEPA.[21] Instead, MEPA's threshold of harm has been imposed by the courts which distinguish between actions that merely impact natural resources and those that meet MEPA's threshold. As the Michigan Supreme Court stated, "virtually all human activities can be found to adversely impact natural resources in some way or other."[22] The test, therefore, is not whether a natural resource is impacted or affected, but whether it is polluted, impaired, or destroyed to a level justifying judicial intervention.[23]

It is well settled that appellate courts review MEPA decisions of trial courts de novo.[24] It is less clear whether courts should independently review the MEPA decisions of agencies de novo or whether the court should use the substantial evidence standard.[25]

In reviewing a claim under MEPA to determine whether the plaintiff made a prima facie showing that the defendant polluted, impaired, or destroyed a natural resource, a court determines first, whether a natural resource is involved, and second, whether the level of impairment alleged justifies judicial intervention.[26]

To satisfy the first part of the test, a natural resource must be adversely affected. The terms "air, water and other natural resources" in MEPA do not include effects on the social and cultural environment.[27] Aesthetic considerations, standing alone, do not trigger MEPA.[28] If the proposed action will not affect a natural resource, the plaintiff's claim fails.[29] For example, rezoning has been held not to trigger MEPA because the act of rezoning did not destroy or impair natural resources.[30] If the court finds that it is unlikely that natural resources will be impaired, polluted, or destroyed, the court may decide that judicial intervention is not warranted.[31]

In order to satisfy the second part of the test, a court considers several factors, including whether the natural resource is "rare, unique, endangered, or has historical significance"; the resource is easily replaceable; there will be any significant indirect effects on other natural resources; and whether the direct or indirect effects of the proposed action will impact on a critical number of animals or plants.[32] A statewide, rather than a local, perspective is generally applied in determining whether a natural resource is impaired.[33]

In essence, the test is a restatement of MEPA case law. Michigan courts have found that development of a small area of wildlife habitat was not an impairment when the same species of wildlife could be maintained on other natural areas within Michigan[34]; the loss of trout caused by impoundment of a stream was not an impairment when the trout stream was marginal and trout had to be restocked to survive as a species in the stream[35]; destruction of a small number of animals or plants in a common species was not an impairment[36]; removal of trees from a nonwilderness area was not a "significant consequential impact on the environment justifying judicial intervention"[37]; and destruction of trees from a roadway was not an impairment when the trees were replaceable.[38] In contrast, the courts found that the risk to the last wild elk herd east of the Mississippi River would impair or destroy a natural resource[39]; as would continued gill net fishing in the Great Lakes when the fish population would probably be injured if the fishing continued.[40]

If a plaintiff presents a prima facie case of pollution, impairment or destruction of natural resources, a defendant may rebut the prima facie case or may establish an affirmative defense by a preponderance of the evidence.[41] In making a determination of whether a feasible and prudent alternative to the continued action exists, a court may examine other alternatives attempted by the defendant to mitigate the pollution, impairment, or destruction[42] in addition to alternatives presented by the plaintiffs. The court may prevent the action from proceeding if a feasible and prudent alternative to the action exists. The court may not choose among feasible and prudent alternatives. That choice is for the defendant if he wishes to continue the action.[43] As long as the alternative chosen by the defendant does not violate MEPA, a court may not order a defendant to adopt another alternative even if the suggested alternative is considered better by the court.[44]

7.2.2 Comparison with NEPA

MEPA and NEPA are dissimilar. Whereas MEPA is substantive, NEPA is essentially procedural. MEPA's substantive quality means that the courts may enjoin actions or conduct permanently, whereas under NEPA actions may proceed after adequate environmental analysis. Under NEPA, ongoing conduct may not be permanently enjoined. The power of the courts to order natural resources to be restored is also not contained in NEPA, nor is the power granted to the judiciary to impose pollution standards.

The scope of MEPA is broader than that of NEPA, covering private as well as public actions. Whereas NEPA creates no private right to environmental quality and imposes no duty on private individuals and entities to prevent or minimize environmental degradation caused by them, MEPA does both. Thus, under MEPA, agencies may sue private parties to reduce pollution,[45] a cause of action not available under NEPA.

Under MEPA there is no equivalent of a CEQ and no agency regulations and standards exist which must be complied with before actions may proceed. The courts generally make the significance decisions rather than the agencies. This difference results in the avoidance of lawsuits involving purely procedural issues and it generally permits the courts to exercise independent review of actions instead of being limited to judicially reviewing agency decisions. However, the lack of procedural provisions means that agency decisions that may significantly affect the environment may be made without public participation unless other laws or regulations require such participation.

Whereas the threshold for NEPA is whether a proposed federal action significantly affects the quality of the human environment, MEPA is not triggered unless a plaintiff shows that an action "has, or is likely to pollute, impair or destroy the air, water or other natural resources or the public trust therein."[46] Because MEPA is expressly intended to be enforced by citizens as well as others, the MEPA threshold is low. However, not just any pollution, impairment, or destruction of natural resources triggers MEPA. If a resource is common in Michigan, courts require a higher level of pollution, impairment, or destruction than if the resource is rare. In addition, the requirement that a resource must be threatened statewide rather than locally raises the threshold level for triggering MEPA.

7.3 THE CALIFORNIA ENVIRONMENTAL QUALITY ACT

7.3.1 Overview

The California Environmental Quality Act (CEQA)[47] was enacted in 1970. CEQA is procedural and substantive. If projects will have significant effects on the environment, "an agency should not approve [the] projects as proposed if there are feasible alternatives or feasible mitigation measures available which would substantially lessen the significant environmental effects of such projects."[48] If factors such as specific economic or social conditions make it infeasible for an agency to adopt mitigation measures or to choose alternatives to its project, the agency may approve the project in spite of its significant environmental effects.[49] Agencies thus have a duty to avoid or minimize adverse environmental impacts when it is feasible to do so.[50] This duty and the authority connected with it supplement the agencies' other statutory duties and authority.[51]

"Projects" covered by CEQA include activities that a public agency undertakes directly; supports in whole or in part by grants, loans, contracts, subsidies, or other forms of assistance; or for which an agency issues permits, leases, licenses, certificates, or other entitlements.[52] If a proposed action is one of a series of actions that ultimately may significantly affect the environment when the actions are carried out by the agency, the proposed action is a project for purposes of CEQA.[53] Projects may not be segmented to avoid preparing an environmental impact report (EIR).[54]

The "environment" means "the physical conditions which exist within the area which will be affected by a proposed project, including land, air, water, minerals, flora, fauna, noise, [and] objects of historic or aesthetic significance."[55] A project's significant effects on historic and prehistoric archaeological resources must also be considered.[56] A project affects the environment if it culminates in an environmental impact.[57]

In order to aid state and local agencies in complying with CEQA, the California Legislature ordered the California Office of Planning and Research to develop guidelines implementing CEQA.[58] It is not settled whether the guidelines are binding regulations or whether they are interpretive aids.[59] Courts grant great weight to the guidelines unless a guideline is "clearly unauthorized or erroneous under CEQA."[60] The guidelines include aids for complying with

CEQA such as an environmental checklist. In addition to the CEQA guidelines, individual agencies adopt objectives, procedures, and criteria for complying with CEQA.[61] State and local agencies are agencies for the purpose of CEQA.[62]

Certain actions are statutorily exempt from CEQA.[63] Such actions include certain environmental regulatory programs that are certified as meeting the requirements of CEQA.[64] This exemption, which is a statutory version of the functional equivalency doctrine of NEPA case law, applies to agencies with environmental responsibilities.[65] To qualify for the functional equivalency exemption in proposing a project, an agency must show that it followed the procedures specified in CEQA.[66]

Purely ministerial actions are exempt from CEQA.[67] Courts have construed this exemption narrowly.[68] If an agency has any discrimination to reject or change a project, the project is subject to CEQA.[69] Other statutory exemptions include projects as diverse as the institution or increase of passenger or commuter services on rail or highway rights-of-way already in use,[70] and actions, except for the construction of facilities, necessary for bidding for and hosting the Olympic Games.[71]

Agencies must not expand exemption categories beyond the reasonable scope of the categories' statutory language.[72] In particular, agencies must read the exemption for emergency actions narrowly and, if they categorize an action as falling in this exemption, they must include substantial evidence in the record to support a finding that an emergency exists.[73]

The California Legislature ordered the California Office of Planning and Research to prepare and adopt a list of categorical exemptions in the guidelines.[74] The list is extensive.[75] When projects that are listed as categorical exemptions are conducted successively in one location so that they have a significant cumulative effect on the environment, the projects are not exempt from CEQA.[76] If unusual circumstances exist such that there is a reasonable possibility that an action will significantly affect the environment, the proposed project may not be treated as a categorical exemption.[77]

The agency must base its decision that an action is categorically exempt on substantial evidence.[78] When an agency proceeds with a project on the basis of an exemption, it may publicly file a notice of exemption.[79] If a notice is filed, a 35-day statute of limitations on judicial challenges applies; if no notice is filed, the statute of limitations is 180 days.[80] Exemptions may be challenged either on the basis that the exemption itself is improper or that an action is improperly categorized under an exemption.[81]

If there is a possibility that a project may have a significant effect on the environment, the lead agency must conduct an initial threshold study.[82] An initial threshold study must consider all phases of the planning, implementation, and operation of the proposed project.[83] The guidelines facilitate compliance by applicants by providing an environmental information form and an environmental checklist form.[84] The checklist may be used to identify environmental effects for the initial study. Answers to the questions in the environmental checklist must disclose the data or other evidence that they are based on; they may not be conclusory.[85]

In conducting an initial study, an agency consults informally with all responsible agencies and with agencies responsible for resources affected by a proposed project.[86] If, on the basis of the initial study, the agency determines that substantial evidence exists on which it could be fairly argued "that any aspect of the project, either individually or cumulatively, may cause a significant effect on the environment, regardless of whether the overall effect of the project is adverse or beneficial," the agency must prepare an EIR.[87]

CEQA defines a "significant effect on the environment" as "a substantial, or potentially substantial, adverse change in the environment."[88] Courts have interpreted this language as setting a low threshold of harm for a determination of significance.[89] A project may have a significant effect on the environment if

(a) A proposed project has the potential to degrade the quality of the environment, curtail the range of the environment, or to achieve short-term, to the disadvantage of long-term, environmental goals.

(b) The possible effects of a project are individually limited but cumulatively considerable. As used in this subdivision, 'cumulatively considerable' means that the incremental effects of an individual project are considerable when viewed in connection with the effects of past projects, the effects of other current projects, and the effects of probable future projects.

(c) The environmental effects of a project will cause substantial adverse effects on human beings, either directly or indirectly."[90]

Findings of significance must be based on substantial evidence in the agency's record.[91]

After conducting an initial study, if an agency "perceives no substantial evidence that the project or any of its aspects may cause a significant effect on the environment," it prepares a negative declaration.[92] Alternatively, the agency may prepare a negative declaration if the study identifies potentially significant effects but measures to mitigate or avoid the effects are made or agreed to before the proposed negative declaration is publicly released.[93] In the second situation, there must not be substantial evidence before the agency that the revised project may significantly affect the environment.[94] A copy of the initial study containing reasons to support the negative declaration must be attached to the negative declaration.[95]

Agencies have 105 days from completion of a permit application in which to file a negative declaration.[96] Agencies must publish their intent to adopt a negative declaration within a reasonable period of time prior to the adoption.[97] The negative declaration must be published for review and any comments to it considered by the decision-maker in approving the project.[98] If the decision-maker approves the project on the basis of a negative declaration, the agency must file a notice of determination. Filing and posting the notice begins the running of a thirty-day statute of limitations for judicial challenges to the project's approval on the basis of CEQA.[99] If the agency adopts a negative declaration in which mitigation measures reduce the environmental effects below the significance level, the agency shall adopt a reporting or monitoring program for those changes to ensure compliance with the conditions during implementation of the project.[100]

The public plays an essential role in the CEQA process. If an agency prepares an EIR it must make the draft EIR available for public review.[101] The draft EIR must adequately inform the public of the environmental consequences of the agency's proposed project.[102] Following public review, the agency must evaluate the draft EIR in light of any comments received by it,[103] and must notify the public a reasonable time before it adopts the EIR.[104] The final EIR must incorporate any comments received and respond to significant environmental points raised in the CEQA review process.[105]

The agency must certify that the final EIR was completed in compliance with CEQA and that the decision maker reviewed and considered the information in the final EIR before approving the project.[106] Delegation of consideration of environmental effects by the lead agency is prohibited.[107] Before approving the project, the decision maker must make findings either that the significant environmental effects identified in the EIR were avoided or mitigated, or that the benefits of the project outweigh the unmitigated effects.[108] If the agency requires mitigation measures in a project, it shall adopt a reporting or monitoring program for those changes to ensure compliance with the mitigation measures during implementation of the project.[109]

If the EIR identifies mitigation measures or alternatives that are not adopted by the agency, the agency must state why the mitigation measures or alternatives were infeasible and why overriding considerations justified approval of the project.[110] Findings must be made for each significant effect that is identified.[111] The findings must be supported by substantial evidence.[112] If feasible mitigation measures are adopted, the agency need not discuss the feasibility of environmentally superior alternatives to the project in the findings.[113]

A reviewing court may set aside, void or annul an agency's decision under CEQA if "there was a prejudicial abuse of discretion. Abuse of discretion is established if the agency has not proceeded in a manner required by law or if the determination or decision is not supported by substantial evidence."[114] This standard does not permit a court to weigh conflicting evidence of whether adverse environmental effects could be mitigated better or whether they were mitigated.[115] Reasonable doubts are resolved in favor of the agency's finding and decision.[116]

An agency decision may be set aside if the agency prepared an EIR that omitted discussion required by CEQA. An EIR must contain discussion of significant environmental effects of the proposed project, any significant environmental effects that cannot be avoided if the proposal is implemented, proposed mitigation measures, alternatives to the proposed action, and the growth-inducing effect of the proposed project.[117] The cumulative effects analysis must include consideration of reasonably foreseeable projects in addition to the proposed project.[118]

Consideration of alternatives and mitigation measures is governed by the rule of reason.[119] The decision makers must be provided with enough information to be able to intelligently take account of the significant environmental effects of the proposed project.[120] A range of alternatives must be considered,[121] including the no action alternative.[122] In order for the decision maker and the public to make "an independent reasoned judgment" regarding a projected project, the EIR must include facts and analysis rather than conclusions or opinions.[123]

A judicial challenge to an EIR must be made within thirty days of the date the agency files the notice of approval of the project.[124] If potential plaintiffs have not objected to the project's approval, they may be precluded from judicially challenging the agency's action.[125] The grounds for judicially challenging an agency's project must have been presented to the agency.[126]

If an agency substantially changes a project, thus requiring major revisions of the EIR, or if significant new information becomes available, an agency must prepare a supplemental EIR.[127] If minor additions or changes to the EIR would make it apply to the changed project, the agency may supplement the EIR instead of preparing a subsequent EIR.[128] The agency's decision, which should be made after an opportunity for public review,[129] must be supported by substantial evidence.[130] The statute of limitations for challenging a project begun pursuant to an EIR when a supplemental EIR should have been, but was not, prepared, begins to run on the date that the plaintiff knew or reasonably should have known that the project differed from the project described in the EIR.[131]

When a project is subject to NEPA as well as CEQA, an EIS that is prepared for NEPA compliance may be used for CEQA compliance provided that the EIS adequately complies with CEQA.[132] Thus, information required by CEQA that is not required by NEPA must be included.[133]

7.3.2 Comparison with NEPA

CEQA was modeled on NEPA[134] and its "purposes are almost identical to those of NEPA."[135] CEQA is a procedural statute as is NEPA, but differs from NEPA in that it has a substantive mandate.[136] In addition to granting injunctive relief, courts may declare actions void, annul, or set them aside under CEQA,[137] a remedy that is not available under NEPA. Like NEPA, CEQA supplements other statutes.[138] A major purpose of both CEQA and NEPA is the disclosure to the public and other governmental agencies of the environmental impacts of a proposed project.[139] Because of the acts' similarities, California courts often use NEPA precedent in establishing CEQA case law.[140]

CEQA is much more detailed than NEPA, and the procedures and criteria in the CEQA guidelines are more extensive than the criteria in the federal CEQ regulations under NEPA. Part of CEQA's additional length comes from the incorporation into CEQA of the procedures and principles of the federal CEQ guidelines.

The California Office of Planning and Research codifies some of CEQA's case law into its guidelines. Thus, the CEQA guidelines evolve in response to judicial precedent, whereas the CEQ regulations have been revised only once since their promulgation. The CEQA guidelines also contain many categorical exemptions whereas, under NEPA categorical exclusions are included in the procedures of individual agencies not the regulations of the CEQ. CEQA also contains provisions concerning matters such as the judicial review standard for EIRs[141] and codification of the exhaustion of remedies doctrine[142] that exist in NEPA case law but are not in the statute or regulations.

An EIR under CEQA is analogous to an EIS under NEPA and a negative declaration under CEQA is analogous to a FONSI under NEPA. However, the initial study established by the CEQA guidelines has an additional use than the EA established by the federal CEQ regulations. In addition to being prepared to determine whether a negative declaration or an EIR is necessary, an initial study may be prepared to determine if a previously prepared EIR may apply to a proposed project.[143]

The public participation procedures under CEQA are more detailed than those under NEPA. Public review is statutorily required for negative declarations as well as for EIRs. Another feature of CEQA not found in NEPA is the requirement that agency decision makers must certify that they have complied with CEQA in making their decisions. Under NEPA, the record of decision fulfills a similar purpose. However, while the accountability provided by the certification is clearly defined under CEQA, the role of the record of decision as a means of ensuring agency accountability under NEPA is not developed. Due to CEQA's substantive nature, an agency decision maker under the California law has a wider area of accountability than under NEPA.

In contrast to NEPA, CEQA includes time limits for the preparation of environmental documents as well as statutes of limitations for judicial challenges to agency projects. Thus the doctrine of laches is rarely argued in CEQA causes of action.

7.4 THE NEW YORK STATE ENVIRONMENTAL QUALITY REVIEW ACT

7.4.1 Overview

The New York State Environmental Quality Review Act (SEQRA) was enacted in 1975 "to declare a state policy which will encourage productive and enjoyable harmony between man and his environment; to promote efforts which will prevent or eliminate damage to the environment and enhance human and community resources; and to enrich the understanding of the ecological systems, natural, human and community resources important to the people of the state."[144] SEQRA was phased in with all sections of it finally becoming effective by November 1978.[145]

SEQRA is substantive as well as procedural.[146] Agencies must "'act and choose alternatives which, consistent with social, economic and other essential considerations, to the maximum extent practicable, minimize or avoid adverse environmental effects.'"[147] This substantive mandate enables agencies to impose mitigation measures as a condition of granting a permit.[148] This power is limited to the action under SEQRA review and not prior development at the site that was the subject of a prior SEQRA review.[149] SEQRA's substantive mandate authorizes reviewing courts to declare agency actions in violation of SEQRA null and void.[150]

"Actions" covered by SEQRA include activities that an agency directly undertakes; supports in whole or in part by funding; or actions involving the issuance of leases, permits, licenses, certificates, or other entitlements. Policy making, rule making, and procedure making are also actions for purposes of SEQRA.[151] Preliminary activities that do not commit an agency to commence, engage in, or conduct actions are not actions for purposes of SEQRA.[152] Conversely, a decision that commits an agency to a course of action is an action under SEQRA.[153] Related actions must be considered together in one EIS.[154] If a proposed action has no independent utility without other proposed agency actions, the cumulative environmental effects of the actions must be considered together.[155]

SEQRA defines the "environment" as "the physical conditions which will be affected by a proposed action, including land, air, water, minerals, flora, fauna, noise, objects of historic or aesthetic significance, existing patterns of population concentration, distribution, or growth, and existing community or neighborhood character."[156] Thus, SEQRA covers certain socio-economic impacts as well as effects on the physical environment.[157] Cumulative as well as individual environmental effects must be considered.[158]

The New York Legislature ordered the Commissioner of the New York State Department of Environmental Conservation to issue regulations implementing SEQRA.[159] The final regulations were issued in September 1978. The regulations contain appendices of model forms to aid applicants and agencies in complying with SEQRA.[160] Individual agencies may adopt procedures for complying with SEQRA.[161] The procedures must be consistent with the SEQRA regulations and at least as stringent.[162] If an agency does not adopt individual regulations[163] or if, in a given case, its procedures may be applied less stringently than the Department of Environmental Conservation's SEQRA regulations,[164] it must comply with the SEQRA regulations.

Certain actions and types of actions are statutorily exempt from compliance with SEQRA.[165] Such actions include enforcement proceedings[166] and "official acts of a ministerial nature."[167] Actions are considered on a case-by-case basis. Thus, a specific action, such as the issuance of a building permit, may be ministerial in some instances but not in others.[168]

An agency must prepare an EIS if a proposed action may significantly affect the environment.[169] The threshold for significance is "relatively low."[170] The SEQRA regulations contain a list of criteria considered to be indicators of significant environmental effects.[171] Based on these criteria, the regulations divide actions into three categories: type I actions, type II actions, and unlisted actions.

Type I actions are more likely to require preparation of an EIS than an unlisted action but do not necessarily require preparation of an EIS.[172] Type II actions have been determined not to significantly affect the environment. Type II actions are those actions that are exempt from SEQRA by virtue of the SEQRA regulations.[173] If an action is of a type listed as a type II action, the agency need not prepare an EIS or any other SEQRA documentation before proceeding with the action.[174] Unlisted actions may be either type I or type II actions depending on their environmental effects.

In determining whether a type I or unlisted action has significant environmental effects, an agency or an applicant uses full or short environmental assessment forms (EAFs). Full EAFs are used for type I actions, and either short or full EAFs are used for unlisted actions depending on the nature of the action.[175] An agency action that is based on an improperly completed EAF may be found to be arbitrary and capricious.[176]

The lead agency, that is, the agency principally responsible for approving an action,[177] compares the action's potential environmental effects against the criteria for determining significance in the SEQRA regulations.[178] If type I actions and unlisted actions are determined not to significantly affect the environment, a negative declaration must be prepared.[179] The negative declaration must contain a reasoned elaboration of the basis for the declaration.[180] If an applicant or another agency prepares the negative declaration, the lead agency must independently review and analyze the issues in it.[181] If the agency action is subject to SEQRA and an EIS is not prepared, the negative declaration must be prepared by the agency prior to the time it decides whether to proceed with the action.[182] A conditioned negative declaration may be prepared for unlisted actions in which mitigation measures will reduce the effect below the significance level and for which a full EAF has been prepared.[183]

If an agency decides that an action may significantly affect the environment, it must prepare a draft and final EIS.[184] The EISs must contain a discussion of the proposed action and its environmental setting, its environmental effects, adverse environmental effects which cannot be avoided if the proposal is implemented, alternatives, irreversible and irretrievable commitments of resources if the action is implemented, proposed mitigation measures, growth-inducing aspects, and effects of the proposed action on the use and conservation of energy resources where appropriate.[185] A defect in a draft EIS is not necessarily cured by correcting the defect in the final EIS.[186]

The agency must make the draft and final EISs publicly available and receive comments on them[187] before "'any significant authorization is granted for a specific proposal.'"[188] If the agency holds a hearing on a draft EIS, it must prepare the final EIS within forty-five days from the close of the hearing. If the agency does not hold a hearing, it must as a general rule prepare the draft EIS and make it publicly available within sixty days after filing the draft EIS.[189] After filing a final EIS, the agency must wait at least ten days before making a decision based on the EIS.[190] If the EIS is based on an application by a private party, the agency must file its written findings statement and its decision within thirty days after filing the final EIS.[191]

SEQRA does not mention supplemental EISs but, if environmentally significant modifications are made to a proposed action after a final EIS has been issued, the agency must take a hard look at the need for a supplemental EIS.[192] The requirement for a supplemental EIS if the above conditions exist was added to the SEQRA regulations effective mid-1987. Under the regulations, a supplemental EIS must also be prepared if information about significant adverse effects is newly discovered or if a change in circumstances arises that may result in a significant adverse environmental effect.[193] If a supplemental EIS is required, the agency must comply with SEQRA procedures applicable to the preparation of EISs.[194]

An agency may not approve an action subject to SEQRA "unless it makes 'an explicit finding that the requirements of [SEQRA] have been met and that consistent with social, economic and other essential considerations, to the maximum extent practicable, adverse environmental effects revealed in the environmental impact statement process will be minimized or avoided' and that 'consistent with social, economic and other essential considerations, to the maximum extent practicable, adverse environmental effects revealed in the environmental impact statement process will be minimized or avoided by incorporating as conditions to the decision those mitigative measures which were identified as practicable.'"[195] "To the maximum extent practicable" does not mean that an agency must impose any particular mitigation measures. The agency satisfies SEQRA by taking a hard look at potential mitigation measures. If there is substantial evidence that an agency has done this, a reviewing court will not upset the agency's choice of mitigation measure.[196]

To challenge an agency's action under SEQRA, a plaintiff must have standing. That is, the plaintiff must suffer an actual injury that is within the zone of interests protected by SEQRA.[197] Alternatively, the plaintiff must have a substantial interest in the proposed action, such as owning the property at issue.[198] The New York Attorney General has standing to sue to protect resources for the people of New York State.[199]

Reviewing courts determine whether an agency has complied with SEQRA procedurally and substantively.[200] The courts do not determine whether an action may have a significant effect.[201] The agency's decision may be declared null and void if it is arbitrary, capricious, or unsupported by substantial evidence.[202] This scope of review is "very limited."[203] Under New York law, judicial challenges to alleged SEQRA violations must generally be filed within four months of the agency action that allegedly violated SEQRA.[204]

In determining whether an agency has complied with SEQRA in making a determination, the courts determine whether the agency identified the relevant areas of concern, took a "hard look" at those areas, and made a "reasoned elaboration" of the basis for its determination.[205] In determining if the agency identified and considered EIS contents such as alternatives and potential mitigation measures, the courts follow the rule of reason.[206] The requisite detail required differs according to a proposal's circumstances and nature.[207]

When a proposed action is subject to NEPA as well as SEQRA, an agency may coordinate the procedures under both acts.[208]

7.4.2 Comparison with NEPA

SEQRA was modeled on NEPA.[209] It not only contains provisions drawn from NEPA itself; it contains provisions drawn from NEPA case law and the CEQ guidelines. For example, SEQRA's definition of environment includes quality of life language drawn from NEPA case law.[210] Thus, SEQRA specifically requires consideration of significant socio-economic effects, whereas NEPA only requires consideration of socio-economic effects if the action affects the physical environment. In addition, the rule of reason that applies to alternatives considered in an EIS under NEPA is adopted by SEQRA and its implementing regulations.[211]

New York courts frequently interpret phrases in SEQRA that are drawn from NEPA by referring to NEPA case law interpreting the provisions. Thus, the phrase "to the fullest extent possible," which appears in both NEPA[212] and SEQRA,[213] requires entities subject to SEQRA to comply literally and not merely substantially with SEQRA.[214]

SEQRA case law tracks NEPA case law in other major areas. For example, the judicial tests adopted by New York courts in reviewing negative declarations (that is, determinations of nonsignificance)[215] and EISs[216] are drawn from NEPA case law. Determinations of whether a plaintiff has standing under SEQRA also track NEPA case law.[217] The level of significance of an environmental concern necessary to be accorded standing to sue appears to be about the same under NEPA as it is under SEQRA.[218] However, under SEQRA, the owner of property at issue in the proposed action may have standing without having to demonstrate the likelihood of environmental harm to his property if his interest in the proposed action is substantial.[219]

SEQRA is triggered when a proposed action may have a significant environmental effect.[220] Thus, the threshold level for triggering SEQRA is the same as the threshold level for triggering NEPA in the Fifth and Ninth Circuits and probably in the First Circuit also.[221] However, SEQRA's threshold is probably lower than NEPA's threshold in other circuits,[222] particularly the Second Circuit.[223]

A major potential difference between SEQRA and NEPA is that SEQRA has substantive provisions whereas NEPA is essentially procedural. The inclusion of substantive provisions in SEQRA means that agencies have a duty to mitigate or avoid adverse environmental effects to the maximum extent practicable. Before deciding to proceed with an action, the agency must explicitly find that this has been done and that the requirements of SEQRA have been met, procedures which do not exist under NEPA.[224]

The substantive provisions also affect the type of remedies available. Under SEQRA, a reviewing court has the power to declare an action null and void if the agency violates SEQRA, a remedy that is not available under NEPA. In contrast, the injunctive relief typically applicable under NEPA may be inappropriate in certain SEQRA cases.[225]

Apart from the difference in available remedies, SEQRA has been interpreted in much the same way as NEPA. The substantive provisions of SEQRA are not well-developed by the courts. However, the duty to mitigate or avoid environmental harm to the maximum extent practicable places a duty on agencies to act as well as to disclose that is not contained in NEPA. In addition, the New York Department of Environmental Conservation's power to require applicants for permits to mitigate or avoid environmental harm contrasts with the procedural limits of NEPA, and empowers the Department to ensure that SEQRA's purposes are complied with.

The New York Department of Environmental Conservation plays a similar role under SEQRA to the CEQ under NEPA. The Department has promulgated regulations under SEQRA but does not enforce them. As in NEPA, enforcement rests with individual plaintiffs. In contrast to the CEQ, however, the Department of Environmental Conservation has regulatory powers under other statutes. Thus, courts may find that the Department has violated SEQRA regarding actions under these other statutes.[226]

The SEQRA regulations categorize agency actions into equivalents of the three groups of actions identified by the CEQ under NEPA. Type II actions are equivalent to categorical exclusions; type I actions are equivalent to those actions generally requiring an EIS; and unlisted actions are equivalent to those requiring an EA or EIS. The CEQ regulations under NEPA do not list such actions as do the SEQRA regulations. Rather, under NEPA the lists are contained in the procedures of individual agencies.

SEQRA contrasts with NEPA by establishing agency time limits for the preparation of EISs. Thus, under SEQRA, the EIS process may be substantially more abbreviated than the NEPA process. In general, however, SEQRA's procedures have more similarities to NEPA than dissimilarities.

NOTES

1. See generally Hagman, NEPA's Progeny Inhabit the States—Were the Genes Defective?, 1974 Urb. L. Ann. 3, 7–10.

2. Mich. Stat. Ann. §§ 14.528(201) to (207) (Callaghan 1989).

3. Id. § 14.528(202)(1).

4. Ray v. Mason County Drain Comm'r, 393 Mich. 294, 224 N.W.2d 883, 888 n.8 (1975) (citing Sax & Conner, Michigan's Environmental Protection Act of 1970: A Progress Report, 70 Mich. L. Rev. 1003, 1005 (1972); Press Release, Representative Thomas J. Anderson, Michigan Passes Landmark Environmental Law, July 2, 1970).

5. Id. at 888.

6. See Stevens v. Creek, 121 Mich. App. 503, 328 N.W.2d 672, 674 (1982).

7. In re Highway US-24 v. Vanderkloot, 392 Mich. 159, 220 N.W.2d 416, 427–28 (1974); see Ray v. Mason County Drain Comm'r, 393 Mich. 294, 224 N.W.2d 883, 888 (1975); Her Majesty the Queen in Right of the Province of Ontario, 874 F.2d 332, 337 (6th Cir. 1989) (citing Mich. Const. art. 4, § 52).

8. Mich. Stat. Ann. § 14.528(204) (Callaghan 1989).

9. Stevens v. Creek, 121 Mich. App. 503, 328 N.W.2d 672, 675 (1982).

10. Mich. Stat. Ann. § 14.528(202a) (Callaghan 1989).

11. Id. § 14.528(203)(3); see Superior Public Rights, Inc. v. Department of Natural Resources, 80 Mich. App. 72, 263 N.W.2d 290, 298 (1978); Taxpayers & Citizens in Public Interest v. Department of State Highways, 70 Mich. App. 385, 245 N.W.2d 761, 762 (1976).

12. Mich. Stat. Ann. § 14.528(202)(2) (Callaghan 1989).

13. Her Majesty the Queen in Right of the Province of Ontario v. City of Detroit, 874 F.2d 332, 344 (6th Cir. 1989).

14. Mich. Stat. Ann. § 14.528(203)(1) (Callaghan 1989). A prima facie case is one in which a plaintiff establishes sufficient evidence in a trial to require its rebuttal

by the defendant. Ray v. Mason County Drain Comm'r, 393 Mich. 294, 224 N.W.2d 883, 890 (1975).

15. Mich. Stat. Ann. § 14.528(203)(1) (Callaghan 1989); see Dwyer v. City of Ann Arbor, 79 Mich. App. 113, 261 N.W.2d 231, 237 (1978).

16. See Wayne County Dep't of Health v. Olsonite Corp., 79 Mich. App. 668, 263 N.W.2d 778, 792–93 (1978). See generally Slone, The Michigan Environmental Protection Act: Bringing Citizen-Initiated Environmental Suits Into the 1980's, 12 Ecology L.Q. 271, 278–79 (1985).

17. West Mich. Envtl. Action Council v. Natural Resources Comm'n, 405 Mich. 741, 275 N.W.2d 538, 542, cert. denied, 444 U.S. 941 (1979).

18. People ex rel. Attorney General v. Clinton County Drain Comm'r, 91 Mich. App. 630, 283 N.W.2d 815, 817 (1979).

19. Sax & DiMento, Environmental Citizen Suits: Three Years' Experience Under the Michigan Environmental Protection Act, 4 Ecology L.Q. 1, 5 (1974).

20. See Abrams, Thresholds of Harm in Environmental Litigation: The Michigan Environmental Protection Act as Model of a Minimal Requirement, 7 Harv. Envtl. L. Rev. 107, 110 (1983).

21. See id. at 111 (legislature expressly rejected imposing threshold of harm).

22. West Mich. Envtl. Action Council, Inc. v. Natural Resources Comm'n, 405 Mich. 741, 275 N.W.2d 538, 545, cert. denied, 444 U.S. 941 (1979).

23. See id.; Kent County Road Comm'n v. Hunting, 170 Mich. App. 222, 428 N.W.2d 353, 358 (1988).

24. See Thomas Township v. John Sexton Corp., 173 Mich. App. 507, 434 N.W.2d 644, 645–46 (1988); Eyde v. State, 82 Mich. App. 531, 267 N.W.2d 442, 447 (1978).

25. Compare Thomas Township v. John Sexton Corp., 173 Mich. App. 507, 434 N.W.2d 644, 645 (1988) (substantial evidence standard is appropriate) with Citizens Disposal, Inc. v. Department of Natural Resources, 172 Mich. App. 541, 432 N.W.2d 315, 317 (1988) (court should review agency decision de novo).

26. See Kent County Road Comm'n v. Hunting, 170 Mich. App. 222, 428 N.W.2d 353, 358 (1988).

27. Poletown Neighborhood Council v. City of Detroit, 410 Mich. 616, 304 N.W.2d 455, 460 (1981).

28. City of Portage v. Kalamazoo County Road Comm'n, 136 Mich. App. 276, 355 N.W.2d 913, 916 (1984).

29. See Whittaker Gooding Co. v. Scio Township Zoning Bd. of Appeals, 117 Mich. App. 18, 323 N.W.2d 574, 576 (1982).

30. See Committee for Sensible Land Use v. Garfield Township, 124 Mich. App. 559, 335 N.W.2d 216, 218 (1983).

31. Oscoda Chapter of PBB Action Comm., Inc. v. Department of Natural Resources, 403 Mich. 215, 268 N.W.2d 240, 246 (1978).

32. See Kent County Road Comm'n v. Hunting, 170 Mich. App. 222, 428 N.W.2d 353, 358 (1988).

33. See Thomas Township v. John Sexton Corp., 173 Mich. App. 507, 434 N.W.2d 644, 648 (1988) (declaring that proper standard is statewide perspective rather than local perspective). Cf. Rush v. Sterner, 143 Mich. App. 672, 373

N.W.2d 183, 187 n.1 (1985) (noting that statewide perspective is not always appropriate).

34. *See* Kimberly Hills Neighborhood Ass'n v. Dion, 114 Mich. App. 495, 320 N.W.2d 668, 674 (1982).

35. Rush v. Sterner, 143 Mich. App. 672, 373 N.W.2d 183, 187 (1985).

36. Cook v. Grand River Hydroelectric Power Co., 131 Mich. App. 821, 346 N.W.2d 881, 885 (1984); Kimberly Hills Neighborhood Ass'n v. Dion, 114 Mich. App. 495, 320 N.W.2d 668, 673 (1982).

37. Highland Recreation Defense Found'n v. Natural Resources Comm'n, 180 Mich. App. 324, 446 N.W.2d 895, 898 (1989).

38. City of Portage v. Kalamazoo County Road Comm'n, 136 Mich. App. 276, 355 N.W.2d 913, 916 (1984).

39. West Mich. Envtl. Action Council, Inc. v. Natural Resources Comm'n, 405 Mich. 741, 275 N.W.2d 538, 545, *cert. denied*, 444 U.S. 941 (1979).

40. Michigan United Conservation Clubs v. Anthony, 90 Mich. App. 99, 280 N.W.2d 883, 889 (1979).

41. Mich. Stat. Ann. § 14.528(203)(1) (Callaghan 1989); *see* Wayne County Dep't of Health v. Olsonite Corp., 79 Mich. App. 668, 263 N.W.2d 778, 795 (1978).

42. *See* Wayne County Dep't of Health v. Olsonite Corp., 79 Mich. App. 668, 263 N.W.2d 778, 797 (1978).

43. Oscoda Chapter of PBB Action Comm., Inc. v. Department of Natural Resources, 403 Mich. 215, 268 N.W.2d 240, 247 (1978).

44. *Id.* at 246.

45. *See generally* Slone, *The Michigan Environmental Protection Act: Bringing Citizen-Initiated Environmental Suits into the 1980's*, 12 Ecology L.Q. 271, 295–96 (1985).

46. Mich. Stat. Ann. § 14.528(203)(1) (Callaghan 1989).

47. Cal. Pub. Res. Code §§ 21000–21177 (West 1986 & Supp. 1990).

48. *Id.* § 21002 (West 1986).

49. *Id.*

50. Cal. Code Regs. tit. 14, § 15021(a) (1990).

51. *Id.* §§ 15040(a), (c), 15041; *see* Cal. Pub. Res. Code § 21004 (West 1986).

52. Cal. Pub. Res. Code § 21065 (West 1986).

53. *See* Bozung v. Local Agency Formation Comm'n, 13 Cal. 3d 263, 279-81, 118 Cal. Rptr. 249, 259-61, 529 P.2d 1017, 1027–29 (1975); *see also* McQueen v. Board of Directors, 202 Cal. App. 3d 1136, 1143–44, 249 Cal. Rptr. 439, 443 (1988) (citing cases interpreting "project" broadly). *Cf.* City of Agoura Hills v. Local Agency Formation Comm'n, 198 Cal. App. 3d 480, 493–94, 243 Cal. Rptr. 740, 748 (1988) (upholding agency's determination that action could not significantly affect the environment); Simi Valley Recreation & Park Dist. v. Local Agency Formation Comm'n, 51 Cal. App. 3d 648, 664–66, 124 Cal. Rptr. 635, 646–47 (1975) (action was not a project because it was not an action proposed to be carried out by the agency).

54. *See* Laurel Heights Improvement Ass'n of San Francisco, Inc. v. Regents of Univ. of Cal., 47 Cal. 3d 376, 396–99, 253 Cal. Rptr. 426, 433–35, 764 P.2d 278, 285–88 (1988); Christward Ministry v. Superior Court, 184 Cal. App. 3d 180, 195–96, 228 Cal. Rptr. 868, 876–77 (1986); Orinda Ass'n v. Board of Supervisors,

182 Cal. App. 3d 1145, 1171–72, 227 Cal. Rptr. 688, 705–06 (1986); Citizens Ass'n for Sensible Dev. v. County of Inyo, 172 Cal. App. 3d 151, 166–67, 217 Cal. Rptr. 893, 902–03 (1985); *see also* City of Santee v. County of San Diego, 214 Cal. App. 3d 1438, 263 Cal. Rptr. 340, 349 (1989) (future actions and their cumulative effects on temporary project must be considered).

55. Cal. Pub. Res. Code § 21060.5 (West 1986).

56. *Id.* § 21083.2; Cal. Code Regs. tit. 14, app. K (1990).

57. *See* Fullerton Joint Union High School Dist. v. State Bd. of Educ., 32 Cal. 3d 779, 797, 187 Cal. Rptr. 398, 410, 654 P.2d 168, 180 (1982) (approval of secession plan); Bozung v. Local Agency Formation Comm'n, 13 Cal. 3d 263, 281, 118 Cal. Rptr. 249, 261, 529 P.2d 1017, 1029 (1975) (annexation); City of Carmel-by-the-Sea v. Board of Supervisors, 183 Cal. App. 3d 229, 243, 227 Cal. Rptr. 899, 909 (1986) (rezoning); Terminal Plaza Corp. v. City & County of San Francisco, 177 Cal. App. 3d 892, 905–06, 223 Cal. Rptr. 379, 385–86 (1986) (ordinance); Pistoresi v. City of Madera, 138 Cal. App. 3d 284, 288, 188 Cal. Rptr. 136, 138–39 (1982) (annexation); City of Santa Ana v. City of Garden Grove, 100 Cal. App. 3d 521, 534, 160 Cal. Rptr. 907, 914 (1979) (adoption or amendment to city's general plan).

58. Cal. Pub. Res. Code § 21083 (West 1986).

59. *See* Laurel Heights Improvement Ass'n of San Francisco, Inc. v. Regents of Univ. of Cal., 47 Cal. 3d 376, 391 n.2, 253 Cal. Rptr. 426, 430 n.2, 764 P.2d 278, 282 n.2 (1988).

60. *Id.*

61. Cal. Pub. Res. Code § 21082 (West 1986); Cal. Code Regs. tit. 14, § 15022 (1990).

62. Cal. Pub. Res. Code §§ 21062, 21063 (West 1986); *see* Bozung v. Local Agency Formation Comm'n, 13 Cal. 3d 263, 276, 118 Cal. Rptr. 249, 257, 529 P.2d 1017, 1025 (1975).

63. Cal. Pub. Res. Code §§ 21080.01–.21 (West 1986 & Supp. 1990); *see* City of South Gate v. Los Angeles Unified School Dist., 184 Cal. App. 3d 1416, 1425, 229 Cal. Rptr. 568, 573 (1986).

64. Cal. Code Regs. tit. 14, §§ 15250–15251 (1990); *see* Cal. Pub. Res. Code § 21080.5 (West 1986 & Supp. 1990).

65. Wildlife Alive v. Chickering, 18 Cal. 3d 190, 203, 132 Cal. Rptr. 377, 383, 553 P.2d 537, 543 (1976).

66. *See* Citizens for Non-Toxic Pest Control v. California Dep't of Food & Agric., 187 Cal. App. 3d 1575, 1587–88, 232 Cal. Rptr. 729, 735 (1987).

67. Cal. Pub. Res. Code § 21080(b)(1) (West 1986).

68. *See* Friends of Westwood, Inc. v. City of Los Angeles, 191 Cal. App. 3d 259, 271, 235 Cal. Rptr. 788, 796 (1987); Natural Resources Defense Council, Inc. v. Arcata Nat'l Corp., 59 Cal. App. 3d 959, 970, 131 Cal. Rptr. 172, 179 (1976).

69. *See* People v. Department of Housing & Community Dev., 45 Cal. App. 3d 185, 193–94, 119 Cal. Rptr. 266, 272 (1975).

70. Cal. Pub. Res. Code § 21080(b)(11) (West 1986); *see* Napa Valley Wine Train, Inc. v. Public Utilities Comm'n, 50 Cal. 3d 370, 267 Cal. Rptr. 569, 577, 787 P.2d 976, 984 (1990).

71. Cal. Pub. Res. Code § 21080(b)(7) (West 1986).

72. *See* Hans-Joachim Dehne v. County of Santa Clara, 115 Cal. App. 3d 827, 842, 171 Cal. Rptr. 753, 762 (1981); *see also* City of Santa Clara v. Santa Clara County Local Agency Formation Comm'n, 139 Cal. App. 3d 923, 929-30, 189 Cal. Rptr. 112, 115-16 (1983).

73. Western Municipal Water Dist. v. Superior Court, 187 Cal. App. 3d 1104, 1113, 232 Cal. Rptr. 359, 364 (1986).

74. Cal. Code Regs. tit. 14, §§ 15061(c) (1990).

75. *Id.* §§ 15300-15329.

76. *Id.* § 15300.2(b).

77. *Id.* § 15300.2(c); *see* McQueen v. Board of Directors, 202 Cal. App. 3d 1136, 1148-49, 249 Cal. Rptr. 439, 446 (1988); Lewis v. Seventeenth Dist. Agric. Ass'n, 165 Cal. App. 3d 823, 828-29, 211 Cal. Rptr. 884, 887 (1985).

78. *See* McQueen v. Board of Directors, 202 Cal. App. 3d 1136, 1148, 249 Cal. Rptr. 439, 446 (1988); Simons v. City of Los Angeles, 72 Cal. App. 3d 924, 939, 140 Cal. Rptr. 484, 492 (1977).

79. Cal. Code Regs. tit. 14, § 15062(a) (1990).

80. *Id.* § 15062(d).

81. *See, e.g.,* International Longshoremen's & Warehousemen's Union v. Board of Supervisors, 116 Cal. App. 3d 265, 276-77, 171 Cal. Rptr. 875, 881-82 (1981) (categorical exemption was improper); Myers v. Board of Supervisors, 58 Cal. App. 3d 413, 424, 129 Cal. Rptr. 902, 907 (1976) (same).

82. Cal. Code Regs. tit. 14, § 15063(a) (1990); *see* Merz v. Monterey County Bd. of Supervisors, 147 Cal. App. 3d 933, 936, 195 Cal. Rptr. 370, 372 (1983).

83. Cal. Code Regs. tit. 14, § 15063(a) (1990).

84. *Id.* § 15063(f), apps. H, I.

85. Citizens Ass'n for Sensible Dev. v. County of Inyo, 172 Cal. App. 3d 151, 171, 217 Cal. Rptr. 893, 906 (1985).

86. Cal. Code Regs. tit. 14, § 15063(g) (1990).

87. Cal. Pub. Res. Code § 21100 (West 1986); Cal. Code Regs. tit. 14, §§ 15063(b)(1), 15064(g)(1) (1990); *see* Heninger v. Board of Supervisors, 186 Cal. App. 3d 601, 605-06, 231 Cal. Rptr. 11, 13 (1986); Friends of "B" Street v. City of Hayward, 106 Cal. App. 3d 988, 1002, 165 Cal. Rptr. 514, 523 (1980).

88. Cal. Pub. Res. Code § 21068 (West 1986).

89. *See* No Oil, Inc. v. City of Los Angeles, 13 Cal. 3d 68, 85-86, 118 Cal. Rptr. 34, 45, 529 P.2d 66, 77 (1974); Simons v. City of Los Angeles, 63 Cal. App. 3d 455, 465, 133 Cal. Rptr. 721, 727 (1976).

90. Cal. Pub. Res. Code § 21083 (West 1986).

91. *Id.* § 21082.2(a).

92. Cal. Code Regs. tit. 14, § 15063(b)(2) (1990); *see* Newberry Springs Water Ass'n v. County of San Bernardino, 150 Cal. App. 3d 740, 748-49, 198 Cal. Rptr. 100, 104-05 (1984).

The guidelines define "substantial evidence" as: "enough relevant information and reasonable inferences from this information that a fair argument can be made to support a conclusion, even though other conclusions might also be reached. Whether a fair argument can be made is to be determined by examining the entire record. Mere uncorroborated opinion or rumor does not constitute substantial evidence." Cal. Code Regs. tit. 14, § 15384(a) (1990).

93. Cal. Code Regs. tit. 14, § 15070(b) (1990).

94. *Id.*

95. *Id.* § 15071(d).

96. *Id.* § 15107.

97. *Id.* § 15072(a).

98. Cal. Pub. Res. Code § 21091 (West Supp. 1990); Cal. Code Regs. tit. 14, §§ 15073–15074 (1990).

99. Cal. Code Regs. tit. 14, § 15075 (1990).

100. Cal. Pub. Res. Code § 21081.6 (West Supp. 1990).

101. *Id.* § 21091; *see also* Sutter Sensible Planning, Inc. v. Sutter County Bd. of Supervisors, 122 Cal. App. 3d 813, 823, 176 Cal. Rptr. 342, 347 (1981) (revised final EIR containing comments was required to be circulated).

102. Mountain Lion Coalition v. California Fish & Game Comm'n, 214 Cal. App. 3d 1043, 263 Cal. Rptr. 104, 108–10 (1989).

103. Cal. Code Regs. tit. 14, § 15088 (1990).

104. Cal. Pub. Res. Code § 21092 (West Supp. 1990).

105. *See* Society for California Archaeology v. County of Butte, 65 Cal. App. 3d 832, 839, 135 Cal. Rptr. 679, 683 (1977); People v. County of Kern, 62 Cal. App. 3d 761, 770, 133 Cal. Rptr. 389, 395 (1976); Cal. Code Regs. tit. 14, § 15132 (1990); *see also* Twain Harte Homeowners Ass'n, Inc. v. County of Tuolumne, 138 Cal. App. 3d 664, 686, 188 Cal. Rptr. 233, 246 (1982) (response to comments was adequate even though comments were not exhaustive or thorough in all respects).

106. Cal. Code Regs. tit. 14, § 15090 (1990).

107. *See* Kleist v. City of Glendale, 56 Cal. App. 3d 770, 778–79, 128 Cal. Rptr. 781, 787 (1976).

108. Laurel Heights Improvement Ass'n of San Francisco, Inc. v. Regents of Univ. of Cal., 47 Cal. 3d 376, 391, 253 Cal. Rptr. 426, 430, 764 P.2d 278, 282 (1988) (citing Cal. Pub. Res. Code §§ 21002, 21002.1, 21081 (West 1986); Cal. Code Regs. tit. 14, §§ 15091–15093 (1990)).

109 .Cal. Pub. Res. Code § 21081.6 (West Supp. 1990).

110. *See* Village Laguna of Laguna Beach, Inc. v. Board of Supervisors, 134 Cal. App. 3d 1022, 1034, 185 Cal. Rptr. 41, 48 (1982).

111. Cal. Code Regs. tit. 14, § 15091 (1990); *see* Citizens for Quality Growth v. City of Mount Shasta, 198 Cal. App. 3d 433, 440–41, 243 Cal. Rptr. 727, 730–31 (1988).

112. *See* Towards Responsibility in Planning v. City Council, 200 Cal. App. 3d 671, 683–85, 246 Cal. Rptr. 317, 323–24 (1988); No Oil, Inc. v. City of Los Angeles, 196 Cal. App. 3d 223, 239, 242 Cal. Rptr. 37, 45 (1988); *see also* Burger v. County of Mendocino, 45 Cal. App. 3d 322, 326–37, 119 Cal. Rptr. 568, 570 (1975) (no evidence to support agency's override of adverse recommendations in EIR).

113. Laurel Hills Homeowners Ass'n v. City Council, 83 Cal. App. 3d 515, 521, 147 Cal. Rptr. 842, 845 (1978); *see* Stevens v. City of Glendale, 125 Cal. App. 3d 986, 995–96, 178 Cal. Rptr. 367, 372 (1981); San Diego Trust & Savings Bank v. Friends of Gill, 121 Cal. App. 3d 203, 213–14, 174 Cal. Rptr. 784, 789-90 (1981).

114. Cal. Pub. Res. Code § 21168.5 (West 1986).

115. Laurel Heights Improvement Ass'n of San Francisco, Inc. v. Regents of Univ. of Cal., 47 Cal. 3d 376, 392, 253 Cal. Rptr. 426, 431, 764 P.2d 278, 283 (1988).

116. *Id.*

117. Cal. Code Regs. tit. 14, § 15126 (1990); *see* Laurel Heights Improvement Ass'n of San Francisco, Inc. v. Regents of Univ. of Cal., 47 Cal. 3d 376, 400–02, 253 Cal. Rptr. 426, 436–38, 764 P.2d 278, 289–91 (1988) (EIR must meaningfully discuss alternatives and mitigation measures).

118. Terminal Plaza Corp. v. City & County of San Francisco, 177 Cal. App. 3d 892, 904, 223 Cal. Rptr. 379, 385 (1986); *see also* Citizens to Preserve the Ojai v. County of Ventura, 176 Cal. App. 3d 421, 430, 222 Cal. Rptr. 247, 252 (1986); San Franciscans for Reasonable Growth v. City & County of San Francisco, 151 Cal. App. 3d 61, 72–77, 198 Cal. Rptr. 634, 638–42 (1984); Whitman v. Board of Supervisors, 88 Cal. App. 3d 397, 409, 151 Cal. Rptr. 866, 872 (1979); Cal. Admin. Code Regs. tit. 14, § 15130 (1990).

119. *See* Citizens of Goleta Valley v. Board of Supervisors, 197 Cal. App. 3d 1167, 1177–78, 243 Cal. Rptr. 339, 345 (1988); Bowman v. City of Petaluma, 185 Cal. App. 3d 1065, 1083–84, 230 Cal. Rptr. 413, 424 (1986); Foundation for San Francisco's Architectural Heritage v. City & County of San Francisco, 106 Cal. App. 3d 893, 909–11, 165 Cal. Rptr. 401, 410–11 (1980); Cal. Code Regs. tit. 14, § 15126(d)(5) (1990).

120. Citizens of Goleta Valley v. Board of Supervisors, 197 Cal. App. 3d 1167, 1179, 243 Cal. Rptr. 339, 346 (1988); *see also* El Dorado Union High School Dist. v. City of Placerville, 144 Cal. App. 3d 123, 132–33, 192 Cal. Rptr. 480, 485 (1983) (EIR contained insufficient information to permit decision makers to make a decision of the project's environmental effects).

121. *See* Citizens of Goleta Valley v. Board of Supervisors, 216 Cal. App. 3d 48, 264 Cal. Rptr. 587, 592 (1989).

122. *See* County of Inyo v. City of Los Angeles, 124 Cal. App. 3d 1, 12–14, 177 Cal. Rptr. 479, 485–87 (1981).

123. Concerned Citizens of Costa Mesa, Inc. v. 32nd Dist. Agricultural Ass'n, 42 Cal. 3d 929, 935, 231 Cal. Rptr. 748, 751, 727 P.2d 1029, 1032 (1987).

124. Cal. Pub. Res. Code § 21167(c) (West 1986).

125. *Id.* § 21177; *see* California Aviation Council v. County of Amador, 200 Cal. App. 3d 337, 342–44, 246 Cal. Rptr. 110, 113–15 (1988); Browning-Ferris Indus. of Cal., Inc. v. City Council, 181 Cal. App. 3d 852, 859–60, 226 Cal. Rptr. 575, 579 (1986); Kane v. Redevelopment Agency, 179 Cal. App. 3d 899, 904–08, 224 Cal. Rptr. 922, 924–26 (1986); Environmental Law Fund, Inc. v. Town of Corte Madera, 49 Cal. App. 3d 105, 114, 122 Cal. Rptr. 282, 287 (1975).

126. Cal. Pub. Res. Code § 21177(a) (West 1986).

127. *Id.* § 21166; Cal. Code Regs. tit. 14, § 15162 (1990); *see* Mira Monte Homeowners Ass'n v. County of San Buenaventura, 165 Cal. App. 3d 357, 364–65, 212 Cal. Rptr. 127, 132 (1985).

128. Cal. Code Regs. tit. 14, § 15163 (1990).

129. *See* City of San Jose v. Great Oaks Water Co., 192 Cal. App. 3d 1005, 1017, 237 Cal. Rptr. 845, 852 (1987).

130. Bowman v. City of Petaluma, 185 Cal. App. 3d 1065, 1075, 230 Cal. Rptr. 413, 418 (1986); *see* Fund for Envt'l Defense v. County of Orange, 204 Cal. App. 3d 1538, 1552–53, 252 Cal. Rptr. 79, 87–88 (1988).

131. Concerned Citizens of Costa Mesa, Inc. v. 32nd Dist. Agricultural Ass'n, 42 Cal. 3d 929, 939, 231 Cal. Rptr. 748, 754, 727 P.2d 1029, 1035 (1987).

132. Cal. Pub. Res. Code §§ 21083.5–.7 (West 1986 & Supp. 1990); *see* Bakman v. State Dep't of Transp., 99 Cal. App. 3d 665, 680, 160 Cal. Rptr. 583, 591 (1979); Cal. Code Regs. tit. 14, § 15170 (1990).

133. Cal. Code Regs. tit. 14, § 15221(b) (1990).

134. Wildlife Alive v. Chickering, 18 Cal. 3d 190, 201, 132 Cal. Rptr. 377, 383, 553 P.2d 537, 543 (1976).

135. City of Davis v. Coleman, 521 F.2d 661, 672 (9th Cir. 1975).

136. *See* Selmi, *The Judicial Development of the California Environmental Quality Act,* 18 U.C. Davis L. Rev. 197, 259-76 (1984); Comment, *Substantive Enforcement of the California Environmental Quality Act,* 69 Cal. L. Rev. 112, 115–16 (1981).

137. Cal. Pub. Res. Code § 21168.5 (West 1986).

138. Cal. Code Regs. tit. 14, §§ 15040(a), (c) (1990); *see also* Environmental Protection Information Center, Inc. v. Johnson, 170 Cal. App. 3d 604, 616–17, 216 Cal. Rptr. 502, 509 (1985).

139. *See* Laurel Heights Improvement Ass'n of San Francisco, Inc. v. Regents of Univ. of Cal., 47 Cal. 3d 376, 402, 253 Cal. Rptr. 426, 439, 764 P.2d 278, 291 (1988); No Oil, Inc. v. City of Los Angeles, 13 Cal. 3d 68, 86–87, 118 Cal. Rptr. 34, 46, 529 P.2d 66, 78 (1974); Cal. Code Regs. tit. 14, § 15201 (1990).

140. *See, e.g.,* No Oil, Inc. v. City of Los Angeles, 13 Cal. 3d 68, 81, 118 Cal. Rptr. 34, 42, 529 P.2d 66, 74 (1974); Friends of Mammoth v. Board of Supervisors, 8 Cal. 3d 247, 261–63, 104 Cal. Rptr. 761, 769-71, 502 P.2d 1049, 1057–59 (1972).

141. Cal. Pub. Res. Code § 21168.5 (West 1986).

142. *Id.* § 21177.

143. Cal. Code Regs. tit. 14, § 15063(b)(1)(B) (1990); *see id.* § 15153.

144. N.Y. Envtl. Conserv. Law § 8–0101 (McKinney 1984).

145. *Id.* § 8–0117.

146. *Id.* §§ 8–0103(9), 8–0109(1); *see* E.F.S. Ventures Corp. v. Foster, 71 N.Y.2d 359, 371, 526 N.Y.S.2d 56, 62, 550 N.E.2d 1345, 1351 (1988); Town of Henrietta v. Department of Environmental Conservation, 76 A.D.2d 215, 430 N.Y.S.2d 440, 447 (1980).

147. Jackson v. New York State Urban Dev. Corp., 67 N.Y.2d 400, 416, 503 N.Y.S.2d 298, 304, 494 N.E.2d 429, 435 (1986) (quoting N.Y. Envtl. Conserv. Law § 8–0109(1)).

148. Town of Henrietta v. Department of Environmental Conservation, 76 A.D.2d 215, 430 N.Y.S.2d 440, 447 (1980).

149. E.F.S. Ventures Corp. v. Foster, 71 N.Y.2d 359, 526 N.Y.S.2d 56, 63–64, 520 N.E.2d 1345, 1352–53 (1988).

150. *See id.* at 371, 526 N.Y.S.2d at 62, 520 N.E.2d at 1351; Chinese Staff & Workers Ass'n v. City of New York, 68 N.Y.2d 359, 369, 509 N.Y.S.2d 499, 505, 502 N.E.2d 176, 182 (1986); *see also* Dreves v. New York Power Auth., 131 A.D.2d 182, 520 N.Y.S.2d 956, 958 n.1 (1987).

151. N.Y. Envtl. Conserv. Law § 8–0105(4) (McKinney 1984).

152. N.Y. Comp. R. & Regs. tit. 6, § 617.3(c)(1) (1987); *see* Nassau/Suffolk Neighborhood Network v. Town of Oyster Bay, 134 Misc. 2d 979, 513 N.Y.S.2d 921, 923 (1987).

153. *See* Bardon v. Town of North Dansville, 134 Misc. 2d 927, 513 N.Y.S.2d 584, 588 (1987).

154. Save the Pine Bush, Inc. v. City of Albany, 70 N.Y.2d 193, 206, 518 N.Y.S.2d 943, 948, 512 N.E.2d 526, 531 (1987).

155. Village of Westbury v. Department of Transp., 75 N.Y.2d 62, 69, 550 N.Y.S.2d 604, 607 (1989).

156. N.Y. Envtl. Conserv. Law § 8–0105(6) (McKinney 1984).

157. *See* Chinese Staff & Workers Ass'n v. City of New York, 68 N.Y.2d 359, 366, 509 N.Y.S.2d 499, 503, 502 N.E.2d 176, 180 (1986). *See generally* Ulasewicz, *The Department of Environmental Conservation and SEQRA: Upholding Its Mandates and Charting Parameters for the Elusive Socio-Economic Assessment*, 46 Albany L. Rev. 1255, 1266 (1982).

158. Save the Pine Bush, Inc. v. City of Albany, 70 N.Y.2d 193, 200, 206–07, 518 N.Y.S.2d 943, 944, 948–49, 512 N.E.2d 526, 527, 530–31 (1987); Village of Westbury v. Department of Transp., 146 A.D.2d 578, 536 N.Y.S.2d 502, 504 (1989); Guptill Holding Corp. v. Williams, 140 A.D.2d 12, 531 N.Y.S.2d 648, 651 (1988).

159. N.Y. Envtl. Conserv. Law § 8–0113 (McKinney 1984); *see* N.Y. Comp. Codes R. & Regs. tit. 6, pt. 617 (1987).

160. N.Y. Comp. Codes R. & Regs. tit. 6, § 617.21 (1987).

161. N.Y. Envtl. Conserv. Law § 8–0113(3) (McKinney 1984); *see* N.Y. Comp. Codes R. & Regs. tit. 6, § 617.4 (1987).

162. N.Y. Envtl. Conserv. Law § 8–0113(3)(a) (McKinney 1984); N.Y. Comp. Codes R. & Regs. tit. 6, § 617.4(b) (1987).

163. N.Y. Envtl. Conserv. Law § 8–0117(5) (McKinney 1984); N.Y. Comp. Codes R. & Regs. tit. 6, § 617.4(a) (1987).

164. *See* Village of Westbury v. Department of Transp., 75 N.Y.2d 62, 71–72, 550 N.Y.S.2d 604, 608–09 (1989).

165. N.Y. Envtl. Conserv. Law §§ 8–0105(5), 8–0111(5) (McKinney 1984).

166. *Id.* § 8–0105(5)(i); *see* New York Public Interest Research Group, Inc. v. Town of Islip, 71 N.Y.2d 292, 525 N.Y.S.2d 798, 805–06, 520 N.E.2d 517, 524 (1988).

167. N.Y. Envtl. Conserv. Law § 8–0105(5)(ii) (McKinney 1984); *see* Pius v. Bletsch, 70 N.Y.2d 920, 922, 524 N.Y.S.2d 395, 396, 519 N.E.2d 306, 307 (1987); Queensbury Ass'n v. Town Bd., 141 A.D.2d 997, 530 N.Y.S.2d 861, 863 (1988); Citizens for the Preservation of Windsor Terrace v. Smith, 122 A.D.2d 827, 505 N.Y.S.2d 896, 898 (1986).

168. Pius v. Bletsch, 70 N.Y.2d 920, 922, 524 N.Y.S.2d 395, 396, 519 N.E.2d 306, 307 (1987).

169. N.Y. Envtl. Conserv. Law § 8–0109(2) (McKinney 1984); Inland Vale Farm Co. v. Stergianopoulos, 65 N.Y.2d 718, 720, 492 N.Y.S.2d 7, 8, 481 N.E.2d 547, 548 (1985).

170. Chinese Staff & Workers Ass'n v. City of New York, 68 N.Y.2d 359, 364–65, 509 N.Y.S.2d 499, 502, 502 N.E.2d 176, 179 (1986).

171. N.Y. Comp. Codes R. & Regs. tit. 6, § 617.11 (1987).

172. *Id.* § 617.12(a); *see* Jaffee v. RCI Corp., 119 A.D.2d 854, 500 N.Y.S.2d 427, 429 (1986).

173. N.Y. Comp. Codes R. & Regs. tit. 6, § 617.13 (1987).

174. *Id.* § 617.13(a); *see* Anderberg v. New York Dep't of Environmental Conservation, 141 Misc. 2d 594, 533 N.Y.S.2d 828, 831 (1988) (action was type II not type I action). *See, e.g.,* Spring-Gar Community Civic Ass'n, Inc. v. Homes for the Homeless, Inc., 149 A.D.2d 581, 540 N.Y.S.2d 453, 454 (1989) (emergency action); Silver v. Koch, 137 A.D.2d 467, 525 N.Y.S.2d 186, 188 (1988) (same); Davis v. Board of Educ., 125 A.D.2d 534, 509 N.Y.S.2d 612, 613 (1986) (routine activity of educational institution).

175. N.Y. Comp. Codes R. & Regs., tit. 6, § 617.5 (1987).

176. *See* Kirk-Astor Drive Neighborhood Ass'n v. Town Bd., 106 A.D.2d 868, 483 N.Y.S.2d 526, 528–29 (1984); *see also* Tehan v. Scrivani, 97 A.D.2d 769, 468 N.Y.S.2d 402, 405–06 (1983); Kanaley v. Brennan, 119 Misc. 2d 1003, 465 N.Y.S.2d 130, 133–34 (1983), *aff'd,* 120 A.D.2d 974, 502 N.Y.S.2d 880 (1986); Meschi v. New York State Dep't of Environmental Conservation, 114 Misc. 2d 877, 452 N.Y.S.2d 553, 554–55 (1982).

177. N.Y. Envtl. Conserv. Law 8–0111(6) (McKinney 1984); N.Y. Comp. Codes R. & Regs., tit. 6, § 617.2(v) (1987); *see* Coca-Cola Bottling Co. of New York, Inc. v. Board of Estimate, 72 N.Y.2d 674, 536 N.Y.S.2d 33, 37, 532 N.E.2d 1261, 1265 (1988); Glen Head-Glenwood Landing Civic Council, Inc. v. Town of Oyster Bay, 88 A.D.2d 484, 453 N.Y.S.2d 732, 738 (1982).

178. *See* Di Veronica v. Arsenault, 124 A.D.2d 442, 507 N.Y.S.2d 541, 543 (1986); N.Y. Comp. Codes R. & Regs., tit. 6, § 617.11 (1987); *see also* Nielsen v. Planning Bd., 110 A.D.2d 767, 487 N.Y.S.2d 845, 847 (1985) (agency must take designated environmental criteria into account in making significance decision).

179. N.Y. Comp. Codes R. & Regs., tit. 6, § 617.10 (1987).

180. *See* Di Veronica v. Arsenault, 124 A.D.2d 442, 507 N.Y.S.2d 541, 543 (1986); Fernandez v. Planning Bd., 122 A.D.2d 139, 504 N.Y.S.2d 524, 526 (1986); *see also* Desmond-Americana v. Jorling, 153 A.D.2d 4, 550 N.Y.S.2d 94, 98–99 (1989) (negative declaration indicated cursory examination of potential environmental effects).

181. *See* Martin v. Koppelman, 124 A.D.2d 24, 510 N.Y.S.2d 881, 884 (1987).

182. Devitt v. Heimbach, 58 N.Y.2d 925, 460 N.Y.S.2d 512, 513, 447 N.E.2d 59, 60 (1983).

183. N.Y. Comp. Codes R. & Regs., tit. 6, §§ 617.2(h), 617.6(h) (1987).

184. N.Y. Envtl. Conserv. Law § 8–0109 (McKinney 1984 & Supp. 1990).

185. *Id.* § 8–0109(2) (McKinney 1984).

186. *See* Webster Assocs. v. Town of Webster, 59 N.Y.2d 220, 228–29, 464 N.Y.S.2d 431, 433–34, 451 N.E.2d 189, 191–92 (1983).

187. N.Y. Envtl. Conserv. Law §§ 8–0109(4), (5), (6) (McKinney 1984).

188. Programming & Systems, Inc. v. New York State Urban Dev. Corp., 61 N.Y.2d 738, 472 N.Y.S.2d 912, 913, 460 N.E.2d 1347, 1348 (1984) (quoting Tri-County Taxpayers Ass'n v. Town Bd., 55 N.Y.2d 41, 447 N.Y.S.2d 699, 432 N.E.2d 592 (1982)).

189. N.Y. Envtl. Conserv. Law § 8–0109(5) (McKinney 1984).

190. N.Y. Comp. Codes R. & Regs., tit. 6, § 617.9(a) (1987).

191. *Id.* § 617.9(b).

192. *See* Coalition for Responsible Planning, Inc. v. Koch, 148 A.D.2d 230, 543 N.Y.S.2d 653, 656 (1989); *see also* Main Seneca Corp. v. Erie County Industrial

Dev. Agency, 125 A.D.2d 930, 510 N.Y.S.2d 326, 327 (1986) (agency reasonably found that repositioning stadium caused no significant effect).

193. N.Y. Comp. Codes R. & Regs., tit. 6, § 617.8(g) (1987).

194. *Id.* § 617.8(g)(3); *see* Glen Head-Glenwood Landing Civic Council, Inc. v. Town of Oyster Bay, 88 A.D.2d 484, 453 N.Y.S.2d 732, 739 (1982).

195. Jackson v. New York State Urban Dev. Corp., 67 N.Y.2d 400, 416, 503 N.Y.S.2d 298, 304, 494 N.E.2d 429, 435 (1986) (quoting N.Y. Envtl. Conserv. Law § 8–0109(8); N.Y. Comp. Codes R. & Regs. tit. 6, § 617.9(c)(2)).

196. *Id.* at 421–22, 503 N.Y.S.2d at 308, 494 N.E.2d at 439.

197. *See* Battenkill Ass'n of Concerned Citizens v. Town of Greenwich Planning Bd., ___ A.D.2d ___, 550 N.Y.S.2d 86, 88 (1989); Big V Supermarkets, Inc. v. Town of Wallkill, 154 A.D.2d 669, 546 N.Y.S.2d 668, 669-70 (1989); Niagara Recycling, Inc. v. Town Bd., 83 A.D.2d 335, 443 N.Y.S.2d 951, 955 (1981).

198. *See* Har Enterprises v. Town of Brookhaven, 74 N.Y.2d 524, 549 N.Y.S.2d 638, 641–42, 548 N.E.2d 1289, 1292–93 (1989).

199. Abrams v. Love Canal Area Revitalization Agency, 134 A.D.2d 885, 522 N.Y.S.2d 53, 54 (1987).

200. Jackson v. New York State Urban Dev. Corp., 67 N.Y.2d 400, 416, 503 N.Y.S.2d 298, 304–05, 494 N.E.2d 429, 435–36 (1986).

201. Greenpoint Renaissance Enterprise Corp. v. City of New York, 137 A.D.2d 597, 524 N.Y.S.2d 488, 491 (1988).

202. Jackson v. New York State Urban Dev. Corp., 67 N.Y.2d 400, 417, 503 N.Y.S.2d 298, 305, 494 N.E.2d 429, 436 (1986).

203. Orchards Assocs. v. Planning Bd., 114 A.D.2d 850, 494 N.Y.S.2d 760, 761 (1985).

204. N.Y. Civ. Prac. L. & R. §§ 7801–7806 (McKinney 1981 & Supp. 1990); *see* Save the Pine Bush, Inc. v. City of Albany, 70 N.Y.2d 193, 200, 518 N.Y.S.2d 943, 944, 512 N.E.2d 526, 527 (1987); *see also* Village of Westbury v. Department of Transp., 75 N.Y.2d 62, 72–73, 550 N.Y.S.2d 604, 609-10 (1989) (triggering date for limitations to begin running on negative declaration was date aggrieved political subdivision was served; notice by publication was insufficient).

205. Har Enterprises v. Town of Brookhaven, 74 N.Y.2d 524, 549 N.Y.S.2d 638, 642, 548 N.E.2d 1289, 1293 (1989); Jackson v. New York State Urban Dev. Corp., 67 N.Y.2d 400, 417, 503 N.Y.S.2d 298, 305, 494 N.E.2d 429, 436 (1986); H.O.M.E.S. v. New York State Urban Dev. Corp., 69 A.D.2d 222, 418 N.Y.S.2d 827, 832 (1979); *see also* Save the Pine Bush, Inc. v. City of Albany, 141 A.D.2d 949, 530 N.Y.S.2d 295, 298 (1988) (agency did not take hard look at cumulative environmental effects).

206. Jackson v. New York State Urban Dev. Corp., 67 N.Y.2d 400, 417, 421, 503 N.Y.S.2d 298, 305, 307, 494 N.E.2d 429, 436, 438 (1986); *see* Coalition Against Lincoln West, Inc. v. City of New York, 94 A.D.2d 483, 465 N.Y.S.2d 170, 176, *aff'd*, 60 N.Y.S.2d 805, 469 N.Y.S.2d 689, 457 N.E.2d 795 (1983).

207. Jackson v. New York State Urban Dev. Corp., 67 N.Y.2d 400, 417, 503 N.Y.S.2d 298, 305, 494 N.E.2d 429, 436 (1986); *see* Horn v. International Business Machines Corp., 110 A.D.2d 87, 493 N.Y.S.2d 184, 190–91 (1985) (comparing consideration of alternatives by private developer and governmental agency).

208. N.Y. Envtl. Conserv. Law § 8–0111(1) (McKinney 1984).

209. *See* Jackson v. New York State Urban Dev. Corp., 67 N.Y.2d 400, 415, 503 N.Y.S.2d 298, 303, 494 N.E.2d 429, 434 (1986); Levine, *The New York State Environmental Quality Review Act of 1975: An Analysis of the Parties' Responsibilities in the Review/Permit Request Process*, 12 Fordham Urb. L.J. 1, 20 (1984).

210. *See* Marsh, *Symposium on the New York State Environmental Quality Review Act: Introduction-SEQRA's Scope and Objectives*, 46 Albany L. Rev. 1097, 1100 n.21 (1982) (citing Hanly v. Marsh, 460 F.2d 640, 647 (2d Cir.), *cert. denied*, 409 U.S. 990 (1972)).

211. N.Y. Envtl. Conserv. Law § 8–0109(4) (McKinney 1984) (agency must consider reasonable alternatives); N.Y. Comp. Codes R. & Regs., tit. 6, § 617.14(f)(5) (1987) (same); *see* Horn v. International Business Machines Corp., 110 A.D.2d 87, 493 N.Y.S.2d 184, 190 (1985).

212. 42 U.S.C. § 4332 (1988).

213. N.Y. Envtl. Conserv. Law § 8–0103(6) (McKinney 1984).

214. Holmes v. Brookhaven Town Planning Bd., 137 A.D.2d 601, 524 N.Y.S.2d 492, 493 (1988); Rye Town/King Civic Ass'n v. Town of Rye, 82 A.D.2d 474, 442 N.Y.S.2d 67, 71 (1981). *Cf.* Calvert Cliffs' Coordinating Comm. v. AEC, 449 F.2d 1109, 1115 (D.C. Cir. 1971) (section 102 duties under NEPA "must be complied with to the fullest extent possible").

215. *See* H.O.M.E.S. v. New York State Urban Dev. Corp., 69 A.D.2d 222, 418 N.Y.S.2d 827, 832 (1979).

216. *See* Town of Henrietta v. Department of Environmental Conservation, 76 A.D.2d 215, 430 N.Y.S.2d 440, 447–48 (1980); *see also* Aldrich v. Pattison, 107 A.D.2d 258, 486 N.Y.S.2d 23, 29 (1985) (applying hard look standard to final EIS).

217. *See* Bliek v. Town of Webster, 104 Misc. 2d 852, 429 N.Y.S.2d 811, 817 (1980).

218. *See* section 6.3.2; *but see* Industrial Liaison Comm. v. Williams, 131 A.D.2d 205, 521 N.Y.S.2d 321, 324–25 (1987) (considering level under NEPA to be higher), *aff'd*, 72 N.Y.2d 137, 531 N.Y.S.2d 791, 527 N.E.2d 274 (1988).

219. Har Enterprises v. Town of Brookhaven, 74 N.Y.2d 524, 549 N.Y.S.2d 638, 641–42, 548 N.E.2d 1289, 1292–93 (1989).

220. *See* Chinese Staff & Workers Ass'n v. City of New York, 68 N.Y.2d 359, 509 N.Y.S.2d 499, 502, 502 N.E.2d 176, 179 (1986).

221. *See* Fritiofson v. Alexander, 772 F.2d 1225, 1238 n.7 (5th Cir. 1985) ("test is whether there is a possibility not a certainty of significant impacts"); Sierra Club v. Marsh, 769 F.2d 868, 870 (1st Cir. 1985) (plaintiffs must show "substantial possibility" that action could significantly affect quality of human environment); Steamboaters v. FERC, 759 F.2d 1382, 1392 (9th Cir. 1985) ("plaintiff need not show that significant effects *will in fact occur*" (emphasis original)).

222. *See* Town of Huntington v. Marsh, 884 F.2d 648, 653 (2d Cir. 1989) (requiring showing of irreparable harm for injunction), *cert. denied*, 110 S. Ct. 1296 (1990).

223. *See* Chinese Staff & Workers Ass'n v. City of New York, 68 N.Y.2d 359, 509 N.Y.S.2d 499, 502 n.6, 502 N.E.2d 176, 179 n.6 (1986). *Cf.* Kentucky *ex rel.* Beshear v. Alexander, 655 F.2d 714, 720 (6th Cir. 1981) (plaintiffs presented no evidence that action had a significant environmental effect); Greenwood Utilities Comm'n v. Hodel, 764 F.2d 1459, 1465 (11th Cir. 1985) (no evidence that action would significantly affect environment); International Detective Serv., Inc. v. ICC, 595

F.2d 862, 865 n.5 (D.C. Cir. 1979) (same); Plaza Bank v. Board of Governors of Federal Reserve System, 575 F.2d 1248, 1251 (8th Cir. 1978) (same).

224. *See* Jackson v. New York State Urban Dev. Corp., 67 N.Y.S.2d 400, 503 N.Y.S.2d 298, 303, 494 N.E.2d 429, 434 (1986).

225. *See* Chinese Staff & Workers Ass'n v. City of New York, 68 N.Y.2d 359, 509 N.Y.S.2d 499, 505, 502 N.E.2d 176, 182 (1986); City of Glens Falls v. Board of Educ., 88 A.D.2d 233, 453 N.Y.S.2d 891, 894 (1982). *Cf.* Federation to Preserve Greenwich Village Waterfront v. New York State Dep't of Transp., 150 A.D.2d 225, 541 N.Y.S.2d 394, 395–96 (1989) (declining to disturb denial of injunctive relief pending trial on the merits and setting early trial date).

226. *See, e.g.,* Desmond-Americana v. Jorling, 153 A.D.2d 4, 550 N.Y.S.2d 94, 98–99 (1989) (Commissioner of Department of Environmental Conservation violated SEQRA when promulgating regulations concerning pesticide application). *Cf.* Industrial Liaison Comm. of Niagara Falls Area Chamber of Commerce v. Williams, 72 N.Y.2d 137, 146, 531 N.Y.S.2d 791, 795, 527 N.E.2d 274, 278 (1988) (Department of Environmental Conservation complied with SEQRA in promulgating ambient water quality standards).

8

Conclusion

NEPA case law is voluminous. It is impossible to understand how to comply with NEPA merely by reading the statute. This book has attempted to provide a practical guide to the NEPA process and an in-depth legal analysis of NEPA, its implementing regulations, and case law. Chapter 8 concludes the book by briefly summarizing the role of the CEQ, the courts, plaintiffs, and Congress in NEPA's development and future. Finally, this chapter discusses several major themes that flow through judicial interpretations of NEPA.

NEPA provided the federal agencies with authority and a duty to consider the significant environmental effects of their proposed actions. NEPA did not provide an explicit substantive mandate, authority to a regulatory agency to enforce the statute, an explicit jurisdictional base, or even an attorney fee provision to encourage plaintiffs to enforce NEPA's provisions. NEPA did provide procedural requirements but did not directly tie those requirements to NEPA's policies and purposes.

If Congress expected the federal agencies to necessarily alter their proposed actions to comply with NEPA's policies and purposes once the agencies had completed NEPA's procedural requirements, it was mistaken. Although NEPA has altered the way in which most agencies propose actions, some agencies continue to have a poor reputation for complying with NEPA.[1] In the face of this continuing reluctance on the part of some agencies to comply with NEPA, the CEQ, the courts, Congress, environmental organizations and citizen groups have played a pivotal role in developing and enforcing the act.

The CEQ formulated standard guidelines and regulations applicable to all federal agencies, issued guidance memoranda, and aided agencies in adopting implementing procedures. Indeed, were it not for the CEQ's foresight and persistence during the 1970s in guiding agency compliance with NEPA, the procedures adopted by the various federal agencies would probably vary greatly because of the discretion NEPA accords to the federal agencies to formulate their individual NEPA procedures. The CEQ guidance and regulations transformed the broad language of NEPA into workable procedures that, perhaps most importantly, assured public participation in all stages of the NEPA process.

The CEQ probably could not have persuaded federal agencies to follow its guidelines and advice if the courts had not reinforced the CEQ's somewhat dubious authority under NEPA. Fortunately for the CEQ, the District of Columbia Circuit strongly endorsed the CEQ's interpretation of NEPA in 1971, causing federal agencies to adopt stricter procedures to comply with NEPA and persuading other circuits to follow the District of Columbia Circuit's interpretation of NEPA as more than "a paper tiger."

The courts and the CEQ have acted symbiotically throughout NEPA's history. The courts set out principles of NEPA law, which were given nationwide application by the CEQ during the 1970s. In turn, the courts deferred to the CEQ's interpretation of NEPA and further developed the CEQ's codification of NEPA case law.

The role of environmental organizations and citizen groups in the evolution of NEPA law is enormous. The legal arguments of these plaintiffs form the basis for much of NEPA case law. The organizations and groups have participated in countless NEPA processes, thus raising the level of the agencies' consideration of the environmental effects of their proposed actions. Judicial challenges to an agency's procedures often mean that future agency compliance with NEPA must meet a higher standard. In effect, the environmental organizations and citizens groups, with the aid of the courts, have enforced NEPA and the CEQ regulations, thus ensuring NEPA's continued vitality and integration into the procedures of the federal agencies.

The role of Congress in NEPA's evolution is less clear than that of the CEQ, the courts, and environmental organizations and citizens groups. In the twenty years since NEPA's enactment, Congress has rejected attempts to dilute NEPA's purpose and scope. However, Congress has failed to clarify the relationship between NEPA's strong declaration of policy and the action-forcing provisions designed to integrate NEPA's policy into the agency decision-making process.

Congress clearly wished to strengthen NEPA's enforcement in 1970 after it became apparent that federal agencies were not fully complying with NEPA.[2] By enacting section 309 of the Clean Air Act, Congress gave the EPA authority to review and comment on major federal actions significantly affecting the quality of the human environment as well as certain other federal actions. This review, together with the potential referral of environmentally unsatisfactory actions to the CEQ, goes beyond NEPA's action-forcing procedures. Thus Congress clearly intended the EPA and the CEQ, upon referral of an action, to have the power to participate in agencies' substantive decisions.

The issue of whether Congress intended courts to have the power to prevent an agency from proceeding with an action if the agency followed all NEPA's action-forcing procedures is still not squarely answered, although the United States Supreme Court has strongly implied that NEPA does not provide the courts with such authority. If an agency action is directly contrary to NEPA's purposes, proceeding with the action would arguably be arbitrary and capricious because Congress surely did not intend agencies to be able to follow the action-forcing procedures of NEPA merely to accord no weight to the environmental consequences of their proposed actions.

Congress added the action-forcing procedures to NEPA "[t]o insure that the policies and goals defined in [NEPA were] infused into the ongoing programs and actions of the Federal Government."[3] NEPA would be nothing more than a "paper tiger" if Congress did not also intend the agencies to infuse the policies and goals defined in NEPA into their decisions. In introducing the version of NEPA revised by the conference committee to the Senate floor, Senator Jackson, one of NEPA's authors, declared a purpose of NEPA to be "[t]hat we will not intentionally initiate actions which will do irreparable damage to the air, land, and water which supports life on earth."[4] If an agency decision maker may proceed with an action that will do irreparable environmental damage, and if that decision maker makes that decision after following all NEPA's action-forcing procedures, the result of Congress' adding action-forcing provisions to NEPA will have been merely to ensure that the irreparable environmental damage was conducted intentionally and not unintentionally. Congress surely cannot have intended NEPA to have this result. However, as NEPA is presently written, agencies that comply with its procedures by spending millions of dollars analyzing proposed actions, do not violate NEPA if they proceed with environmentally destructive actions contrary to NEPA's policies and purposes.[5]

Congress' intent that NEPA applies to all major federal actions significantly affecting the quality of the human environment is clearer than the relationship Congress failed to adequately express between NEPA's purposes and its action-forcing procedures. NEPA has proven to be resilient to challenges from federal agencies seeking to gain a blanket exemption from NEPA's reach. Compliance with NEPA is only rarely prohibited because of the mandate of another statute. Even when the action involves classified data, the courts have held that NEPA still applies to the action.

Legislation pending in Congress in 1990 would finally bridge the gap between NEPA's policies and purposes and its action-forcing procedures. The proposed legislation appears to provide NEPA with a substantive mandate by requiring agencies to consider mitigation measures they "will" adopt. Other provisions in the proposed legislation call for a review of past mitigation measures to determine the extent to which they were implemented and their effectiveness. Provisions clarifying existing case law would grant regulatory authority to the CEQ and require agencies to consider the significant effects of their proposed actions on the extraterritorial and global environments.[6] These amendments should be enacted. It is time for Congress to signal congressional support for NEPA and to end a chain of United States Supreme Court cases that have created an ever-widening chasm between NEPA's action-forcing provisions and its purposes and policies.

While strengthening NEPA, the amendments would not affect several major themes that run through NEPA case law. It is well settled that NEPA protects only environmental interests. By limiting standing to plaintiffs with at least some environmental interests, the courts have ensured that NEPA has not been trivialized by plaintiffs with purely economic interests or used as a tool for nonenvironmental purposes. NEPA's purpose of protecting environmental not pecuniary interests extends to other aspects of NEPA case law besides standing. For example, damages are not appropriate under NEPA because remedies under NEPA are designed solely to protect the environment.

NEPA's requirement that federal agencies consider proposed actions on a site-specific basis except for broad programs is well established. The agencies and courts have recognized that an interpretation of a "significant" environmental effect invariably changes from one action in one location to another action in the same or different location. This requirement recognizes that the knowledge of ecological processes is inexact and no one is able to accurately determine the ecological effects of various actions merely by using an analysis of an action at one location.

NEPA opened up the federal agencies' decision-making process to the public by requiring agencies to disclose information on proposed actions' environmental consequences to the public and by allowing the public to participate in the process. When the public participates in the decision-making process, the exchange of ideas and different views on the environmental effects of a proposed action and alternatives to it means that the public may help shape actions that will affect their community. Thus, the level of consideration of the environmental effects of a proposed agency action is invariably enhanced when both the public and the agency analyze the action's environmental effects.

Public participation carries a liability with it as well, however. If members of the public fail to participate in the NEPA process and fail to offer their views on the adequacy of the agency's process, or the agency's consideration of environmental effects and alternatives, or if they fail to bring relevant information to the attention of the agency, they may jeopardize their right to subsequently object in a court to the agency action. A tension thus exists between the agency's duty to comply with NEPA and the role of the public in participating in the agency's decision-making process. Participation by the public ensures that the agency will respond to public concerns and often means that the agency will modify its action to reflect the concerns. However, the agency's duty to comply with NEPA exists whether or not the public participates in the NEPA process. Therefore, regardless of whether the public participates, the agency must comply with NEPA albeit with a potentially reduced level of consideration of environmental effects and alternatives.

NEPA's purpose is only served in a decision on a proposed action when an agency can factor the results of the NEPA process into its decision making. Therefore, courts do not require agencies to comply with NEPA when this purpose cannot be served, either because an agency decision maker has no discretionary authority, because an action is too far advanced, or because a decision has already been made.

Post-EIS remedies are not generally recognized. Obviously, if an agency action requiring an EIS is complete, the physical environment is already significantly affected. However, if the agency prepares an EIS for one action and conducts another by substantially changing the action it proposed in the EIS, the affected public should have some remedy for the agency's failure to prepare a supplemental EIS, or for any bad faith on the part of the agency in conducting an action different from that contained in the final EIS. Similarly, if an agency issues an EA and FONSI for a proposed action and then changes the action so that it has significant environmental effects, the affected public should have some remedy for the agency's failure to prepare an EIS for an action significantly affecting the quality of the human environment. One remedy could be to require the agency to modify the conducted action to conform with the action the agency purportedly proposed. Even though the physical environment would have already been affected by the conducted action, the consequences of those effects on the human environment could still be mitigated.

The involvement in government decision making triggered by NEPA is far reaching. Many states have adopted mini-NEPAs, thus opening up state and local governmental decision making to the public in those states. Often the mini-NEPAs require agencies to mitigate the environmental effects of their actions if feasible. Thus, the mini-NEPAs of some states protect the environment to a greater degree than can NEPA. Even in states that do not have a mini-NEPA, applicants for state permits or funding sometimes use the processes established under NEPA to meet requirements to consider environmental effects and to allow public participation in the permitting process. Thus, NEPA affects not only federal actions, but in its role as a model for analyzing environmental consequences of agency actions it indirectly affects many state and local government actions nationwide.

NOTES

1. *See* Congressional Research Service, *NEPA Compliance at Department of Energy Defense Production Facilities* CRS-1 (1990).

2. *See generally* Andreen, *In Pursuit of NEPA's Promise: The Role of Executive Oversight in the Implementation of Environmental Policy,* 64 Ind. L.J. 205, 223–29 (1989).

3. 115 Cong. Rec. 40,416 (1969) (remarks of Sen. Jackson).

4. *Id.*

5. *See* Caldwell, *20 Years with NEPA Indicates the Need,* 31 Environment 7, 26 (Dec. 1989); *see also* Blumm, *The National Environmental Policy Act at Twenty: A Preface,* 20 Envtl. L. (NEPA Symposium) (1990).

6. S. 1089, 101st Cong., 1st Sess. (1989); H.R. 1113, 101st Cong., 1st Sess. (1989); H.R. 3847, 101st Cong., 2d Sess. (1990).

The National Environmental Policy Act of 1969

Section 1. That this Act may be cited as the "National Environmental Policy Act of 1969."

Section 2 (42 U.S.C. § 4321). Congressional declaration of purpose.

The purposes of this chapter are: To declare a national policy which will encourage productive and enjoyable harmony between man and his environment; to promote efforts which will prevent or eliminate damage to the environment and biosphere and stimulate the health and welfare of man; to enrich the understanding of the ecological systems and natural resources important to the Nation; and to establish a Council on Environmental Quality.

SUBCHAPTER I

Section 101 (42 U.S.C. § 4331). Congressional declaration of national environmental policy.

(a) The Congress, recognizing the profound impact of man's activity on the interrelations of all components of the natural environment, particularly the profound influences of population growth, high-density urbanization, industrial expansion, resource exploitation, and new and expanding technological advances and recognizing further the critical importance of restoring and maintaining environmental quality to the overall welfare and development of man, declares that it is the continuing policy of the Federal Government, in cooperation with State and local governments, and other concerned public and private organizations, to use all practicable means and measures, including financial and technical assistance, in a manner calculated to foster and promote the general welfare, to create and maintain conditions under which man and nature can exist in productive harmony, and fulfill the social, economic, and other requirements of present and future generations of Americans.

(b) In order to carry out the policy set forth in this Act, it is the continuing responsibility of the Federal Government to use all practicable means, consistent with other essential considerations of national policy, to improve and coordinate Federal plans, functions, programs, and resources to the end that the Nation may

> (1) fulfill the responsibilities of each generation as trustee of the environment for succeeding generations;
> (2) assure for all Americans safe, healthful, productive, and esthetically and culturally pleasing surroundings;
> (3) attain the widest range of beneficial uses of the environment without degradation, risk to health or safety, or other undesirable and unintended consequences;
> (4) preserve important historic, cultural, and natural aspects of our national heritage, and maintain, wherever possible, an environment which supports diversity, and variety of individual choice;
> (5) achieve a balance between population and resource use which will permit high standards of living and a wide sharing of life's amenities; and
> (6) enhance the quality of renewable resources and approach the maximum attainable recycling of depletable resources.

(c) The Congress recognizes that each person should enjoy a healthful environment and that each person has a responsibility to contribute to the preservation and enhancement of the environment.

Section 102 (42 U.S.C. § 4332). Cooperation of agencies; reports; availability of information; recommendations; international and national coordination of efforts.

The Congress authorizes and directs that, to the fullest extent possible: (1) the policies, regulations, and public laws of the United States shall be interpreted and administered in accordance with the policies set forth in this chapter, and (2) all agencies of the Federal Government shall

(a) utilize a systematic, interdisciplinary approach which will insure the integrated used of the natural and social sciences and the environmental design arts in planning and in decisionmaking which may have an impact on man's environment;

(b) identify and develop methods and procedures, in consultation with the Council on Environmental Quality established by subchapter II of this chapter, which will insure that presently unquantified environmental amenities and values may be given appropriate consideration in decisionmaking along with economic and technical considerations;

(c) include in every recommendation or report on proposals for legislation and other major Federal actions significantly affecting the quality of the human environment, a detailed statement by the responsible official on

>(i) the environmental impact of the proposed action,
>(ii) any adverse environmental effects which cannot be avoided should the proposal be implemented,
>(iii) alternatives to the proposed action,
>(iv) the relationship between local short-term uses of man's environment and the maintenance and enhancement of long-term productivity, and
>(v) any irreversible and irretrievable commitments of resources which would be involved in the proposed action should it be implemented.

Prior to making any detailed statement, the responsible Federal official shall consult with and obtain the comments of any Federal agency which has jurisdiction by law or special expertise with respect to any environmental impact involved. Copies of such statement and the comments and views of the appropriate Federal, State, and local agencies, which are authorized to develop and enforce environmental standards, shall be made available to the President, the Council on Environmental Quality and to the public as provided by section 552 of title 5, United States Code, and shall accompany the proposal through the existing agency review processes;

(d) Any detailed statement required under subparagraph (C) after January 1, 1970, for any major Federal action funded under a program of grants to States shall not be deemed to be legally insufficient solely by reason of having been prepared by a State agency or official, if:

(i) the State agency or official has statewide jurisdiction and has the responsibility for such action,

(ii) the responsible Federal official furnishes guidance and participates in such preparation,

(iii) the responsible Federal official independently evaluates such statement prior to its approval and adoption, and

(iv) after January 1, 1976, the responsible Federal official provides early notification to, and solicits the views of, any other State or any Federal land management entity of any action or any alternative thereto which may have significant impacts upon such State or affected Federal land management entity and, if there is any disagreement on such impacts, prepares a written assessment of such impacts and views for incorporation into such detailed statement.

The procedures in this subparagraph shall not relieve the Federal official of his responsibilities for the scope, objectivity, and content of the entire statement or of any other responsibility under this chapter; and further, this subparagraph does not affect the legal sufficiency of statements prepared by State agencies with less than statewide jurisdiction.

(e) study, develop, and describe appropriate alternatives to recommended courses of action in any proposal which involves unresolved conflicts concerning alternative uses of available resources;

(f) recognize the worldwide and long-range character of environmental problems and, where consistent with the foreign policy of the United States, lend appropriate support to initiatives, resolutions, and programs designed to maximize international cooperation in anticipating and preventing a decline in the quality of mankind's world environment;

(g) make available to States, counties, municipalities, institutions, and individuals, advice and information useful in restoring, maintaining, and enhancing the quality of the environment;

(h) initiate and utilize ecological information in the planning and development of resource-oriented projects; and

(i) assist the Council on Environmental Quality established by subchapter II of this chapter.

Section 103 (42 U.S.C. § 4333). Conformity of administrative procedures to national environmental policy.

All agencies of the Federal Government shall review their present statutory authority, administrative regulations, and current policies and procedures for the purpose of determining whether there are any deficiencies or inconsistencies therein which prohibit full compliance with the purposes and provisions of this chapter and shall propose to the President not later than July 1, 1971, such measures as may be necessary to bring their authority and policies into conformity with the intent, purposes, and procedures set forth in this chapter.

Section 104 (42 U.S.C. § 4334). Other statutory obligations of agencies.

Nothing in section 4332 or 4333 of this title shall in any way affect the specific statutory obligations of any Federal agency (1) to comply with criteria or standards of environmental quality, (2) to coordinate or consult with any other Federal or State agency, or (3) to act, or refrain from acting contingent upon the recommendations or certification of any other Federal or State agency.

Section 105 (42 U.S.C. § 4335). Efforts supplemental to existing authorizations.

The policies and goals set forth in this chapter are supplementary to those set forth in existing authorizations of Federal agencies.

SUBCHAPTER II - COUNCIL ON ENVIRONMENTAL QUALITY

Section 201 (42 U.S.C. § 4341). Reports to Congress; recommendations for legislation.

The President shall transmit to the Congress annually beginning July 1, 1970, an Environmental Quality Report (hereinafter referred to as the "report") which shall set forth (1) the status and condition of the major natural, manmade, or altered environmental classes of the Nation, including, but not limited to, the air, the aquatic, including marine, estuarine, and fresh water, and the terrestrial environment, including, but not limited to, the forest, dryland, wetland, range, urban, suburban and rural environment; (2) current and foreseeable trends in the quality, management and utilization of such environments and the effects of those trends on the social, economic, and other requirements of the Nation; (3) the adequacy of available natural resources for fulfilling human and economic requirements of the Nation in the light of expected population pressures; (4) a review of the programs and activities (including regulatory activities) of the Federal Government, the State and local governments, and nongovernmental entities or individuals with particular reference to their effect on the environment and on the conservation, development and utilization of natural resources; and (5) a program for remedying the deficiencies of existing programs and activities, together with recommendations for legislation.

Section 202 (42 U.S.C. § 4342). Establishment; membership; Chairman; appointments.

There is created in the Executive Office of the President a Council on Environmental Quality (hereinafter referred to as the "Council"). The Council shall be composed of three members who shall be appointed by the President to serve at his pleasure, by and with the advice and consent of the Senate. The President shall designate one of the members of the Council to serve as Chairman. Each member shall be a person who, as a result of his training, experience, and attainments, is exceptionally well qualified to analyze and interpret environmental trends and information of all kinds; to appraise programs and activities of the Federal Government in the light of the policy set forth in subchapter I of this chapter; to be conscious of and responsive to the scientific, economic, social, esthetic, and cultural needs and interests of the Nation; and to formulate and recommend national policies to promote the improvement of the quality of the environment.

Section 203 (42 U.S.C. § 4343). Employment of personnel, experts and consultants.

(a) The Council may employ such officers and employees as may be necessary to carry out its functions under this chapter. In addition, the Council may employ and fix the compensation of such experts and consultants as may be necessary for the carrying out of its functions under this chapter, in accordance with section 3109 of title 5 (but without regard to the last sentence thereof).

(b) Notwithstanding section 1342 of title 31, the Council may accept and employ voluntary and uncompensated services in furtherance of the purposes of the Council.

Section 204 (42 U.S.C. § 4344). Duties and functions.

It shall be the duty and function of the Council

(1) to assist and advise the President in the preparation of the Environmental Quality Report required by section 4341 of this title;

(2) to gather timely and authoritative information concerning the conditions and trends in the quality of the environment both current and prospective, to analyze and interpret such information for the purpose of determining whether such conditions and trends are interfering, or are likely to interfere, with the achievement of the policy set forth in subchapter I of this chapter, and to compile and submit to the President studies relating to such conditions and trends;

(3) to review and appraise the various programs and activities of the Federal Government in the light of the policy set forth in subchapter I of this chapter for the purpose of determining the extent to which such programs and activities are contributing to the achievement of such policy, and to make recommendations to the President with respect thereto;

(4) to develop and recommend to the President national policies to foster and promote the improvement of environmental quality to meet the conservation, social, economic, health, and other requirements and goals of the Nation;

(5) to conduct investigations, studies, surveys, research, and analyses relating to ecological systems and environmental quality;

(6) to document and define changes in the natural environment, including the plant and animal systems, and to accumulate necessary data and other information for a continuing analysis of these changes or trends and an interpretation of their underlying causes;

(7) to report at least once each year to the President on the state and condition of the environment; and

(8) to make and furnish such studies, reports thereon, and recommendations with respect to matters of policy and legislation as the President may request.

Section 205 (42 U.S.C. § 4345). Consultation with the Citizens' Advisory Committee on Environmental Quality and other representatives.

In exercising its powers, functions, and duties under this chapter, the Council shall

(1) consult with the Citizens' Advisory Committee on Environmental Quality established by Executive Order numbered 11472, dated May 29, 1969, and with such representatives of science,

industry, agriculture, labor, conservation organizations, State and local governments and other groups, as it deems advisable; and

(2) utilize, to the fullest extent possible, the services, facilities and information (including statistical information) of public and private agencies and organizations, and individuals, in order that duplication of effort and expense may be avoided, thus assuring that the Council's activities will not unnecessarily overlap or conflict with similar activities authorized by law and performed by established agencies.

Section 206 (42 U.S.C. § 4346). Tenure and compensation of members.

Members of the Council shall serve full time and the Chairman of the Council shall be compensated at the rate provided for Level II of the Executive Schedule Pay Rates (5 U.S.C. 5313). The other members of the Council shall be compensated at the rate provided for Level IV [of] the Executive Schedule Pay Rates (5 U.S.C. 5315).

Section 207 (42 U.S.C. § 4346a). Travel reimbursement by private organizations and Federal, State, and local governments.

The Council may accept reimbursements from any private non-profit organization or from any department, agency, or instrumentality of the Federal Government, any State, or local government, for the reasonable travel expenses incurred by an officer or employee of the Council in connection with his attendance at any conference, seminar, or similar meeting conducted for the benefit of the Council.

Section 208 (42 U.S.C. § 4346b). Expenditures in support of international activities.

The Council may make expenditures in support of its international activities, including expenditures for: (1) international travel; (2) activities in implementation of international agreements; and (3) the support of international exchange programs in the United States and in foreign countries.

Section 209 (42 U.S.C. § 4347). Authorization of appropriations.

There are authorized to be appropriated to carry out the provisions of this chapter not to exceed $300,000 for fiscal year 1970, $700,000 for fiscal year 1971, and $1,000,000 for each fiscal year thereafter.

Appendix B

The Council on Environmental Quality Regulations

PART 1500--PURPOSE, POLICY, AND MANDATE

§ 1500.1   Purpose.

(a) The National Environmental Policy Act (NEPA) is our basic national charter for protection of the environment.   It establishes policy, sets goals (section 101), and provides means (section 102) for carrying out the policy.   Section 102(2) contains "action-forcing" provisions to make sure that federal agencies act according to the letter and spirit of the Act.   The regulations that follow implement section 102(2).   Their purpose is to tell federal agencies what they must do to comply with the procedures and achieve the goals of the Act.   The President, the federal agencies, and the courts share responsibility for enforcing the Act so as to achieve the substantive requirements of section 101.

(b) NEPA procedures must insure that environmental information is available to public officials and citizens before decisions are made and before actions are taken.   The information must be of high quality.   Accurate scientific analysis, expert agency comments, and public scrutiny are essential to implementing NEPA. Most important, NEPA documents must concentrate on the issues that are truly significant to the action in question, rather than amassing needless detail.

(c) Ultimately, of course, it is not better documents but better decisions that count.   NEPA's purpose is not to generate paperwork--even excellent paperwork--but to foster excellent action.   The NEPA process is intended to help public officials make decisions that are based on understanding of environmental consequences, and take actions that protect, restore, and enhance the environment.   These regulations provide the direction to achieve this purpose.

§ 1500.2   Policy.

Federal agencies shall to the fullest extent possible:

(a) Interpret and administer the policies, regulations, and public laws of the United States in accordance with the policies set forth in the Act and in these regulations.

(b) Implement procedures to make the NEPA process more useful to decisionmakers and the public; to reduce paperwork and the accumulation of extraneous background data; and to emphasize real environmental issues and alternatives.   Environmental impact statements shall be concise, clear, and to the point, and shall be supported by evidence that agencies have made the necessary environmental analyses.

(c) Integrate the requirements of NEPA with other planning and environmental review procedures required by law or by agency practice so that all such procedures run concurrently rather than consecutively.

(d) Encourage and facilitate public involvement in decisions which affect the quality of the human environment.

(e) Use the NEPA process to identify and assess the reasonable alternatives to proposed actions that will avoid or minimize adverse effects of these actions upon the quality of the human environment.

(f) Use all practicable means, consistent with the requirements of the Act and other essential considerations of national policy, to restore and enhance the quality of the human environment and avoid or minimize any possible adverse effects of their actions upon the quality of the human environment.

§ 1500.3 **Mandate.**

Parts 1500 through 1508 of this title provide regulations applicable to and binding on all Federal agencies for implementing the procedural provisions of the National Environmental Policy Act of 1969, as amended (Pub. L. 91-190, 42 U.S.C. 4321 et seq.) (NEPA or the Act) except where compliance would be inconsistent with other statutory requirements. These regulations are issued pursuant to NEPA, the Environmental Quality Improvement Act of 1970, as amended (42 U.S.C. 4371 et seq.) section 309 of the Clean Air Act, as amended (42 U.S.C. 7609) and Executive Order 11514, Protection and Enhancement of Environmental Quality (March 5, 1970, as amended by Executive Order 11991, May 24, 1977). These regulations, unlike the predecessor guidelines, are not confined to sec. 102(2)(C) (environmental impact statements). The regulations apply to the whole of section 102(2). The provisions of the Act and of these regulations must be read together as a whole in order to comply with the spirit and letter of the law. It is the Council's intention that judicial review of agency compliance with these regulations not occur before an agency has filed the final environmental impact statement, or has made a final finding of no significant impact (when such a finding will result in action affecting the environment), or takes action that will result in irreparable injury. Furthermore, it is the Council's intention that any trivial violation of these regulations not give rise to any independent cause of action.

§ 1500.4 **Reducing paperwork.**

Agencies shall reduce excessive paperwork by:

(a) Reducing the length of environmental impact statements (§ 1502.2(c)), by means such as setting appropriate page limits (§§ 1501.7(b)(1) and 1502.7).

(b) Preparing analytic rather than encyclopedic environmental impact statements (§ 1502.2(a)).

(c) Discussing only briefly issues other than significant ones (§ 1502.2(b)).

(d) Writing environmental impact statements in plain language (§ 1502.8).

(e) Following a clear format for environmental impact statements (§ 1502.10).

(f) Emphasizing the portions of the environmental impact statement that are useful to decisionmakers and the public (§§ 1502.14 and 1502.15) and reducing emphasis on background material (§ 1502.16).

(g) Using the scoping process, not only to identify significant environmental issues deserving of study, but also to deemphasize insignificant issues, narrowing the scope of the environmental impact statement process accordingly (§ 1501.7).

(h) Summarizing the environmental impact statement (§ 1502.12) and circulating the summary instead of the entire environmental impact statement if the latter is unusually long (§ 1502.19).

(i) Using program, policy, or plan environmental impact statements and tiering from statements of broad scope to those of narrower scope, to eliminate repetitive discussions of the same issues (§§ 1502.4 and 1502.20).

(j) Incorporating by reference (§ 1502.21).

(k) Integrating NEPA requirements with other environmental review and consultation requirements (§ 1502.25).

(l) Requiring comments to be as specific as possible (§ 1503.3).

(m) Attaching and circulating only changes to the draft environmental impact statement, rather than rewriting and circulating the entire statement when changes are minor (§ 1503.4(c)).

(n) Eliminating duplication with State and local procedures, by providing for joint preparation (§ 1506.2), and with other Federal procedures, by providing that an agency may adopt appropriate environmental documents prepared by another agency (§ 1506.3).

(o) Combining environmental documents with other documents (§ 1506.4).

(p) Using categorical exclusions to define categories of actions which do not individually or cumulatively have a significant effect on the human environment and which are therefore exempt from requirements to prepare an environmental impact statement (§ 1508.4).

(q) Using a finding of no significant impact when an action not otherwise excluded will not have a significant effect on the human environment and is therefore exempt from requirements to prepare an environmental impact statement (§ 1508.13).

§ 1500.5 Reducing delay.

Agencies shall reduce delay by:

(a) Integrating the NEPA process into early planning (§ 1501.2).

(b) Emphasizing interagency cooperation before the environmental impact statement is prepared, rather than submission of adversary comments on a completed document (§ 1501.6).

(c) Insuring the swift and fair resolution of lead agency disputes (§ 1501.5).

(d) Using the scoping process for an early identification of what are and what are not the real issues (§ 1501.7).

(e) Establishing appropriate time limits for the environmental impact statement process (§§ 1501.7(b)(2) and 1501.8).

(f) Preparing environmental impact statements early in the process (§ 1502.5).

(g) Integrating NEPA requirements with other environmental review and consultation requirements (§ 1502.25).

(h) Eliminating duplication with State and local procedures by providing for joint preparation (§ 1506.2) and with other Federal procedures by providing that an agency may adopt appropriate environmental documents prepared by another agency (§ 1506.3).

(i) Combining environmental documents with other documents (§ 1506.4).

(j) Using accelerated procedures for proposals for legislation (§ 1506.8).

(k) Using categorical exclusions to define categories of actions which do not individually or cumulatively have a significant effect on the human environment (§ 1508.4) and which are therefore exempt from requirements to prepare an environmental impact statement.

(l) Using a finding of no significant impact when an action not otherwise excluded will not have a significant effect on the human environment (§ 1508.13) and is therefore exempt from requirements to prepare an environmental impact statement.

§ 1500.6   Agency authority.

Each agency shall interpret the provisions of the Act as a supplement to its existing authority and as a mandate to view traditional policies and missions in the light of the Act's national environmental objectives. Agencies shall review their policies, procedures, and regulations accordingly and revise them as necessary to insure full compliance with the purposes and provisions of the Act. The phrase "to the fullest extent possible" in section 102 means that each agency of the Federal Government shall comply with that section unless existing law applicable to the agency's operations expressly prohibits or makes compliance impossible.

PART 1501--NEPA AND AGENCY PLANNING

§ 1501.1   Purpose.

The purposes of this part include:

(a) Integrating the NEPA process into early planning to insure appropriate consideration of NEPA's policies and to eliminate delay.

(b) Emphasizing cooperative consultation among agencies before the environmental impact statement is prepared rather than submission of adversary comments on a completed document.

(c) Providing for the swift and fair resolution of lead agency disputes.

(d) Identifying at an early stage the significant environmental issues deserving of study and deemphasizing insignificant issues, narrowing the scope of the environmental impact statement accordingly.

(e) Providing a mechanism for putting appropriate time limits on the environmental impact statement process.

§ 1501.2   Apply NEPA early in the process.

Agencies shall integrate the NEPA process with other planning at the earliest possible time to insure that planning and decisions reflect environmental values, to avoid delays later in the process, and to head off potential conflicts. Each agency shall:

(a) Comply with the mandate of section 102(2)(A) to "utilize a systematic, interdisciplinary approach which will insure the integrated use of the natural and social sciences and the environmental design arts in planning and in decisionmaking which may have an impact on man's environment," as specified by § 1507.2.

(b) Identify environmental effects and values in adequate detail so they can be compared to economic and technical analyses. Environmental documents and appropriate analyses shall be circulated and reviewed at the same time as other planning documents.

(c) Study, develop, and describe appropriate alternatives to recommended courses of action in any proposal which involves unresolved conflicts concerning alternative uses of available resources as provided by section 102(2)(E) of the Act.

(d) Provide for cases where actions are planned by private applicants or other non-Federal entities before Federal involvement so that:

(1) Policies or designated staff are available to advise potential applicants of studies or other information foreseeably required for later Federal action.

(2) The Federal agency consults early with appropriate State and local agencies and Indian tribes and with interested private persons and organizations when its own involvement is reasonably foreseeable.

(3) The Federal agency commences its NEPA process at the earliest possible time.

§ 1501.3   When to prepare an environmental assessment.

(a) Agencies shall prepare an environmental assessment (§ 1508.9) when necessary under the procedures adopted by individual agencies to supplement these regulations as described in § 1507.3. An assessment is not necessary if the agency has decided to prepare an environmental impact statement.

(b) Agencies may prepare an environmental assessment on any action at any time in order to assist agency planning and decisionmaking.

§ 1501.4 **Whether to prepare an environmental impact statement.**

In determining whether to prepare an environmental impact statement the Federal agency shall:

(a) Determine under its procedures supplementing these regulations (described in § 1507.3) whether the proposal is one which:

(1) Normally requires an environmental impact statement, or

(2) Normally does not require either an environmental impact statement or an environmental assessment (categorical exclusion).

(b) If the proposed action is not covered by paragraph (a) of this section, prepare an environmental assessment (§ 1508.9). The agency shall involve environmental agencies, applicants, and the public, to the extent practicable, in preparing assessments required by § 1508.9(a)(1).

(c) Based on the environmental assessment make its determination whether to prepare an environmental impact statement.

(d) Commence the scoping process (§ 1501.7), if the agency will prepare an environmental impact statement.

(e) Prepare a finding of no significant impact (§ 1508.13), if the agency determines on the basis of the environmental assessment not to prepare a statement.

(1) The agency shall make the finding of no significant impact available to the affected public as specified in § 1506.6.

(2) In certain limited circumstances, which the agency may cover in its procedures under §1507.3, the agency shall make the finding of no significant impact available for public review (including State and areawide clearinghouses) for 30 days before the agency makes its final determination whether to prepare an environmental impact statement and before the action may begin. The circumstances are:

(i) The proposed action is, or is closely similar to, one which normally requires the preparation of an environmental impact statement under the procedures adopted by the agency pursuant to § 1507.3, or

(ii) The nature of the proposed action is one without precedent.

§ 1501.5 **Lead agencies.**

(a) A lead agency shall supervise the preparation of an environmental impact statement if more than one Federal agency either:

(1) Proposes or is involved in the same action; or

(2) Is involved in a group of actions directly related to each other because of their functional interdependence or geographical proximity.

(b) Federal, State, or local agencies, including at least one
Federal agency, may act as joint lead agencies to prepare an
environmental impact statement (§ 1506.2).

(c) If an action falls within the provisions of paragraph (a)
of this section the potential lead agencies shall determine by
letter or memorandum which agency shall be the lead agency and
which shall be cooperating agencies. The agencies shall resolve
the lead agency question so as not to cause delay. If there is
disagreement among the agencies, the following factors (which are
listed in order of descending importance) shall determine lead
agency designation:

(1) Magnitude of agency's involvement.
(2) Project approval/disapproval authority.
(3) Expertise concerning the action's environmental effects.
(4) Duration of agency's involvement.
(5) Sequence of agency's involvement.

(d) Any Federal agency, or any State or local agency or private
person substantially affected by the absence of lead agency
designation, may make a written request to the potential lead
agencies that a lead agency be designated.

(e) If Federal agencies are unable to agree on which agency
will be the lead agency or if the procedures described in
paragraph (c) of this section has not resulted within 45 days in
a lead agency designation, any of the agencies or persons
concerned may file a request with the Council asking it to
determine which Federal agency shall be the lead agency.

A copy of the request shall be transmitted to each potential lead
agency. The request shall consist of:

(1) A precise description of the nature and extent of the
proposed action.
(2) A detailed statement of why each potential lead agency
should or should not be the lead agency under the criteria
specified in paragraph (c) of this section.

(f) A response may be filed by any potential lead agency
concerned within 20 days after a request is filed with the
Council. The Council shall determine as soon as possible but not
later than 20 days after receiving the request and all responses
to it which Federal agency shall be the lead agency and which
other Federal agencies shall be cooperating agencies.

§ 1501.6 Cooperating agencies.

The purpose of this section is to emphasize agency cooperation
early in the NEPA process. Upon request of the lead agency, any
other Federal agency which has jurisdiction by law shall be a
cooperating agency. In addition any other Federal agency which
has special expertise with respect to any environmental issue,
which should be addressed in the statement may be a cooperating
agency upon request of the lead agency. An agency may request
the lead agency to designate it a cooperating agency.

(a) The lead agency shall:

(1) Request the participation of each cooperating agency in the NEPA process at the earliest possible time.

(2) Use the environmental analysis and proposals of cooperating agencies with jurisdiction by law or special expertise, to the maximum extent possible consistent with its responsibility as lead agency.

(3) Meet with a cooperating agency at the latter's request.

(b) Each cooperating agency shall:

(1) Participate in the NEPA process at the earliest possible time.

(2) Participate in the scoping process (described below in § 1501.7).

(3) Assume on request of the lead agency responsibility for developing information and preparing environmental analyses including portions of the environmental impact statement concerning which the cooperating agency has special expertise.

(4) Make available staff support at the lead agency's request to enhance the latter's interdisciplinary capability.

(5) Normally use its own funds. The lead agency shall, to the extent available funds permit, fund those major activities or analyses it requests from cooperating agencies. Potential lead agencies shall include such funding requirements in their budget requests.

(c) A cooperating agency may in response to a lead agency's request for assistance in preparing the environmental impact statement (described in paragraph (b)(3), (4), or (5) of this section) reply that other program commitments preclude any involvement or the degree of involvement requested in the action that is the subject of the environmental impact statement. A copy of this reply shall be submitted to the Council.

§ 1501.7 Scoping.

There shall be an early and open process for determining the scope of issues to be addressed and for identifying the significant issues related to a proposed action. This process shall be termed scoping. As soon as practicable after its decision to prepare an environmental impact statement and before the scoping process the lead agency shall publish a notice of intent (§ 1508.22) in the Federal Register except as provided in § 1507.3(e).

(a) As part of the scoping process the lead agency shall:

(1) Invite the participation of affected Federal, State, and local agencies, any affected Indian tribe, the proponent of the action, and other interested persons (including those who might not be in accord with the action on environmental grounds), unless there is a limited exception under § 1507.3(c). An agency may give notice in accordance with § 1506.6.

(2) Determine the scope (§ 1508.25) and the significant issues to be analyzed in depth in the environmental impact statement.

(3) Identify and eliminate from detailed study the issues which are not significant or which have been covered by prior

environmental review (§ 1506.3), narrowing the discussion of
these issues in the statement to a brief presentation of why they
will not have a significant effect on the human environment or
providing a reference to their coverage elsewhere.

(4) Allocate assignments for preparation of the environmental
impact statement among the lead and cooperating agencies, with
the lead agency retaining responsibility for the statement.

(5) Indicate any public environmental assessments and other
environmental impact statements which are being or will be
prepared that are related to but are not part of the scope of the
impact statement under consideration.

(6) Identify other environmental review and consultation
requirements so the lead and cooperating agencies may prepare
other required analyses and studies concurrently with, and
integrated with, the environmental impact statement as provided
in § 1502.25.

(7) Indicate the relationship between the timing of the
preparation of environmental analyses and the agency's tentative
planning and decisionmaking schedule.

(b) As part of the scoping process the lead agency may:

(1) Set page limits on environmental documents (§ 1502.7).

(2) Set time limits (§ 1501.8).

(3) Adopt procedures under § 1507.3 to combine its
environmental assessment process with its scoping process.

(4) Hold an early scoping meeting or meetings which may be
integrated with any other early planning meeting the agency has.
Such a scoping meeting will often be appropriate when the impacts
of a particular action are confined to specific sites.

(c) An agency shall revise the determinations made under
paragraphs (a) and (b) of this section if substantial changes are
made later in the proposed action, or if significant new
circumstances or information arise which bear on the proposal or
its impacts.

§ 1501.8 Time limits.

Although the Council has decided that prescribed universal time
limits for the entire NEPA process are too inflexible, Federal
agencies are encouraged to set time limits appropriate to
individual actions (consistent with the time intervals required
by § 1506.10). When multiple agencies are involved the reference
to agency below means lead agency.

(a) The agency shall set time limits if an applicant for the
proposed action requests them: _Provided_, That the limits are
consistent with the purposes of NEPA and other essential
considerations of national policy.

(b) The agency may:

(1) Consider the following factors in determining time limits:

(i) Potential for environmental harm.

(ii) Size of the proposed action.

(iii) State of the art of analytic techniques.

(iv) Degree of public need for the proposed action, including
the consequences of delay.

(v) Number of persons and agencies affected.

(vi) Degree to which relevant information is known and if not
known the time required for obtaining it.

(vii) Degree to which the action is controversial.

(viii) Other time limits imposed on the agency by law,
regulations, or executive order.

(2) Set overall time limits or limits for each constituent part
of the NEPA process, which may include:

(i) Decision on whether to prepare an environmental impact
statement (if not already decided).

(ii) Determination of the scope of the environmental impact
statement.

(iii) Preparation of the draft environmental impact statement.

(iv) Review of any comments on the draft environmental impact
statement from the public and agencies.

(v) Preparation of the final environmental impact statement.

(vi) Review of any comments on the final environmental impact
statement.

(vii) Decision on the action based in part on the environmental
impact statement.

(3) Designate a person (such as the project manager or a person
in the agency's office with NEPA responsibilities) to expedite
the NEPA process.

(c) State or local agencies or members of the public may
request a Federal Agency to set time limits.

PART 1502--ENVIRONMENTAL IMPACT STATEMENT

§ 1502.1 Purpose.

The primary purpose of an environmental impact statement is to
serve as an action-forcing device to insure that the policies and
goals defined in the Act are infused into the ongoing programs
and actions of the Federal Government. It shall provide full and
fair discussion of significant environmental impacts and shall
inform decisionmakers and the public of the reasonable
alternatives which would avoid or minimize adverse impacts or
enhance the quality of the human environment. Agencies shall
focus on significant environmental issues and alternatives and
shall reduce paperwork and the accumulation of extraneous
background data. Statements shall be concise, clear, and to the
point, and shall be supported by evidence that the agency has
made the necessary environmental analyses. An environmental
impact statement is more than a disclosure document. It shall be
used by Federal officials in conjunction with other relevant
material to plan actions and make decisions.

§ 1502.2 Implementation.

To achieve the purposes set forth in § 1502.1 agencies shall prepare environmental impact statements in the following manner:

(a) Environmental impact statements shall be analytic rather than encyclopedic.

(b) Impacts shall be discussed in proportion to their significance. There shall be only brief discussion of other than significant issues. As in a finding of no significant impact, there should be only enough discussion to show why more study is not warranted.

(c) Environmental impact statements shall be kept concise and shall be no longer than absolutely necessary to comply with NEPA and with these regulations. Length should vary first with potential environmental problems and then with project size.

(d) Environmental impact statements shall state how alternatives considered in it and decisions based on it will or will not achieve the requirements of sections 101 and 102(1) of the Act and other environmental laws and policies.

(e) The range of alternatives discussed in environmental impact statements shall encompass those to be considered by the ultimate agency decisionmaker.

(f) Agencies shall not commit resources prejudicing selection of alternatives before making a final decision (§ 1506.1).

(g) Environmental impact statements shall serve as the means of assessing the environmental impact of proposed agency actions, rather than justifying decisions already made.

§ 1502.3   Statutory requirements for statements.

As required by sec. 102(2)(C) of NEPA environmental impact statements (§ 1508.11) are to be included in every recommendation or report.

On proposals (§ 1508.23).

For legislation and (§ 1508.17).

Other major Federal actions (§ 1508.18).

Significantly (§ 1508.27).

Affecting (§§ 1508.3, 1508.8).

The quality of the human environment (§ 1508.14).

§ 1502.4   Major Federal actions requiring the preparation of environmental impact statements.

(a) Agencies shall make sure the proposal which is the subject of an environmental impact statement is properly defined. Agencies shall use the criteria for scope (§ 1508.25) to determine which proposal(s) shall be the subject of a particular statement. Proposals or parts of proposals which are related to each other closely enough to be, in effect, a single course of action shall be evaluated in a single impact statement.

(b) Environmental impact statements may be prepared, and are sometimes required, for broad Federal actions such as the adoption of new agency programs or regulations (§ 1508.18). Agencies shall prepare statements on broad actions so that they are relevant to policy and are timed to coincide with meaningful points in agency planning and decisionmaking.

(c) When preparing statements on broad actions (including proposals by more than one agency), agencies may find it useful to evaluate the proposal(s) in one of the following ways.

(1) Geographically, including actions occurring in the same general location, such as body of water, region, or metropolitan area.

(2) Generically, including actions which have relevant similarities, such as common timing, impacts, alternatives, methods of implementation, media, or subject matter.

(3) By stage of technological development including federal or federally assisted research, development or demonstration programs for new technologies which, if applied, could significantly affect the quality of the human environment. Statements shall be prepared on such programs and shall be available before the program has reached a stage of investment or commitment to implementation likely to determine subsequent development or restrict later alternatives.

(d) Agencies shall as appropriate employ scoping (§ 1501.7), tiering (§ 1502.20), and other methods listed in §§ 1500.4 and 1500.5 to relate broad and narrow actions and to avoid duplication and delay.

§ 1502.5 Timing.

An agency shall commence preparation of an environmental impact statement as close as possible to the time the agency is developing or is presented with a proposal (§ 1508.23) so that preparation can be completed in time for the final statement to be included in any recommendation or report on the proposal. The statement shall be prepared early enough so that it can serve practically as an important contribution to the decisionmaking process and will not be used to rationalize or justify decisions already made (§§ 1500.2(c), 1501.2, and 1502.2). For instance:

(a) For projects directly undertaken by Federal agencies the environmental impact statement shall be prepared at the feasibility analysis (go-no go) stage and may be supplemented at a later stage if necessary.

(b) For applications to the agency appropriate environmental assessments or statements shall be commenced no later than immediately after the application is received. Federal agencies are encouraged to begin preparation of such assessments or statements earlier, preferably jointly with applicable State or local agencies.

(c) For adjudication, the final environmental impact statement shall normally precede the final staff recommendation and that portion of the public hearing related to the impact study. In appropriate circumstances the statement may follow preliminary hearings designed to gather information for use in the statements.

(d) For informal rulemaking the draft environmnental impact statement shall normally accompany the proposed rule.

§ 1502.6   **Interdisciplinary preparation.**

Environmental impact statements shall be prepared using an inter-disciplinary approach which will insure the integrated use of the natural and social sciences and the environmental design arts (section 102(2)(A) of the Act). The disciplines of the preparers shall be appropriate in the scope and issues identified in the scoping process (§ 1501.7).

§ 1502.7   **Page limits.**

The text of final environmental impact statements (e.g., paragraphs (d) through (g) of § 1502.10) shall normally be less than 150 pages and for proposals of unusual scope or complexity shall normally be less than 300 pages.

§ 1502.8   **Writing.**

Environmental impact statements shall be written in plain language and may use appropriate graphics so that decisionmakers and the public can readily understand them. Agencies should employ writers of clear prose or editors to write, review, or edit statements, which will be based upon the analysis and supporting data from the natural and social sciences and the environmental design arts.

§ 1502.9   **Draft, final, and supplemental statements.**

Except for proposals for legislation as provided in § 1506.8 environmental impact statements shall be prepared in two stages and may be supplemented.
   (a) Draft environmental impact statements shall be prepared in accordance with the scope decided upon in the scoping process. The lead agency shall work with the cooperating agencies and shall obtain comments as required in Part 1503 of this chapter. The draft statement must fulfill and satisfy to the fullest extent possible the requirements established for final statements in section 102(2)(C) of the Act. If a draft statement is so inadequate as to preclude meaningful analysis, the agency shall prepare and circulate a revised draft of the appropriate portion. The agency shall make every effort to disclose and discuss at appropriate points in the draft statement all major points of view on the environmental impacts of the alternatives including the proposed action.
   (b) Final environmental impact statements shall respond to comments as required in Part 1503 of this chapter. The agency shall discuss at appropriate points in the final statement any responsible opposing view which was not adequately discussed in

the draft statement and shall indicate the agency's response to
the issues raised.
   (c) Agencies:
   (1) Shall prepare supplements to either draft or final
environmental impact statements if:
   (i) The agency makes substantial changes in the proposed action
that are relevant to environmental concerns; or
   (ii) There are significant new circumstances or information
relevant to environmental concerns and bearing on the proposed
action or its impacts.
   (2) May also prepare supplements when the agency determines
that the purposes of the Act will be furthered by doing so.
   (3) Shall adopt procedures for introducing a supplement into
its formal administrative record, if such a record exists.
   (4) Shall prepare, circulate, and file a supplement to a
statement in the same fashion (exclusive of scoping) as a draft
and final statement unless alternative procedures are approved by
the Council.

§ 1502.10   Recommended format.

   Agencies shall use a format for environmental impact statements
which will encourage good analysis and clear presentation of the
alternatives including the proposed action. The following
standard format for environmental impact statements should be
followed unless the agency determines that there is a compelling
reason to do otherwise:
   (a) Cover sheet.
   (b) Summary.
   (c) Table of contents.
   (d) Purpose and need for action.
   (e) Alternatives including proposed action (sections
102(2)(C)(iii) and 102(2)(E) of the Act).
   (f) Affected environment.
   (g) Environmental consequences (especially sections
102(2)(C)(i), (ii), (iv), and (v) of the Act).
   (h) List of preparers.
   (i) List of Agencies, Organizations, and persons to whom copies
of the statement are sent.
   (j) Index.
   (k) Appendices (if any).

If a different format is used, it shall include paragraphs (a),
(b), (c), (h), (i), and (j), of this section and shall include
the substance of paragraphs (d), (e), (f), (g), and (k) of this
section, as further described in §§ 1502.11 through 1502.18, in
any appropriate format.

§ 1502.11   Cover sheet.

   The cover sheet shall not exceed one page. It shall include:

(a) A list of the responsible agencies including the lead agency and any cooperating agencies.

(b) The title of the proposed action that is the subject of the statement (and if appropriate the titles of related cooperating agency actions), together with the State(s) and county(ies) (or other jurisdiction if applicable) where the action is located.

(c) The name, address, and telephone number of the person at the agency who can supply further information.

(d) A designation of the statement as a draft, final, or draft or final supplement.

(e) A one paragraph abstract of the statement.

(f) The date by which comments must be received (computed in cooperation with EPA under § 1506.10).

The information required by this section may be entered on Standard Form 424 (in items 4, 6, 7, 10, and 18).

§ 1502.12 Summary.

Each environmental impact statement shall contain a summary which adequately and accurately summarizes the statement. The summary shall stress the major conclusions, areas of controversy (including issues raised by agencies and the public), and the issues to be resolved (including the choice among alternatives). The summary will normally not exceed 15 pages.

§ 1502.13 Purpose and need.

The statement shall briefly specify the underlying purpose and need to which the agency is responding in proposing the alternatives including the proposed action.

§ 1502.14 Alternatives including the proposed action.

This section is the heart of the environmental impact statement. Based on the information and analysis presented in the sections on the Affected Environment (§ 1502.15) and the Environmental Consequences (§ 1502.16), it should present the environmental impacts of the proposal and the alternatives in comparative form, thus sharply defining the issues and providing a clear basis for choice among options by the decisionmaker and the public. In this section agencies shall:

(a) Rigorously explore and objectively evaluate all reasonable alternatives, and for alternatives which were eliminated from detailed study, briefly discuss the reasons for their having been eliminated.

(b) Devote substantial treatment to each alternative considered in detail including the proposed action so that reviewers may evaluate their comparative merits.

(c) Include reasonable alternatives not within the jurisdiction of the lead agency.

(d) Include the alternative of no action.

(e) Identify the agency's preferred alternative or alternatives, if one or more exists, in the draft statement and identify such alternative in the final statement unless another law prohibits the expression of such a preference.

(f) Include appropriate mitigation measures not already included in the proposed action or alternatives.

§ 1502.15 Affected environment.

The environmental impact statement shall succinctly describe the environment of the area(s) to be affected or created by the alternatives under consideration. The descriptions shall be no longer than is necessary to understand the effects of the alternatives. Data and analyses in a statement shall be commensurate with the importance of the impact, with less important material summarized, consolidated, or simply referenced. Agencies shall avoid useless bulk in statements and shall concentrate effort and attention on important issues. Verbose descriptions of the affected environment are themselves no measure of the adequacy of an environmental impact statement.

§ 1502.16 Environmental consequences.

This section forms the scientific and analytic basis for the comparisons under § 1502.14. It shall consolidate the discussions of those elements required by sections 102(2)(C)(i), (ii), (iv), and (v) of NEPA which are within the scope of the statement and as much of section 102(2)(C)(iii) as is necessary to support the comparisons. The discussion will include the environmental impacts of the alternatives including the proposed action, any adverse environmental effects which cannot be avoided should the proposal be implemented, the relationship between short-term uses of man's environment and the maintenance and enhancement of long-term productivity, and any irreversible or irretrievable commitments of resources which would be involved in the proposal should it be implemented. This section should not duplicate discussions in § 1502.14. It shall include discussions of:

(a) Direct effects and their significance (§ 1508.8).

(b) Indirect effects and their significance (§ 1508.8).

(c) Possible conflicts between the proposed action and the objectives of Federal, regional, State, and local (and in the case of a reservation, Indian tribe) land use plans, policies and controls for the area concerned. (See § 1506.2(d)).

(d) The environmental effects of alternatives including the proposed action. The comparisons under § 1502.14 will be based on this discussion.

(e) Energy requirements and conservation potential of various alternatives and mitigation measures.

(f) Natural or depletable resource requirements and conservation potential of various alternatives and mitigation measures.

(g) Urban quality, historic and cultural resources, and the design of the built environment, including the reuse and conservation potential of various alternatives and mitigation measures.

(h) Means to mitigate adverse environmental impacts (if not fully covered under § 1502.14(f)).

§ 1502.17 List of preparers.

The environmental impact statement shall list the names, together with their qualifications (expertise, experience, professional disciplines), of the persons who were primarily responsible for preparing the environmental impact statement or significant background papers, including basic components of the statement (§§ 1502.6 and 1502.8). Where possible the persons who are responsible for a particular analysis, including analyses in background papers, shall be identified. Normally the list will not exceed two pages.

§ 1502.18 Appendix.

If an agency prepares an appendix to an environmental impact statement the appendix shall:

(a) Consist of material prepared in connection with an environmental impact statement (as distinct from material which is not so prepared and which is incorporated by reference (§ 1502.21)).

(b) Normally consist of material which substantiates any analysis fundamental to the impact statement.

(c) Normally be analytic and relevant to the decision to be made.

(d) Be circulated with the environmental impact statement or be readily available on request.

§ 1502.19 Circulation of the environmental impact statement.

Agencies shall circulate the entire draft and final environmental impact statements except for certain appendices as provided in § 1502.18(d) and unchanged statements as provided in § 1503.4(c). However, if the statement is unusually long, the agency may circulate the summary instead, except that the entire statement shall be furnished to:

(a) Any Federal agency which has jurisdiction by law or special expertise with respect to any environmental impact involved and any appropriate Federal, State or local agency authorized to develop and enforce environmental standards.

(b) The applicant, if any.

(c) Any person, organization, or agency requesting the entire environmental impact statement.

(d) In the case of a final environmental impact statement any person, organization, or agency which submitted substantive comments on the draft.

If the agency circulates the summary and thereafter receives a timely request for the entire statement and for additional time to comment, the time for that requestor only shall be extended by at least 15 days beyond the minimum period.

§ 1502.20 Tiering.

Agencies are encouraged to tier their environmental impact statements to eliminate repetitive discussions of the same issues and to focus on the actual issues ripe for decision at each level of environmental review (§ 1508.28). Whenever a broad environmental impact statement has been prepared (such as a program or policy statement) and a subsequent statement or environmental assessment is then prepared on an action included within the entire program or policy (such as a site specific action) the subsequent statement or environmental assessment need only summarize the issues discussed in the broader statement and incorporate discussions from the broader statement by reference and shall concentrate on the issues specific to the subsequent action. The subsequent document shall state where the earlier document is available. Tiering may also be appropriate for different stages of actions. (Section 1508.28).

§ 1502.21 Incorporation by reference.

Agencies shall incorporate material into an environmental impact statement by reference when the effect will be to cut down on bulk without impeding agency and public review of the action. The incorporated material shall be cited in the statement and its content briefly described. No material may be incorporated by reference unless it is reasonably available for inspection by potentially interested persons within the time allowed for comment. Material based on proprietary data which is itself not available for review and comment shall not be incorporated by reference.

§ 1502.22 Incomplete or unavailable information.

When an agency is evaluating reasonably foreseeable significant adverse effects on the human environment in an environmental impact statement and there is incomplete or unavailable information, the agency shall always make clear that such information is lacking.

(a) If the incomplete information relevant to reasonably foreseeable significant adverse impacts is essential to a reasoned choice among alternatives and the overall costs of obtaining it are not exorbitant, the agency shall include the information in the environmental impact statement.

(b) If the information relevant to reasonably foreseeable significant adverse impacts cannot be obtained because the overall costs of obtaining it are exorbitant or the means to

obtain it are not known, the agency shall include within the
environmental impact statement:
(1) A statement that such information is incomplete or
unavailable; (2) a statement of the relevance of the incomplete
or unavailable information to evaluating reasonably foreseeable
significant adverse impacts on the human environment; (3) a
summary of existing credible scientific evidence which is
relevant to evaluating the reasonably foreseeable significant
adverse impacts on the human environment, and (4) the agency's
evaluation of such impacts based upon theoretical approaches or
research methods generally accepted in the scientific community.
For the purposes of this section, "reasonably foreseeable"
includes impacts which have catastrophic consequences, even if
their probability of occurrence is low, provided that the
analysis of the impacts is supported by credible scientific
evidence, is not based on pure conjecture, and is within the rule
of reason.
(c) The amended regulation will be applicable to all
environmental impact statements for which a Notice of Intent (40
CFR 1508.22) is published in the _Federal Register_ on or after May
27, 1986.   For environmental impact statements in progress,
agencies may choose to comply with the requirements of either the
original or amended regulation.

§ 1502.23   Cost-benefit analysis.

If a cost-benefit analysis relevant to the choice among
environmentally different alternatives is being considered for
the proposed action, it shall be incorporated by reference or
appended to the statement as an aid in evaluating the
environmental consequences.   To assess the adequacy of compliance
with section 102(2)(B) of the Act the statement shall, when a
cost-benefit analysis is prepared, discuss the relationship
between that analysis and any analyses of unquantified
environmental impacts, values, and amenities.   For purposes of
complying with the Act, the weighing of the merits and drawbacks
of the various alternatives need not be displayed in a monetary
cost-benefit analysis and should not be when there are important
qualitative considerations.   In any event, an environmental
impact statement should at least indicate those considerations,
including factors not related to environmental quality, which are
likely to be relevant and important to a decision.

§ 1502.24   Methodology and scientific accuracy.

Agencies shall insure the professional integrity, including
scientific integrity, of the discussions and analyses in
environmental impact statements.   They shall identify any
methodologies used and shall make explicit reference by footnote
to the scientific and other sources relied upon for conclusions
in the statement.   An agency may place discussion of methodology
in an appendix.

§ 1502.25 Environmental review and consultation requirements.

(a) To the fullest exent possible, agencies shall prepare draft environmental impact statements concurrently with and integrated with environmental impact analyses and related surveys and studies required by the Fish and Wildlife Coordination Act (16 U.S.C. 661 et seq.), the National Historic Preservation Act of 1966 (16 U.S.C. 470 et seq), the Endangered Species Act of 1973 (16 U.S.C. 1531 et seq.), and other environmental review laws and executive orders.

(b) The draft environmental impact statement shall list all Federal permits, licenses, and other entitlements which must be obtained in implementing the proposal. If it is uncertain whether a Federal permit, license, or other entitlement is necessary, the draft environmental impact statement shall so indicate.

PART 1503--COMMENTING

§ 1503.1 Inviting comments.

(a) After preparing a draft environmental impact statement and before preparing a final environmental impact statement the agency shall:

(1) Obtain the comments of any Federal agency which has jurisdiction by law or special expertise with respect to any environmental impact involved or which is authorized to develop and enforce environmental standards.

(2) Request the comments of:

(i) Appropriate State and local agencies which are authorized to develop and enforce environmental standards;

(ii) Indian tribes, when the effects may be on a reservation; and

(iii) Any agency which has requested that it receive statements on actions of the kind proposed.

Office of Management and Budget Circular A-95 (Revised), through its system of clearinghouses, provides a means of securing the views of State and local environmental agencies. The clearinghouses may be used, by mutual agreement of the lead agency and the clearinghouse, for securing State and local reviews of the draft environmental impact statements.

(3) Request comments from the applicant, if any.

(4) Request comments from the public, affirmatively soliciting comments from those persons or organizations who may be interested or affected.

(b) An agency may request comments on a final environmental impact statement before the decision is finally made. In any case other agencies or persons may make comments before the final decision unless a different time is provided under § 1506.10.

§ 1503.2 Duty to comment.

Federal agencies with jurisdiction by law or special expertise with respect to any environmental impact involved and agencies which are authorized to develop and enforce environmental standards shall comment on statements within their jurisdiction, expertise, or authority. Agencies shall comment within the time period specified for comment in § 1506.10. A Federal agency may reply that it has no comment. If a cooperating agency is satisfied that its views are adequately reflected in the environmental impact statement, it should reply that it has no comment.

§ 1503.3 Specificity of comments.

(a) Comments on an environmental impact statement or on a proposed action shall be as specific as possible and may address either the adequacy of the statement or the merits of the alternatives discussed or both.
(b) When a commenting agency criticizes a lead agency's predictive methodology, the commenting agency should describe the alternative methodology which it prefers and why.
(c) A cooperating agency shall specify in its comments whether it needs additional information to fulfill other applicable environmental reviews or consultation requirements and what information it needs. In particular, it shall specify any additional information it needs to comment adequately on the draft statement's analysis of significant site-specific effects associated with the granting or approving by that cooperating agency of necessary Federal permits, licenses, or entitlements.
(d) When a cooperating agency with jurisdiction by law objects to or expresses reservations about the proposal on grounds of environmental impacts, the agency expressing the objection or reservation shall specify the mitigation measures it considers necessary to allow the agency to grant or approve applicable permit, license, or related requirements or concurrences.

§ 1503.4 Response to comments.

(a) An agency preparing a final environmental impact statement shall assess and consider comments both individually and collectively, and shall respond by one or more of the means listed below, stating its response in the final statement. Possible responses are to:
(1) Modify alternatives including the proposed action.
(2) Develop and evaluate alternatives not previously given serious consideration by the agency.
(3) Supplement, improve, or modify its analyses.
(4) Make factual corrections.
(5) Explain why the comments do not warrant further agency response, citing the sources, authorities, or reasons which

support the agency's position and, if appropriate, indicate those
circumstances which would trigger agency reappraisal or further
response.

(b) All substantive comments received on the draft statement
(or summaries thereof where the response has been exceptionally
voluminous), should be attached to the final statement whether or
not the comment is thought to merit individual discussion by the
agency in the text of the statement.

(c) If changes in response to comments are minor and are
confined to the responses described in paragraphs (a)(4) and (5)
of this section, agencies may write them on errata sheets and
attach them to the statement instead of rewriting the draft
statement. In such cases only the comments, the responses, and
the changes and not the final statement need be circulated (§
1502.19). The entire document with a new cover sheet shall be
filed as the final statement (§ 1506.9).

**PART 1504--PREDECISION REFERRALS TO THE COUNCIL OF PROPOSED
FEDERAL ACTIONS DETERMINED TO BE ENVIRONMENTALLY UNSATISFACTORY**

§ 1504.1 Purpose.

(a) This part establishes procedures for referring to the
Council Federal interagency disagreements concerning proposed
major Federal actions that might cause unsatisfactory
environmental effects. It provides means for early resolution of
such disagreements.

(b) Under section 309 of the Clean Air Act (42 U.S.C. 7609),
the Administrator of the Environmental Protection Agency is
directed to review and comment publicly on the environmental
impacts of Federal activities, including actions for which
environmental impact statements are prepared. If after this
review the Administrator determines that the matter is
"unsatisfactory from the standpoint of public health or welfare
or environmental quality," section 309 directs that the matter be
referred to the Council (hereinafter "environmental referrals").

(c) Under section 102(2)(C) of the Act other Federal agencies
may make similar reviews of environmental impact statements,
including judgments on the acceptability of anticipated
environmental impacts. These reviews must be made available to
the President, the Council and the public.

§ 1504.2 Criteria for referral.

Environmental referrals should be made to the Council only
after concerted, timely (as early as possible in the process),
but unsuccessful attempts to resolve differences with the lead
agency. In determining what environmental objections to the
matter are appropriate to refer to the Council, an agency should
weigh potential adverse environmental impacts, considering:

(a) Possible violations of national environmental standards or
policies.
(b) Severity.
(c) Geographical scope.
(d) Duration.
(e) Importance as precedents.
(f) Availability of environmentally preferable alternatives.

§ 1504.3 Procedure for referrals and response.

(a) A Federal agency making the referral to the Council shall:
(1) Advise the lead agency at the earliest possible time that
it intends to refer a matter to the Council unless a satisfactory
agreement is reached.
(2) Include such advice in the referring agency's comments on
the draft environmental impact statement, except when the
statement does not contain adequate information to permit an
assessment of the matter's environmental acceptability.
(3) Identify any essential information that is lacking and
request that it be made available at the earliest possible time.
(4) Send copies of such advice to the Council.
(b) The referring agency shall deliver its referral to the
Council not later than twenty-five (25) days after the final
environmental impact statement has been made available to the
Environmental Protection Agency, commenting agencies, and the
public. Except when an extension of this period has been granted
by the lead agency, the Council will not accept a referral after
that date.
(c) The referral shall consist of:
(1) A copy of the letter signed by the head of the referring
agency and delivered to the lead agency informing the lead agency
of the referral and the reasons for it, and requesting that no
action be taken to implement the matter until the Council acts
upon the referral. The letter shall include a copy of the
statement referred to in (c)(2) of this section.
(2) A statement supported by factual evidence leading to the
conclusion that the matter is unsatisfactory from the standpoint
of public health or welfare or environmental quality. The
statement shall:
(i) Identify any material facts in controversy and incorporate
(by reference if appropriate) agreed upon facts,
(ii) Identify any existing environmental requirements or
policies which would be violated by the matter,
(iii) Present the reasons why the referring agency believes the
matter is environmentally unsatisfactory,
(iv) Contain a finding by the agency whether the issue raised
is of national importance because of the threat to national
environmental resources or policies or for some other reason,
(v) Review the steps taken by the referring agency to bring its
concerns to the attention of the lead agency at the earliest
possible time, and

(vi) Give the referring agency's recommendations as to what mitigation alternative, further study, or other course of action (including abandonment of the matter) are necessary to remedy the situation.

(d) Not later than twenty-five (25) days after the referral to the Council the lead agency may deliver a response to the Council, and the referring agency. If the lead agency requests more time and gives assurance that the matter will not go forward in the interim, the Council may grant an extension. The response shall:

(1) Address fully the issues raised in the referral.

(2) Be supported by evidence.

(3) Give the lead agency's response to the referring agency's recommendations.

(e) Interested persons (including the applicant) may deliver their views in writing to the Council. Views in support of the referral should be delivered not later than the referral. Views in support of the response shall be delivered not later than the response.

(f) Not later than twenty-five (25) days after receipt of both the referral and any response or upon being informed that there will be no response (unless the lead agency agrees to a longer time), the Council may take one or more of the following actions:

(1) Conclude that the process of referral and response has successfully resolved the problem.

(2) Initiate discussions with the agencies with the objective of mediation with referring and lead agencies.

(3) Hold public meetings or hearings to obtain additional views and information.

(4) Determine that the issue is not one of national importance and request the referring and lead agencies to pursue their decision process.

(5) Determine that the issue should be further negotiated by the referring and lead agencies and is not appropriate for Council consideration until one or more heads of agencies report to the Council that the agencies' disagreements are irreconcilable.

(6) Publish its findings and recommendations (including where appropriate a finding that the submitted evidence does not support the position of an agency).

(7) When appropriate, submit the referral and the response together with the Council's recommendation to the President for action.

(g) The Council shall take no longer than 60 days to complete the actions specified in paragraph (f)(2), (3), or (5) of this section.

(h) When the referral involves an action required by statute to be determined on the record after opportunity for agency hearing, the referral shall be conducted in a manner consistent with 5 U.S.C. 557(d) (Administrative Procedure Act).

PART 1505--NEPA AND AGENCY DECISIONMAKING

§ 1505.1 Agency decisionmaking procedures.

Agencies shall adopt procedures (§ 1507.3) to ensure that decisions are made in accordance with the policies and purposes of the Act. Such procedures shall include but not be limited to:

(a) Implementing procedures under section 102(2) to achieve the requirements of sections 101 and 102(1).

(b) Designating the major decision points for the agency's principal programs likely to have a significant effect on the human environment and assuring that the NEPA process corresponds with them.

(c) Requiring that relevant environmental documents, comments, and responses be part of the record in formal rulemaking or adjudicatory proceedings.

(d) Requiring that relevant environmental documents, comments, and responses accompany the proposal through existing agency review processes so that agency officials use the statement in making decisions.

(e) Requiring that the alternatives considered by the decisionmaker are encompassed by the range of alternatives discussed in the relevant environmental documents and that the decisionmaker consider the alternatives described in the environmental impact statement. If another decision document accompanies the relevant environmental documents to the decisionmaker, agencies are encouraged to make available to the public before the decision is made any part of that document that relates to the comparison of alternatives.

§ 1505.2 Record of decision in cases requiring environmental impact statements.

At the time of its decision (§ 1506.10) or, if appropriate, its recommendation to Congress, each agency shall prepare a concise public record of decision. The record, which may be integrated into any other record prepared by the agency, including that required by OMB Circular A-95 (Revised), part I, sections 6(c) and (d), and Part II, section 5(b)(4), shall:

(a) State what the decision was.

(b) Identify all alternatives considered by the agency in reaching its decision, specifying the alternative or alternatives which were considered to be environmentally preferable. An agency may discuss preferences among alternatives based on relevant factors including economic and technical considerations and agency statutory missions. An agency shall identify and discuss all such factors including any essential considerations of national policy which were balanced by the agency in making its decision and state how those considerations entered into its decision.

(c) State whether all practicable means to avoid or minimize environmental harm from the alternative selected have been

adopted, and if not, why they were not. A monitoring and
enforcement program shall be adopted and summarized where
applicable for any mitigation.

§ 1505.3   Implementing the decision.

Agencies may provide for monitoring to assure that their
decisions are carried out and should do so in important cases.
Mitigation (§ 1505.2(c)) ad other conditions established in the
environmental impact statement or during its review and committed
as part of the decision shall be implemented by the lead agency
or other appropriate consenting agency. The lead agency shall:
   (a) Include appropriate conditions in grants, permits or other
approvals.
   (b) Condition funding of actions on mitigation.
   (c) Upon request, inform cooperating or commenting agencies on
progress in carrying out mitigation measures which they have
proposed and which were adopted by the agency making the
decision.
   (d) Upon request, make available to the public the result of
relevant monitoring.

PART 1506--OTHER REQUIREMENTS OF NEPA

§ 1506.1   Limitations on actions during NEPA process.

   (a) Until an agency issues a record of decision as provided in
§ 1505.2 (except as provided in paragraph (c) of this section),
no action concerning the proposal shall be taken which would:
   (1) Have an adverse environmental impact; or
   (2) Limit the choice of reasonable alternatives.
   (b) If any agency is considering an application from a non-
Federal entity, and is aware that the applicant is about to take
an action within the agency's jurisdiction that would meet either
of the criteria in paragraph (a) of this section, then the agency
shall promptly notify the applicant that the agency will take
appropriate action to insure that the objectives and procedures
of NEPA are achieved.
   (c) While work on a required program environmental impact
statement is in progress and the action is not covered by an
existing program statement, agencies shall not undertake in the
interim any major Federal action covered by the program which may
significantly affect the quality of the human environment unless
such action:
   (1) Is justified independently of the program;
   (2) Is itself accompanied by an adequate environmental impact
statement; and
   (3) Will not prejudice the ultimate decision on the program.
Interim action prejudices the ultimate decision on the program
when it tends to determine subsequent development or limit
alternatives.

(d) This section does not preclude development by applicants of plans or designs or performance of other work necessary to support an application for Federal, State or local permits or assistance. Nothing in this section shall preclude Rural Electrification Administration approval of minimal expenditures not affecting the environment (e.g. long leadtime equipment and purchase options) made by nongovernmental entities seeking loan guarantees from the Administration.

§ 1506.2 Elimination of duplication with State and local procedures.

(a) Agencies authorized by law to cooperate with State agencies of statewide jurisdiction pursuant to section 102(2)(D) of the Act may do so.
(b) Agencies shall cooperate with State and local agencies to the fullest extent possible to reduce duplication between NEPA and State and local requirements, unless the agencies are specifically barred from doing so by some other law. Except for cases covered by paragraph (a) of this section, such cooperation shall to the fullest extent possible include:
(1) Joint planning processes.
(2) Joint environmental research and studies.
(3) Joint public hearings (except where otherwise provided by statute).
(4) Joint environmental assessments.
(c) Agencies shall cooperate with State and local agencies to the fullest extent possible to reduce duplication between NEPA and comparable State and local requirements, unless the agencies are specifically barred from doing so by some other law. Except for cases covered by paragraph (a) of this section, such cooperation shall to the fullest extent possible include joint environmental impact statements. In such cases one or more Federal agencies and one or more State or local agencies shall be joint lead agencies. Where State laws or local ordinances have environmental impact statement requirements in addition to but not in conflict with those in NEPA, Federal agencies shall cooperate in fulfilling these requirements as well as those of Federal laws so that one document will comply with all applicable laws.
(d) To better integrate environmental impact statements into State or local planning processes, statements shall discuss any inconsistency of a proposed action with any approved State or local plan and laws (whether or not federally sanctioned). Where an inconsistency exists, the statement should describe the extent to which the agency would reconcile its proposed action with the plan or law.

§ 1506.3 Adoption.

(a) An agency may adopt a Federal draft or final environmental impact statement or portion thereof provided that the statement

or portion thereof meets the standards for an adequate statement
under these regulations.

(b) If the actions covered by the original environmental impact
statement and the proposed action are substantially the same, the
agency adopting another agency's statement is not required to
recirculate it except as a final statement. Otherwise the
adopting agency shall treat the statement as a draft and
recirculate it (except as provided in paragraph (c) of this
section).

(c) A cooperating agency may adopt without recirculating the
environmental impact statement of a lead agency when, after an
independent review of the statement, the cooperating agency
concludes that its comments and suggestions have been satisfied.

(d) When an agency adopts a statement which is not final within
the agency that prepared it, or when the action it assesses is
the subject of a referral under Part 1504, or when the
statement's adequacy is the subject of a judicial action which is
not final, the agency shall so specify.

§ 1506.4   Combining documents.

Any environmental document in compliance with NEPA may be
combined with any other agency document to reduce duplication and
paperwork.

§ 1506.5   Agency responsibility.

(a) _Information_. If an agency requires an applicant to submit
environmental information for possible use by the agency in
preparing an environmental impact statement, then the agency
should assist the applicant by outlining the types of information
required. The agency shall independently evaluate the
information submitted and shall be responsible for its accuracy.
If the agency chooses to use the information submitted by the
applicant in the environmental impact statement, either directly
or by reference, then the names of the persons responsible for
the independent evaluation shall be included in the list of
preparers (§ 1502.17). It is the intent of this paragraph that
acceptable work not be redone, but that it be verified by the
agency.

(b) _Environmental assessments_. If an agency permits an
applicant to prepare an environmental assessment, the agency,
besides fulfilling the requirements of paragraph (a) of this
section, shall make its own evaluation of the environmental
issues and take responsibility for the scope and content of the
environmental assessment.

(c) _Environmental impact statements_. Except as provided in §§
1506.2 and 1506.3 any environmental impact statement prepared
pursuant to the requirements of NEPA shall be prepared directly
by or by a contractor selected by the lead agency or where
appropriate under § 1501.6(b), a cooperating agency. It is the
intent of these regulations that the contractor be chosen solely

by the lead agency, or by the lead agency in cooperation with cooperating agencies, or where appropriate by a cooperating agency to avoid any conflict of interest. Contractors shall execute a disclosure statement prepared by the lead agency, or where appropriate the cooperating agency, specifying that they have no financial or other interest in the outcome of the project. If the document is prepared by contract, the responsible Federal official shall furnish guidance and participate in the preparation and shall independently evaluate the statement prior to its approval and take responsibility for its scope and contents. Nothing in this section is intended to prohibit any agency from requesting any person to submit information to it or to prohibit any person from submitting information to any agency.

§ 1506.6 Public involvement.

Agencies shall:
(a) Make diligent efforts to involve the public in preparing and implementing their NEPA procedures.
(b) Provide public notice of NEPA-related hearings, public meetings, and the availability of environmental documents so as to inform those persons and agencies who may be interested or affected.
(1) In all cases the agency shall mail notice to those who have requested it on an individual action.
(2) In the case of an action with effects of national concern notice shall include publication in the Federal Register and notice by mail to national organizations reasonably expected to be interested in the matter and may include listing in the 102 Monitor. An agency engaged in rulemaking may provide notice by mail to national organizations who have requested that notice regularly be provided. Agencies shall maintain a list of such organizations.
(3) In the case of an action with effects primarily of local concern the notice may include:
(i) Notice to State and areawide clearinghouses pursuant to OMB Circular A-95 (Revised).
(ii) Notice to Indian tribes when effects may occur on reservations.
(iii) Following the affected State's public notice procedures for comparable actions.
(iv) Publication in local newspapers (in papers of general circulation rather than legal papers).
(v) Notice through other local media.
(vi) Notice to potentially interested community organizations including small business associations.
(vii) Publication in newsletters that may be expected to reach potentially interested persons.
(viii) Direct mailing to owners and occupants of nearby or affected property.

(ix) Posting of notice on and off site in the area where the
action is to be located.

(c) Hold or sponsor public hearings or public meetings whenever
appropriate or in accordance with statutory requirements
applicable to the agency.   Criteria shall include whether there
is:

(1) Substantial environmental controversy concerning the
proposed action or substantial interest in holding the hearing.

(2) A request for a hearing by another agency with jurisdiction
over the action supported by reasons why a hearing will be
helpful.   If a draft environmental impact statement is to be
considered at a public hearing, the agency should make the
statement available to the public at least 15 days in advance
(unless the purpose of the hearing is to provide information for
the draft environmental impact statement).

(d) Solicit appropriate information from the public.

(e) Explain in its procedures where interested persons can get
information or status reports on environmental impact statements
and other elements of the NEPA process.

(f) Make environmental impact statements, the comments
received, and any underlying documents available to the public
pursuant to the provisions of the Freedom of Information Act (5
U.S.C. 552), without regard to the exclusion for interagency
memoranda where such memoranda transmit comments of Federal
agencies on the environmental impact of the proposed action.
Materials to be made available to the public shall be provided to
the public without charge to the extent practicable, or at a fee
which is not more than the actual costs of reproducing copies
required to be sent to other Federal agencies, including the
Council.

§ 1506.7   Further guidance.

The Council may provide further guidance concerning NEPA and
its procedures including:

(a) A handbook which the Council may supplement from time to
time, which shall in plain language provide guidance and
instructions concerning the application of NEPA and these
regulations.

(b) Publication of the Council's Memoranda to Heads of
Agencies.

(c) In conjunction with the Environmental Protection Agency and
the publication of the 102 Monitor, notice of:

(1) Research activities;

(2) Meetings and conferences related to NEPA; and

(3) Successful and innovative procedures used by agencies to
implement NEPA.

§ 1506.8   Proposals for legislation.

(a) The NEPA process for proposals for legislation (§ 1508.17)
significantly affecting the quality of the human environment

shall be integrated with the legislative process of the Congress. A legislative environmental impact statement is the detailed statement required by law to be included in a recommendation or report on a legislative proposal to Congress. A legislative environmental impact statement shall be considered part of the formal transmittal of a legislative proposal to Congress; however, it may be transmitted to Congress up to 30 days later in order to allow time for completion of an accurate statement which can serve as the basis for public and Congressional debate. The statement must be available in time for Congressional hearings and deliberations.

(b) Preparation of a legislative environmental impact statement shall conform to the requirements of these regulations except as follows:

(1) There need not be a scoping process.

(2) The legislative statement shall be prepared in the same manner as a draft statement, but shall be considered the "detailed statement" required by statute; Provided, That when any of the following conditions exist both the draft and final environmental impact statement on the legislative proposal shall be prepared and circulated as provided by §§ 1503.1 and 1506.10.

(i) A Congressional Committee with jurisdiction over the proposal has a rule requiring both draft and final environmental impact statements.

(ii) The proposal results from a study process required by statute (such as those required by the Wild and Scenic Rivers Act (16 U.S.C. 1271 et seq.) and the Wilderness Act (16 U.S.C. 1131 et seq.)).

(iii) Legislative approval is sought for Federal or federally assisted construction or other projects which the agency recommends be located at specific geographic locations. For proposals requiring an environmental impact statement for the acqusition of space by the General Services Administration, a draft statement shall accompany the Prospectus or the 11(b) Report of Building Project Surveys to the Congress, and a final statement shall be completed before site acquisition.

(iv) The agency decides to prepare draft and final statements.

(c) Comments on the legislative statement shall be given to the lead agency which shall forward them along with its own responses to the Congressional committees with jurisdiction.

§ 1506.9 Filing requirements.

Environmental impact statements together with comments and responses shall be filed with the Environmental Protection Agency, attention Office of Federal Activities (A-104), 401 M Street SW., Washington, DC 20460. Statements shall be filed with EPA no earlier than they are also transmitted to commenting agencies and made available to the public. EPA shall deliver one copy of each statement to the Council, which shall satisfy the requirement of availability to the President. EPA may issue

guidelines to agencies to implement its responsibilities under
this section and § 1506.10.

§ 1506.10 Timing of agency action.

(a) The Environmental Protection Agency shall publish a notice
in the <u>Federal Register</u> each week of the environmental impact
statements filed during the preceding week. The minimum time
periods set forth in this section shall be calculated from the
date of publication of this notice.

(b) No decision on the proposed action shall be made or
recorded under § 1505.2 by a Federal agency until the later of
the following dates:

(1) Ninety (90) days after publication of the notice described
above in paragraph (a) of this section for a draft environmental
impact statement.

(2) Thirty (30) days after publication of the notice described
above in paragraph (a) of this section for a final environmental
impact statement.

An exception to the rules on timing may be made in the case of an
agency decision which is subject to a formal internal appeal.
Some agencies have a formally established appeal process which
allows other agencies or the public to take appeals on a decision
and make their views known, after publication of the final
environmental impact statement. In such cases, where a real
opportunity exists to alter the decision, the decision may be
made and recorded at the same time the environmental impact
statement is published. This means that the period for appeal of
the decision and the 30-day period prescribed in paragraph (b)(2)
of this section may run concurrently. In such cases the
environmental impact statement shall explain the timing and the
public's right of appeal. An agency engaged in rulemaking under
the Administrative Procedure Act or other statute for the purpose
of protecting the public health or safety, may waive the time
period in paragraph (b)(2) of this section and publish a decision
on the final rule simultaneously with publication of the notice
of the availability of the final environmental impact statement
as described in paragraph (a) of this section.

(c) If the final environmental impact statement is filed within
ninety (90) days after a draft environmental impact statement is
filed with the Environmental Protection Agency, the minimum
thirty (30) day period and the minimum ninety (90) day period may
run concurrently. However, subject to paragraph (d) of this
section agencies shall allow not less than 45 days for comments
on draft statements.

(d) The lead agency may extend prescribed periods. The
Environmental Protection Agency may upon a showing by the lead
agency of compelling reasons of national policy reduce the
prescribed periods and may upon a showing by any other Federal
agency of compelling reasons of national policy also extend
prescribed periods, but only after consultation with the lead

agency. (Also see § 1507.3(d).) Failure to file timely comments shall not be a sufficient reason for extending a period. If the lead agency does not concur with the extension of time, EPA may not extend it for more than 30 days. When the Environmental Protection Agency reduces or extends any period of time it shall notify the Council.

§ 1506.11 Emergencies.

Where emergency circumstances make it necessary to take an action with significant environmental impact without observing the provisions of these regulations, the Federal agency taking the action should consult with the Council about alternative arrangements. Agencies and the Council will limit such arrangements to actions necessary to control the immediate impacts of the emergency. Other actions remain subject to NEPA review.

§ 1506.12 Effective date.

The effective date of these regulations is July 30, 1979, except that for agencies that administer programs that qualify under section 102(2)(D) of the Act or under section 104(h) of the Housing and Community Development Act of 1974 an additional four months shall be allowed for the State or local agencies to adopt their implementing procedures.

(a) These regulations shall apply to the fullest extent practicable to ongoing activities and environmental documents begun before the effective date. These regulations do not apply to an environmental impact statement or supplement if the draft statement was filed before the effective date of these regulations. No completed environmental documents need be redone by reasons of these regulations. Until these regulations are applicable, the Council's guidelines published in the Federal Register of August 1, 1973, shall continue to be applicable. In cases where these regulations are applicable the guidelines are superseded. However, nothing shall prevent an agency from proceeding under these regulations at an earlier time.

(b) NEPA shall continue to be applicable to actions begun before January 1, 1970, to the fullest extent possible.

PART 1507--AGENCY COMPLIANCE

§ 1507.1 Compliance.

All agencies of the Federal Government shall comply with these regulations. It is the intent of these regulations to allow each agency flexibility in adapting its implementing procedures authorized by § 1507.3 to the requirements of other applicable laws.

§ 1507.2 Agency capability to comply.

Each agency shall be capable (in terms of personnel and other resources) of complying with the requirements enumerated below. Such compliance may include use of other's resources, but the using agency shall itself have sufficient capability to evaluate what others do for it. Agencies shall:

(a) Fulfill the requirements of section 102(2)(A) of the Act to utilize a systematic, interdisciplinary approach which will insure the integrated use of the natural and social sciences and the environmental design arts in planning and in decisionmaking which may have an impact on the human environment. Agencies shall designate a person to be responsible for overall review of agency NEPA compliance.

(b) Identify methods and procedures required by section 102(2)(B) to insure that presently unquantified environmental amenities and values may be given appropriate consideration.

(c) Prepare adequate environmental impact statements pursuant to section 102(2)(C) and comment on statements in the areas where the agency has jurisdiction by law or special expertise or is authorized to develop and enforce environmental standards.

(d) Study, develop, and describe alternatives to recommended courses of action in any proposal which involves unresolved conflicts concerning alternative uses of available resources. This requirement of section 102(2)(E) extends to all such proposals, not just the more limited scope of section 102(2)(C)(iii) where the discussion of alternatives is confined to impact statements.

(e) Comply with the requirements of section 102(2)(H) that the agency initiate and utilize ecological information in the planning and development of resource-oriented projects.

(f) Fulfill the requirements of sections 102(2)(F), 102(2)(G), and 102(2)(I), of the Act and of Executive Order 11514, Protection and Enhancement of Environmental Quality, Sec. 2.

§ 1507.3 Agency procedures.

(a) Not later than eight months after publication of these regulations as finally adopted in the _Federal Register_, or five months after the establishment of an agency, whichever shall come later, each agency shall as necessary adopt procedures to supplement these regulations. When the agency is a department, major subunits are encouraged (with the consent of the department) to adopt their own procedures. Such procedures shall not paraphrase these regulations. They shall confine themselves to implementing procedures. Each agency shall consult with the Council while developing its procedures and before publishing them in the _Federal Register_ for comment. Agencies with similar programs should consult with each other and the Council to coordinate their procedures, especially for programs requesting similar information from applicants. The procedures shall be adopted only after an opportunity for public review and after review by the Council for conformity with the Act and these regulations. The Council shall complete its review within 30 days. Once in effect they shall be filed with the Council and made readily available to the public. Agencies are encouraged to publish explanatory guidance for these regulations and their own procedures. Agencies shall continue to review their policies and procedures and in consultation with the Council to revise them as necessary to ensure full compliance with the purposes and provisions of the Act.

(b) Agency procedures shall comply with these regulations except where compliance would be inconsistent with statutory requirements and shall include:

(1) Those procedures required by §§ 1501.2(d), 1502.9(c)(3), 1505.1, 1506.6(e), and 1508.4.

(2) Specific criteria for and identification of those typical classes of action:

(i) Which normally do require environmental impact statements.

(ii) Which normally do not require either an environmental impact statement or an environmental assessment (categorical exclusions § 1508.4)).

(iii) Which normally require environmental assessments but not necessarily environmental impact statements.

(c) Agency procedures may include specific criteria for providing limited exceptions to the provisions of these regulations for classified proposals. They are proposed actions which are specifically authorized under criteria established by an Executive Order or statute to be kept secret in the interest of national defense or foreign policy and are in fact properly classified pursuant to such Executive Order or statute. Environmental assessments and environmental impact statements which address classified proposals may be safeguarded and restricted from public dissemination in accordance with agencies' own regulations applicable to classified information. These documents may be organized so that classified portions can be included as annexes, in order that the unclassified portions can be made available to the public.

(d) Agency procedures may provide for periods of time other than those presented in § 1506.10 when necessary to comply with other specific statutory requirements.

(e) Agency procedures may provide that where there is a lengthy period between the agency's decision to prepare an environmental impact statement and the time of actual preparation, the notice of intent required by § 1501.7 may be published at a reasonable time in advance of preparation of the draft statement.

PART 1508--TERMINOLOGY AND INDEX

§ 1508.1   Terminology.

The terminology of this part shall be uniform throughout the Federal Government.

§ 1508.2   Act.

"Act" means the National Environmental Policy Act, as amended (42 U.S.C. 4321, et seq.) which is also referred to as "NEPA."

§ 1508.3   Affecting.

"Affecting" means will or may have an effect on.

§ 1508.4   Categorical exclusion.

"Categorical exclusion" means a category of actions which do not individually or cumulatively have a significant effect on the human environment and which have been found to have no such effect in procedures adopted by a Federal agency in implementation of these regulations (§ 1507.3) and for which, therefore, neither an environmental assessment nor an environmental impact statement is required. An agency may decide in its procedures or otherwise, to prepare environmental assessments for the reasons stated in § 1508.9 even though it is not required to do so. Any procedures under this section shall provide for extraordinary circumstances in which a normally excluded action may have a significant environmental effect.

§ 1508.5   Cooperating agency.

"Cooperating agency" means any Federal agency other than a lead agency which has jurisdiction by law or special expertise with respect to any environmental impact involved in a proposal (or a reasonable alternative) for legislation or other major Federal action significantly affecting the quality of the human environment. The selection and responsibilities of a cooperating agency are described in § 1501.6. A State or local agency of similar qualifications or, when the effects are on a reservation, an Indian Tribe, may by agreement with the lead agency become a cooperating agency.

§ 1508.6   Council.

"Council" means the Council on Environmental Quality established by Title II of the Act.

§ 1508.7   Cumulative impact.

"Cumulative impact" is the impact on the environment which results from the incremental impact of the action when added to other past, present, and reasonably foreseeable future actions regardless of what agency (Federal or non-Federal) or person undertakes such other actions. Cumulative impacts can result from individually minor but collectively significant actions taking place over a period of time.

§ 1508.8 Effects.

"Effects" include:
(a) Direct effects, which are caused by the action and occur at the same time and place.
(b) Indirect effects, which are caused by the action and are later in time or farther removed in distance, but are still reasonably foreseeable. Indirect effects may include growth inducing effects and other effects related to induced changes in the pattern of land use, population density or growth rate, and related effects on air and water and other natural systems, including ecosystems.

Effects and impacts as used in these regulations are synonymous. Effects includes ecological (such as the effects on natural resources and on the components, structures, and functioning of affected ecosystems), aesthetic, historic, cultural, economic, social, or health, whether direct, indirect, or cumulative. Effects may also include those resulting from actions which may have both beneficial and detrimental effects, even if on balance the agency believes that the effect will be beneficial.

§ 1508.9 Environmental assessment.

"Environmental assessment":
(a) Means a concise public document for which a Federal agency is responsible that serves to:
(1) Briefly provide sufficient evidence and analysis for determining whether to prepare an environmental impact statement or a finding of no significant impact.
(2) Aid an agency's compliance with the Act when no environmental impact statement is necessary.
(3) Facilitate preparation of a statement when one is necessary.
(b) Shall include brief discussions of the need for the proposal, of alternatives as required by section 102(2)(E), of the environmental impacts of the proposed action and alternatives, and a listing of agencies and persons consulted.

§ 1508.10 Environmental document.

"Environmental document" includes the documents specified in § 1508.9 (environmental assessment), § 1508.11 (environmental impact statement, § 1508.13 (finding of no significant impact), and § 1508.22 (notice of intent).

§ 1508.11 Environmental impact statement.

"Environmental impact statement" means a detailed written statement as required by section 102(2)(C) of the Act.

§ 1508.12 Federal agency.

"Federal agency" means all agencies of the Federal Government. It does not mean the Congress, the Judiciary, or the President, including the performance of staff functions for the President in his Executive Office. It also includes for purposes of these regulations States and units of general local government and Indian tribes assuming NEPA responsibilities under section 104(h) of the Housing and Community Development Act of 1974.

§ 1508.13 Finding of no significant impact.

"Finding of no significant impact" means a document by a Federal agency briefly presenting the reasons why an action, not otherwise excluded (§ 1508.4), will not have a significant effect on the human environment and for which an environmental impact statement therefore will not be prepared. It shall include the environmental assessment or a summary of it and shall note any other environmental documents related to it (§ 1501.7(a)(5)).   If the assessment is included, the finding need not repeat any of the discussion in the assessment but may incorporate it by reference.

§ 1508.14 Human environment.

"Human environment" shall be interpreted comprehensively to include the natural and physical environment and the relationship of people with that environment. (See the definition of "effects" (§ 1508.8).) This means that economic or social effects are not intended by themselves to require preparation of an environmental impact statement. When an environmental impact statement is prepared and economic or social and natural or physical environmental effects are interrelated, then the environmental impact statement will discuss all of these effects on the human environment.

§ 1508.15 Jurisdiction by law.

"Jurisdiction by law" means agency authority to approve, veto, or finance all or part of the proposal.

§ 1508.16 Lead agency.

"Lead agency" means the agency or agencies preparing or having taken primary responsibility for preparing the environmental impact statement.

§ 1508.17 Legislation.

"Legislation" includes a bill or legislative proposal to Congress developed by or with the significant cooperation and support of a Federal agency, but does not include requests for

appropriations. The test for significant cooperation is whether
the proposal is in fact predominantly that of the agency rather
than another source. Drafting does not by itself constitute
significant cooperation. Proposals for legislation include
requests for ratification of treaties. Only the agency which has
primary responsibility for the subject matter involved will
prepare a legislative environmental impact statement.

§ 1508.18 Major Federal action.

"Major federal action" includes actions with effects that may
be major and which are potentially subject to Federal control and
responsibility. Major reinforces but does not have a meaning
independent of significantly (§ 1508.27). Actions include the
circumstance where the responsible officials fail to act and that
failure to act is reviewable by courts or administrative
tribunals under the Administrative Procedure Act or other
applicable law as agency action.
  (a) Actions include new and continuing activities, including
projects and programs entirely or partly financed, assisted,
conducted, regulated, or approved by federal agencies; new or
revised agency rules, regulations, plans, policies, or
procedures; and legislative proposals (§§ 1506.8, 1508.17).
Actions do not include funding assistance solely in the form of
general revenue sharing funds, distributed under the State and
Local Fiscal Assistance Act of 1972, 31 U.S.C. 1221 et seq., with
no Federal agency control over the subseqent use of such funds.
Actions do not include bringing judicial or administrative civil
or criminal enforcement actions.
  (b) Federal actions tend to fall within one of the following
categories:
  (1) Adoption of official policy, such as rules, regulations,
and interpretations adopted pursuant to the Administrative
Procedure Act, 5 U.S.C. 551 et seq.; treaties and international
conventions or agreements; formal documents establishing an
agency's policies which will result in or substantially alter
agency programs.
  (2) Adoption of formal plans, such as official documents
prepared or approved by federal agencies which guide or prescribe
alternative uses of Federal resources, upon which future agency
actions will be based.
  (3) Adoption of programs, such as a group of concerted actions
to implement a specific policy or plan; systematic and connected
agency decisions allocating agency resources to implement a
specific statutory program or executive directive.
  (4) Aproval of specific projects, such as construction or
management activities located in a defined geographic area.
Projects include actions approved by permit or other regulatory
decision as well as federal and federally assisted activities.

§ 1508.19 Matter.

"Matter" includes for purposes of Part 1504:
(a) With respect to the Environmental Protection Agency, any proposed legislation, project, action or regulation as those terms are used in section 309(a) of the Clean Air Act (42 U.S.C. 7609).
(b) With respect to all other agencies, any proposed major federal action to which section 102(2)(C) of NEPA applies.

§ 1508.20 Mitigation.

"Mitigation" includes:
(a) Avoiding the impact altogether by not taking a certain action or parts of an action.
(b) Minimizing impacts by limiting the degree or magnitude of the action and its implementation.
(c) Rectifying the impact by repairing, rehabilitating, or restoring the affected environment.
(d) Reducing or eliminating the impact over time by preservation and maintenance operations during the life of the action.
(e) Compensating for the impact by replacing or providing substitute resources or environments.

§ 1508.21 NEPA process.

"NEPA process" means all measures necessary for compliance with the requirements of section 2 and Title I of NEPA.

§ 1508.22 Notice of intent.

"Notice of intent" means a notice that an environmental impact statement will be prepared and considered. The notice shall briefly:
(a) Describe the proposed action and possible alternatives.
(b) Describe the agency's proposed scoping process including whether, when, and where any scoping meeting will be held.
(c) State the name and address of a person within the agency who can answer questions about the proposed action and the environmental impact statement.

§ 1508.23 Proposal.

"Proposal" exists at that stage in the development of an action when an agency subject to the Act has a goal and is actively preparing to make a decision on one or more alternative means of accomplishing that goal and the effects can be meaningfully evaluated. Preparation of an environmental impact statement on a proposal should be timed (§ 1502.5) so that the final statement may be completed in time for the statement to be included in any recommendation or report on the proposal. A proposal may exist in fact as well as by agency declaration that one exists.

§ 1508.24 Referring agency.

"Referring agency" means the federal agency which has referred any matter to the Council after a determination that the matter is unsatisfactory from the standpoint of public health or welfare or environmental quality.

§ 1508.25 Scope.

Scope consists of the range of actions, alternatives, and impacts to be considered in an environmental impact statement. The scope of an individual statement may depend on its relationships to other statements (§§ 1502.20 and 1508.28). To determine the scope of environmental impact statements, agencies shall consider 3 types of actions, 3 types of alternatives, and 3 types of impacts. They include:

(a) Actions (other than unconnected single actions) which may be:

(1) Connected actions, which means that they are closely related and therefore should be discussed in the same impact statement. Actions are connected if they:

(i) Automatically trigger other actions which may require environmental impact statements.

(ii) Cannot or will not proceed unless other actions are taken previously or simultaneously.

(iii) Are interdependent parts of a larger action and depend on the larger action for their justification.

(2) Cumulative actions, which when viewed with other proposed actions have cumulatively significant impacts and should therefore be discussed in the same impact statement.

(3) Similar actions, which when viewed with other reasonably foreseeable or proposed agency actions, have similarities that provide a basis for evaluating their environmental consequences together, such as common timing or geography. An agency may wish to analyze these actions in the same impact statement. It should do so when the best way to assess adequately the combined impacts of similar actions or reasonable alternatives to such actions is to treat them in a single impact statement.

(b) Alternatives, which include: (1) No action alternative.

(2) Other reasonable courses of actions.

(3) Mitigation measures (not in the proposal action).

(c) Impacts, which may be: (1) Direct; (2) indirect; (3) cumulative.

§ 1508.26 Special expertise.

"Special expertise" means statutory responsibility, agency mission, or related program experience.

§ 1508.27 Significantly.

"Significantly" as used in NEPA requires considerations of both context and intensity:

(a) <u>Context.</u> This means that the significance of an action must be analyzed in several contexts such as society as a whole (human, national), the affected region, the affected interests, and the locality. Significance varies with the setting of the proposed action. For instance, in the case of a site-specific action, significance would usually depend upon the effects in the locale rather than in the world as a whole. Both short- and long-term effects are relevant.

(b) <u>Intensity.</u> This refers to the severity of impact. Responsible officials must bear in mind that more than one agency may make decisions about partal aspects of a major action. The following should be considered in evaluating intensity:

(1) Impacts that may be both beneficial and adverse. A significant effect may exist even if the Federal agency believes that on balance the effect will be beneficial.

(2) The degree to which the proposed action affects public health or safety.

(3) Unique characteristics of the geographic area such as proximity to historic or cultural resources, park lands, prime farmlands, wetlands, wild and scenic rivers, or ecologically critical areas.

(4) The degree to which the effects on the quality of the human environment are likely to be highly controversial.

(5) The degree to which the possible effects on the human environment are highly uncertain or involve unique or unknown risks.

(6) The degree to which the action may establish a precedent for future actions with significant effects or represents a decision in principle about a future consideration.

(7) Whether the action is related to other actions with individually insignificant but cumulatively significant impacts. Significance exists if it is reasonable to anticipate a cumulatively significant impact on the environment. Significance cannot be avoided by terming an action temporary or by breaking it down into small component parts.

(8) The degree to which the action may adversely affect districts, sites, highways, structures, or objects listed in or eligible for listing in the National Register of Historic Places or may cause loss or destruction of significant scientific, cultural, or historical resources.

(9) The degree to which the action may adversely affect an endangered or threatened species or its habitat that has been determined to be critical under the Endangered Species Act of 1973.

(10) Whether the action threatens a violation of Federal, State, or local law or requirements imposed for the protection of the environment.

§ 1508.28 **Tiering.**

"Tiering" refers to the coverage of general matters in broader environmental impact statements (such as national program or policy statements) with subsequent narrower statements or environmental analyses (such as regional or basinwide program statements or ultimately site-specific statements) incorporating by reference the general discussions and concentrating solely on the issues specific to the statement subsequently prepared. Tiering is appropriate when the sequence of statements or analyses is:

(a) From a program, plan, or policy environmental impact statements to a program, plan, or policy statement or analysis of lesser scope or to a site-specific statement or analysis.

(b) From an environmental impact statement on a specific action at an early stage (such as need and site selection) to a supplement (which is preferred) or a subsequent statement or analysis at a later stage (such as environmental mitigation). Tiering in such cases is appropriate when it helps the lead agency to focus on the issues which are ripe for decision and exclude from consideration issues already decided or not yet ripe.

Bibliography

Abrams, *Thresholds of Harm in Environmental Litigation: The Michigan Environmental Protection Act as Model of a Minimal Requirement*, 7 Harv. Envtl. L. Rev. 107 (1983).

Andreen, *In Pursuit of NEPA's Promise: The Role of Executive Oversight in the Implementation of Environmental Policy*, 64 Ind. L.J. 205 (1989).

R. Andrews, *Environmental Policy and Administrative Change* (Lexington Books 1976).

Andrews, *NEPA in Practice: Environmental Policy or Administrative Reform?*, 6 Envtl. L. Rep. (Envtl. L. Inst.) 50,001 (1976).

Arnold, *The Substantive Right to Environmental Quality Under the National Environmental Policy Act*, 3 Envtl. L. Rep. (Envtl. L. Inst.) 50,028 (1973).

Blumm & Brown, *Pluralism and the Environment: The Role of Comment Agencies in NEPA Litigation*, 14 Harv. Envtl. L. Rev. no. 2 (1990).

Caldwell, *20 Years with NEPA Indicates the Need*, 31 Environment 7 (Dec. 1989).

Congressional Research Service, *NEPA Compliance at Department of Energy Defense Production Facilities* (90–127 ENR, Mar. 6, 1990).

Council on Environmental Quality, *Environmental Quality 1970: First Annual Report.*

Council on Environmental Quality, *Environmental Quality 1972: Third Annual Report.*

Council on Environmental Quality, *Environmental Quality 1979: Tenth Annual Report.*

Council on Environmental Quality, *Environmental Quality 1984: Fifteenth Annual Report.*

Davies & Lettow, *The Impact of Federal Institutional Arrangements* in *Federal Environmental Law* 126 (Envtl. L. Inst. 1974).

Druley, *Federal Agency NEPA Procedures*, Envt't Rep. (BNA) Monograph No. 23 (1976).

General Accounting Office, *The Council on Environmental Quality: A Tool in Shaping National Policy* (CED-81–66 1981).

Hagman, *NEPA's Progeny Inhabit the States—Were the Genes Defective?*, 1974 Urb. L. Ann. 3.

Karp, *The NEPA Regulations*, 19 Am. Bus. L.J. 295 (1981).

Levine, *The New York State Environmental Quality Review Act of 1975: An Analysis of the Parties' Responsibilities in the Review/Permit Request Process*, 12 Fordham Urb. L.J. 1 (1984).

Liebesman, *The Council on Environmental Quality's Regulations to Implement the National Environmental Policy Act—Will They Further NEPA's Substantive Mandate*, 10 Envtl. L. Rep. (Envtl. L. Inst.) 50,039 (1980).

Liroff, *The Council on Environmental Quality*, 3 Envtl. L. Rep. (Envtl. L. Inst.) 50,051 (1973).

Lynch, *The 1973 CEQ Guidelines: Cautious Updating of the Environmental Impact Statement Process*, 11 Cal. Western L. Rev. 297 (1975).

Marsh, *Symposium on the New York State Environmental Quality Review Act: Introduction—SEQRA's Scope and Objectives*, 46 Albany L. Rev. 1097 (1982).

Sax & DiMento, *Environmental Citizen Suits: Three Years' Experience Under the Michigan Environmental Protection Act*, 4 Ecology L.Q. 1 (1974).

Selmi, *The Judicial Development of the California Environmental Quality Act*, 18 U.C. Davis L. Rev. 197 (1984)

Slone, *The Michigan Environmental Protection Act: Bringing Citizen-Initiated Environmental Suits Into the 1980's*, 12 Ecology L.Q. 271 (1985).

Symposium on NEPA at Twenty: The Past, Present, and Future of the National Environmental Policy Act, 20 Envtl. L. no. 3 (1990).

Ulasewicz, *The Department of Environmental Conservation and SEQRA: Upholding Its Mandates and Charting Parameters for the Elusive Socio-Economic Assessment*, 46 Albany L. Rev. 1255 (1982).

Yarrington, *The National Environmental Policy Act*, 4 Env't Rep. (BNA) Monograph No. 17 (1974).

Yost, *Don't Gut Worst Case Analysis*, 13 Envtl. L. Rep. (Envtl. L. Inst.) 10,394 (1983).

Comment, *CEQ Proposes New Guidelines for NEPA*, 3 Envtl. L. Rep. (Envtl. L. Inst.) 10,056 (1973).

Comment, *Reinvigorating the NEPA Process: CEQ's Draft Compliance Regulations Stir Controversy*, 8 Envtl. L. Rep. (Envtl. L. Inst.) 10,045 (1978).

Comment, *Substantive Enforcement of the California Environmental Quality Act*, 69 Cal. L. Rev. 112 (1981).

Comment, *Supreme Court Ushers in New Era for CEQ in* Warm Springs *Case*, 4 Envtl. L. Rep. (Envtl. L. Inst.) 10,130 (1974).

Comment, *The Council on Environmental Quality's Guidelines and Their Influence on the National Environmental Policy Act*, 23 Catholic Univ. L. Rev. 547 (1974).

Note, *Program Environmental Impact Statements: Review and Remedies*, 75 Mich. L. Rev. 107 (1976)

Note, *The CEQ Regulations: New Stage in the Evolution of NEPA*, 3 Harv. Envtl. L. Rev. 347 (1979).

Agencies Revised NEPA Procedural Compliance Guidelines Near Completion, Months After Deadline for Submission to CEQ, 1 Envtl. L. Rep. (Envtl. L. Inst.) 10,167 (1971).

CEQ Proposes Ambitious NEPA Regulations for Comment, Stands Ground Despite Agency Criticism, 8 Envtl. L. Rep. (Envtl. L. Inst.) 10,129 (1978).

CEQ's Role Declines Under Carter, Reagan After Serving as Major Policy-Making Body, 16 Env't Rep. (BNA) 10 (1985).

CEQ Staggering Under Latest Budget Cut, 221 Science 529 (1983).

CEQ to Work Closely with White House, EPA to Define its Focus, New Chairman Deland Says, 20 Env't Rep. (BNA) 688 (1989).

CEQ Will Grow, Have Bigger Policy Role, Nominee for Chairman Tells Senate Panel, 20 Env't Rep. (BNA) 598 (1989).

EPA's Responsibilities Under the National Environmental Policy Act: Further Developments, 3 Envtl. L. Rep. (Envtl. L. Inst.) 10,157 (1973).

Federal Agencies Begin to Consider Global Warming in Impact Statements, 20 Envt. Rep. (BNA) 1271 (1989).

Index

ABOUT THE AUTHOR

VALERIE M. FOGLEMAN is an associate with the law firm of Gary, Thomasson, Hall & Marks Professional Corporation in Corpus Christi, Texas, where she specializes in environmental law. Previously, she was Visiting Instructor at the University of Illinois College of Law and Natural Resources Law Fellow at the Northwestern School of Law at Lewis and Clark College. She is the author of numerous articles on environmental law.